LET'S GO

www.letsgo.com

Withdrawn

PARIS

researcher-writers
Ama R. Francis
Edward Monahan

staff writers
Juan Cantu
Dorothy McLeod
Qichen Zhang
Whitney Donaldson
Alexandra Perloff-Giles

research manager
Joseph B. Gaspard

editor
Teresa Cotsirilos

managing editor
Daniel C. Barbero

W9-BRO-942

Tel: 33 (0)1 42 60 79 04
Fax: 33 (0)1 42 60 09 04

office@hoteldiliondor.com

Hotel du Lion D'Or
5 rue de la Sourdiere
75001 PARIS

Budget Hotel in the Heart of Paris

Minutes from the most beautiful landmarks in Paris, with its own CyberCafe, Hotel du Lion D'Or is the perfect choice for Let's Go Travelers. Only steps away from the Louvre, the Tuileries Gardens, the Place Vendome and the Opera Garnier.

Breakfast Buffet

Petit Salon

Room (Double)

Studio Apartment

www.hoteldiliondor.com

CONTENTS

RESEARCHER-WRITERS

AMA R. FRANCIS. A childhood on the lovely island of Dominica left Ama with fabulous French skills, a love for the beach, and a taste for mangoes. Her time in France was spent balancing newfound friendships with fellow students and her steady (verging on dependent) relationship with pain au chocolat.

EDWARD MONAHAN. Born Edward Monahan III, Ned is truly Boston's boy. A hip-hop enthusiast with a habit of befriending strangers on the street, Ned once spent a summer working on a champagne vineyard in France. When he returned to France for Let's Go, he knew he'd be in for a whole new experience (and a very different final product).

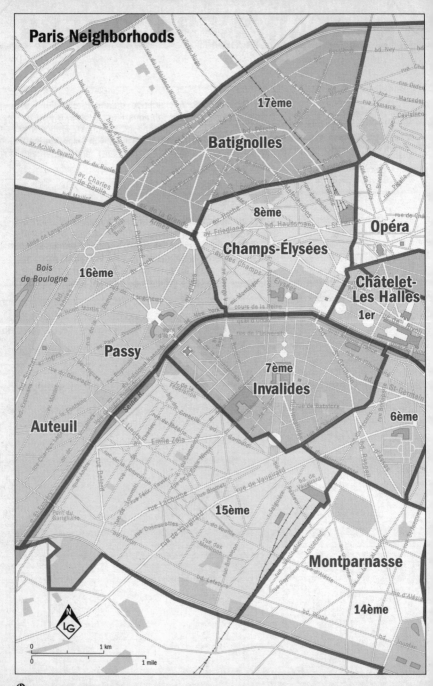

Paris Neighborhoods

17ème

Batignolles

8ème

Opéra

Champs-Élysées

Bois de Boulogne

16ème

Châtelet-Les Halles

1er

Passy

7ème

Invalides

6ème

Auteuil

15ème

Montparnasse

14ème

0   1 km
0   1 mile

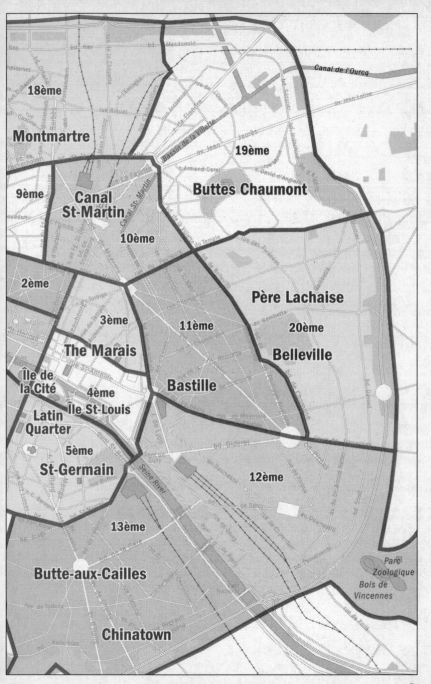

PARIS

If you are lucky enough to have lived in Paris as a young man, then wherever you go for the rest of your life, it stays with you, for Paris is a moveable feast.

-Ernest Hemingway

Think of a famous idea. Any famous idea. Or for that matter any brushstroke, article of clothing, architectural style, camera technique, great thinker that should have been medicated, or hip reason to brew a Molotov cocktail. If that famous idea is Western, then it is probably rooted in Paris, one way or another. It's no secret that young Americans migrate to France to lose their virginity and construct their identity at a safe distance from their parents. The successes of James Baldwin, Gertrude Stein, and Ernest Hemingway suggest that we couldn't have chosen a better spot. Your first walk around Paris will be defined by a paralyzing level of excitement; there is a pervading sense in France that *everything* is here.

Students might go to Paris to be fashionably disaffected artists in boho-chic corner cafes, but Paris is also, increasingly, the city of parkour and veil bans, a sprawling Chinatown, and the Marie Leonie case of 2004. This diversity and intense progressivism sharply contrasts with a carefully guarded and insular local culture (yes, for the record, the waiters are judging you). These rapid transitions have created a cultural patchwork that is safe and affordable for the average backpacker to thoroughly explore.

when to go

Spring weather in Paris is fickle and punctuated by unexpected rain. Of the summer months, June is notoriously rainy, while high temperatures tend to hit in July and August. Occasional heat waves can be uncomfortable, and muggy weather aggravates Paris's pollution problem. By fall, a fantastic array of auburn foliage brightens up the parks, and the weather becomes dry and temperate. Rain is more common than snow in the winter, though heavy snowfalls do happen—and as demonstrated last winter, the city is not necessarily equipped to deal with them.

As far as the crowds are concerned, tourists move in and Parisians move out in the summertime, and smaller hotels, shops, and services usually close for the month of August. Many of Paris' best festivals are held during the summer (see Festivals, p. 254), and parts of the city can be quite peaceful. In the fall, the tourist madness begins to calm down—airfares and hotel rates drop, travel is less congested, and the museum lines are shorter. The winter is pretty low-key and less touristed but, as expected, many people love Paris in the springtime.

top five affairs to remember

"A Frenchman's home is where another man's wife is." - Mark Twain

5. GERTRUDE STEIN AND ALICE B. TOKLAS. In an era when homosexuality was illegal in most of America, Gertrude and Alice were referred to by Hemingway as "husband and wife." Take that, Focus on the Family!

4. HÉLOÏSE AND ABELARD. It doesn't get racier than this. He was a 12th-century monk. She was his student. Their torrid love affair was discovered by Héloïse's uncle, who didn't take the news well and castrated Abelard in his sleep. Héloïse fled from her uncle to an abbey in Brittany, became a nun, and secretly had Abelard's child. Whom she named Astrolabius. Apple Martin's name has never seemed more okay.

3. JEAN SARTRE AND SIMONE DE BEAUVOIR. The creators of existentialist thought and second-wave feminism maintained a famously open relationship, then shared the same under-aged mistresses.

2. CATHERINE BELLIER AND LOUIS XIV. Fearing that her son would be as inept in the bedroom as her husband, Queen Anne of Austria allegedly asked her handmaid, the hideous Bellier, to deflower her 16-year-old son Louis XIV. Bellier's husband was subsequently promoted to royal advisor. Best. Cougar. Ever.

1. RICK BLAINE AND ILSA LUND LAZLO. They'll always have Paris.

what to do

THE ART OF FRENCH COOKING

Crème brulee. Merlot. Chocolate crêpes. Escargot. France's famed kitchens should be named World Heritage Sites, and we cannot think of a better place to gain weight than Paris, which hosts some of the best restaurants France has to offer. Though French food is generally associated with white tablecloths and steep prices in the US, an appreciation of fine dining is evident throughout Parisian society, right down to its chaotic street markets; it's both cheaper and more convenient to buy a loaf of baguette and a roll of brie than a microwave dinner. Paris additionally boasts a myriad of other culinary traditions, due to its extensive immigrant populations. Try some of the hot falafel and mom-and-pop Moroccan while you're in town.

- **CHEZ JANOU:** Specializing in traditional French food, our Researcher-Writers report that Chez Janou is so good it "inspires desert-island hypotheticals" (p. 139).
- **MARCHÉ DES ENFANTS ROUGES:** Get fresh groceries from singing street vendors at Paris' oldest covered market (p. 141).
- **LE CAMBODGE:** Join the hordes of locals in a mad rush for well priced and mouth-watering Cambodian (p. 156).
- **BERTHILLON:** The best homemade ice cream in the Île de la Cité, or maybe anywhere (p. 134).
- **LA BAGUE DE KENZA:** Choose from sticky pyramids of Algerian pastries (p. 157).

GET LOST IN THE LOUVRE

The Chuck Norris of revolutionary thought, Paris generates more creativity than the world knows what to do with. Spend as much time as humanly possible in the Louvre and the Pompidou, and be sure to visit the Sorbonne, Balzac's quarters, and other famed sites of innovation. Paris is home to a lot more than several hundred years of Western painting, and the city's famed retro movie theaters, elite fashionistas, and (stolen) collections of indigenous art yield a more panoramic view of its history.

- **THE LOUVRE:** Do we even need to tell you why to come here? (p. 68).
- **THE POMPIDOU:** A veritable theme park of artistic innovation (p. 76).
- **SAINTE-CHAPELLE:** You've heard a lot more about its neighbor Notre Dame (apparently a hunchback with issues lives there), but we'd take Sainte-Chapelle's floor-to-ceiling stained glass windows any day (p. 64).
- **MUSÉE DE RODIN:** Contemplate the universe alongside *The Thinker* (p. 97).
- **QUAI D'ANJOU:** It doesn't get more Parisian than this. This single street was once home to John Dos Passos, Charles Baudelaire, Voltaire and his married mistress, and a publishing press edited by Ezra Pound. Imagine the drama at that neighborhood block party (p. 67).

POISONING PIGEONS IN THE PARK

Okay, only Weird Al does that, but we still recommend that you explore Paris' public spaces anyway. The city's spectacular gardens were originally the pet projects of tyrannical royals and feature everything from moats to topiary mazes. Though the **Jardin des Tuileries** (p. 71) and **Jardin du Luxembourg** (p. 86) are endlessly photographed, we also recommend that you visit some of the city's less touristed squares and local parks, which provide a more intimate window into the city's daily rhythm and contradictions. Several thousand years of history intersect with the daily lives of joggers, street musicians, teen punks, local suits, and women in hijabs pushing strollers. Especially in comparison to most modern American cities, Paris is also meticulously well-organized, and its promenades and gardens are maintained to the point of anal retention. Grab a bottle of wine and go enjoy the sunshine.

- **LE JARDIN DU LUXEMBOURG:** Once the private gardens of Marie de Médicis, the gardens are an endless maze of manicured lawns and winding pathways (p. 86).
- **JARDIN DES TUILERIES:** The elaborate fountains and wide walkways make Central Park look provincial (p. 71).
- **PLACE DES VOSGES:** This bustling square boasts arguably the best people watching in the city (p. 78).

BEYOND TOURISM

If you're interested in more than a snapshot of the Eiffel Tower, we suggest that you enroll in a semester program and submerge yourself in Paris properly. Study abroad programs in Paris really have their act together; the majority of them involve intensive language immersion programs, place students with host families, and offer cross-enrollment in partner French institutions. Programs aimed at advanced speakers offer work placement and direct enrollment opportunities. Volunteer work in Paris is harder to come by for foreigners, but the country does boast several venerated outreach programs for those who get riled up about social justice. Work as au pairs or English teaching assistants is also readily available.

- **CUPA:** Enroll directly in French universities (p. 257).
- **AGENCY AU PAIR FLY:** Perfect your language skills with the aid of small children (p. 262).

student superlatives

- **BEST PLACE TO HAVE A POLITICALLY SUBVERSIVE CONVERSATION:** Try the backstreets of Butte-aux-Cailles (p. 16) or the 6ème's St-Michel Place (p. 15), where the left wing riots of 1871 and 1968 both began.
- **BEST PLACE TO INDULGE YOUR INNER DISNEY PRINCESS:** The Palais-Royal (p. 73).
- **BEST GENDER-BENDING:** It's definitely a toss up, but we're going with the Pigalle (p. 111).
- **BEST PLACE TO DRINK UNTIL YOU CAN'T REMEMBER HAVING BEEN THERE:** Le Caveau de la Huchette; the basements once housed the prisoners of Robespierre (p. 176).
- **BEST PLACE TO SERIOUSLY NERD OUT:** Deconstruct *Finnegan's Wake* with the "tumbleweeds" of Shakespeare and Co. Bookstore in the Latin Quarter, a former haven for the alcoholic expats of the Lost Generation (p. 200).

suggested itineraries

BEST OF PARIS

1. NOTRE DAME: Joan of Arc was tried for heresy here. Quasimodo tried to rescue Esmeralda here. Thousands of Parisians prayed for deliverance from the invading Germans here—twice. Does God just like Sainte-Chapelle better or something?

2. SAINTE-CHAPELLE: The kaleidoscope of blue stained glass will leave you speechless.

3. CENTRE POMPIDOU: It looks like an epic game of shoots and ladders and houses the largest modern art museum in Europe.

4. MUSÉE DU LOUVRE: There's a good chance that this museum is the reason you're in Paris. We recommend pulling a Mrs. Basil E. Frankweiler, hiding out in the bathrooms, and living in here for as long as you can.

5. MUSÉE D'ORSAY: The core works of this museum's collection were originally Louvre rejects. Which really says something about the Louvre.

6. TOUR D'EIFFEL: It may have been derisively referred to as "metal asparagus" when it was first built, but this monument is not overrated.

7. ARC DE TRIOMPHE

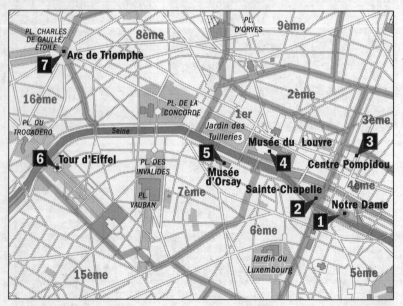

THE INSIDE SKINNY

1. CIMETIÈRE DU PÈRE LACHAISE: Kiss Oscar Wilde's tombstone and then mob Jim Morrison's.

2. MAHLIA KENT: Witness the production of high fashion up close and personal at this artisan workshop.

3. PLACE DES VOSGES: Parisian daily life collides with centuries of history in this lovely and bustling city square and picnic spot.

4. MUSÉE PICASSO: A museum dedicated to the master's take on the city of lights, his many mistresses, and other things.

5. EGLISE ST-EUSTACHE: Richelieu, Molière, Louis XIV, and Mme. de Pompadour were all baptized and/or received communion here. We think this church might be lucky.

6. PLACE DE LA CONCORDE: With views of the Champs-Élysées, Arc de Triomphe, Jardin de Tuileries, and sumptuous Belle-Epoque buildings, this gold-speckled square is a focal point of Paris.

7. MUSÉE DU QUAI BRANLY: The museum showcases a stunning 300,000 artifacts and works of art from around the world, all of which were questionably acquired during France's period of colonial expansion.

8. MUSÉE DE RODIN: Contemplate *The Thinker* and stare down into the *Gates of Hell*.

9. CATACOMBS: Navigate your way through the city of tunnels in this underground graveyard.

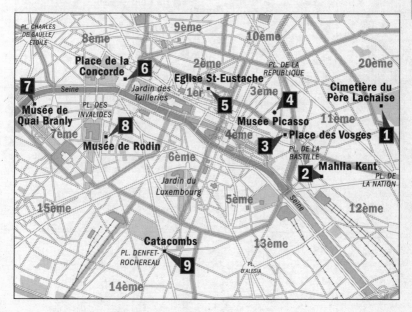

THE BOOZER-FLOOZER

1. AU RENDEZ-VOUS DES AMIS: You know you're in for a wild night when the owner threatens to drink you under the table.

2. L'ABRACADABAR: This funky bar attracts its fair share of shameless stoners.

3. RAIDD BAR: If you want a penis or just want to see one, come here.

4. FAVELA CHIC: An Afro-Brazilian bar that is jam-packed with hot, gyrating bodies.

5. CHAMPS DE MARS: The best place to drink in Paris that isn't a bar.

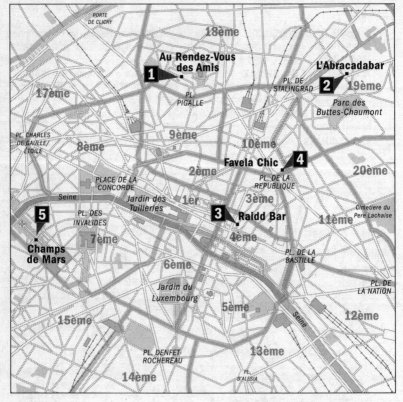

discover paris

LIBERTÉ, ÉGALITÉ, FRATERNITÉ

1. THÉÂTRE DES CHAMPS-ÉLYSÉES: Igor Stravinsky's *Rite of Spring* premiered here in 1913. The audience was so scandalized that they rioted, as disgruntled Parisians will do.

2. PLACE DE LA CONCORDE: Commissioned by King Louis XV in honor of, well, himself, the Concorde was a potent symbol of the French monarchy, and was naturally co-opted by the Revolution. King Louis XVI, Marie Antoinette, Robespierre, and 1,343 other aristocrats were executed in this plaza during the Reign of Terror.

3. PLACE D'ITALIE

4. THE BASTILLE: ...Or what's left of it anyway. The huddled masses were mighty thorough when they stormed this place.

5. CIMETIÈRE DU PÈRE LACHAISE: In 1871, the disenfranchised workers of Paris staged a massive revolt against France's lackluster Third Republic, and attempted to establish the socialist and democratic Paris Commune in its place. Their state was short-lived and ended brutally; 147 Communards were summarily executed against a wall in the Père Lachaise. The Mur des Fédérés has been a rallying point for the French Left ever since.

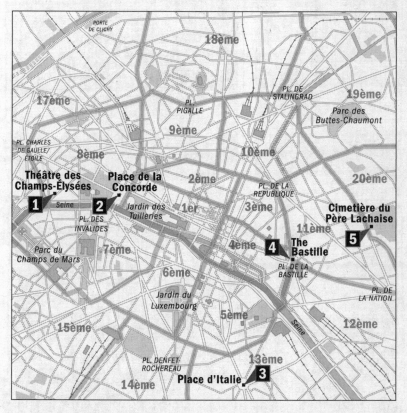

how to use this book

CHAPTERS

In the next few pages, the travel coverage chapters—the meat of any *Let's Go* book—begin with budget-friendly **Accommodations** (yes, they do exist, even in Paris). Your inner nerd will go gaga as you move into our **Sights** coverage, taking you through the best that each arrondissement has to offer. In **Food** you'll find everything from crêperies to romantic bistros to erotic bakeries, depending on what your stomach (or libido) is craving. **Nightlife** will help you plan out your debauched activities in the city of lights. When you're looking to class it up a little, check **Arts and Culture**—Parisians do it right. If you think your travel-worn wardrobe needs an update, our **Shopping** coverage should help you look *très chic*. If city life is getting you down, or you're just looking to spice it up a bit, **Excursions** shows you just what's waiting for you outside the city limits.

But that's not all, folks. We also have a few extra chapters for you to peruse:

CHAPTER	DESCRIPTION
Discover Paris	Discover tells you what to do, when to do it, and where to go for it. The absolute coolest things about any destination get highlighted in this chapter at the front of all *Let's Go* books.
Essentials	Essentials contains the practical info you need before, during, and after your trip—visas, regional transportation, health and safety, phrasebooks, and more.
Paris 101	Paris 101 is just what it sounds like—a crash course in where you're traveling. This short chapter on Paris's history and culture makes great reading on a long plane ride.
Beyond Tourism	As students ourselves, we at *Let's Go* encourage studying abroad, or going beyond tourism more generally, every chance we get. This chapter lists ideas for how to study, volunteer, or work abroad with other young travelers in Paris to get more out of your trip.

LISTINGS

Listings—a.k.a. reviews of individual establishments—constitute a majority of *Let's Go* coverage. Our Researcher-Writers list establishments in order from **best to worst value**—not necessarily quality. (Obviously a five-star hotel is nicer than a hostel, but it would probably be ranked lower because it's not as good a value.) Listings pack in a lot of information, but it's easy to digest if you know how they're constructed:

ESTABLISHMENT NAME 💳🚫♿⊗📶🍸❄⛅▼ type of establishment ❶

Address ☎phone number 🖥website

Editorial review goes here.

⇄ Directions to the establishment. ℹ Other practical information about the establishment, like age restrictions at a club or whether breakfast is included at a hostel. $ Prices for goods or services. ⏰ Hours or schedules.

ICONS

First things first: places and things that we absolutely love, sappily cherish, generally obsess over, and wholeheartedly endorse are denoted by the all-empowering **👍Let's Go thumbs-up.** In addition, the icons scattered throughout a listing (as you saw in the sample above) can tell you a lot about an establishment. The following icons answer a series of yes-no questions about a place:

💳	Credit cards accepted	🚫	Cash only	♿	Wheelchair-accessible
⊗	Not wheelchair-accessible	📶	Internet access available	🍸	Alcohol served
❄	Air-conditioned	⛅	Outdoor seating available	▼	GLBT or GLBT-friendly

The rest are visual cues to help you navigate each listing:

☎	Phone numbers	🖥	Websites	⇄	Directions
ℹ	Other hard info	$	Prices	⏰	Hours

OTHER USEFUL STUFF

Area codes for each destination appear opposite the name of the city and are denoted by the ☎ icon. Finally, in order to pack the book with as much information as possible, we have used a few **standard abbreviations.** Ave. for Avenue, bld. for Boulevard, pl. for Place. *Entrées* mean appetizers in French, whereas *plats* are main dishes.

PRICE DIVERSITY

A final set of icons corresponds to what we call our "price diversity" scale, which approximates how much money you can expect to spend at a given establishment. For **accommodations,** we base our range on the cheapest price for which a single traveler can stay for one night. For **food,** we estimate the average amount one traveler will spend in one sitting. The table below tells you what you'll *typically* find in Paris at the corresponding price range, but keep in mind that no system can allow for the quirks of individual establishments.

ACCOMMODATIONS	RANGE	WHAT YOU'RE LIKELY TO FIND
❶	under €25	Campgrounds and dorm rooms, both in hostels and actual universities. Expect bunk beds and a communal bath. You may have to provide or rent towels and sheets.
❷	€25-€40	Upper-end hostels or lower-end hotels. You may have a private bathroom, or there may be a sink in your room and a communal shower in the hall.
❸	€40-€60	A small room with a private bath. Should have decent amenities, such as phone and TV. Breakfast may be included.
❹	€60-€80	Should have bigger rooms than a 3, with more amenities or in a more convenient location. Breakfast probably included.
❺	over €80	Large hotels or upscale chains. If it's a 5 and it doesn't have the perks you want (and more), you've paid too much.
FOOD	**RANGE**	**WHAT YOU'RE LIKELY TO FIND**
❶	under €15	Probably street food or a fast-food joint, but also university cafeterias and bakeries (yum). Usually takeout, but you may have the option of sitting down.
❷	€15-€25	Sandwiches, pizza, appetizers at a bar, or low-priced entrees. Most ethnic eateries are a 2. Either takeout or a sit-down meal, but only slightly more fashionable decor.
❸	€25-€35	Mid-priced entrees, seafood, and exotic pasta dishes. More upscale ethnic eateries. Since you'll have the luxury of a waiter, tip will set you back a little extra.
❹	€35-€45	A somewhat fancy restaurant. Entrees tend to be heartier or more elaborate, but you're really paying for decor and ambience. Few restaurants in this range have a dress code, but some may look down on T-shirts and sandals.
❺	over €45	Your meal might cost more than your room, but there's a reason—it's something fabulous, famous, or both. Slacks and dress shirts may be expected. Offers foreign-sounding food and a decent wine list. Don't order a PB and J!

discover paris

ORIENTATION

In comparison to any sprawling post-war American cities, Paris is both dense and meticulously planned. The Seine river ("SEN") flows from east to west, and slices through the middle of Paris, dividing the city into two main sections: the Rive Gauche (Left Bank) to the north, and the Rive Droite (Right Bank) to the south. The two islands in the center of the Seine, the Ile de la Cité and Ile St-Louis, are both the geographical and historical heart of the city. The rest of Paris proper is divided into 20 arrondissements (districts), which spiral clockwise outwards from the center of the city, like a snail shell. Each arrondissement is usually referred to by an assigned number. For example, the Eiffel Tower is located in the seventh arrondissement of Paris; this district is simply referred to as le septième ("the seventh"), abbreviated 7ème. The city's first arrondissement is the only one that is not abbreviated by the grammatical form ème; it is known as the premier ("PREM-yay") and abbreviated 1er.

The city's organization may sound eminently reasonable, but Paris can be plenty hard to navigate in practice. Just to make things more difficult for travelers, Paris's most prominent neighborhoods regularly bleed into different arrondissements, and do not abide by their numerical divisions. The Marais, for example, spans both the 3ème and the 4ème. We have divided our coverage by both neighborhood and arrondissement, to keep our readers in the know. The most historic areas in Paris can devolve into a maze of narrowed cobbled streets, which can be poorly marked. The city is eminently walkable, however, so we recommend that newbies put away the map and just go with it. Getting lost in Paris is the reason you flew to France in the first place, isn't it?

île de la cité and île st-louis

Marooned in the middle of the Seine and tethered to the mainland by arched bridges, Île de la Cité is situated at the physical center of Paris. The island hosted Paris's first ramshackle settlement in 300 BCE, and became the seat of the French monarchy in the sixth century CE when Clovis crowned himself king of the Franks; it remained a hotbed of French political power until Charles V abandoned it in favor of the **Louvre** in the 14th century. The stunning **Notre Dame,** as well as the **Sainte-Chapelle** and the **Conciergerie,** ensured that the island would remain a center of Parisian religious, political, and cultural life; unsurprisingly, it is now a major center of tourism. All distances in France are measured from *kilomètre zéro,* a circular sundial in front of Notre Dame.

As it often goes with twins, the neighboring Île St-Louis is less illustrious. Originally two small islands—**Île aux Vâches** (Cow Island) and **Île de Notre Dame**—Île St-Louis was considered a suitable location for duels, cows, and not much else throughout the Middle Ages. In 1267 CE, the area was renamed for Louis IX after he departed for the Crusades. The two islands merged in the 17th century under the direction of architect Louis Le Vau, and Île St-Louis became a residential district. The island's *hôtels particuliers* (mansions, many of which were also designed by Le Vau) attracted a fair share of uppity citizenry including Voltaire, Mme. de Châtelet, Daumier, Ingres, Baudelaire, Balzac, Courbet, Sand, Delacroix, and Cézanne. The 1930s, the idiosyncratic and artistic inhabitants declared the island an independent republic. The island still retains a certain remoteness from the rest of Paris; older residents still say *"Je vais à Paris"* ("I'm going to Paris") when they leave the neighborhood by one of the four bridges linking Île St-Louis and the mainland. All in all, the island looks remarkably similar to its 17th-century self and retains both its history and genteel tranquility. See neighborhood map, p. 19.

châtelet-les halles *(1er, 2ème)*

Paris's Châtelet-Les Halles is famous for turning Paris's pet vices into beloved institutions. Its most famous sight, the **Louvre,** was home to French kings for four centuries; absolute monarchy has since gone out of fashion, and the bedchambers and dining rooms of the *ancien régime* palace now house the world's finest art. The surrounding **Jardin des Tuileries** was redesigned in 1660 by Louis XIV's favorite architect, André Le Nôtre. The Sun King's prized grounds are now a public park, hosting crowds of strolling plebeians like ourselves that Louis probably wouldn't touch with a 10 ft. pole. Still, the arrondissement's legacy of excess is certainly alive and well; we suspect that toilet paper rolls are made of €1000 notes around the **Bourse de Valeurs,** and the world's oldest profession reigns supreme along the curbs of **Rue St-Denis.** One of Paris' main tourist hubs, Châtelet-Les Halles is heavily frequented by travelers, locals, and lots of scam artists. Seeing somebody run after a pickpocket is not an uncommon occurrence here, so move cautiously and confidently. See neighborhood map, p. 20–21.

the marais *(3ème, 4ème)*

The Marais is the ultimate ugly duckling tale. Originally all bog—the name "Marais" literally translates to "swamp"—the area became remotely livable in the 13th century, when monks drained the land to provide building space for the **Right Bank.** With Henri IV's construction of the glorious **Place des Vosges** at the beginning of the 17th century, the area ironically became the city's center of fashionable living; *hôtels particuliers* built by leading architects and sculptors abounded, as did luxury and scandal. During the Revolution, former royal haunts gave way to slums and tenements, and the majority of the *hôtels* fell into ruin or disrepair. The Jewish population, a presence in the Marais since the 12th century, grew with influxes of immigrants from Russia and North Africa but suffered tragic losses during the Holocaust. In the 1960s, the Marais was once again revived when declared a historic neighborhood. Since then, more than 30 years of gentrification, renovation, and fabulous-ization has restored the Marais to its pre-Revolutionary glory. Once-palatial mansions have become exquisite museums, and the tiny twisting streets are covered with hip bars, avant-garde galleries, and some of the city's most unique boutiques. **Rue des Rosiers,** in the heart of the *4ème*, is still the center of the city's Jewish population, though the steady influx of hyper-hip clothing stores threatens its existence. Superb kosher delicatessens neighbor Middle Eastern and Eastern European restaurants, and on Sundays, when much of the city is closed, the Marais remains lively. As if it didn't already have it all, the Marais is also unquestionably the center of gay Paris, with its hub at the intersection of **rue Sainte-Croix de la Brettonerie** and **rue Vieille du Temple.** Though the steady stream of tourists has begun to wear away the Marais's eclectic personality, the district retains its signature charm: an accessible and fun mix of old and new, queer and straight, cheap and chic. See neighborhood map, p. 22–23.

latin quarter and st-germain *(5ème, 6ème)*

The Latin Quarter and St-Germain tend to be two of Paris's primary tourist neighborhoods. From the hustle and bustle of the predatory cafes around **St-Michel** to the residential areas around **Cardinal Lemoine** and **Jussieu,** the schmoozy galleries of **Odéon** to two of the best museums in Paris **(Musee de Cluny, Musee Delacroix),** the fifth and sixth arrondissements truly have it all. The arrondissements are also eminently walkable, offering a wide variety of different neighborhoods to explore. Don't head underground during the day; you'll only encounter pickpockets, scammers, crowds, and, in the summertime, sweaty Metro rides. See neighborhood map, p. 24–25.

invalides *(7ème)*

With tourist attractions and museums at every corner, the *7ème* bustles with activity but could use some personality. French military prowess (stop laughing, that's not nice) is celebrated at **Invalides, École Militaire,** and **Champ de Mars,** while the nation's artistic legacy is shown full force at the **Musee d'Orsay** and the **Quai Voltaire.** Formerly one of Paris's most elegant residential districts, the neighborhood is now home to many of the city's embassies. The **Tour Eiffel** appropriately towers over it all, securing the area as one of the most popular destinations. See neighborhood map, p. 26–27.

champs-élysées *(8ème)*

If the Champs-Élysées was a supermodel, it would have been forced to retire for being well past its prime. The *arrondissemont* was synonymous with fashion throughout the 19th century, and the boulevards here are still lined with the vast mansions, expensive shops, and grandiose monuments that keep the tourists coming. But the sense of sophistication and progress has since devolved into charmless boutiques, office buildings, and car dealerships; these areas are comatose after dark. Only the **Champs** itself throbs late into the night, thanks to its unparalleled nightclubs and droves of tourists. A stroll along **avenue Montaigne, rue du Faubourg St-Honoré,** or around the **Madeleine** will give you a taste of what life in Paris for the excessively rich. While low prices usually mean low quality here—particularly for accommodations—there are a few good restaurants and many great museums. The northern part of the neighborhood, near the **Parc Monceau,** is a lovely and less-touristed area for walking. See neighborhood map, p. 28–29.

opéra (9ème)

The 9th arrondissement is (surprise surprise) best known for the **Opéra National Garnier,** a magnificent structure steeped in history that is difficult to top in terms of architectural triumph and OCD attention to detail. While the Opera National is the 9*ème*'s crown jewel, however, Opera is more aptly characterized by a juxtaposition of opposing worlds. One of Paris' chic shopping districts on the Grands Boulevards and the anything-but-classy **Pigalle,** encompassing the red light district and a sickening amount of shops catering to tourists. A residential neighborhood is just a stone's throw away, with the St. Georges Metro at its center, as is the beautiful **Moreau Museum,** housed in the famous painter's former home. A couple days in the Opéra will probably leave you thinking that it's among the most bizarre city neighborhoods in the world. One comes to learn that the comfortable coexistence of opposing worlds is *très* French. See neighborhood map, p. 30.

canal st-martin and surrounds (10ème)

The Canal St-Martin, i.e., the 10th arrondissement, is undeniably one of the sketchier neighborhoods in Paris. During the day as well as at night, you have to constantly watch your back for pickpockets, muggers, and swaying drunks. That being said, the neighborhood boasts some fantastic restaurants around the **Canal St-Martin** itself and some great hotel deals around **Gare du Nord.** The canal is like a mini-Seine; it's smaller, less touristed, and has just as much trash in it. It becomes a more peaceful area on Sundays, when cars are barred from the streets that run alongside the water. See neighborhood map, p. 31.

bastille (11ème, 12ème)

As its name attests, the Bastille (bah-steel) area is most famous for hosting the Revolution's kick-off at its prison on July 14, 1789. Hundreds of years later, the French still storm this neighborhood nightly in search of the latest cocktail, culinary innovation, and up-and-coming artist. Five Metro lines converge at **République** and three at Bastille, making the Bastille district a transport hub and mammoth center of action—the hangout of the young, the fun, and the frequently drunk. The 1989 opening of the glassy **Opéra Bastille** on the bicentennial of the Revolution was supposed to breathe new cultural life into the area, but the party atmosphere has yet to give way to galleries and string quartets. Today, with numerous bars along **Rue de Lappe,** manifold original dining options on **Rue de la Roquette** and **Rue J.P. Timbaud,** and young designer boutiques, the Bastille is a great area for unwinding after a day at the museums. See neighborhood map, p. 32.

butte-aux-cailles and chinatown (13ème)

The 13*ème* may have served as the setting of Victor Hugo's *Les Miserables*, but these days you're more likely to see a postmodern performance of *Les Miz* than any fashionably-starving children. Once one of Paris' poorest arrondissements, the arrival of the high-speed metro line and the ZAC Paris Rive Gauche redevelopment project has since transformed the neighborhood into a dynamic community and colorful hub of food and culture. Butte-Aux-Cailles attracts a young, artsy crowd who lovingly tags the walls with graffiti. Across the way, Chinatown stretches across multiple metro stops and is defined by a unique cultural hybridization rarely seen among immigrant enclaves, in both Paris and beyond. See neighborhood map, p. 33.

montparnasse (14ème, 15ème)

The Montparnasse area is home to two of Paris's most celebrated institutions, the **Catacombs** and the **Cité Universitaire,** and one of its most profitable tourist areas, **Montparnasse Bienvenue.** While the 14th arrondissement has historically been home to a trendy bohemian crowd, especially in the 1920s, the 15ème is generally residential and less exciting. Your key objective here is to avoid getting dragged into the touristy vortex of Montparnasse—you'll get fleeced by obnoxiously expensive restaurants and tourist outlets, and you'll think that Parisians are even snootier than they actually are.

One of Paris's more dynamic neighborhoods, the 14ème provides all the things any self-respecting arrondissement has to offer: a fairly diverse population, fantastic local restaurants, neighborhood specialty shops, leafy parks, mischievous children, and drunks. We recommend staying on the Metro's line 4 past Montparnasse and hopping off at Denfert, or, better yet, Mouton Duvernet. Check out the open-air markets on rue Daguerre, or stroll down **Avenue René Coty,** and go strike up a conversation on the *grande pelouse* at the Cité Universitaire. The 15ème isn't that exciting after hours, and doesn't boast much excitement in terms of people watching, unless you enjoy seeing women struggle to carry the fruits of their daily labor (read: Cartier, Dior, and Kooples bags). But the area does boast some of Paris's best-priced fine dining (Le Troquet, Le Dix Vins) and a somewhat vibrant nighttime bar scene on **Bld. Pasteur.** Stick a baguette in your bag, a cigarette in your mouth, a copy of *Le Monde* (or, if you're for Sarkozy, *Le Figaro*) under your arm, and hit the road. See neighborhood map, p. 34.

passy and auteuil (16ème)

Perhaps one of the swankiest neighborhoods in Paris, the 16ème is home to the ladies who lunch, their beautiful children, and their overworked husbands. Its elegant, boutique-lined streets are calmer than surrounding areas, and offer a glimpse into the lives of Parisian elites. Backlit by fabulous views of the Eiffel Tower, the neighborhood is home to a number of museums and attractions, and elderly local pedestrians are often swamped by mobs of eager sightseers. **Trocadero** witnesses the heaviest tourist traffic, with breakdancing street performers, sprawling gardens, and the best "I've been to Paris" photo opps. See neighborhood map, p. 35.

batignolles (17ème)

Far away from Paris' most touristed destinations, the 17ème offers a pleasant respite from the mobs of fellow tourists, and provides the chance to rub elbows, or other appendages, if you so choose, with the locals. A diverse group of Parisians are in residence here; bourgeois promenades with flowered trees are abruptly juxtaposed with working-class areas and immigrant neighborhoods. The eastern and southern parts of the arrondissement share the bordering 8ème and 16ème's aristocratic feel, while the *quartier*'s western edge resembles the shoddier 18ème and **Pigalle.** In the lively **Village Batignolles,** parents and their overly-earnest teenagers take leisurely strolls or sit in the many cafes. Unlike other, more crowded arrondissements, there is a real community vibe here. Families walk or lounge around, smile at their neighbors, and enjoy some good Parisian living. See neighborhood map, p. 36.

montmartre *(18ème)*

Montmartre might just be the most eccentric of Paris's neighborhoods. From the scenic vistas at the **Basilique de Sacre-Coeur,** to the historic **cabarets** and **Butte vineyard,** to the (ahem) colorful establishments in the **Red Light District** on Bld. de Clichy, you'll see it all in the 18th. Tourism in this part of town can be very difficult. While there aren't too many great options for staying in Montmartre, there are some fantastic sights, decent food, and fun local bars. Keep in mind that while wandering through this neighborhood, you might have to occasionally hike the 130m hill, or *butte,* **Montmartre.** See neighborhood map, p. 37.

buttes chaumont *(19ème)*

In the mid-19th century, Baron Haussman's architectural reforms paved the way for a new working-class neighborhood to be settled in the 19th arrondissement, on the northeastern outskirts of Paris. A quiet family neighborhood with a surprisingly lovely Parc des Buttes Chaumont, the 19*ème* is now making its best effort at a bohemian revival. The area is rapidly becoming the trendy new hot spot for young professionals and students and now boasts a diverse slew of growing Asian and North African communities. The modern macro-social engineering feat that is the Parc de la Villette is also well worth a visit.

orientation

skating through the streets

You know those Friday nights when you just get the urge to blaze through Paris riding roller blades? Well apparently, approximately 15,000 Parisians do, and they skate 19 miles around the city, from 10pm until late. While these tours all across Paris are free, you are encouraged to become a member of **Pari Roller** for a small fee. The organization has a few rules and guidelines to keep you safe:

- **WEAR BRIGHT NEON CLOTHING.** As it is probably fashionable in Paris and will be easier to spot in the nighttime.

- **GO AT YOUR OWN SPEED.** Don't push yourself too hard, since you can't really impress anyone while roller-skating.

- **PROTECT THOSE DAINTY WRISTS.** The majority of injuries occur there. Also wear protective padding on your head, knees and elbows.

- **DON'T SKATE ON THE SIDEWALK.** Pedestrians can be very big roadblocks. Injuries can happen and may be disastrous—don't go splat.

Even though there are more rules, concentrate on having a good time. Since the route changes weekly, you won't get bored if you go more than once. And remember, the Friday Night Fever tour is growing in popularity, so don't be shocked to see someone from your tour group skating alongside you. Hopefully they won't make fun of for your bright orange shorts and twenty wrist pads.

belleville and père lachaise *(20ème)*

Belleville is one of Paris's most legendary working-class neighborhoods. Although far from the city center, it is home to one of Paris's most visited tourist sights, the Cimetière du Père Lachaise (i.e., that cemetery where Jim Morrison was buried). During the late Second Republic, the *20ème* became a "red" arrondissement and was characterized as proletarian and **radical.** The fighting that occurred during the Commune suppression caught the neighborhood reds between the Versaillais troops to the west and the Prussian lines outside the city walls. Forts at Parc des Buttes-Chaumont and the Cimetière du Père Lachaise expired, and on May 28, 1871, the Communards abandoned their last barricade and surrendered. Their legacy of class solidarity and progressivism still characterizes the "red" arrondissement today. See neighborhood map, p. 38.

neighborhood maps

Île de la Cité and Île St-Louis

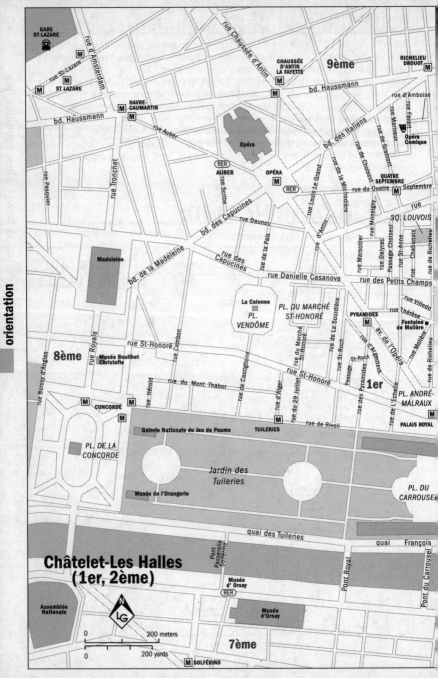

Châtelet-Les Halles (1er, 2ème)

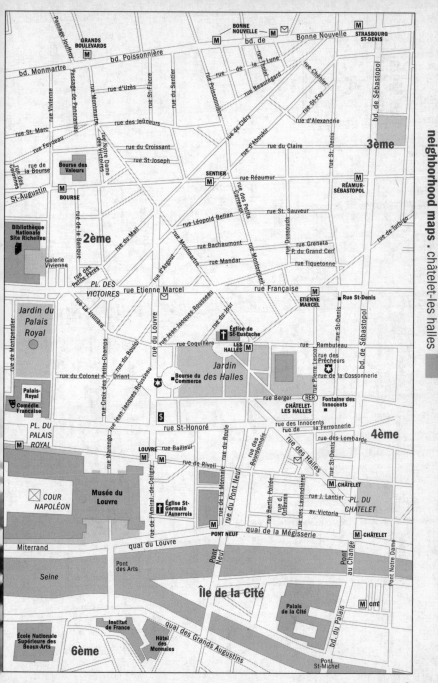

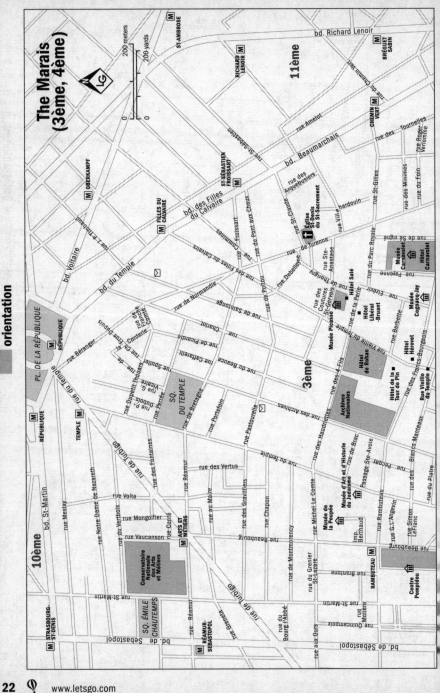

The Marais
(3ème, 4ème)

200 meters
200 yards

10ème

11ème

3ème

bd. Richard Lenoir

ST-AMBROSE Ⓜ

BRÉGUET SABIN Ⓜ

RICHARD LENOIR Ⓜ

bd. Beaumarchais

ST-SÉBASTIEN FROISSART Ⓜ

CHEMIN VERT Ⓜ

OBERKAMPF Ⓜ

FILLES DU CALVAIRE Ⓜ

bd. des Filles du Calvaire

bd. du Temple

rue du Pont-aux-Choux

rue St-Sébastien

rue Amelot

bd. Voltaire

av. de la République

PL. DE LA RÉPUBLIQUE

RÉPUBLIQUE Ⓜ

RÉPUBLIQUE Ⓜ

TEMPLE Ⓜ

rue du Temple

rue Béranger

rue de Franche-Comté

rue de Normandie

rue Debelleyme

rue de Saintonge

rue Charlot

rue de Picardie

rue de Bretagne

SQ. DU TEMPLE

rue du Temple

rue de Turenne

rue St-Claude

rue des Arquebusiers

rue des Tournelles

rue des Minimes

rue du Foin

rue St-Gilles

rue du Roger Verlomme

rue Ste-Anastase

Église St-Denis du St-Sacrement ⛪

rue de la Ville Hardouin

rue Villehardouin

rue Payenne

rue Elzévir

rue du Parc Royale

rue de Sévigné

Musée Carnavalet 🏛

Hôtel Carnavalet 🏛

Musée Cognacq-Jay 🏛

Hôtel Salé

Musée Picasso 🏛

Hôtel Libéral Bruant

Hôtel Hérovet

Hôtel de Rohan

Hôtel de la Tour du Pin

rue Vieille du Temple

rue de la Perle

rue des Coutures St-Gervais

rue Barbette

rue des Francs-Bourgeois

rue des 4-Fils

Rue Vieille du Temple

Archives Nationales

rue des Archives

rue des Haudriettes

rue des Blancs Manteaux

rue des Guillemites

rue Ste-Avoie

rue de Braq

rue du Temple

Musée d'Art et d'Historie du Judaïsme 🏛

Musée de la Poupée 🏛

Passage Ste-Avoie

rue Rambuteau

rue du Grenier St-Lazare

rue Aubriot

rue Pecquay

rue des Guillemites

rue des Archives

rue Simon LeFranc

rue G.-L'Argent

rue Geoffroy L'Angevin

rue du Renard

rue Beaubourg

rue Brantôme

RAMBUTEAU Ⓜ

Centre Pompidou 🏛

rue St-Martin

bd. de Sébastopol

STRASBOURG-ST-DENIS Ⓜ

RÉAUMUR-SÉBASTOPOL Ⓜ

SQ. ÉMILE CHAUTEMPS

bd. St-Martin

bd. St-Denis

bd. de Sébastopol

rue St-Denis

rue Quincampoix

rue aux Ours

rue St-Martin

rue Grenéta

rue du Bourg-l'Abbé

rue Réaumur

rue Volta

rue Notre-Dame de Nazareth

rue du Vertbois

rue Meslay

rue de Turbigo

ARTS ET MÉTIERS Ⓜ

Conservatoire Nationale des Arts et Métiers

rue Vaucanson

rue Conté

rue Mongolfier

rue Borda

rue des Fontaines

rue Réaumur

rue au Maire

rue des Gravilliers

rue Chapon

rue des Vertus

rue Dupetit-Thouars

rue G. Dubois

rue de la Corderie

rue Perrée

rue Dupetit-Thouars

rue Chrt. rue Dupuis

rue Paul Dubois

rue Portefoin

rue de Beauce

rue de Montmorency

rue Michel le Comte

rue Rambuteau

rue du Temple

rue de Montmorency

rue Beaubourg

Imp. Berthaud

rue du Bourg-l'Abbé

rue Molière

N

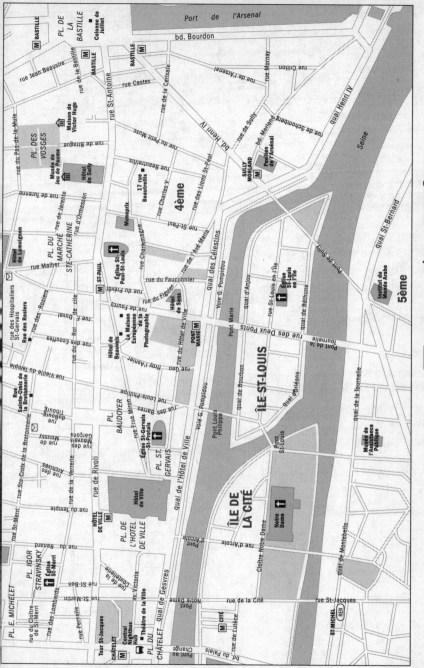

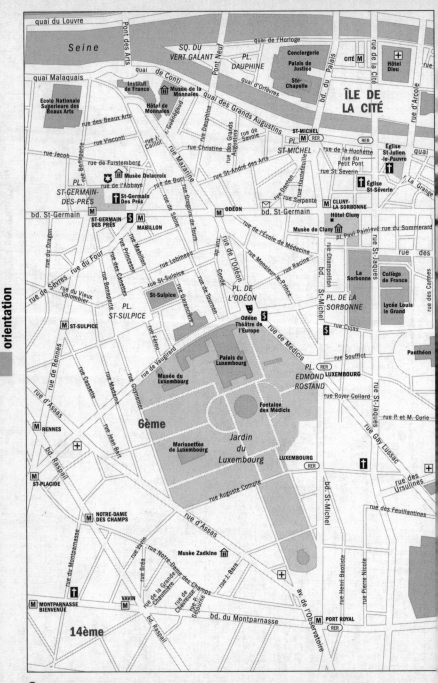

Seine

quai du Louvre

Pont des Arts

quai de l'Horloge

SQ. DU
VERT GALANT

Pont Neuf

PL.
DAUPHINE

Conciergerie

Palais de
Justice

CITÉ [M]

Hôtel
Dieu

Ste-
Chapelle

quai Malaquais

quai de Conti

quai d'Orfèvres

Palais

bd. du Palais

ÎLE DE
LA CITÉ

quai des Grands Augustins

rue de la Cité

rue d'Arcole

Institut
de France

quai des Grands Augustins

Musée de la
Monnaies

Hôtel de
Monnaies

Ecole Nationale
Superieure des
Beaux Arts

rue des Beaux Arts

rue de la Monnaie

rue Dauphine

rue J.
Caillot

rue Visconti

rue Mazarine

rue Christine

rue des Grands Augustins

rue de
Savoie

ST-MICHEL

PL.

ST-MICHEL

RER

rue de la Huchette

Église
St-Julien
le-Pauvre

rue Jacob

rue de Bonaparte

rue de Furstemberg

rue de l'Abbaye

Musée Delacroix

rue St-André des Arts

rue du
Petit Pont

rue St Séverin

r. La Grange

PL.

ST-GERMAIN-
DES-PRÉS

St-Germain
Des Prés

rue de Buci

rue Danton

rue Serpente

rue Hautefeuille

Église
St-Séverin

bd. St-Germain

ST-GERMAIN
DES PRÉS

[S] [M]

rue de Grégoire de Tours

ODÉON

bd. St-Germain

CLUNY-
LA SORBONNE

Hôtel Cluny

MABILLON

rue du Dragon

rue de Seine

rue de l'Ecole de Médecine

Musée de Cluny

pl. Paul Painlevé

rue du Sommerard

rue des

rue de Sèvres

rue du Four

rue du Vieux
Colombier

rue Mabillon

rue Princesse

rue des Canettes

rue St-Sulpice

rue Lobineau

rue de l'Odéon

rue Monsieur-le-Prince

rue Racine

La
Sorbonne

rue St-Jacques

Collège
de France

rue des Carmes

PL.
ST-SULPICE

rue Bonaparte

St-Sulpice

PL. DE
L'ODÉON

Condé

rue de Tournon

PL. DE LA
SORBONNE

Lycée Louis
le Grand

[M] ST-SULPICE

rue de Rennes

rue de Vaugirard

rue Férou

rue Garancière

Odéon
Théâtre de
l'Europe

[S]

rue de Médicis

rue Cujas

Panthéon

rue de Vaugirard

Palais du
Luxembourg

Musée du
Luxembourg

rue Soufflot

PL.
EDMOND
ROSTAND

RER

LUXEMBOURG

[M] RENNES

rue Cassette

rue Madame

rue Jean Bart

Fontaine
des Médicis

rue Royer Collard

rue Gay Lussac

[M]
ST-PLACIDE

bd. Raspail

6ème

Marionettes
de Luxembourg

Jardin
du
Luxembourg

LUXEMBOURG

RER

rue P. et M. Curie

rue des
Ursulines

NOTRE-DAME
DES CHAMPS

rue d'Assas

rue Auguste Compte

bd. St-Michel

rue des Feuillantines

[M]

rue du Montparnasse

rue Vavin

rue Bréa

rue Notre-Dame des Champs

Musée Zadkine

rue d'Assas

rue J. Bara

rue Henri-Baptiste

rue Pierre Nicole

[M] MONTPARNASSE
BIENVENUE

VAVIN
[M]

rue de la Grande Chaumière

rue
de
Chevreuse

rue P.
Séguine

PORT ROYAL
RER

av. de l'Observatoire

14ème

bd. Raspail

bd. du Montparnasse

orientation

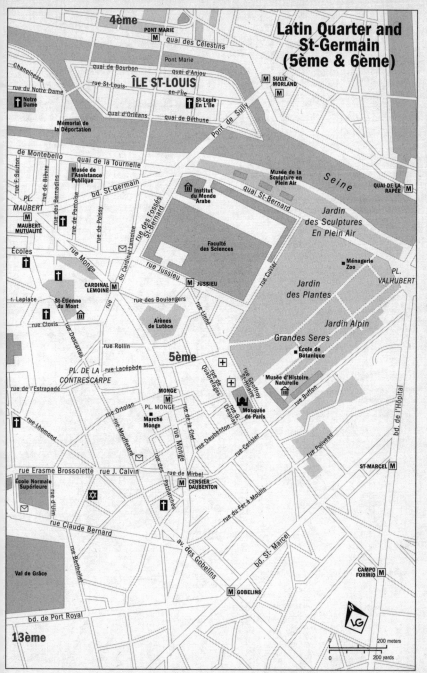

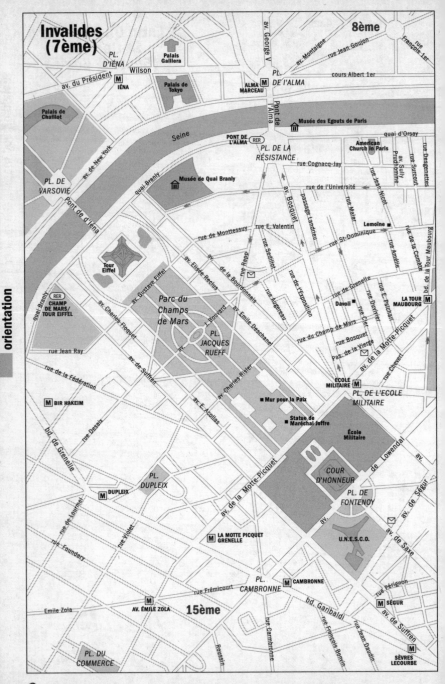

Invalides (7ème)

8ème

orientation

PL. D'IÉNA
Palais Galliera
Wilson
av. du Président
IÉNA
Palais de Tokyo
Palais de Chaillot
PL. DE VARSOVIE
Pont de d'Iéna
Tour Eiffel
RER CHAMP DE MARS/ TOUR EIFFEL
rue Jean Ray
rue de la Fédération
BIR HAKEIM
bd. de Grenelle
rue Desaix
PL. DUPLEIX
DUPLEIX
rue de Lourmel
rue Violet
rue Foundary
Emile Zola
AV. ÉMILE ZOLA
PL. DU COMMERCE
rue Frémicourt
PL. CAMBRONNE
CAMBRONNE
15ème

av. George V
av. Montaigne
rue Jean Goujon
rue François 1er
cours Albert 1er
PL. DE L'ALMA
ALMA MARCEAU
Pont de l'Alma
Musée des Egouts de Paris
quai d'Orsay
PONT DE L'ALMA RER
PL. DE LA RÉSISTANCE
American Church in Paris
rue Cognacq-Jay
av. Sully Prudhomme
rue des Desgentes
av. Surcouf
rue de l'Université
Seine
quai Branly
Musée de Quai Branly
av. Bosquet
passage Landrieu
rue de Montessuy
rue E. Valentin
rue de la Comète
rue Jean Nicot
rue Malar
rue St-Dominique
Lemoine
rue Amélie
rue de l'Exposition
rue de Grenelle
rue Cler
Davoli
rue Duvivier
rue E. Fabriani
LA TOUR MAUBOURG
av. de la Bourdonnais
av. de la Motte-Picquet
av. de Suffren
av. Elisée Reclus
av. Gustave Eiffel
av. Charles Floquet
Parc du Champs de Mars
J. Bouvard
PL. JACQUES RUEFF
av. Emile Deschanel
av. Charles Rister
av. de la Motte-Picquet
rue de la Vierge
rue du Champ de Mars
rue Bosquet
rue Chevert
ÉCOLE MILITAIRE
PL. DE L'ECOLE MILITAIRE
Mur pour la Paix
Statue de Maréchal Joffre
av. E. Acollas
École Militaire
COUR D'HONNEUR
de Lowendal
PL. DE FONTENOY
PL. DE LOWENDAL
av. de Ségur
av. de Saxe
U.N.E.S.C.O.
LA MOTTE PICQUET GRENELLE
bd. Garibaldi
SÉGUR
rue Pérignon
av. de Suffren
rue Jean Daudin
rue François Bonvin
Roussin
rue Cambronne
SÈVRES LECOURBE

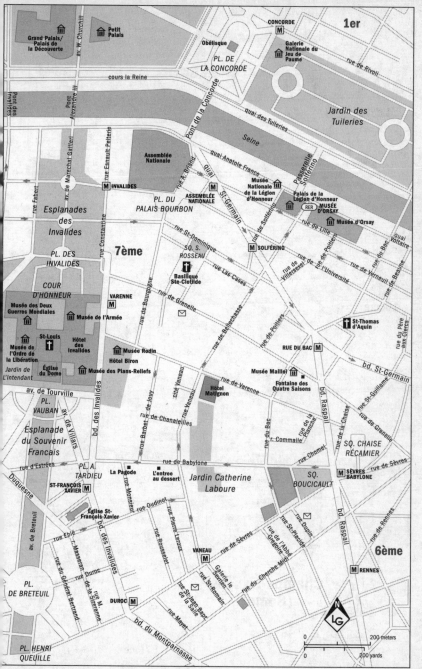

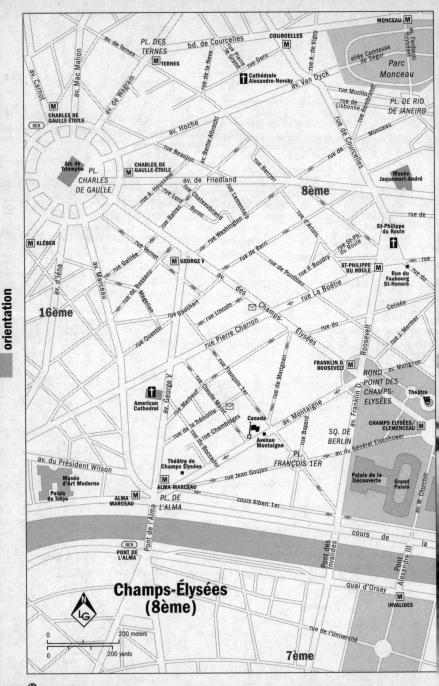

orientation

Champs-Élysées (8ème)

N L G

0   200 meters
0   200 yards

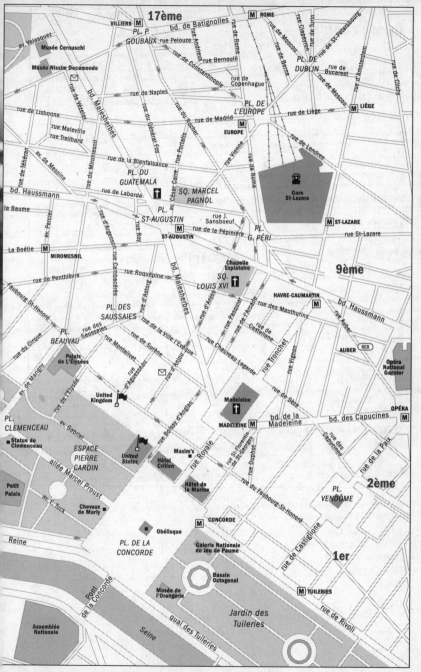

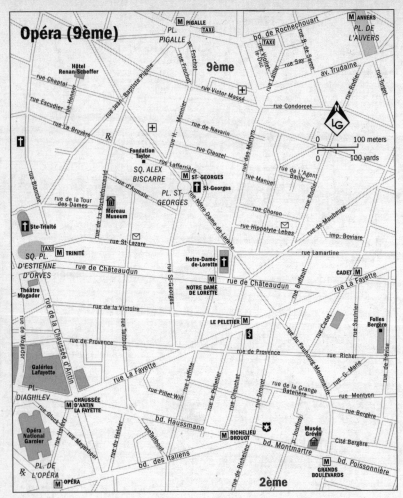

Opéra (9ème)

orientation

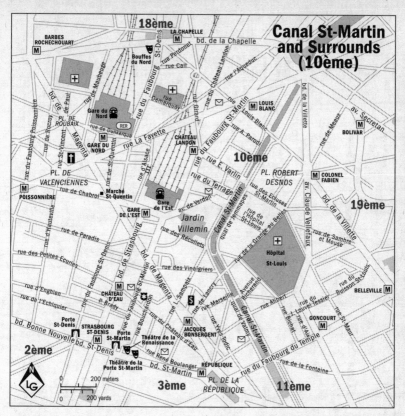

Canal St-Martin and Surrounds (10ème)

18ème

BARBES ROCHECHOUART Ⓜ

LA CHAPELLE Ⓜ

bd. de la Chapelle

rue St-Denis

Bouffes du Nord

rue Pordone

rue Cail

rue de la Chapelle

rue du Château-Landon

rue de l'Aqueduc

bd. de la Villette

av. Secretan

bd. de Maubeuge

bd. de Maux

rue Demarquay

rue Girard

rue St-Martin

LOUIS BLANC Ⓜ

BOLIVAR

bd. de Magenta

PL. DE ROUBAIX

rue de Paul

✚

Gare du Nord 🚂

RER

rue de Dunkerque

Gare du Nord

Ⓜ

rue La Fayette

rue du Faubourg St-Denis

rue du Faubourg St-Martin

rue Louis-Blanc

rue A.-Paroli

rue E. Varlin

PL. ROBERT DESNOS

COLONEL FABIEN Ⓜ

bd. du Faubourg Poissonnière

rue de Rocroy

rue St-Vincent

CHÂTEAU LANDON Ⓜ

rue d'Alsace

rue du Terrage

rue des Écluses St-Martin

av. Claude Vellefaux

19ème

PL. DE VALENCIENNES

Ⓜ POISSONNIÈRE

rue de Chabrol

Marché St-Quentin

rue du Quentin

10ème

Canal St-Martin

av. de Verdun

rue de l'Hôpital St-Louis

bd. de la Villette

rue de Sambre et Meuse

GARE DE L'EST Ⓜ

Gare de l'Est 🚂

Jardin Villemin

quai de Jemmapes

Hôpital St-Louis ✚

rue de Paradis

rue des Récollets

rue de la Grange au Belles

rue des Petites Écuries

bd. de Strasbourg

bd. de Magenta

rue des Vinaigriers

rue du Buisson St-Louis

BELLEVILLE Ⓜ

rue d'Enghien

rue de l'Échiquier

CHÂTEAU D'EAU Ⓜ P. Brady

rue du Faubourg St-Martin

-Sampoix

rue de Lancry

$

rue Marseille

Avenue Richerand

rue Alibert

rue du J.-Louvel-Tesier

rue du Bichat

GONCOURT Ⓜ

rue St-Maur

Porte St-Denis

STRASBOURG ST-DENIS Ⓜ

Porte St-Martin

rue du Château d'Eau

rue du Bouchardon

JACQUES BONSERGENT Ⓜ

rue Yves Toudic

Canal St-Martin

quai de Valmy

bd. Bonne Nouvelle bd. St-Denis

Théâtre de la Renaissance

rue René Boulanger

RÉPUBLIQUE

rue du Faubourg du Temple

rue de la Fontaine

2ème

Théâtre de la Porte St-Martin

bd. St-Martin

Ⓜ

3ème

PL. DE LA RÉPUBLIQUE

11ème

N

⚐LG

0   200 meters

0   200 yards

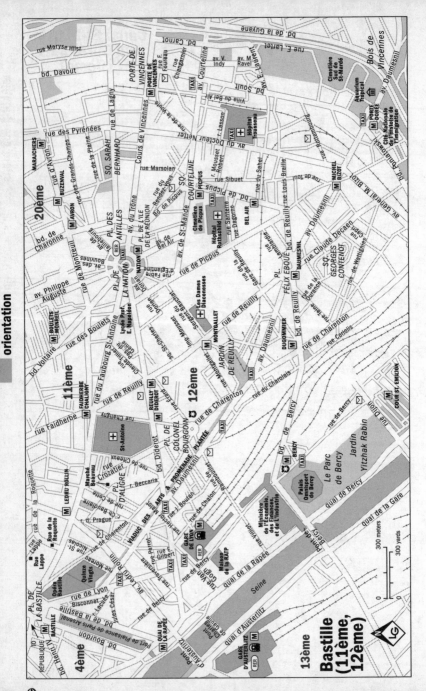

Bastille
(11ème,
12ème)

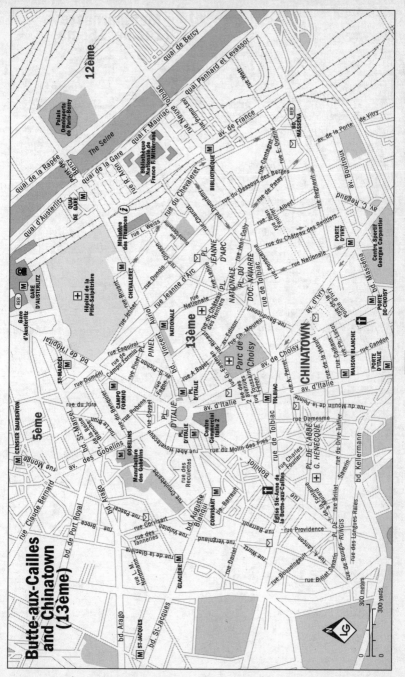

Butte-aux-Cailles and Chinatown (13ème)

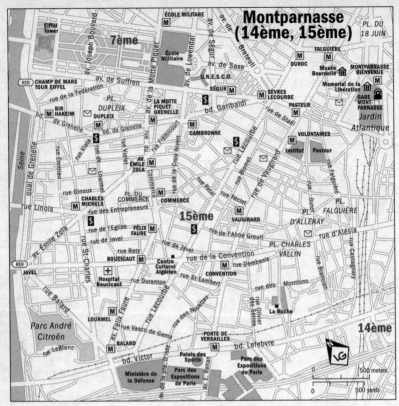

Montparnasse (14ème, 15ème)

orientation

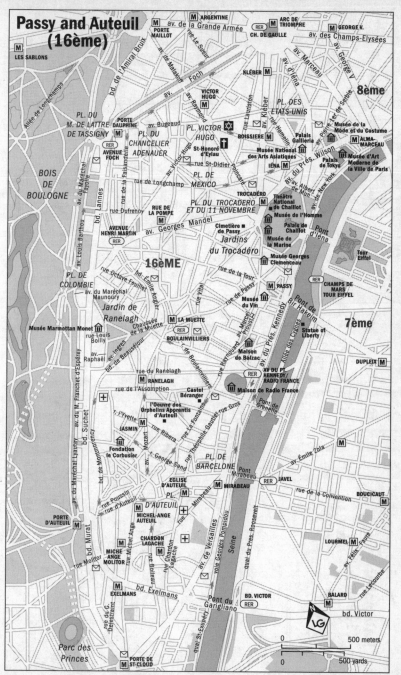

Passy and Auteuil (16ème)

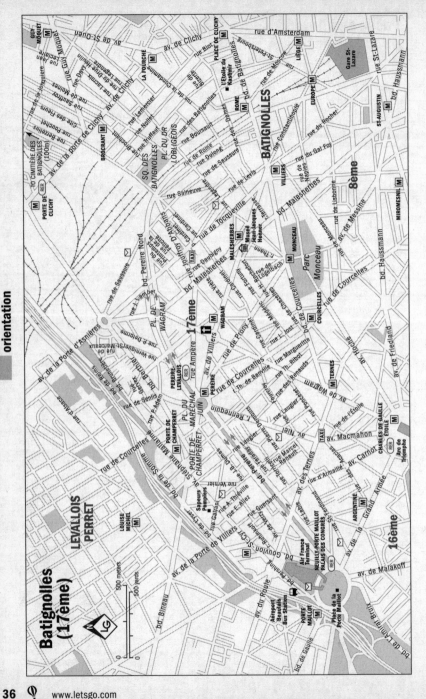

Batignolles (17ème)

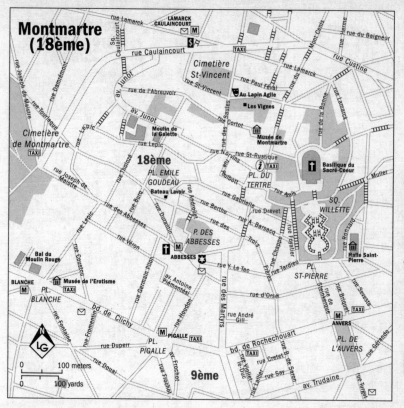

Montmartre
(18ème)

rue Lamarck

LAMARCK CAULAINCOURT

Sq. Caulaincourt

rue Caulaincourt

av. Junot

rue de l'Abreuvoir

av. Junot

rue Lepic

Cimetière de Montmartre

TAXI

rue Joseph de Maistre

rue Joseph de Maistre

rue Tourlaque

rue de Damrémont

Cimetière St-Vincent

rue Paul Féval

rue St-Vincent

rue Lamarck

rue Custine

Mont Cenis

rue Hermel

rue du Baigneur

Au Lapin Agile

Les Vignes

rue Cortot

Musée de Montmartre

Moulin de la Galette

rue Lepic

18ème

PL. EMILE GOUDEAU

Bateau Lavoir

rue Norvins

rue St-Rustique

Talbott

PL. DU TERTRE

rue des Saules

rue de la Bonne

Basilique du Sacré-Coeur

Muller

rue Lepic

rue Tholoze

rue des Abbesses

rue Burq

rue Berthe

rue Androuet

rue Durantin

rue Gabrielle

rue Drevet

rue A. Barsacq

rue Trois

SQ. WILLETTE

rue Foyatier

rue Ronsard

rue Chappe

rue Veron

P. DES ABBESSES

ABBESSES

rue des

rue Y. Le Tac

rue Tardieu

PL. ST-PIERRE

Halle Saint-Pierre

PL. DE L'AUVERS

rue Coustou

rue Lepic

Bal du Moulin Rouge

Museé de l'Erotisme

TAXI

BLANCHE

PL. BLANCHE

rue Fontaine

rue Fromentin

av. Antoine Plemontsai

rue Germain Pilon

rue Houdon

rue des Martyrs

rue Chappe

rue Frères

rue d'Orsel

rue André Gill

rue de Steinkerque

rue Steinkerque

rue Briquet

TAXI

ANVERS

rue Seveste

rue Gérando

bd. de Clichy

rue Duperr

PL. PIGALLE

PIGALLE

TAXI

av. Frochot

rue Douai

rue Frochot

bd. de Rochechouart

TAXI

rue Violet le-Duc

rue Cretet

rue B. de Séron

rue Say

av. Trudaine

rue de Lattre

rue Turgot

9ème

0 ——— 100 meters

0 ——— 100 yards

N

LG

neighborhood maps · montmartre

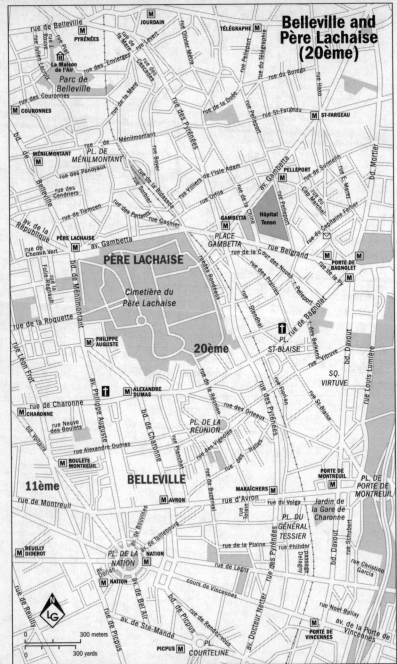

Belleville and Père Lachaise (20ème)

orientation

ACCOMMODATIONS

Budget accommodations (or for that matter, budget anything) can be pretty hard to find in this city. Hostels and hotels generally get cheaper as you journey farther out into the less trafficked arrondissements. Once you get out to the 17ème, however, you're looking at a pretty long Metro ride, and an inconvenient location doesn't always translate into decent prices here; a case in point Passy and Auteuil (16ème), whose residents make the kids on Gossip Girl look like tacky members of the nouveau riche. That being said, Paris has its fair share of steals. Both Châtelet-

greatest hits

- **WE'RE TRIPPIN' OUT, MAN:** The **(BVJ): Paris Louvre** in Châtelet-Les Halles is called the Louvre for a reason—short of becoming a character in a Dan Brown novel, this hostel is the closest you'll get to actually sleeping in the museum. The exceptionally youthful atmosphere and 60s vibe are both a plus.

- **KOWTOW TO THE CONVENT:** You'll have plenty to pray about in the **Maubuisson,** a renovated convent and monastery in the Marais. The hotel's on the pricey side for students, but if you're willing to splurge, the historic building and courtyard provide a peaceful respite from one of Paris's most fun and frenetic arrondissements.

- **COOKING UP PERFECTION:** Our researchers report that the **Perfect Hotel** in Champs-Élysées "is, well, practically perfect." Ideally located and super cheap, the hotel comes with free kitchen access.

- **OOPS!:** One of the few hostels in Paris with A/C, **Oops!** hostel is a little removed from downtown in the Butte-Aux-Cailles, but has unbeatable prices. And (we quote) "has fashion sense of a teen with an attitude problem." We like.

- **SCOOBY GANG SOLD SEPARATELY:** Yes, you're all the way in the 20th arrondissement, near Père Lachaise's fabled cemetery. But the wonderfully-named **Le D'Artagnan** hostel is cheap, enormous, and cultivates an exceptional young community, even by Paris standards. Besides, we've always wanted to talk smack with the ghost of Oscar Wilde.

Les Hailes and Bastille are home to youth hostels with rock bottom prices (around €20), ridiculously close to Paris's main attractions. When it comes to hotels, be on the lookout for exceptionally good two-stars. The great deals tend to be either very quirky or very forgettable, but are always clean and more peaceful than the alternatives; expect to pay about €40-60. Free Wi-Fi and cheap (or free) breakfasts are almost always provided, and it's not uncommon for hostels to host an adjoining bar. But if you're doing Paris on the cheap, be warned that you can't always count on having your own bathroom or shower, even if you shell it out for a single; A/C is also not as common a luxury as you might want it to be.

île de la cité and île st-louis

One of the romantic centers of Paris, the isles attracts honeymooners, swooners, and the like; the hoteliers more than make good on it. Rooms are generally anything but budget and more in the "I need to seduce her" price range.

▨ HÔTEL HENRI IV
☛ HOTEL ❸

25 pl. Dauphine ☎01 43 54 44 53 ▣www.henri4hotel.fr

It may not have modern-day "necessities" like TVs and hair dryers, but it does have some of the best located, least expensive rooms in Paris. Henry IV's printing presses once occupied this 400-year-old and off-beat building; the hotel's porthole doors and a winding staircase make it look like an ancient ship. Spacious rooms have large windows and charming views.

✚ ⓜPont Neuf. *i* Breakfast included. ⓢ Singles €42-59; doubles €49-78; twins €76-81.

châtelet-les halles

While affordable hotels in this trendy neighborhood tend to be pretty hard to come by, there are a few high-quality budget addresses that are worth checking out. Be sure to make your reservations far in advance—cheap spots in such a central location fill up rapidly at any time of the year. Also, be sure to watch yourself around Châtelet. Other tourists will not stick up for you (or even tell you) when a pickpocket or mugger is about to pounce.

▨ HOTEL DE ROUEN
☛(ⁿ)⊗ HOTEL ❷

42 Rue Croix des Petits Champs ☎01 42 61 38 21 ▣www.hotelderouen.net

This cozy two-star boasts the lowest prices you'll find in the 1st arrondissement for hotel accommodations. The friendly owner speaks English and is more than happy to tell you about the virtues of all the different rooms. Some of the rooms are decorated with liberated Metro signs and maps, so you won't even have to

accommodations

take advantage of the free Wi-Fi to plan your itinerary. While most rooms come equipped with showers, beware of getting the room without the shower on the first floor; you'll have to walk up five floors (the hotel doesn't have an elevator) to the hallway shower.

⚡ Ⓜ*Palais Royal Musée du Louvre, Les Halles.* *i* *Breakfast €6.* Ⓢ *Singles €40-60; doubles €45-75.* Ⓩ *Reception 24hr.*

HOTEL TIQUETONNE ☞👤 HOTEL ❸
6 rue Tiquetonne ☎01 42 36 94 58

Located a stone's throw from Marché Montorgueil and rue St-Denis' sex shops, Hotel Tiquetonne is surrounded by so many hip shopping spots it could send its hipster clientele into bankruptcy. Simple rooms are generously sized and boast unusually high ceilings (by Parisian standards). Amenities can be hit or miss; the hotel has an elevator, but some rooms don't have showers. Unbeatable prices for this location.

⚡ Ⓜ*Étienne-Marcel.* *i* *Breakfast €6. Hall showers €6.* Ⓢ *Singles €35, with shower €45; doubles with shower €55.* Ⓩ *Reception 24hr.*

CENTRE INTERNATIONALE DE PARIS (BVJ): PARIS LOUVRE ☺(ᴘ) HOSTEL ❶
20 rue Jean-Jacques Rousseau ☎01 53 00 90 90

In an unbeatable location right down the street from the Louvre, this massive hostel has taken over three buildings in total. All guests must be younger than 35, ensuring a young and international crowd. The decor in the lobby, dining hall, and rooms is utilitarian and vaguely influenced by the '60s. Spacious single-sex rooms are available with 2-8 beds. A new location is coming to the Opera district, stay tuned.

⚡ Ⓜ*Louvre.* *i* *Breakfast included. Reservations can be made no more than 15 days in advance by phone or internet, except Jul-Aug, when they can be made 2 months in advance. Wi-Fi in dining hall €2/1hr., €3/2hr.* Ⓢ *Dorms €29, €35 for bed in double.* Ⓩ *Reception 24hr. 3-day max. stay; extensions can be arranged on arrival.*

HOTEL MONTPENSIER ☞(ᴘ) HOTEL ❸
12 rue de Richelieu ☎01 42 96 28 50 🖳www.montpensierparis.com

Hotel Montpensier is a swanky and relatively affordable option on a quiet street, only a few blocks from the Louvre and other sights of the *2ème.* Tall ceilings and savvy old-school decor grace the first two floors of the hotel. While the rooms upstairs aren't quite as gracefully decorated (and have spots on the walls), they offer much lovelier views of rue de Richelieu, if you can negotiate with the doors' elusively complex locks. The staff is warm and eager to help you get around the arrondissement and Paris at large. 35 of the hotel's 43 rooms have ensuite bath.

⚡Ⓜ*Palais Royal Musée du Louvre.* *i* *Breakfast €9. Free Wi-Fi.* Ⓢ *Singles €71; doubles €76-118; triples €139; quads €159.* Ⓩ *Reception 24hr.*

HOTEL DU LION D'OR ☞(ᴘ) HOTEL ❹
5 Rue de La Sourdière ☎01 42 60 79 04 🖳www.hotel-louvre-paris.com

Hotel du Lion d'Or isn't a budget hotel, but its location on a deliciously tranquil street in the 1st arrondissement is worth the price. The breakfast area and rooms are richly decorated and sunny. All rooms equipped with a full bathroom. There are some great deals available for three-night stays; check the website.

⚡ Ⓜ*Pyramides.* Ⓢ *Breakfast €9.50. Singles €90-145; studio €155-175; duplex €250-285; large apartment €430. Extra bed €15.* Ⓩ*24-hr. reception.*

HOTEL HENRI-IV ☞ HOTEL ❸
25 Pl. Dauphine ☎01 43 54 44 53 🖳henri4hotel.fr

Located on the beautiful, leafy *place* Dauphine, Hotel Henri-IV has been a family business since 1937, so expect a warm welcome. All rooms come with shower and all except for the cheapest single with a toilet. There's no elevator, but the view from the 5th floor of place Dauphine's treetops and the Cathedral of Notre Dame is spectacular.

✻ ⓂPont Neuf. *i* Breakfast included. Ⓢ Singles €59-72; doubles €74-81. ⌚ Reception 24hr.

HOTEL DES BOULEVARDS
⌖⟨⟩ HOTEL ❸

10 rue de la Ville-Neuve ☎01 42 36 02 29 🖳www.hoteldesboulevards.com

Located on the outskirts of the 2*éme's* fabric and rug district, Hotel des Boulevards keeps it simple, with sparse and generously sized rooms at rock-bottom prices (for the Chatelet-Les Halles, anyway). Expect a warm welcome from the personable staff.

✻ ⓂBonne Nouvelle. *i* Breakfast included. Ⓢ Singles and doubles €50-65.

HOTEL VIVIENNE
⌖⊗ HOTEL ❸

40 rue Vivienne ☎01 42 33 13 26 🖳www.hotel-vivienne.com

Located on a quiet street in the 2*éme*, Hotel Vivienne boasts lush decor, a very warm welcome, and showers in every room. The owner is proud of the hotel's rooms; six are renovated per year. Several of the rooms include lovely balconies that overlook rue Vivienne. If you want one of these—or a room period—you'll have to make your reservations up to several months in advance.

✻ ⓂBourse, Grands Boulevards, or Richelieu. *i* Continental breakfast €11. Ⓢ Singles with shower €64; doubles €92-118. Extra bed 30%.

the marais

As would be expected, the Marais and its surroundings provide budget accommodations with a bit of flair. Many basic rooms are wallet-friendly, done up in style, and situated in the center of Parisian action. The trendy yet down to earth 4*ème* is also home to some of the best deals and worthwhile splurges in the city. There's a lot of good stuff to take home.

▨ MAUBUISSON
⌖⟨⟩ HOSTEL ❸

12 rue des Barres ☎01 42 74 23 45 🖳www.mije.com

Recognized as a 17th-century historical monument, Maubisson is a former convent on a quiet street by the St-Gervais monastery. In keeping with the pious theme, the hostel only accommodates individual travelers rather than groups. A member of the MJIE hostel group. Airport pickup and drop-off can be arranged, as can reservations for area attractions; call for details.

✻ ⓂHôtel de Ville or ⓂPont Marie. From ⓂPont Marie, walk opposite traffic on rue de l'Hôtel-de-Ville and turn right on rue des Barres. *i* Breakfast, in-room shower, and sheets included (no towels). No smoking. English spoken. Public phones and free lockers (with €1 deposit). Internet access €0.10 per min. with €0.50 initial connection fee. MIJE membership required (€2.50). Arrive before noon the 1st day of reservation (call in advance if you'll be late). Reserve months ahead online and 2-3 weeks ahead by phone. Ⓢ 4- to 9-bed dorms €30; singles €49; doubles €72; triples €96. ⌚ Reception 7am-1am. Lockout noon-3pm. Curfew 1am; notify in advance if coming back after this time. Quiet hours after 10pm. 7-night max. stay.

▨ LE FOURCY
⌖⟨⟩ HOSTEL ❸

6 rue de Fourcy ☎01 42 74 23 45 🖳www.mjie.com

Le Fourcy surrounds a large, charming, mansion-worthy courtyard ideal for meeting travelers or for open-air picnicking. The adjoining restaurant is located in an authentic vaulted cellar and offers a main course with drink (lunch only) and a three-course "hosteler special" (€10.50).

➜ ⓂSt-Paul or ⓂPont Marie. From ⓂSt-Paul, walk opposite the traffic for a few meters down rue St-Antoine and turn left on rue de Fourcy. i Breakfast, in-room shower, and sheets included (no towels). No smoking. English spoken. Public phones and free lockers (with €1 deposit). Internet access €0.10 per min. with €0.50 initial connection fee. MIJE membership required (€2.50). Arrive before noon the 1st day of reservation (call in advance if you'll be late). Reserve months ahead online and 2-3 weeks ahead by phone. Ⓢ 4- to 9-bed dorms €30; singles €49; doubles €72; triples €96. ⏰ Reception 7am-1am. Lockout noon-3pm. Curfew 1am; notify in advance if coming back after this time. Quiet hours after 10pm. 7-night max. stay.

✍ HOTEL PICARD — 🔌📶 HOTEL [4]

26 rue de Picardie ☎01 48 87 53 82 💻www.hotelpicardparis.com

A welcoming, family-owned hotel that's run more like a home with an open-door policy. Let's Go readers will definitely feel like a member of the family; a 5% discount is given if you flash your copy (yeah, yeah, we know, shameless product pushing). Bright and adorable rooms vary in size, but all are comfy. Many of them have private bathrooms, most of which have been recently renovated. TVs and safes in rooms with showers.

➜ ⓂRépublique. Follow bd. du Temple and turn right on rue Charlot. Take the first right on rue de Franche Comte, which becomes rue de Picardie. i Shower €3. Breakfast €5. Reserve 1 week ahead in summer and 2 weeks ahead the rest of the year. Ⓢ Singles with sink €53-68, with bath €74-93; doubles €59-74/89-112; triples €124-155.

✍ HÔTEL JEANNE D'ARC — 🔌📶 HOTEL [4]

3 rue de Jarente ☎01 48 87 62 11 💻www.hoteljeannedarc.com

Joan of Arc may have been one, but you certainly won't be a martyr for staying in this quaint hotel. Charming rooms decorated in mismatched patterns all come with bath or shower, toilet, cable TV, safe, and hair dryer. Despite its modern amenities, the place feels more like a home-style inn than a two-star hotel; the dining area boasts an absurdly funky mosaic mirror and serves a country-style breakfast.

➜ ⓂSt-Paul. From ⓂSt-Paul, walk against traffic on rue de Rivoli; turn left on rue de Sévigné, then right on rue de Jarente. i Breakfast €7. English spoken. Reserve 2-3 months in advance (longer for stays in Sept-Oct) by emailing or calling with credit card. Ⓢ Singles €62-90; doubles €90-116; triples €146; quads €160.

✍ HÔTEL DU SÉJOUR — 🔌 HOTEL [3]

36 rue du Grenier St-Lazare ☎01 48 87 40 36 💻www.hoteldusejour.com

Bringing the spirit of minimalism to the service industry, this trendy hotel features 20 basic rooms with a colorful and urban decor. Ideally located a block away from Les Halles and the Centre Pompidou. You'll be pleased with the warm staff at reception and the young clientele.

➜ ⓂÉtienne-Marcel. i Reserve 2-3 weeks in advance. Ⓢ Singles €42-85; doubles €44-90, with shower and toilet €56-95. Best rates online. ⏰ Reception 7:30am-10:30pm.

LE FAUCONNIER — 🔌📶 HOSTEL [2]

11 rue du Fauconnier ☎01 42 74 23 45 💻www.mjie.com

Le Fauconnier is an ivy-covered, sun-drenched building just steps away from the Seine and Île St-Louis. All rooms have shower and sink.

➜ ⓂSt-Paul or ⓂPont Marie. From ⓂSt-Paul, walk opposite the traffic for a few meters down rue St-Antoine and turn left on rue de Fourcy. i Breakfast, in-room shower, and sheets included (no towels). No smoking. English spoken. Public phones and free lockers (with €1 deposit). Internet access €0.10 per min. with €0.50 initial connection fee. MIJE membership required (€2.50). Arrive before noon the 1st day of reservation (call in advance if you'll be late). Reserve months ahead online and 2-3 weeks ahead by phone. Ⓢ 4- to 9-bed dorms €30; singles €49; doubles €72; triples €96. ⏰ Reception 7am-1am. Lockout noon-3pm. Curfew 1am; notify in advance if coming back after this time. Quiet hours after 10pm. 7-night max. stay.

HÔTEL ANDRÉA RIVOLI

◆(((•)))❄ HOTEL ❹

3 rue St-Bon ☎01 42 78 43 93 🖳www.hotel-andrea-rivoli.com

Living proof that well-run businesses don't have to be soulless, this modern hotel has a friendly and family-run vibe. Rooms are clean, carpeted, and softly decorated with phone, hairdryer, TV, A/C, and bath. Some rooms have a sleek, black-and-white zebra motif. Top floor rooms have balconies. Conveniently located on a quiet street two blocks from Hotel de Ville.

⚡ Ⓜ*Hôtel de Ville.* *i* *Breakfast €8.50.* Ⓢ *Singles €70-82; doubles €90-130.*

HÔTEL SÉVIGNÉ

◆(((•)))❄ HOTEL ❷

2 rue Malher ☎01 42 72 76 17 🖳www.le-sevigne.com

Everyone knows that French people are skinny, but even Twiggy would have a hard time squeezing around this hotel. The absurdly tiny but brightly decorated rooms are all equipped with A/C, hair dryers, telephone, TV and bath. Ideally located in the center of the Marais, which means you'll probably be spending most of your time outside anyway.

⚡ Ⓜ*St-Paul.* *i* *Breakfast €8.* Ⓢ *Singles €69; doubles €84-95; triples €113.*

HÔTEL DE NICE

◆(((•)))❄ HOTEL ❺

42bis rue de Rivoli ☎01 42 78 55 29 🖳www.hoteldenice.com

This quirky and extravagantly decorated hotel off the adorable Pl. du Bourg-Tibourg prides itself on its "old-time Paris" appeal. Heavily wallpapered and painted rooms feature vintage prints, satellite TV, toilet, shower or bath, hair dryer, phone, and A/C. A few have balconies with great views, but the beauty comes at a price.

⚡ Ⓜ*Hôtel de Ville.* *i* *Breakfast (€8) served in a gorgeous salon. Reserve 2-4 weeks in advance.* Ⓢ *Singles €80-95; doubles €110-120; triples €135-145.*

HÔTEL DE ROUBAIX

◆ HOTEL ❹

6 rue Greneta ☎01 42 72 89 91 🖳www.hotel-de-roubaix.com

The rooms here are small and may look like your grandmother decorated them (check out the flowered wallpaper), but they are also clean, with high ceilings and soundproof windows. All have bathrooms, phone, locker, and satellite TV; some have balconies.

⚡ Ⓜ*Réaumur-Sébastopol.* *i* *Breakfast €7.* Ⓢ *Singles €64-74; doubles €74; triples €84.*

HÔTEL BELLEVUE ET DU CHARIOT D'OR

◆ HOTEL ❹

39 rue de Turbigo ☎01 48 87 45 60 🖳www.hotelbellevue75.com

Standard rooms are short on light but clean, with phone and cable TV. More time may be spent in the spacious bathrooms, many of which have full baths. Some rooms have balconies.

⚡ Ⓜ*Étienne-Marcel.* *i* *Breakfast €7. Reserve 3 weeks in advance.* Ⓢ *Singles €64; doubles €72-75; triples €87; quads €98. 5% discount if you flash your Let's Go.*

HOTEL PRATIC

◆ HOTEL ❹

9 rue d'Ormesson ☎01 48 87 80 47 🖳www.hotelpratic.com

Tiny, tiny rooms with busy, busy decor in a timbered hotel on a redeeming cobblestone square in the Marais. A dark retreat from the colorful 4ème, the business of the patterns creates a cozy feel. All guest rooms have TVs, direct-dial phones, hair dryers, safes, and soundproof windows.

⚡ Ⓜ*St-Paul.* *i* *Breakfast included for long stays, €6 for stays under 5 days. Reserve online or by phone 2-3 weeks in advance. English spoken.* Ⓢ *Doubles €79-89; triples €98. Book online for best rates.*

HÔTEL DE LA HERSE D'OR

◆(((•))) HOTEL ❸

20 rue St-Antoine ☎01 48 87 84 09 🖳www.hotel-herse-dor.com

A decent hotel in every way—decent location, decent rooms, decent service—it becomes more exceptional when you remember it's technically a one-star estab-

the marais

lishment. Small, clean, slightly dark rooms with low ceilings and a cute timbered dining area and two courtyards. All rooms have Wi-Fi, hair dryer, phone, and TV.

⌗ ⓂBastille. *i* Breakfast €6. Ⓢ Singles with sink €65; doubles with sink €75, with full bath €99; triples with bath €129.

latin quarter and st-germain

While hotels are generally a bit overpriced in these neighborhoods, it's to be expected given their central location in Paris. Nonetheless, the area boasts some truly luxurious accommodations at very reasonable prices. If you want to be well located while living the (somewhat) high life, *Let's Go* has a few good recommendations for you.

▨ HÔTEL DE NESLE ✦ HOTEL ❸
7 rue du Nesle   ☎01 43 54 62 41 ▣www.hoteldenesleparis.com

An absolutely phenomenal place to stay. Every room is unique and represents a particular time period or locale. The Molière room is ideal for the comically minded, and an Oriental room is available for undying proponents of the colonial lifestyle (don't let that be you). The lobby's ceiling is adorned with bouquets of dried flowers, and the peaceful garden has terraced seating and a duck pond. Reserve a good deal in advance, because this unforgettable accommodation fills up quickly, especially during the summertime.

⌗ ⓂOdéon. *i* Laundry facilities on-site. Ⓢ Singles €55-65; doubles €75-100. Extra bed €12.

HOTEL DES ARGONAUTS ✦♿ HOTEL ❸
12 rue de la Huchette   ☎01 43 54 09 82 ▣www.hotel-les-argonautes.com

A hotel with extremely reasonable prices, especially considering its location on one of Paris's main thoroughfares. The intriguing decor includes leopard-print chairs perched under traditional rustic wood-beamed ceilings and insulates the guest from the hustle and bustle of rue de la Huchette. Keep in mind that rue de la Huchette is almost always buzzing with activity; if you need your peace and quiet, search elsewhere. All rooms have showers; more expensive options have toilets and bathtubs.

⌗ ⓂSt-Michel. *i* Breakfast €5. Ⓢ Singles €55-80; doubles €65-90; triples €90.

HÔTEL ESMERALDA ✦ HOTEL ❹
4 rue St-Julien-le-Pauvre   ☎01 43 54 19 20

The rooms here are potentially awesome. Antique wallpaper, rope staircase railings (geezers, beware), exposed wooden ceiling beams, and red velvet make Esmeralda a cozy and refined place to stay, if not always a top-of-the-line one. Rooms range from palatial suites to singles with doors so narrow that most Americans won't be able to squeeze through them. Great location near a small park, within sight of the Seine and earshot of Notre Dame's bells.

⌗ⓂSt. Michel. *i* Breakfast €7. Ⓢ Singles €75-90; doubles €100-110; triples €130; quads €150. ⌚ Reception 24hr.

DELHY'S HÔTEL ✦ HOTEL ❷
22 rue de l'Hirondelle   ☎01 43 26 58 25 ▣www.delhyshotel.com

A stone's throw from pl. St-Michel and the Seine, Delhy's is situated on a quiet cobblestone alleyway. Wood-paneled and often palatial stone-walled rooms come at decent prices in a surprisingly quiet location. All basic amenities are covered, with a TV with a satellite dish and a phone in every room. Cheapest singles and doubles come with sink only.

⌗ⓂSt-Michel. *i* Breakfast €7. Ⓢ Singles €46-56, with shower €66-71; doubles €62-82; triples €111-121. Extra bed €15.

HÔTEL BRÉSIL

📶 📶 HOTEL ❷

10 rue Le Goff ☎01 43 54 76 11 🖳 www.bresil-paris-hotel.com

While only a block away from the Metro and Luxembourg Garden, Hôtel Brésil feels far removed from the clamoring *5ème*. If the luxurious wood-paneled lobby and the rooms with sound-proof windows, hair dryers, and cable TVs aren't enough, sleeping in the same chamber as the hotel's famous past occupant, Sigmund Freud, may appeal to your subconscious.

✚ *RER: Luxembourg.* *i* *Breakfast €6.* Ⓢ *Singles €85; doubles €95-110; triples €135. Up to €35 off 3-night weekend stays and high-season promotions.*

HOTEL GAY LUSSAC

📶 📶 HOTEL ❷

29 rue Gay Lussac ☎01 43 54 23 96 🖳www.paris-hotel-gay-lussac.com

An older folks' place (owned by old folks, not inhabited by them) that hosts a younger crowd. The hotel has been around for 50 years, and the rooms' classic French doors, creaky floors, no-frills dining room, and old-school charm are a throwback to a previous age. Rock-bottom prices for rooms that vary widely in size, equipped with only a WC.

✚Ⓜ *RER: Luxembourg.* *i* *Breakfast €6. Wi-Fi €3 per 24hrs, €5 per 48hrs.* Ⓢ *singles €50-65; doubles €60-80; triples €100; quad €120.*

HÔTEL STELLA

📶 HOTEL ❶

41 rue Monsieur-le-Prince ☎01 40 51 00 25 🖳site.voila.fr/hotel-stella

The rooms here are huge, boasting high ceilings, lots of exposed beams, the occasional piano, and rich oriental rugs. Sun flows into the rooms in the afternoon; this is budget paradise. All rooms are equipped with shower and WC.

✚Ⓜ *Odéon.* Ⓢ *Singles €30-50; doubles €60; triples €80; quads €100.*

HÔTEL ST-ANDRÉ DES ARTS

📶 HOTEL ❸

66 rue St-André-des-Arts ☎01 43 26 96 16

Stone walls, high ceilings, and exposed beams make this surprising hotel feel like a country inn, despite its location in the heart of St-Germain. The hotel is exceptionally fancy for a one-star; you'll feel like royalty mounting the red-carpeted stairs to your rather spacious room.

✚Ⓜ*Odéon.* *i* *Breakfast included.* Ⓢ *Singles €73; doubles €93-98; triples €117; quads €129.*

HOTEL ST-JACQUES

📶 📶 ❄ HOTEL ❸

35 rue des Écoles ☎01 44 07 45 45 🖳www.paris-hotel-stjacques.com

A perfect hotel for those who are accustomed to enjoying, and paying for, the finer things in life. Audrey Hepburn and Cary Grant fans may recognize this chic hotel from the 1963 romantic murder mystery *Charade*. Spacious, elegant rooms with balcony, bath, and TV come at reasonable, if by no means cheap, rates. Chandeliers, Belle Époque frescoes, and walls decorated with *trompe-l'oeil* designs create a regal feel; it's not quite Versailles, but it's a pretty good deal for €125. A/C is an unusual amenity, and perhaps worth the extra buck for those steamy summer nights.

✚Ⓜ*Maubert-Mutualité.* *i* *Breakfast €12.50. English spoken. Online discounts up to 25%.* Ⓢ *Singles €125; doubles €145-250; triples €250.*

HÔTEL DU LYS

📶 HOTEL ❺

23 rue Serpente ☎01 43 26 97 57 🖳www.hoteldulys.com

If relative luxury in lodging is important to you, this semi-splurge is well worth it. Spacious rooms, tall ceilings, colorful wall-prints, rustic beams, antique tiles, and a slightly crooked staircase will make you feel like you're staying in someone's château. All rooms come with bathtub or shower, TV, and phone; some come with doors so narrow they must be anti-American. Reserve well in advance during the summer.

✚Ⓜ*Odéon or* Ⓜ*St-Michel.* Ⓢ *Singles €100; doubles €105 for 1 bed, €120 for 2; triples €140.*

latin quarter and st-germain

HÔTEL MARIGNAN 💳📶 HOTEL [3]

13 rue du Sommerard ☎01 43 54 63 81 💻www.hotel-marignan.com

This family-owned hotel offers a few rare amenities. Clean, freshly decorated rooms can sleep up to five—a rare find in Paris. Backpackers and families can enjoy hostel friendliness and rates without sacrificing hotel privacy. The hotel also offers free laundry *(8am-8pm)*, so you can wash the pajamas you sweat out in the A/C-less rooms as many times as you want. The floor bathrooms might occasionally be a bit grimy, but nothing truly bothersome. The fluent English-speaking owners will gladly chat with you, suggest sightseeing activities and restaurants.

*‡ ⓂMaubert-Mutualité. **i** Breakfast included. Kitchen available for use 12:45-9:30pm. Hall showers open until 10:45pm. Reserve ahead. Ⓢ Apr-July singles €52-65; doubles €68-95; triples €90-120; quads €115-140; quints €135-160. Prices vary in low season.*

YOUNG AND HAPPY HOSTEL 💳📶 HOSTEL [1]

80 rue Mouffetard ☎01 47 07 47 07 💻www.youngandhappy.fr

A funky, lively hostel with 21 clean—if basic—rooms, some with showers and toilets. Friendly staff speaks English. A kitchen is available for guest use; the hostel is building a bar in the breakfast room which should be installed by late 2010.

*‡ ⓂMonge. **i** Breakfast included. Internet €2 per 30min. Ⓢ Sheets €2.50 with €5 deposit, towels €1. Ⓢ 2-, 3-, 4-, 5-, 6-, 8-, or 10-bed dorms in high season €28-85. 🕐 Strict lockout 11am-4pm.*

invalides

Budget travel isn't exactly synonymous with the elegant *7ème*. Still, the centrally located arrondissement hosts a number of modern and decently affordable hotels with a friendly staff committed to good service. Many rooms also come with a view of the gilded dome of Invalides.

GRAND HÔTEL LÉVÊQUE 💳 HOTEL [4]

28 rue Cler ☎01 47 05 49 15 💻www.hotel-leveque.com

Centrally located on the quaint and cobblestoned Rue de Cler, this richly decorated hotel is just steps away from many of the arrondissement's main attractions. The hotel offers rooms with views of the street and courtyard, and some include full baths.

*‡ ⓂÉcole Militaire. **i** Breakfast €9. Ⓢ Singles €62-74; doubles €95-130; twins €95-134; triples €132-155; quads €154-159.*

HOTEL DE TURENNE 💳 HOTEL [3]

20 Ave. de Tourville ☎01 47 05 99 92

Somewhere between nice and nice enough, this hotel almost has a personality. It may have the squeaky floors and pin-striped wallpaper of forgettable hotels everywhere, but the bathrooms are huge and rooms are well kept.

‡ ⓂÉcole Militaire. Ⓢ Singles €69; doubles €87; twins €100; triples €130.

HOTEL MONTEBELLO 🚫💳 HOTEL [2]

18 rue Pierre Leroux ☎01 47 34 41 18 💻hmontebello@aol.com

From the worn leather couch in the lobby to the faded old photographs lining the walls, Hotel Montebello feels more like a haven for long-lost French grandchildren than an actual hotel. Montebello provides clean and colorful rooms with purple curtains at some of the best prices in the *7ème*. It's a bit far from most of the neighborhood sights, but the elderly proprietor lends a genuine taste of old Paris. Be warned that credit cards are still considered a bit too new-fangled for this place; you will have to pay by check.

*‡ ⓂVaneau. **i** All rooms with bath. Ⓢ Singles €49; doubles €59; triples €79.*

pardonnez-moi

Expect not only your fashion tastes and sense of cafe culture to be upended when perusing the City of Lights—your personal boundaries will be redrawn as well. French people possess a different sense of space and etiquette that won't bode well for the Aunt Mildred at the family reunion pressing up against all the second cousins. The next time you're shouting to your bartender for your order of *pastis*, you'll know why you're hearing expletives from everyone else. Follow the below advice to avoid pulling an Aunt Millie of your own.

- **BEHIND CLOSED DOORS.** French people like their privacy, so don't take the long corridor of shut doors in an office building to heart. Most employees keep their door shut for mere privacy and not because they're reading up on celebrity gossip on the entertainment section of *Le Figaro*. Don't be alarmed if someone beckons you in and shuts the door behind them—he or she probably isn't suggesting anything serious. Unless you're lucky.

- **KNOCK, DON'T STOP.** Like in most other Western countries, don't forget to knock prior to entering a closed door, whether in a guest's home or in a public building. But unlike the American courtesy, don't linger outside waiting for an answer. Most French people rap on the door as more of a signal to enter, not a request. Dawdle outside only if you're willing to risk looking like, well, an American.

- **LOOK, DON'T TOUCH.** When at a friend's Parisian home, do not wander around from room to room, prodding her Napoleon porcelain or commenting on his grandma's mole in the family photo. The French consider it rude and intrusive for guests to roam without their permission or guidance. Instead, wait for the hospitality of your host to kick in and allow them to personally show you the weird fetishistic chinaware and the unfortunate snapshot of Grandma.

- **KEEP IT MODERATE.** People in public consider raised voices extremely inconsiderate, so keep the vocal decibels to a minimum. At the same time, conspicuous whispering also implies a rude, gossipy mannerism. If you find yourself with an inkling to point out the Audrey Tautou doppelganger at the next cafe table, just remember that a little auditory tact never hurt anyone.

- **SUBTLETY OVER SAVAGERY.** In congruence with their vocal mannerisms, the French also like to remain reserved in public in general. Blatant displays of emotion in large crowds testify to a lack of grace, and forceful movements are considered slightly barbaric and impolite. Protesting in the streets for some kind of social reform is the only time when people accept a public proclamation of "*Sacré bleu!*," but outside of boycotting a metro fare hike, save the obnoxious outbursts for your bros.

- **PROXIMITY IS PRECIOUS.** Ironically enough, the individual space of an average French person is surprisingly small. Although most Europeans need about a yard of space when in a social setting, the French like things a little cozier. Well, a lot cozier—when conversing, Parisians like to stand about four inches from the other person. Just don't assume that the guy sidling up to you in the toiletries aisle is suggesting a drugstore makeout session—most likely he just wants to buy some floss.

invalides

HOTEL DE FRANCE
⚔ ♿ (((•))) HOTEL ❖

102 bd. de la Tour Maubourg ☎01 47 05 40 49 ✉www.hoteldefrance.com

Centrally located, Hotel de France prides itself on service. Rooms are on the pricier side and fairly small but come with mini bars, Wi-Fi, and large bathrooms. Many have balconies and amazing views of Invalides; ask when making your reservation.

⚟ ⓂÉcole Militaire. ⓲ Breakfast available. ⓢ July-Aug singles €90; doubles €100; twins €120; triples €130. Sept-June singles €90; doubles €110; twins €140; triples €160. Buffet breakfast €12.

champs-élysées

Catering to the Louis Vuitton clientele, accommodations in the posh 8ème come with a lot of stars and a hell of a nightly rate. Budget travelers might want to look elsewhere. For those absolutely set on location, there are a few quality options.

ⓧ PERFECT HOTEL
⚔⊗ HOTEL ❶

39 rue Rodier ☎01 42 81 18 86

Possibly the best deal in Paris, the Perfect Hotel is, well, practically perfect. For super cheap, visitors have access to a kitchen available for their use whenever they need it. Some of the rooms have balconies, which may be available on request. The cordial owners are enthusiastic when it comes to new visitors; they're so concerned about their guests that they installed a surveillance system of the entire hotel to ensure privacy and safety. Or maybe just to watch you. No Wi-Fi, unfortunately, but it's coming soon with upcoming renovations (new paint, wallpaper, and showers).

⚟ Ⓜ Anvers. ⓲ Reserve 2 months ahead; there are only 10 rooms, and, given the cheap prices, this hotel fills up weeks in advance during summer. Free breakfast. Credit cards only for weeklong stays or longer. ⓢ Doubles €25-35; triples €26-28. Ⓚ No lock-out.

FOYER DE CHAILLOT
♿(((•))) FOYER ❸

28 Ave. George V ☎01 53 67 87 27 ✉www.foyer-galliera.com

At its unbeatable address, the Foyer provides upscale dorm rooms and midbrow apartments that welcome female students or stagières. Well-equipped rooms with sinks and showers are outdone by the communal facilities: a full kitchen is available for breakfast and weekend meals, and the large common rooms are equipped with stereos and TVs. Toilets and additional showers in each hall.

⚟ ⓂGeorge V. In a high-rise silver office building called Eurosite George V; on the 3rd fl. ⓲ Cash and checks only. For women only; residents must be working or holding an internship and be between the ages of 18-25. Dinner included M-F. Full computer lab with internet. Fitness room. Laundry service. Reserve 1-2 months ahead, especially for Sept-Nov. 3-month min. stay; 2-year max. stay. ⓢ €350 deposit required to reserve a room; applications on the website. €35 application/booking fee. Singles for students €600; doubles €670; singles for interns €515; doubles €585. Bulletin boards advertise apartments for rent, theater outings, and other activities. Ⓚ Guests permitted from 9am-9pm.

HÔTEL ALEXANDRINE OPÉRA
⚔ HOTEL ❷

10 rue de Moscou ☎01 43 87 62 21 ✉alexandrineopera@gmail.com

Nothing about this hotel could provoke anger, but you'll still see red (decorators went a little crazy with the color scheme). Apart from that, rooms are well-sized, pleasant and come with a minibar, hair dryer, TV, phone, and shower.

⚟ ⓂLiège. ⓲ Breakfast €9. ⓢ Singles €65-80, doubles €75-100.

HÔTEL EUROPE-LIÈGE
⚔(((•))) HOTEL ❸

8 rue de Moscou ☎01 42 94 01 51; fax 01 43 87 42 18

Though you could certainly get more of a bang for your buck elsewhere, this borderline modern hotel is one of the only affordable options in the pricey 8ème. Rooms are painted lilac, making guests feel slightly more cheerful despite the small size. Rooms come with TV, hair dryer, phone, and shower or bath.

⌗ Ⓜ Liège. *i* Breakfast €7. Wi-Fi €4.50 per hr. Ⓢ Singles €81, doubles €94-120.

UNION CHRÉTIENNE DE JEUNES FILLES (UCJF/YWCA) ⬢📶 FOYER ❷
22 rue de Naples ☎01 53 04 37 47 🖳www.ucjf.net

A spacious and quiet shelter for girls that evokes memories of Madeleine re-runs. Simple rooms have hardwood floors, sinks, and desks, but emphasis is placed on building and sustaining a communal atmosphere. To that end, the large oak-paneled common room is more luscious with fireplace, TV, VCR, and books. Also has theater space and family-style dining room.

⌗ Ⓜ Europe. *i* Free internet in the lobby. 1-month min. stay; 1-year max. stay. Guests permitted until 10pm; men not allowed in bedrooms. No curfew, but ask for key ahead of time. 1 month rent deposit required, which includes processing and membership fees. Shared bathrooms. Kitchen, laundry. Ⓢ Singles, doubles and dorm-style triples €390-505 per month. ⧖ Reception M-F 8am-12:25am, Sa 8:30am-12:30pm and 1:30-12:25am, Su 9am-12:30pm and 1:30pm-12:25am.

HOTEL ANTIN-ST. GEORGES ⬢⊗📶 HOTEL ❸
21 rue Notre Dame de Lorette ☎01 48 78 60 47 🖳www.hotelantinsaintgeorges.com

A cozy two-star located close to the Opéra district in a lively Parisian neighborhood, this 36-room hotel promises a comfortable stay. There's a shower and bath in each of the very spacious rooms. The laundry facilities are a big plus, but other extra amenities are costly.

⌗ Ⓜ Saint-Georges, Pigalle. *i* Breakfast €10. Wi-Fi €3 per 2 hr. Ⓢ Doubles €80; triples €90. Special deals on internet purchases and 3-night deals. ⧖ Reception 24hr.

HOTEL CHOPIN ⬢⊗ HOTEL ❸
10 bd. Montmartre, 46 Passage Jouffroy ☎01 47 70 58 10 🖳www.hotelchopin.fr

Appropriately titled given its location in Opéra, Hotel Chopin is located at the end of a small and hyper-touristy indoor mall. The two-star hotel offers spacious, clean rooms with views of neighboring buildings' rooftops. The staff is fantastic and goes out of its way to enhance your experience. The owner takes great pride in the hotel and showcases his grandmother's paintings in the hallways. Phones, hair dryers, and TVs available in the rooms, but Wi-Fi is not, so geeks beware.

⌗ Ⓜ Grands Boulevards. *i* Breakfast €7. Reserve 2-3 months ahead. Handicapped-inaccessible. Ⓢ Singles €68-84; doubles €92-106; triples €125. ⧖ 24-hour reception. Check-out at noon.

WOODSTOCK HOSTEL ⬢📶 HOSTEL ❶
48 rue Rodier ☎01 48 78 87 76 🖳www.woodstock.fr

You'd think the name would say it all, but not everything is chill here, bro—drugs are absolutely not allowed. A cozy reception instills an intimate vibe to the hostel, and a Beatles-decorated VW bug pays homage to the hippies of old. Rooms are basic but clean, and the outdoors terrace is lovely in the summertime.

⌗ Ⓜ Anvers. *i* Wi-Fi included. Computer €2 per 30min. Ⓢ High season dorm €25; singles €28. Low season dorm €22; doubles €25. Weekend prices €2 higher. Towels €1. ⧖ Lockout from 11am-3pm. Curfew 2am.

champs-élysées

canal st-martin and surrounds

Canal St-Martin offers a wealth of dirt cheap options around **Gare du Nord.** The following accommodations are among the best that the arrondissement has to offer, but if they're full, ask the proprietors to recommend one of their many competing neighbors. People running hotels around here tend to be pretty no-nonsense, so they'll give you the inside skinny.

▨ HOTEL PALACE   ⬦ HOTEL ❶
9 rue Bouchardon   ☎ 01 40 40 09 45

Rock bottom prices and a safe (by 10ème standards), if not central, location are combined with a very warm and comfortable welcome. Prices are stupefyingly low, with singles going for €20; the greater tourist community is beginning to catch on to this bargain, so be sure to make reservations at least two weeks in advance.

⚆ Ⓜ Strasbourg-St-Denis. ⓘ Breakfast €4. ⑤ Singles €20-35; doubles €28-45; triples €60; quads €70.

HOTEL DE MILAN   ⬦ ♿ ((ᵖ)) HOTEL ❷
17 rue de St-Quentin   ☎ 01 40 37 88 50 ▯ www.hoteldemilan.com

Hotel de Milan is a good spot to stay if you feel safe making a short trek from Gare du Nord at night. Prices are really cheap if you can go without a shower (*singles for €36*), and the hotel undoubtedly offers the best accommodations in Paris for patrons with disabilities (the handicapped room is ginormous). Friendly reception.

⚆ Ⓜ Gare du Nord. ⓘ Breakfast €5. Wi-Fi €2 per hr. Shower use (for those without one) €4. ⑤ Singles €36-60; doubles €52-71; triples €90. Extra bed €17. ⚄ Check-out 11am, check-in 2pm.

HOTEL MONTANA LA FAYETTE   ⬦ ✳ HOTEL ❶
164 rue la Fayette   ☎ 01 40 35 80 80 ▯ www.pagesperso-orange.fr/hotelmontana/

Situated in a historic building, Hotel Montana's tall ceilings, cozy breakfast nook, and decent-sized rooms are priced slightly above the neighborhood norm. We guess this is the price you pay for hardwood floors in your room. The warm reception area is a plus. All rooms have bath, shower, and A/C.

⚆ Ⓜ Gare du Nord. ⑤ Singles €51-61; doubles €78-90; triples €90-120. ⚄ Reception 24hr.

CAMBRAI HOTEL   ⬦ ♿ HOTEL ❷
129 bd. Magenta   ☎ 01 48 78 32 13 ▯ www.hotel-cambrai.com

An economical and swankier option for those who are toeing the line between student and professional; deals here are best for those staying in doubles, triples, and quads. All rooms have showers. The rooms are very smartly decorated, and the reception staff is friendly and warm with the clientele. The breakfast room looks like a real restaurant. A huge wheelchair-accessible room awaits clientele with disabilities.

⚆ Ⓜ Gare du Nord. ⓘ Breakfast €6. ⑤ Singles €50-60; doubles €54-65; triples €80-90; quads €100. Extra bed €15.

bastille

The 11ème is littered with hotels (among other things), and offers a little bit of something for everybody. Accommodations range from the very cheap to the very not-cheap, but good quality budget hotels are in abundance. The neighboring 12ème offers relatively inexpensive and simple accommodations, which work hard to make up for being somewhat on the outskirts. The best options cluster around the **Gare de Lyon.**

accommodations

Everyone knows Paris's nickname, **The City of Lights,** and when you think about the number of cigarettes lit daily, or dramatic nighttime views from the **Eiffel Tower,** it seems to make perfect sense. Unfortunately, this interpretation is completely incorrect. The City's famed nickname was originally inspired by its numerous "bright" residents, who were lured to this hub of intellectualism during the **Age of Enlightenment.** Nobody would doubt the aptness of the nickname, but the figurative interpretation is still the most illuminating.

AUBERGE DE JEUNESSE "JULES FERRY" (HI)

🏨📶 HOSTEL ❷

8 bd. Jules Ferry ☎01 43 57 55 60 ✉paris.julesferry@fuaj.org

A noble attempt to brighten up the hostel experience, and we mean that quite literally—the brown bunks have recently been painted neon green. A mural of sharks greets you on your walk up the stairs. Colorful rooms with sinks, mirrors, and tiled floors match the carefree atmosphere, though the sharks don't quite scream, "Welcome Home!"

⚎ Ⓜ*République.* *i* *Breakfast included. Wi-Fi €5 for 2 hours. Kitchen available.* Ⓢ *Dorm €23.* 🕗 *Lockout 10:30am-2pm. Reception 24hr.*

HOTEL BEAUMARCHAIS

🏨⊗📶❄ HOTEL ❺

3 rue Oberkampf ☎01 53 36 86 86 🖥www.hotelbeaumarchais.com

The kind of place that would make hippies who traded their psychedelics for suits nostalgic for the old days. Funky, colorful decor. Spacious rooms come with hair dryers, cable TV, and a safe box.

⚎ Ⓜ*Oberkampf or* Ⓜ*Filles du Calvaire.* *i* *Breakfast €10.* Ⓢ *Singles €90; doubles €130; junior suite €170; triples €190.*

HOTEL MISTRAL

🏨 HOTEL ❹

3 rue Chaligny ☎01 46 28 10 20 🖥www.parishotelmistral.com

Endearingly old-fashioned hotel with airy rooms. Not quite a budget accommodation, but you get what you pay for. All rooms include showers, toilets, TVs, phones, and hair dryers.

⚎ Ⓜ*Reuilly-Diderot.* *i* *Breakfast €7. 24hr. parking €10.* Ⓢ *Singles €56; doubles and twins €61; triples €69.*

HÔTEL PRINCE ALBERT LYON BERCY

🏨📶❄ HOTEL ❺

108 rue de Charenton ☎01 43 45 09 00 🖥www.hotelprincealbert.com

Someone messed up: this 3-star hotel got mistakenly billed as a 2-star. Modern, comfortable, well-decorated rooms with full bath, cable TV, hair dryers, a safe box, and extra pillows.

⚎ Ⓜ*Gare de Lyon.* *i* *Breakfast €10.* Ⓢ *High season singles €110-130; doubles €120-140; triples €140-180. Low season singles €70-100; doubles €80-120; triples €110-140.*

HÔTEL DE L'AVEYRON

🏨📶 HOTEL ❹

5 rue d'Austerlitz ☎01 43 07 86 86 🖥www.hotelaveyron.com

A one-star hotel on a quiet street that makes for a surprisingly good stay once you get past the door. Ornate rooms are fairly large and beautiful.

⚎ Ⓜ*Gare de Lyon.* *i* *Breakfast €5.* Ⓢ *Singles €63; doubles €68-75; triples €80; quads €120.*

HÔTEL RHETIA

🏨 HOTEL ❸

3 rue de Général Blaise ☎01 47 00 47 18 ✉hotel.rhetia@fere.fr

The communal bathroom may not have a toilet seat, but the owners tried damned hard to make all the colors match. Hotel Rhetia is saved from shoddiness by a feminine touch; rooms are surprisingly clean and pleasant, with decorative pillows and matching curtains.

✴ ⓂVoltaire orⓂSt-Ambroise. *i* Breakfast €3. Ⓢ Singles €30-48; doubles €53; twins €55. ⓩ Reception M-F 7:30am-9:30pm, Sa-Su 8am-9:30pm.

HOTEL NOTRE-DAME
📍 HOTEL ❸

51 rue de Malte ☎01 47 00 78 76 🖥www.hotel-notredame.com

Rooms are hit or miss, but the good ones are quaint (read: a little dark). Downstairs you'll find a lounge area with leather couches and paintings on the wall. This hotel is all about location, location, location; the nearby subway makes it easy to get away, if need be.

✴ ⓂRépublique. *i* Breakfast €6.50. Ⓢ Room with sink €40-46, with shower €48-58, with shower and TV €50-70; with bath or shower, bathroom, and TV €52-115.

MODERN HÔTEL
📍 HOTEL ❹

121 rue du Chemin Vert ☎01 47 00 54 05 🖥www.modern-hotel.fr

Contrary to its name, this hotel is all remnants of past grandeur—think worn marble and glass chandeliers. Rooms are clean, with plush carpets that visibly clash with the busy wallpaper and curtains. Avoid if high or suffering from OCD.

✴ ⓂPère-Lachaise. *i* Breakfast included. Ⓢ Singles €61-86; doubles €75-105; twin €78-109; triples €93-129; quads €154.

HÔTEL DE BELFORT
📍 HOTEL ❹

37 rue Servan ☎01 47 00 67 33 🖥hotelbelfortparis.com

Apart from the almost unforgivable faux-silk comforters, this budget hotel is everything you would expect: clean, comfortable, and generally forgettable.

✴ ⓂPère-Lachaise. *i* Internet €3 per hr. Breakfast €6. Ⓢ Singles €55-65; doubles €60-80; twins €60-80; triples €95-105. ⓩ Check-in 2pm.

CISP "MAURICE RAVEL"
📍♿(ᵗᵖ) HOSTEL ❸

6 Ave. Maurice Ravel ☎01 43 58 96 00 🖥www.cisp.fr

A clean place to rest a tired head. Emphasis on quiet; it's kind of in the middle of nowhere. Redeeming features include temporary art displays, auditorium and access to outdoor public pool (€3-4).

✴ ⓂPorte de Vincennes. *i* Max. stay 1 week. Wi-Fi included. Breakfast, sheets, and towels included. Ⓢ Singles with bathroom and shower €40; 2-3 bed dorm with shower, WC €30; 3-5 bed dorm €27; 8-bed dorm room €20. ⓩ Doors open 6:30am-1:30am, night guard after that. Check-out 9:30am.

butte-aux-cailles and chinatown

Though not at the center of it all, the 13ème is home to several inexpensive accomodations in an ethnically-diverse and residential area, providing travelers with an opportunity to escape the steep prices and occasional phoniness of Parisian chic.

🗟 OOPS!
●♿(ᵗᵖ)❊ HOSTEL ❶

50 Ave. des Gobelins ☎01 47 07 47 00 🖥www.oops-paris.com

The first boutique hostel in Paris, Oops! has the fashion sense of a teen with an attitude problem. Animal print wallpaper, bold colors and a kaleidoscope of patterns generate a fun, young feel. Less remarkable than the decor, the rooms are average in size and include a bathroom and shower, though no lockers are available. Guests may use the rainbow-colored lounge and free Wi-Fi.

✴ ⓂLes Gobelins. *i* Breakfast included. Email to make a reservation. No deposit required if booking made through website. Cancel within 24hr. Ⓢ Dorms €23-30; private rooms €60-70.

HOTEL MAGENDIE

♨ HOTEL ❸

2 Rue Magendie, 6 rue Corvisart   ☎01 43 36 13 61

A standard two-star hotel with fake plants and whitewashed, concrete walls of a county hospital, Hotel Magendie offers clean and box-like rooms that are affordable if forgettable. The first floor atmosphere is a lot more welcoming, with warmer colors.

✦ Ⓜ*Les Gobelins*, Ⓜ*Corvisart.* ℹ *Breakfast €8.* ⑤ *M-F singles €75, doubles €89, triples €110; Sa-Su singles €66, doubles €79, triples €98. Dec.27-Dec.31 singles €84, doubles €97, triples €119.* 🕐 *Check-in at noon. Check-out at noon.*

CISP "KELLERMAN"

✦♦((ŋ)) HOSTEL ❶

17 bd. Kellermann   ☎01 44 16 37 38 💻www.cisp.fr

Close to Chinatown in a residential neighborhood, this branch of the Centres Internationaux du Sejour de Paris (CISP) offers sparse dorm-style rooms for up to week-long stays. The industrial metal rods and high-ceilings make it feel like a psych ward.

✦ Ⓜ*Porte d'Italie.* ℹ *Breakfast included. 1-week max. stay. Wi-Fi included.* ⑤ *8-bed dorms €20; 3-5-bed dorms €27; 2-3-bed dorms with shower and bath €30; singles with shower and bath €40.* 🕐 *Reception 24hr.*

ASSOCIATION DES FOYERS DE JEUNES: FOYER TOLBIAC

♨ HOSTEL ❶

234 rue de Tolbiac   ☎01 44 16 22 22; foyer.tolbiac@free.fr 💻www.foyer-tolbiac.com

Normally the Foyer Tolbiac shelters young working girls (no, not the kind you're thinking of), but, travelers staying for at least 3 nights are welcome within the establishment's salmon-pink walls. All rooms are dorm-style, bathrooms are shared, and no boys are allowed. If you're a woman in a bind, you can always rely on a clean, safe place to sleep here.

✦ Ⓜ*Glaciere.* ℹ *Email to make a reservation at least 2 months in advance. One-time €5 fee at arrival.* ⑤*Singles €20; doubles €19.*

montparnasse

HOTEL DE BLOIS

♨Ⓧ((ŋ)) HOTEL ❷

5 Rue des Plantes   ☎01 45 40 99 48 💻www.hoteldeblois.com

Conveniently located a 5min. walk from Denfert-Rochereau, and within walking distances of several tasty restaurants, Hotel de Blois is situated in a largely residential area of the 14*ème* on the popular **Rue des Plantes.** Rooms are well-kept and relatively spacious, with full-sized bathrooms and showers. Amenities include hair dryer, phone, TV, and bathtubs. Don't fret about security—the exceptional hostess is extra vigilant about letting in strangers, given the hotel's central location. Her visitors show their gratitude in a proudly displayed collection of thank you notes. There are five floors and no elevator, so the hotel is far from wheelchair-accessible.

✦ Ⓜ*Mouton Duvernet,* Ⓜ*Alésia.* ℹ *Breakfast €12. Reserve at least one month ahead.* ⑤ *Singles €55-95; doubles €60-98; twin suite 65-80. Extra bed €3-5.* 🕐 *Reception 7am-10:30pm. Check-in 3pm, check-out 11am.*

HOTEL DU PARC

♨((ŋ))❄ HOTEL ❸

6 rue Jolivet   ☎01 43 20 95 54 💻www.hoteldu-parc-paris.com

Located conveniently around the corner from Montparnasse, Hotel du Parc boasts bright red and somewhat small rooms with A/C, hair dryer, phone, and TV. Despite its central location, the setting is relatively tranquil; the sunny rooms overlook the small adjacent park, which doubles as a local pigeon's roost and outdoor bar. The staff is welcoming and eager to make your stay enjoyable.

FIAP JEAN-MONNET

♥(ツ)⛱ HOTEL ❷

30 rue Cabanis   ☎01 43 13 17 00 🖳www.fiap.asso.fr

This student-friendly hotel offers clean rooms and a vibrant social scene. The lobby is high-ceilinged and palatial, and the hotel offers a variety services; there's a bar, two restaurants, an outdoor terrace, and regular parties on Wednesdays and Fridays. Perhaps a lingering remnant of summers past, the hallways have a funky, musty scent, and boast beautiful abstract artwork in an effort to distract from the sweaty musk. Rooms have single beds with a bath/shower and phones. Jean-Monnet boasts fantastic group rates—incredibly, doubles actually cost less than single rooms here, and the price for extra beds decreases in direct proportion to the number you request. Summer travelers beware, though: this place doesn't have air-conditioning.

♯   Ⓜ*Glacière*. *i* *Lockers €3 per day. Lunch €12-14. Dinner €11-30. Reserve at least 1 month in advance.* Ⓢ *Singles €57; doubles €38; triples €34. Extra beds €26-57 per person.* ☒ *Reception 24 hr. Check-in 2:30pm, check-out 9am.*

HOTEL DU MIDI

♥(ツ)❄ HOTEL ❺

4 avenue Ren   ☎01 43 27 23 25 🖳www.midi-hotel-paris.com

Comfortable if unmemorable, Hotel du Midi has clean, air-conditioned rooms equipped with the works (TV, phone, hair dryer, shower, etc.). If you can stand the noise from the bar next door and trains across the street, the hotel is conveniently located across the street from the Denfert Rochereau metro stop, which provides speedy access to both Paris's central attractions and outer suburbs.

♯   Ⓜ*Denfert Rochereau*. *i* *Breakfast €12. Parking €15.* Ⓢ*Singles €88-108; doubles 98€-148€; suites €168.* ☒ *Reception 24hr.*

PACIFIC HÔTEL

♥(ツ)♿ HOTEL ❹

11 rue Fondary   ☎01 45 75 20 49 🖳www.pacifichotelparis.com

Located in a quiet residential area in the 15*ème* within walking distance of the Eiffel Tower, this family-owned and -run hotel offers small rooms fully equipped with full baths, desks, hair dryers, TVs, and so on. Reserve at least a few weeks ahead, as this hotel fills up most nights, especially in the summer and high tourist season.

♯   Ⓜ*Dupleix or* Ⓜ*Emile Zola*. *i* *Breakfast €7. Handicapped-accessible.* Ⓢ *Singles €67; doubles €77. Discounts for three-night stays and internet purchases.* ☒ *Reception 24hr. Check-out 11am, check-in 2pm.*

THREE DUCKS HOSTEL

♥(ツ)⊗ HOSTEL ❷

6 Place Etienne Pernet   ☎01 48 42 04 05 🖳www.3ducks.fr

It's always happy hour at the Three Ducks Hostel. No, really: the concierge desk doubles as a bar (*beer €2.20-7*). A laid-back vibe prevails here, and the rooms and the general decor embody what the attendant describes as a "grunge" attitude. If this is your scene, then the Ducks are for you. Rooms are available in twin, quad, or 6-12 bed formats. Computers and valuables can be stored in a safe at the front desk/bar, and there's a kitchen for guest use.

♯   Ⓜ*Félix Faure*. *i* *Wi-Fi and computer use for guests included. Make sure to reserve at least 1 or 2 months in advance.* Ⓢ *Dorm in high season €24-57 per night, depending on how many people you're willing to shack up with. Off-season €18-23.* ☒ *No curfew, 24hr access.*

ALOHA HOSTEL

⊗⊗(ツ) HOSTEL ❷

1 rue Borromée   ☎01 42 73 03 03 🖳www.aloha.fr

The Aloha Hostel boasts a diverse international crowd, countless recommendations, clean rooms and showers, and a couple of incredibly smelly bathrooms.

If you can stand to bear that last item, you should enjoy your stay here. Located conveniently near the Eiffel Tower on a quiet street near the Place General Beuret, this hotel is walking distance from a vibrant neighborhood of bars and eateries.

⌖ Ⓜ*Volontaires.* *i Breakfast included. Reserve a few weeks in advance.* Ⓢ *Dorms €25; doubles €28.* Ⓩ *Curfew 2am. Lockout 11am-5pm.*

HÔTEL CAMÉLIA
⌖((ᵠ)) HOTEL ❹

24 bd. Pasteur ☎01 47 83 76 35 🖰www.hotel-cameliaparis15.com

Hôtel Camélia is conveniently located a block from the metro, and close to a plentiful collection of eateries and shops, but don't stay here if you're looking for a quiet retreat from the hustle and bustle of Paris. Rooms are comfortable and clean, furnished with a claustrophobic shower and toilet combo, and bizarrely heavy and hard-to-open doors (arthritic readers beware). The hotel boasts free Wi-Fi, but the owner is planning to change during upcoming renovations to cable-based internet, since Wi-Fi is allegedly bad for customers' health.

⌖ Ⓜ*Pasteur.* *i Breakfast €6. Reserve at least a month in advance.* Ⓢ *Doubles €80; triples €100.* Ⓩ *Reception 24hr. Check-out 11:30am, check-in 1:30am.*

passy and auteuil

Prices are as posh as the residents in the 16*ème*, and accommodations are no exception. Budget hotels and hostels are hard to find, and the few options available are a trek from the city's center. On the upside, the neighborhood's more reasonable hotels can offer a welcome respite from the sticky dorms of grungy hostels for those who can afford it.

🏨 HOTELHOME PARIS 16
⌖ HOTEL ❹

36 Rue George Sand ☎01 45 20 61 38 🖰www.hotelhome.fr

As its name would suggest, HotelHome offers a home away from home to the weary traveler. Each of the outfitted apartments come with a kitchen, dishwasher, bathroom, living room, and delicious potpourri aroma. Thick plush carpets, rich colors, and dark wood make for the kind of luxurious atmosphere one wouldn't dream of when traveling on a budget. Varying apartment styles can accommodate a range of people.

⌖ Ⓜ*Jasmin.* *i Breakfast included. Discounts for early bookings.* Ⓢ *Junior suite (1-3 people) €123-260; twin suite €180-345; double suite (1-4 people) €207-385; family suite (1-6 people) €288-580.*

VILLA D'AUTEIL
⌖ HOTEL ❸

28 Rue Poussin ☎01 42 88 30 37 🖰VILLAAUT@aol.com

This two star hotel's uneven stairs will take you to homey, quaint rooms with patterned navy carpets and satellite TVs. All windows facing the street are double-paned for increased safety.

⌖ Ⓜ*Michael-Ange Auteil.* *i Breakfast €6.* Ⓢ *Singles €70; doubles €74-80; triples €92.*

HÔTEL BOILEAU
⌖ HOTEL ❸

81 Rue Boileau ☎01 42 88 83 74 🖰www.hotel-boileau.com

The Hôtel Boileau offers clean, cozy rooms with flatscreen TVs and full baths. A little far out, getting to most Parisian sights from here may be a little difficult, but the free wireless is a plus. Breakfast room overlooks an interior garden.

⌖ Ⓜ*Exelmans, walk down Boulevard Exelmans, take a right onto rue Boileau.* *i Breakfast €9 in dining room, €11.50 in room.* Ⓢ *Singles €70-81; doubles €85-126; twin €100-125; triple €130-150. Extra bed €15.*

batignolles

If you're going to stay this far out from the center of town, there better be something good keeping you here. The 17ème hosts a number of more luxurious budget accommodations that will give you a soft bed to come home to after a long day of sight-seeing, but it'll be a long metro ride.

▨ HOTEL CHAMPERRET HELIOPOLIS
 HOTEL ❹

13 rue d'Héliopolis ☎01 47 64 92 56 ✉www.champerret-heliopolis-paris-hotel.com

Bright blue, white, and gold rooms with plush, comfy beds and flatscreen TVs. The hotel combines an intimate bed and breakfast vibe with the amenities of a modern hotel. Book in advance.

✦ ⓂPorte de Champarret. ⑤ *Singles €77; doubles €90, with bath €96; twin €96; triples with bath €120.*

▨ HOTEL RIVIERA
✦ HOTEL ❹

55 Rue des Acacias ☎01 43 80 45 31 ✉www.hotelriviera-paris.com

An unimpressive hallway opens into princely rooms, or as princely as you'll get on a budget anyway. Rooms include big beds, TVs, thick carpets, and douches (yes, people on the Continent actually appear to use them); some have large baths.

✦ ⓂTernes or ⓂEtoile. ⓘ *Breakfast €7.* ⑤ *Singles with shower €54, singles with bathroom €86-108; doubles €90-136; triples €140-150.*

HÔTEL PRINCE ALBERT WAGRAM
❄ HOTEL ❸

28 Passage Cardinet ☎01 47 54 06 00 ✉hotelprincealbert.com

Located in a quiet alleyway, Hôtel Prince Albert Wagram offers reasonably sized, clean rooms in a quiet neighborhood. Rich dark colors and black leather couches in the lobby make for a more "manly" feel than in other small hotels. Guests are sometimes allowed to use the kitchen microwave. If you are American and of color, the proprietor might ask you if "Obama is your family." Prices negotiable.

✦ ⓂMalesherbes. Walk up bd. Malesherbes. Turn right on rue Cardinet and then left on passage Cardinet. ⓘ *Breakfast €6. A/C €10.* ⑤ *Singles €75-102; doubles €90-110.*

montmartre

Montmartre's accommodations tend to be a bit pricier, given its position near the top of the list of Paris's most heavily touristed neighborhoods. That said, we've picked out a few affordable options if you wish to be in the thick of things. Always remember to evaluate the noise level in the neighborhood of your accommodation; while none of these are located in noisy neighborhoods, most locations in the 18th tend to be a bit rowdy at night.

▨ HOTEL CAULAINCOURT
 HOTEL ❷

2 sq. Caulaincourt ☎ 01 46 06 46 06 ✉www.caulaincourt.com

A friendly, cheap hotel that caters to a slightly younger crowd. Reception will do everything possible to make your stay enjoyable and happy. There's a TV in the lobby, and free internet access up to 30min. Rooms are generally clean, with the exception of a few grimy spots in the bathrooms. Keep in mind that there's a 2am curfew, and 11am-4pm is lockout time; this is not the place to be if you want to party really hard and then sleep in ("*faire la grasse matinée*" in French; doesn't that sound better?). The hotel is located at the top of a long staircase, so its rooms afford some fantastic views.

✦ ⓂLamarck-Caulaincourt. ⑤ *Singles €50-60; doubles €63-76; triples €89.* ☾ *Curfew 2am. Lockout 11am-4pm.*

accommodations

HOTEL ANDRÉ GILL 📶 HOTEL [2]

4 rue André Gill ☎01 42 62 48 48

A cozy family-run budget hotel, André Gill is located on a side street off rue des Martyrs, in the thick of the touristy section of Montmartre. The hotel's well-loved cat adds a homey touch, but travelers with allergies might think about heading somewhere else. The rooms here are clean, and the reception is friendly. The location is a bit busy; if you're a city slicker, you'll be able to sleep like a baby, but country bumpkins should search for something a bit farther out if you want to catch some Z's.

[M]Pigalle, [M]Abesses. i Computer use €1.50 per 30min. Breakfast €4. $ Doubles with sink €60, with full bath €89. ⏰ Reception 24hr.

LE VILLAGE HOSTEL 📶 HOSTEL [1]

20 rue d'Orsel ☎ 01 42 64 22 02 💻www.villagehostel.fr

A clean, friendly hostel that's located in the heart of the tourist district, but Le Village gets quiet at night as the shops that surround it begin to close. Half the rooms overlook the beautiful hilltop of Montmartre, while the other half overlook the lovely patio. Communal kitchen, TV, and telephones in the lounge. The staff speaks English and welcomes an international array of guests. The hostel also boasts a variety of rooms at different price levels; call at least a few weeks ahead, or maybe a month or two in advance during the summer.

[M]Anvers. i Computer use €1 per 15min. $ Dorms €28-40; doubles €70-100; triples €96-117; quads €112-152. ⏰ Reception 24hr.

buttes chaumont

Buttes Chaumont isn't known for its accommodations for a reason. Largely residential and far away from tourist destinations, hotels are generally a bit expensive and impractical for a stay in Paris. La Perdrix Rouge is the great exception.

LA PERDRIX ROUGE 📶 HOTEL [2]

5 rue Lassus ☎01 42 06 09 53 💻www.hotel-perdrixrouge-paris.com

Facing a gorgeous church and just steps from the Metro, La Perdrix Rouge offers a slightly pricey, peaceful home base away from the clamor of central Paris. Surrounded by a bank, grocery store, several bakeries, and restaurants, patrons will find the neighborhood tourist-free and generous in terms of the necessities (fresh bread, pharmacies, crêpes, etc.) Thirty clean, red-carpeted rooms come with bath or shower, hair dryer, toilet, telephone, and TV.

[M]Jourdain. i Breakfast €7.50. Minibar deposit €20. $ Singles €79; doubles €85-92; twins €98. Extra bed €12.

belleville and père lachaise

Belleville is pretty far out from most tourist destinations in Paris. Nonetheless, there are some pretty cheap accommodations here. The **Auberge de Jeunesse** has a fantastic sense of community; if you want to meet people at your hostel but not be able to afford a taxi home after hitting the bars, the 20*ème* is the spot for you.

AUBERGE DE JEUNESSE "LE D'ARTAGNAN" 📶 HOSTEL [1]

80 rue Vitruve ☎01 40 32 34 56 💻www.fuaj.org

A healthy walk from the Metro and a stone's throw from the Cimetière du Père Lachaise, this *auberge* boasts an unbecoming design, a friendly reception, and a huge community of transient students. Claiming to be France's largest youth hostel, this 440-bed backpacker's republic fosters a fun and irreverent atmosphere with flashing neon lights, a free in-house cinema, and a game room complete with those car-driving games you used to stuff with quarters as a kid. Rooms are clean and have all the basics down pat. The jovial elevator/social facilitator man will make otherwise ordinary elevator rides fun.

�» Ⓜ*Porte de Bagnolet.* Ⓢ *Breakfast included. Internet and Wi-Fi €2 per hr. Sheets included. Towel €2.50. Lockers €2-4 per day. Laundry €3 per wash, €1 per dry. Reserve online. Discounts for International Youth Hostels Association members.* Ⓢ *9-bed rooms €21; 3- to 5-bed €23.50; doubles €28.* 🕐 *Lockout noon-3pm. 4-night max. stay.*

SUPER HOTEL
◗•◗◗❄ HOTEL ❷

208 rue des Pyrénées   ☎01 46 36 97 48 ▣http://fr.federal-hotel.com/
hotel_super-hotel-paris_2478.htm

Less than a block from several convenient pharmacies and stores, Super Hotel provides clean rooms with A/C, hair dryer, and TV that vary greatly in size. The lobby boasts bright modern furniture, making it feel a little nicer than your average two-star. Beware of steep Wi-Fi charges.

🚻 Ⓜ*Gambetta. Hotel is right off the Place Gambetta, off rue des Pyrénées.* 𝒊 *Breakfast €8. Wi-Fi €10 per stay; currently only reaches 3rd fl.* Ⓢ *Singles €50.50-55; doubles €60; quads €79.*

EDEN HOTEL
◗ HOTEL ❸

7 rue Jean-Baptiste Dumay   ☎01 46 36 64 22

A good value for two stars, the Eden Hotel's clean rooms each come with a TV and WC and provide a respite from the mobs of tourists outside. Temptation may have you pining to stay longer. Some rooms don't have showers. Dogs welcome for an additional €5 per night.

🚻 Ⓜ*Pyrénées.* 𝒊 *Breakfast €5. Hall showers €4.* Ⓢ *Singles €70-100; doubles/twins €75-120.*

HÔTEL ERMITAGE
◗•◗◗ HOTEL ❷

42bis rue de l'Ermitage   ☎01 46 36 23 44 ▣www.hoteldelermitage.com

Located on the hills of Menilmontant, this simple hotel provides 24 basic rooms with a great view of Sacré-Coeur. Rooms complete with a phone, safe, and TV for cheap. Nothing special, but it gets the job done with bright, sunny rooms, colorful blankets, and a warm atmosphere.

🚻 Ⓜ*Jourdain.* 𝒊 *Wi-Fi €1 per 15min.* Ⓢ *Singles and doubles €65.*

SIGHTS

There are 35,000 works of art in the Louvre, and an estimated 234 lipstick stains on the tomb of Oscar Wilde at all times (okay, the last one's an estimate). More people are buried in the Catacombs than live in the whole of Los Angeles. You know why you're here. Now charge your camera, don some decent walking shoes, and get it together.

greatest hits

- **THE END OF THE WORLD HAS NEVER LOOKED BETTER:** Check out the whimsical renditions of the Apocalypse in the stained glass windows of **Sainte-Chapelle.**

- **WHAT'S WITH THE MISSING EYEBROWS?:** Throw some elbows for a good view of the Mona Lisa in **the Louvre.**

- **"METAL ASPARAGUS" INDEED:** Lord knows the **Eiffel Tower** wasn't popular at first, but these days the number of people that visit the landmark annually is greater than the entire population of Montana.

- **BIGGEST GAME OF CHUTES AND LADDERS EVER:** Wander through the endlessly eccentric exhibits of the **Pompidou.**

- **OFFICIALLY CONQUER FRANCE (EVERYONE ELSE HAS):** The **Arc de Triomphe** is dedicated to the prowess of the French military—so, naturally, every army that has ever conquered the country has ritualistically marched through it. Now you can too.

Your art history professor told you to go to ▩**the Louvre**, and you should but there is so much more to see in Paris than the Mona Lisa - and a lot of it is free. Not nearly as morbid as you might think, ▩**Cimitière du Pere Lachaise** is hauntingly beautiful, and the final resting place of Jim Morrison of The Doors. Though you have to pay to climb up, there's nothing stopping you from admiring the ▩**Arc de Triomphe** from afar. Afterwards, take a stroll down the **Champs-Élysées**, a street which might as well be it's own sight, and at the end you'll hit **Place de la Concorde,** and after that the ▩**Tuileries Garden.** Mona Lisa is the size of a postage stamp (and still worth it) but there's a lot more to see in Paris.

île de la cité and île st-louis

The ground zero of Paris, there are a lot of big hitters on the islands. If you're looking for grand architecture, hundreds of years of history, and mobs of tourists, Île de la Cité is a wonderful place to start. Notre Dame Cathedral is at the center of it all, rising above lesser-known (i.e., not in a Disney movie) but equally impressive locations like Ste-Chapelle. Even without all the grandeur, the Île's sheer level of historical significance makes it worth a visit; the birthplace of Paris, the island's narrow streets offer a glimpse of the city's humble beginnings. Just across the way, the Rue St-Louis-En-L'Île was historically home to some of the most famous *Parisiens* in history. The main thoroughfare strings together a collection of clothing boutiques, gourmet food stores, galleries, and ice-cream shops, including the famous **Berthillon glacerie.**

▩ **NOTRE DAME**   ✒ CATHEDRAL
Île de la Cité   ☎01 53 10 07 00

Centuries before it witnessed Quasimodo's attempted rescue of Esmeralda, Notre Dame was the site of a Roman temple to Jupiter and three different churches. Parisian bishop **Maurice de Sully** initiated the construction of the cathedral in 1163. De Sully took care to avoid the poor interior design that characterized Notre Dame's dark and cramped predecessor and worked to create a more airy structure that would fill with God's light; in the process, he helped engineer a new architectural style that would later be dubbed **Gothic.** De Sully died before his ambitious plan was completed, but the cathedral was reworked over several centuries into the composite masterpiece that stands today.

    Like the Ile de la Cité, Notre Dame has hosted a series of pivotal events in Western history. French royalty used the cathedral for their marital unions, most notably the marriages of François II to **Mary Queen of Scots** in 1558 and of **Henri of Navarre** to Marguerite de Valois in 1572. The cathedral was also the setting for **Joan of Arc's** trial for heresy in 1455. In a fit of logic, secularists renamed the cathedral The Temple of Reason during the Revolution and cleverly encased its Gothic arches in Neoclassical plaster moldings. The church was reconsecrated after the Revolution and was the site of **Napoleon's** famed coronation in 1804. However, the building soon fell into disrepair, and for two decades it was used to shelter livestock. Donkeys and pigs were cleared away when **Victor Hugo,** proving that books can change public opinion, wrote his famed novel *Notre-Dame de Paris (The Hunchback of Notre Dame)* in 1831, reviving the cathedral's popularity and inspiring **Napoleon III** and **Haussmann** to devote financial attention to its restoration. Modifications by **Eugène Viollet-le-Du** included a new spire, gargoyles, and a statue of himself admiring his own work and rejuvenated the cathedral's image in the public consciousness. Notre

sights

Dame once again became a valued symbol of civic unity. In 1870 and again in 1940, thousands of *Parisiens* attended masses in the church to pray for deliverance from the invading Germans; God had a thing and couldn't make it, apparently. On August 26, 1944, **Charles de Gaulle** braved Nazi fire to visit Notre Dame and give thanks for the imminent liberation of Paris. His funeral mass was held there many years later, as was the mass of his successor, **Mitterand.**

Despite these centuries of upheaval—not to mention the herds of tourists who invade its portals every day—Notre Dame remains unscathed and as illustrious as ever. The cathedral continues to keep up its political prominence, and its place in the public consciousness is demonstrated through its pop culture cameos in movies such as *Amélie*, *Before Sunset*, and *Charade* as well as the animated films *The Hunchback of Notre Dame* and *Ratatouille*.

Notre Dame has been undergoing a facelift for a while now. Construction may have started in the 12th century, but detail work was continued all the way into the 17th, when artists were still adding Baroque statues to everything. The oldest part of the cathedral is above the **Porte de Sainte-Anne** (on the right) and dates from 1165-1175. The **Porte de la Vierge** (on the left), which portrays the life of the Virgin Mary, dates from the 13th century. The central **Porte du Jugement** was almost entirely redone in the 19th century; the **figure of Christ** dates from 1885. Irreverent revolutionaries wreaked havoc on the facade during the frenzied rioting of the 1790s; not content with decapitating Louis XVI, Parisians attacked the stone statues of the **Kings of Judah** above the doors, under the mistaken impression that they represented the monarch's ancestors. The heads were found in the basement of the **Banque Française du Commerce** in 1977 and were installed in the **Musée de Cluny.**

Home to the cathedral's fictional resident, Quasimodo the Hunchback, the two **towers** are the cathedral's most prominent features. Streaked with black soot, they cast an imposing shadow on the Paris skyline for years, but after several years of sandblasting, the blackened exterior has been brightened, once again revealing rose windows and rows of holy saints and hideous gargoyles. It's a long way to heaven; there's always a considerable line to make the 422-step climb to the top of the towers, but the view of Paris is worth it (20 visitors are let in every 10min). The narrow staircase leads to a spectacular perch crowded by rows of gargoyles and overlooks the Left Bank's **Latin Quarter** and the Right Bank's **Marais.** In the **South Tower,** a tiny door opens onto the 13-ton bell that even Quasimodo couldn't ring; it requires eight people or one Sumo wrestler to move.

In its interior, Notre Dame can seat over 10,000 churchgoers. The arched ceiling is achieved by the spidery **flying buttresses** that support the vaults of the ceiling from outside, allowing light to fill the cathedral through delicate stained-glass windows. Down the nave is the transept and a view of the **rose windows.** The 21m **north window** (to the left when your back is to the entrance) is still composed almost entirely of 13th-century glass. The Virgin is situated at its center, depicted as the descendant of the Old Testament kings and judges who surround her. While the north window is spectacularly well preserved, the **south and west windows** have had to undergo modern renovations. The base of the south window shows Matthew, Mark, Luke, and John on the shoulders of Old Testament prophets, while the central window depicts Christ surrounded by his 12 apostles. The cathedral's **treasury,** south of the choir, contains an assortment of glittering robes, sacramental chalices, and other gilded artifacts from the cathedral's past. The **Crown of Thorns,** believed to have been worn by Christ himself, is reverentially presented only on the first Friday of every month at 3pm.

[M]Cité. $ €8, ages 18-25 €6, under 18 free. Audio tours €5; includes visit of treasury. Treasury €3, ages 12-25 €2, ages 5-11 €1. ⏰ Cathedral open daily 7:45am-7pm. Towers open Jan-Mar and Oct-Dec 10am-5:30pm; Apr-Sept 10am-6:30pm; June-Aug Sa-Su 10am-11pm. Last entry 45min. before close. Free ours in French M-F 2 and 3pm; call 01 44 54 19 30 for English, Russian, or Spanish tours. Treasury

open M-F 9:30am-6pm, Sa 9:30am-5pm, Su 1-1:30pm and 6-6:30pm; last entry 15min. before close.

📷 SAINTE-CHAPELLE

💳♿ CHURCH

6 bd. du Palais ☎01 53 40 60 97 💻www.monuments-nationaux.fr

Everybody needs the occasional diversion to get through a service. For French royalty in the 13th century, it was the color of the church's walls. When light pours through the floor-to-ceiling stained-glass windows in the **Upper Chapel** of Sainte-Chapelle, illuminating bright dreamscapes of biblical scenes, the church becomes one of the most stunning and mesmerizing sights in Paris. The 15 panes date from 1136 and depict 1113 religious scenes. They narrate the Bible from Genesis to the Apocalypse, and are designed to be read from bottom to top, left to right; the bottom-to-top organization of the stories is meant to represent and enable the elevation of the soul through knowledge. Ste-Chapelle is the foremost example of flamboyant Gothic architecture and a tribute to the craft of medieval stained glass—at 618 sq. m, there's more of it than stone. The chapel was constructed in 1241 to house King Louis IX's most precious possession: the Crown of Thorns from Christ's Passion. Bought along with a section of the Cross by the Emperor of Constantinople in 1239 for the ungodly sum of £135,000 (adjust that puppy for about 800 years of inflation), the crown required an equally grand home, though its cost far exceeded that of the chapel. Although the crown itself—minus a few thorns that St-Louis gave away in exchange for political favors—has been moved to Notre Dame, Ste-Chapelle is still a sight to behold. Down on the bottom floor, the **Lower Chapel** has a blue vaulted ceiling dotted with golden *fleurs-de-lis* and contains a few "treasures"—platter-sized portraits of saints. This was where mortals served God, while royalty got to get a little closer in the Upper Chapel upstairs.

→ [M]Cité. Within Palais de la Cité. $ €8, ages 18-25 €5, EU citizens 18-25 and under 18 free. Twin ticket with Concierge €11, ages 18-25 €7.50, EU citizens aged 18-25 and under 18 free. ⏰ Open daily Nov-Feb 9am-5pm; Mar-Oct 9:30am-6pm, last entry 30min. before closing. Chapel closed M-F 1-2:15pm. Guided tours in French 11am, 3pm, and 4:40pm; in English 3:30pm.

📷 MEMORIAL DE LA DÉPORTATION

♿ HOLOCAUST MEMORIAL

Paris's Holocaust memorial is a claustrophobic and deeply moving experience. Narrow staircases, spiked gates, and high concrete walls are meant to evoke the atmosphere of the concentration camps; only a few visitors are allowed to enter the exhibition at a time, and the solitude that the museum imposes upon its viewers only increases the pervasive sense of sadness. The focal point of the institution is a tunnel lined with 200,000 lit quartz pebbles, one for each of the French citizens who were deported. The pebbles are an homage to the Jewish custom of placing stones on the graves of the deceased. Empty cells and walls bear the names of the most infamous camps, as well as a series of humanitarian statements by famous writers like Jean-Paul Sartre and Antoine de St-Exupéry. Near the exit is the simplest and most arresting of these quotes, *"Pardonne. N'Oublie Pas."* ("Forgive. Do Not Forget.")

→ [M]Cité. At the western tip of the island in square de l'Île de France, on quai de l'Archevêche. A 5min. walk from the back of Notre Dame cathedral and down a narrow flight of steps. $ Free. ⏰ Open Apr-Sept Tu-Su 10am-noon and 2-7pm (last entrance 11:45am and 6:30pm); Oct-Mar 10am-noon and 2-5pm.

PONT NEUF

BRIDGE

Though its name might suggest otherwise, the bridge cutting through the western tip of Île de la Cité is the oldest in Paris. Completed in 1607, the bridge was a marvel at the time because its sides were not lined with houses. Now, less atypically, its sides are lined with lip-locked lovers, seated in the many romantic enclaves overlooking the Seine. Before the construction of the Champs-Élysées, the white stone bridge was Paris's most popular thoroughfare, attracting nobles, peddlers, and street performers. In the middle of the bridge is a towering statue of Henri IV on horseback, commissioned by Henri's widow, Marie de Médicis, perhaps to honor his never-ending vitality. You can see the comic gargoyle faces carved into the supports from a *bâteau-mouche* or from the park at the base of the bridge, Sq. du Vert-Galant.

✠ Ⓜ*Pont Neuf.*

tours

- **BATEAUX-MOUCHES** (*Port de la Conférence, Pont de l'Alma, Rive droite* ☎*01 76 99 73* 🖳*www.bateaux-mouches.fr* Ⓜ*Pont de l'Alma.* **i** *Free parking throughout the duration of the cruise. Tours in English* Ⓢ *€10, children under 12 €5* ⏰ *Apr-Sept 10:15am-7pm, every twenty minutes 7-11pm; Oct-Mar 11am-9pm, weekends 10:15am-9pm.*)

- **CITY SEGWAY TOURS** See Paris from a Segway Human Transporter electric scooter. (*24 rue Edgar Faure* ☎*01 56 58 10 54* 🖳*www.citysegwaytours. com/paris.* **i** *All tours leave from beneath the Eiffel Tower and last 4-5hr.* Ⓢ *€80.* ⏰ *Daily 9:30am, Mar-Dec Daily 9:30am and 2pm.*)

- **CANAUXRAMA** Take a 2hr. boat tour of the St-Martin Canal. (*13 Quai de la Loire* ☎*01 42 39 15 00* 🖳*www.canauxrama.com* Ⓜ *Bastille (Marina Arsenal) or* Ⓜ*Jaurés (Bassin de la Villette).* **i** *Reservations recommended. Ticket desk open 40min. before departure or buy online. Departures either from Marina Arsenal or Bassin de la Villette.* Ⓢ *€16, students €11, children under €12 8.5, under 4 free.* ⏰ *Both locations with tours between 9am and 11pm.*)

- **PARIS Á VÉLO,** C'est sympa! (*37 Bld. Bourdon* ☎*01 48 87 60 01* Ⓜ*Bastille.*)

- **FAT TIRE BIKE TOURS** (*24 rue Edgar Faure, 15éme* ☎*01 56 58 10 54* 🖳*www.fattirebiketours.com* **i** *Tours last 4 hr.* Ⓢ *€28, students €26* ⏰ *Day tour daily 11am; Apr-Nov 11am, 3pm. Night tour Mar-Apr daily 6pm; Apr-Nov daily 7pm; Nov Tu, Th, Sa, Su 6pm.*)

CONCIERGERIE
2 bd. du Palais

🏷 PALACE, PRISON

☎01 53 40 60 97 🖳www.monuments-nationaux.fr

Back in the day, the Conciergerie served as both a palace and a prison, where kings feasted and criminals rotted. Built by Philip the Fair in the 14th century, the building is a good example of secular medieval architecture—heavy, hard, and somber. The name "Conciergerie" refers to the administrative officer of the Crown who acted as the king's steward, the Concierge (Keeper). When Charles V moved the seat of royal power from Île de la Cité to the Louvre after the assassination of his father's advisors, he endowed the Concierge with the power to run the Parliament, Chancery, and Audit Office. Later, this edifice became a royal prison and was taken over by the Revolutionary Tribunal after 1793. Now blackened by auto exhaust, the northern facade casts an appropriate gloom over the building; 2780 people were sentenced to death here between 1792 and 1794. A full list of the bourgeoisie who had their heads chopped up is hung inside. Among its most famous prisoners were Marie-Antoinette—who was kept for five weeks—Robespierre, and 21 Girondins.

At the farthest corner on the right, a stepped parapet marks the oldest tower, the **Tour Bonbec,** which once housed the in-house torture chambers. The modern entrance lies between the **Tour d'Argent,** the stronghold of the royal treasury, and the **Tour de César,** used by the Revolutionary Tribunal. Past the entrance hall, stairs lead to rows of cells complete with somewhat blank-faced replicas of prisoners and prison conditions. Plaques explain how, in a bit of opportunism on the part of the Revolutionary leaders, the rich and famous could buy themselves private cells with cots and tables for writing while the poor slept on straw and with each other in pestilential cells. A model of Marie-Antoinette's rather comfortable-looking room suggests the extent to which class distinction remained preserved during the Revolution. If you follow the corridor named for "Monsieur de Paris," the executioner during the Revolution, you'll be tracing the final footsteps of Marie-Antoinette as she awaited decapitation on October 16, 1793. In 1914, the Conciergerie ceased to be used as a prison. Occasional concerts and wine tastings in the **Salle des Gens d'Armes** have, happily, replaced torture and beheadings.

✦ ⓂCité. ⓈE €7, students €4.50, EU citizens aged 18-25 and under 18 free; includes tour in French, 11am and 3pm. ⏰Open daily Mar-Oct 9:30am-6pm; Nov-Feb 9am-5pm. Last entry 30min. before close.

HOTEL DE DIEU
BUILDING, HOSPITAL

1 pl. du Paris ☎01 42 34 82 34

Upon realizing that it might be helpful to save actual people in addition to their Christian souls (this was the Dark Ages, the idea was new at the time), Bishop St. Landry built this hospital in 651 CE. Today, it is the oldest hospital in Paris. In the Middle Ages, Hôtel de Dieu confined the sick rather than cured them; guards were posted at the doors to keep the patients from escaping and infecting the rest of the city. Over a millennium later, world-renowned chemist and biologist Louis Pasteur utilized the hospital's resources to conduct much of his pioneering research. In 1871, the hospital's proximity to Notre Dame saved the cathedral from the fires of hell, so to speak—Communards were dissuaded from burning the monument for fear that the flames would engulf their hospitalized comrades nearby. The hospital has seen quieter days for some time now. The serene and well-groomed gardens in the inner courtyard feature sculpture exhibits.

✦ ⓂCité. Ⓢ Free. ⏰ Open daily 7am-8pm.

PALAIS DE JUSTICE
COURTHOUSE

4 bd. du Palais ☎01 44 32 51 51

This is *the* place to get a prison sentence. The Palais has witnessed the German spy Mata Hari's death sentence, Sarah Bernhardt's divorce from the Comédie Française, Émile Zola's trial following the Dreyfus Affair, Dreyfus's declaration of his innocence, and the trial of Maréchal Pétain after WWII. The institution's architecture is organized around the theme of—unsurprisingly enough— justice and features symbolic representations of its basic concepts. The portrayals of Zeus and Medusa symbolize royal justice and punishment; the swords and sunlight recall the general concepts of justice and the law. A wide set of stone steps at the main entrance of the Palais de Justice leads to three doorways, each marked with Liberté, Egalité, or Fraternité—words that once signified revolution and now serve as the bedrock of the French legal tradition, not to mention many a photo. All trials are open to the public, and even if your French is not up to legalese, the theatrical sobriety of the interior is worth a quick glance. Plus you don't have to pay to see justice served!

✦ ⓂCité. Within Palais de la Cité. Use Ste-Chapelle entrance at 6 bd. du Palais. Enter through the Ste-Chapelle entrance, go down the hallway after the security check, and turn right onto a double-level courtroom area. To go in the main entrance, turn right into the courtyard after the security check. Ⓢ Free. ⏰ Courtrooms open M-F 9am-noon and 1:30-end of last trial.

CRYPTE ARCHÉOLOGIQUE
✦ MUSEUM

7 parvis Notre-Dame; pl. Jean-Paul II ☎01 55 42 50 10 🖥www.crypte.paris.fr

Far below the cathedral towers, beneath the pavement of the square in front of Notre Dame, the Crypte Archéologique houses artifacts unearthed during the construction of a nearby parking garage. The self proclaimed "more than a museum" is much cooler than its creation story. The crypt provides a virtual tour of the history of Île de la Cité from its initial settlement through the 17th century and features extensive architectural fragments, including the oldest rampart of Paris and a series of 19th-century sewers.

⚓ ⓂCité. Ⓢ €4, ages 14-26 €2, under 14 free. ⏰ Open Tu-Su 10am-6pm. Last entry at 5:30pm.

QUAI BOURBON
Île St-Louis
QUAI

It may seem like any other *quai* along the Seine, but this was where sculptor Camille Claudel lived out the soap opera that was her existence. The protégé, and, as it often goes, lover of famed sculptor Auguste Rodin, worked here at no. 19 from 1899 until 1913. She spent her years on the quai de Bourbon wavering between prolific artistic brilliance and crippling insanity, both of which were probably provoked by her obsessive love for Rodin, who simply refused, as it often goes, to leave his long-time girlfriend Rose Beuret. Finally, following the death of her father in 1913, Claudel's brother committed her to an insane asylum. The wrought-iron and grilled facade of the cafe Au Franc-Pinot, at the intersection of the quai and rue des Deux Ponts, is also high on the historical drama factor. Closed in 1716 after authorities found a basement stash of anti-government tracts, the cafe-cabaret re-emerged as a treasonous address during the Revolution.

⚓ ⓂPont Marie. Immediately to the left after crossing Pont St-Louis. Wraps around the northwest edge of the island.

ÉGLISE ST-LOUIS-EN-L'ÎLE
19bis rue St-Louis-en-l'Île
CHURCH
☎01 46 34 11 60 🖳www.saintlouisenlile.com

Built by Le Vau in 1726 and vandalized during the Revolution, this church seems to prove that God does his work on the sly. Though the building is burdened with a sooty and humdrum facade, the overwhelming Rococo interior is elaborate and occasionally gaudy, with soaring domed ceilings, gilded carvings, and a towering organ. Legendary for its acoustics, the church hosts concerts (usually classical) throughout the year.

⚓ ⓂPont Marie. ℹ Check FNAC (www.fnac.com) or call the church for concert details. Ⓢticket prices vary; around €20, students €15. ⏰ Open M-Sa 9am-1pm and 2-7:30pm, Su 9am-1pm and 2-7pm. Mass M-F 6:45pm, Sa 6:30pm, Su 9:30, 11am.

QUAI D'ANJOU
QUAI

With a row of lovely houses that hug the bank of the Seine, this *quai* embodies exactly what excites us about Paris. No. 37 on this street was once home to Lost Generation writer John Dos Passos. No. 29 housed the Three Mountains Press, which published books by Hemingway and Ford Madox Ford and was edited by Ezra Pound. About 70 years previously, no. 9 was the address of Realist painter and caricaturist Honoré Daumier from 1846 to 1863, during which time he painted, among other works, *La Blanchisseuse* (*The Washer Woman*), now hanging in the Louvre. Poet Charles Baudelaire lived in the Hôtel Lausan (a.k.a. Hôtel Pimodoran) at no. 17 from 1843 to 1845. The Hôtel Lambert, at no. 2, was designed by Le Vau in 1640 for Lambert le Riche and was home to Voltaire and Mme. de Châtelet, his mathematician mistress. If you don't give two cents about all that (though if you're spending any time in Paris, you probably do), some of the city's most beautiful *hôtels particuliers* line the quai as well, and the view of the Seine is quite pleasant.

⚓ ⓂPont Marie. Wraps around the northeast edge of the island to the left after the Pont Marie.

QUAI DE BÉTHUNE
Just about every notable person in Paris lived on the Île St-Louis at some point.

This *quai* had the honor of being home to Marie Curie, who lived at no. 34 until she died of radiation-induced cancer in 1934. French President Georges Pompidou lived at no. 24 for 63 years until his death in 1974.

⚟ Ⓜ*Pont Marie. On the southeast side of Île St-Louis.*

🖐musée du louvre

☎01 40 20 53 17 🖳www.louvre.fr

The cultural importance of the Louvre cannot be overstated. The museum's miles (yes, miles) of galleries stretch seemingly without end, and the depth, breadth, and beauty of their collection spans thousands of years, six continents, countless artistic styles, and a vast range of media. The museum also attracts the sort of crowds that most professional sports teams could only dream of—8.5 million visitors walked through these exhibits in 2010 alone.

Like most of Paris' most spectacular sights, the Louvre was initially commissioned by kings and intended as a tribute to...themselves. The initial foundations of the building were built in the 12th century, and subsequent French monarchs added doses of their own decorative and architectural charm to the Palace—or in the case of the particularly egotistical François I, burned down his predecessors' work to make way for his own. In 1725, after years of relative neglect, the halls were converted into a space for annual salons held by the Royal Academy of Painting and Sculpture to showcase its members' work. In 1793, the Revolutionaries made the exhibit permanent, thus establishing the Musée du Louvre. Napoleon filled the Louvre with plundered art from continental Europe and Egypt, much of which had to be returned after his defeat at Waterloo. In contrast to many of Paris' pristinely preserved monuments, the Louvre continues to be in a constant state of flux and reconstruction. In 1989, American architect I.M. Pei controversially decided to move the museum's entrance to an underground level in the Cour Napoléon, surmounted by his magnificent, devilishly sleek glass pyramid. Traditional French folks were outraged, but the rest of the world thought it was a genius move; the pyramid is now a world-renowned landmark.

Successful trips to the Louvre require two things: a good sense of direction and a great plan of attack. *Let's Go* provides general information about the museum, followed by descriptions of its major collections. Those in search of a more detailed itinerary can choose from a selection of curator-designated "Thematic Trails," described on the Louvre's website. We wish you luck.

ORIENTATION

The Louvre is comprised of three connected wings: **Sully, Richelieu,** and **Denon.** These three buildings are centered on the **Cour Napoleon,** the museum's main entrance, which is accessible through I.M. Pei's large, glass **pyramid** (the Cour Napoleon is also accessible directly from the **Palais-Royal/Musée de Louvre Metro station,** by way of the **Carrousel du Louvre,** an underground gallery with high-end shops and a reasonably priced food court.) The Cour sports two ticket counters, a number of automated ticket machines, and a large information desk. Once you've secured your ticket, proceed up the escalators to Sully, Richelieu, or Denon to enter the museum itself on the basement level. Within the museum, each wing is divided into sections according to period, national origin, and medium. Each room within these thematic sections is assigned a number and color that correspond to the Louvre's free map.

⚟ Ⓜ*Palais-Royal-Musée du Louvre.* ℹ *Audio tour €6, under 18 €2, disabled visitors and unemployed €4, ages 18-25 rent one audioguide get one free. Visitors with disabilities don't have to wait in line. All entrances except the Passage Richelieu have elevators. At the main desk, you can exchange a piece of identification for a temporary wheelchair. Concerts and films are held in the auditorium in the Cour Napoléon. Concerts €3-30; films, lectures, and colloquia €2-10. Check the website for scheduling*

sights

and more information. There is a small theater in the hall with free 1hr. films in French relating to the museum (films every hr. 10am-6pm). 1½hr. tours in English, French, or Spanish daily 11am, 2pm, 3:45pm; sign up at the info desk [$] Admission €9, after 6pm on W and F €6, unemployed free after 6pm, under 26 free after 6pm. Free admission first Su of every month. Prices include both permanent and temporary collections, except for those in the Cour Napoléon. Tickets also allow same-day access to the Musée Delacroix. ⏰ Open M 9am-6pm, W 9am-10pm, Th 9am-6pm, F 9am-10pm, and Sa 9am-6pm. Last entry 45min. before close; closure of rooms begins 30min. before close.

five ways to make the louvre cool

As one of the most famous (and bunion-inducing) museums in the world, the Louvre hosts an exceptional crowd of obnoxious international tourists trampling toward Venus de Milo, rowdy French schoolchildren giggling at every naked statue, and security guards that take personal space too seriously. We offer some advice to make that inevitable visit to I.M. Pei's pyramids a bit more pleasant, albeit more immature:

- **CHECK OUT MONA LISA'S BROWS...** or lack thereof. One painting the size of a mini-magazine. A million American tourists fighting to snap a picture but just getting a shot of each others' cameras. Not enough security guards to fend off the crowd. At some point, should you finding yourself doubting whether you should've just Googled *La Jaconde*, entertain yourself by making a note of her missing eyebrows. The facial aesthetics of the lady in question reflects the style of Florence during an era when it was considered fashionable for women to shave off the only follicular decoration on their face. If only Whoopi Goldberg had been born in the 16th century.
- **MAKE YOUR OWN MUSEUM SOUNDTRACK.** Pick a room on the Richelieu wing on the first floor. Put your iPod on shuffle. Then, for each painting, press next song. As an alternative to stodgy museum cassette tours, your own personalized walk around the museum should make the 400th "Passion of the Christ" triptych more refreshing, especially backed by Nirvana's "Smells Like Teen Spirit."
- **PLAY HIDE AND SEEK IN THE CAROUSEL GARDEN.** Fanning out from the Arc de Triomphe, the outdoor portion of the museum makes botanists everywhere salivate with its various shrubs, trees, flower species, not to mention the naked statues. Find your inner Alice in the Louvre's very own Wonderland. Just don't start painting the roses red or security might ask you to leave—s'il vous plait probably included.
- **ORDER A BEER AT MCDONALD'S.** When the Supersized fast food joint opened up in the Louvre's shopping mall in 2009, the French threw a hissy fit when they realized Americans were trying to make even art connoisseurs fat. But the Mickey D's stayed, and now visitors still have the option of enjoying the European version of the Dollar Menu, as well as the irony of taking a break with a German beverage at an American fast food joint in a French museum.
- **PULL A DUCHAMP.** On your way out, pay a visit to the gift shop in the Allée de Grande Louvre to purchase a postcard of the Mona Lisa. Feel free to add a moustache or a mole here and there, use Duchamp's famous "L.H.O.O.Q"/"Elle a chaud au cou" ("She has a hot ass") pun, or come up with your own version. Either way, you'll have a souvenir that's considerably more cool than an Eiffel Tower keychain.

NEAR EASTERN ANTIQUITIES

The cradle of civilization, the fertile crescent, and the land of epithets, Mesopotamia (known as the Near East) was the birthplace of Western Art. The Louvre's collection is one of the largest agglomerations of Egyptian and Mesopotamian artifacts in the world and includes works that are over ten thousand years old. This area of the museum is generally one of the calmer ones, so you can spend some time marveling at its ancient offerings without feeling overwhelmed by the frenetic crowds. The encyclopedic exhibits include a few terrific *stelas* (no, not the beer you get ripped off for at the cafés around the Louvre; we're talking slabs of wood or stone inscribed with painting, inscription, etc.) The *Victory Stela of Naram Sim (Room 2)* is a highlight of the collection, depicting the Akkadian King ascending to the heavens, trampling his enemies along the way and sporting the crown of a god. One of the Louvre's most historically significant pieces is the *Law Code of Hammurabi*, or the King of Babylon, currently holding things down in Room 3 of the museum's Near East section. The object itself is a modest *stela* inscribed with 282 laws for King Hammurabi's Babylonian civilization. This code was deliberately written in simple language, so that the most people possible could understand it. The code's subjects ranged from family law to slavery to salary-setting. The Babylonians didn't value criminals' civil liberties too highly—dismemberment was the sentence for minor crimes like petty theft.

🏛 *Richelieu. Ground fl.*

GREEK, ETRUSCAN, AND ROMAN ANTIQUITIES

The extensive collection boasts works dating from the Neolithic age, about fourth millennium BCE, up until the sixth century. Many of the works featured here can be traced back to the rich royal collections seized by the rebel government of the French Revolution—which is also, in large part, to thank for transforming the Louvre into a museum. Purchases of various other royal and private collections over the next century solidified the bulk of the modern-day exhibit. The armless *Venus de Milo* is, obviously, the main attraction. As you approach Room 74 on the first floor, you can hear the din of the crowd (not quite Mona Lisa level, but still a din), heartily oohing, ahhing, and snapping pictures of the lady. The *Winged Victory of Samothrace* proves that a head is not a prerequisite for Greek masterpieces; beware of large crowds.

🏛 *Denon and Sully. 1st fl., ground fl., and lower ground fl.*

THE ITALIANS

Da Vinci's *Mona Lisa*, purchased by Francois I in 1518 *(Room 6)* is the most famous painting in the world. While the lady's mysterious smile and plump figure are still charming, there is nothing charming about fighting for a good view of the painting; if you feel comfortable doing so, now's the time to throw some elbows. The crowds are fierce, the painting is hidden in a glass box that constantly reflects hundreds of camera flashes, and you won't be allowed within 15 ft of it. If you're pressed for time and/or physically unimposing, you might consider skipping the lady, or settling for a terrible view of her. In the adjacent hall, an astonishing group of Renaissance masterpieces awaits—everything from Da Vinci's *Virgin on the Rocks* to Raphael's *Grand Saint Michael* to Fra Angelico's *Cavalry*. The rest of the exhibit contains Renaissance masterpieces by Caravaggio, da Vinci, and others, an impressive bunch whose work documents the rise of Humanist art in the West. This wing is best visited as soon as the museum opens, as the entire thing turns into a zoo within 15-30min.; while crowds are smaller on Wednesday and Friday evening visit times, this part of the Museum is always pretty busy.

🏛 *Denon. 1st fl.*

FLANDERS, THE NETHERLANDS

A more relaxed Louvre experience awaits you on the second floor. Vermeer's majestic *Astronomer* and *Lacemaker* occupy Room 38. While Vermeer left behind no sketches or clues related to his preparatory methods, some scholars believe that he used a camera obscura in composing his works; one can make out subtle effects of light that could not have appeared to Vermeer's naked eye without a little assistance, unless he was superhuman (granted, that's a distinct possibility). Also not to be missed is Rubens' *Galerie Médicis*; comprised of 24 huge canvases, the room's paintings are dedicated to episodes from the self-obsessed queen's life. The equally giant tableaux are worth a few minutes of your time. This section of the Museum is also filled with works by Rembrandt, Van Eyck, and Van der Weyden.
✦*Richelieu. 2nd fl.*

AND NOW FOR THE FRENCH

French paintings? In the Louvre? You would never have guessed it. Extravagant works from the 17th, 18th, and 19th centuries dominate the second floor of the Sully wing. A room dedicated to La Tour, once one of the world's leading Caravaggesque painters, showcases his fascination with hidden sources of light, responsible for the haunting works that occupy Room 28. Once you've had your fill of modernity, peace, and quiet, head back to the first floor of Denon, where the French heavyweights neighbor the Mona Lisa. The second most famous painting in these galleries is Delacroix's chaotic *Liberty Leading the People*, in which Liberty is symbolized by a highly liberated (read: partially nude) woman. The rich use of color in the painting is considered seminal in its effect on the Impressionist school of art. Social science types should get a kick out of Ingres's body-twisting *Grande Odalisque* and Delacroix's *Death of Sardanapalus*. The combined chaos and richness of the tableaux are truly fascinating. Both paintings are good examples of Orientalism, a product of France's imperial adventures in North Africa. The latter painting depicts the suicide of Sardanapalus, an Oriental king of Antiquity, on a sacrificial pyre originally built to exterminate his slaves, women, and horses after military defeat. The legacy of French perception of the "Orient" as a paradise of indulgence, sexually generous women, and drugs, remains today.
✦*Sully, 2nd fl. Denon, 1st fl.*

châtelet-les halles

Châtelet-Les Halles is perhaps Paris's most densely touristed area. And that's saying something. From the commercial indulgence of the Place Vendome, to the mind-numbing grandeur and beauty of the Louvre, to the bizarre trends on display at Les Arts Decoratifs, the 1*er* and 2*ème* arrondissements have it all!

▨ JARDIN DES TUILERIES

Pl. de la Concorde, Rue de Rivoli

    ♿ GARDEN
☎01 40 20 90 43

Covering the distance from the Louvre to the place de la Concorde (and the Jeu de Paume and L'Orangerie), the Jardin des Tuileries is a favorite hangout for Parisians and tourists alike. The garden was originally built for Catherine de Medici in 1559, when she moved to the Louvre after the death of her husband, Henri II. The original designer was Italian Bernard de Carnesse, who modeled his masterpiece on the gardens of Catherine's native Florence, and the garden was used mostly for royal occasions. About a hundred years later, Louis XIV's superintendent, Jean-Baptiste Colbert, assigned the task of recreating the Tuileries garden to Le Notre (of Vaux-le-Vicomte and Versailles fame), the grandson of one Catherine's gardeners. Straight lines and sculpted trees became the decorative preference for this majestic plot of land, and several generations of kings employed the new and improved Tuileries for massive parties. You don't want to miss the beautiful views of Paris from the elevated terrace by the Seine. There are extremely expensive cafes scattered throughout the grounds. During the summer, *confiserie* stands, merry-go-rounds and a huge ferris wheel are installed near the rue de Rivoli entrance for the park's younger visitors.

✳ Ⓜ*Tuileries.* Ⓢ *Free entry.* ⓘ *Open daily Apr-May 7am-9pm, June-Aug 7am-11pm, Sept 7am-9pm, Oct-Mar 7:30am-7:30pm. English tours from the Arc de Triomphe du Carrousel. Amusement park open July to mid-Aug.*

⧉ EGLISE ST-EUSTACHE   CHURCH
2 Rue du Jour   ☎01 42 36 31 05 ▣www.saint-eustache.org

There's a reason why Richelieu, Molière, Louis XIV, and Mme. de Pompadour achieved greatness in their lives; they were all baptized and/or received communion in the truly awe-inspiring Église de St-Eustache. Construction of the Gothic structure began in 1532 and dragged on for over a century due to lack of funding. The situation was so dire that its head priest sent a letter to the Les Halles community (which was at that point almost entirely Catholic) soliciting money for the project. Construction was essentially completed in 1633, and the church opened in 1637. In 1754, the unfinished Gothic facade was demolished and replaced with the fantastic Romanesque one that stands here today; in this sense, the Church's dysfunctional building process ended up working in its favor. The chapels contain paintings by Rubens, as well as by the British artist Raymond Mason's seemingly misplaced relief, "Departure of the Fruits and Vegetables from the Heart of Paris," commemorating the closing of the market at Les Halles in February 1969. Today, St. Eustache stands up to almost any other church in terms of its physical beauty. Not to mention that it collects some serious points because it isn't as heavily touristed as the Basilique Sacre-Coeur or, obviously, Notre Dame.

✳ Ⓜ*Les Halles.* Ⓢ *Audio tours available in English; the suggested offering is €3. A piece of identity is required to use one of the guides.* ⓘ*Open M-F 9:30am-7pm, Sa 10am-7pm, Su 9am-7pm. Mass Sa 6pm, Su 9:30, 11am, 6pm.*

PLACE VENDÔME   NEIGHBORHOOD
pl. Vendôme

North of the Jardin des Tuileries, Pl. Vendôme was originally intended by Louis XIV to house the French treasury, embassy, and Royal Library. While there is probably more money walking around the pl. Vendome than there is in any treasury in the world, its modern day uses are more commercially motivated; Dior, Cartier, and Bulgari all hold real estate for their jewelry operations on the *place.* The swankiness of this locale is truly remarkable; this is probably where those girls from MTV's "My Super Sweet Sixteen" came to shop. Despite its more frivolous modern day uses, the Place Vendome's beauty and history must not be neglected; a large sculpture stands tall in the middle of the Place, depicting Napoleon dressed as Caesar. Made out of the bronze from the cannons he captured at the Battle of Austerlitz, Napoleon modeled it after Trojan's column in Rome. While the statue's location and details changed a bit during the tumultuous days of the Revolution, it today remains relatively intact, fittingly colored green (a detail only Americans can appreciate), and majestic. The Place doubles as a tourist attraction and, for those who care, a car show. Dazed tourists gape at the column as businessmen whip out of the Place's garage in late model Mercedes, Bentleys, and Lamborghinis.

✳ Ⓜ*Tuileries or Pyramides.*

JEU DE PAUME   ◆ MUSEUM
1 pl. Concorde   ☎01 41 850 890 ▣www.jeudepaume.org

Originally designed to house Napoleon III's *jeu de paume* courts (an ancestor of

sights

tennis) in 1861, the building was transformed into an art museum in 1909. During World War II, the Nazis used the building as a storage area for confiscated paintings by Jewish artists. The space functioned as an Impressionist art museum from 1947 until 1986, when the Musée d'Orsay stole many of its paintings. In 1990, French politician Jack Lang started an initiative to open the Museum back up, this time as an abstract art space. Since then, it has become dedicated exclusively to the portrayal of photography. Exhibits are entirely rotating; the museum closes for an often significant time between exhibits, so make sure to check the website before visiting.

⚑ ⓜConcorde. ⓢ €7, students €5; ages 25 and under free last Tu every month. ⌚ Open Tu noon-9pm, W-F noon-7pm, Sa-Su 10am-7pm.

MUSÉE DE L'ORANGERIE
Jardin des Tuileries

☞ MUSEUM

☎ 01 44 77 80 07 🖳www.musee-orangerie.fr

Once the greenhouse of the Jardin des Tuileries, l'Orangerie opened as a museum in 1927. Today, it is one of Paris's finest, housing a terrific list of works by Impressionist and post-Impressionist painters like Monet, Matisse, some guy named Pablo Picasso, and Renoir. Since its conversion into a museum, L'Orangerie has been home to Picasso's "The Nymphs" collection, and in the 1960s it received the collection of renowned art collector Paul Guillaume. This impressive list probably explains why it's impossible to enter the Museum without waiting, even on weekdays. On weekends, the wait can last up to two hours, and on Free Sunday (the first Sunday of every month), show up at 9am or roast in the sun for most of the day. In any event, the wait to enter the Museum will definitely figure into your memory of your time at L'Orangerie. The Museum is also fresh off some 2006 renovations, which were designed to increase the amount of natural light inside.

⚑ ⓜConcorde. ⓢ Permanent exhibits €7.50, reduced €5. ⌚ Open M 9am-6pm, W-Su 9am-6pm; free first Su every month.

LES ARTS DECORATIFS
107 rue de Rivoli

☞ MUSEUM

☎01 44 55 57 50 🖳www.lesartsdecoratifs.fr

The fashion-conscious among our *Let's Go* readers could easily spend a full day perusing the Musée des Arts Decoratifs. It itself houses four different museums, in addition to many smaller exhibits: **Arts Decoratifs** (Interior Design), **Mode et Textile** (Fashion and Fabric), **Publicité** (Advertisement), and the **Musée Nissim de Camondo.** The former three are dedicated to some funky, haute couture design that the average tourist has probably never experienced. In the Arts Decoratifs, you'll find sheep-shaped chairs, elephant-shaped fountains, and chairs whittled into the form of birds. The Mode and Textile Museum has exhibits on the evolution of fashion from the 1970s to the 1990s, featuring smaller exhibits on prominent fashion designers, including Yves St.-Laurent. The Advertisement Museum features, you guessed it, lots of ads. Fashion-conscious types balance their time in the museum between scrutinizing the exhibits and finding a mirror to make sure their hair is just so to impress their fellow fashionistas. The latter of the four museums is in the old home of the famous Camondo family; its three floors showcase wonderful artwork, furniture, and woodwork. Don't miss the Galerie des Bijoux; dark-room displays of some of modern mankind's finest jewels are breathtaking even for those helpless dudes who get their significant other a terribly homely piece of jewelry come Christmas and birthday times.

⚑ ⓜPalais Royal-Musée du Louvre. *i* Audio tour included. ⓢ Musées Rivoli (Arts Decoratifs, Mode et Textile, Publicité) €9, reduced €7.50. Musée Nissim Camondo €7, reduced €5. ⌚ Tu-W 11am-6pm, Th 11am-9pm, F-Su 11am-6pm. Last entry 30min. before close.

PALAIS-ROYAL
25 Rue de Valois

♿ HISTORIC SIGHT, PALACE
☎01 42 96 15 35

Palais-Royal is located a block north of the Louvre along rue St-Honoré. The building was originally constructed to be Cardinal Richelieu's residence between 1628 and 1642 by Jacques Lemercier. Richelieu died the same year that the palace was finished, and after Queen Anne d'Autriche lived there, the Palace was home to the exiled Queen of England, Henrietta Maria. Louis XIV was the first king to inhabit the palace. In 1781, a broke Duc d'Orléans rented out the buildings around the palace's formal garden, turning the complex into an 18th-century shopping mall with boutiques, restaurants, theaters, wax museums, and casinos. Its covered arcades were even a favorite of local prostitutes. On July 12, 1789, angered by the dismissal of Louis' reform-minded finance minister Jacques Necker, 26-year-old Camille Desmoulins leapt onto a cafe table here and urged his fellow citizens to arm themselves, shouting, "I would rather die than submit to servitude." After Desmoulins pulled out his guns, the crowd filed out and was soon skirmishing with cavalry in the Jardin des Tuileries. Today, the Palais-Royal plays home to boutiques and cafes in its galleries, while the interior of the Palace itself is inaccessible to the public, inhabited by government offices (oh, the irony of the Revolution!). The black-and-white-striped pillars by Daniel Buren introduce a modern feel (and as a result, a bit of controversy since their installation in 1986). The Palais is mostly a place to wander, window-shop, and relax. The old sight of the National Library is in the back of the Palace.

Ⓜ Palais Royal-Musée du Louvre. Ⓢ Free. Fountain, galleries, and garden open daily June-Aug 7am-11pm; Sept 7am-9:30pm; Oct-Mar 7:30am-8:30pm; Apr-May 7am-10:15pm.

COMÉDIE FRANÇAISE, SALLE RICHELIEU — THEATER

Place Colette, Southwest Corner of Palais-Royal ☎08 25 10 16 80 www.comedie-francaise.fr

In 1680 Louis XIV ordered that Paris's two most prominent acting troupes, that of the Hôtel Guénégaud and that of the Hôtel de Bourgogne, merge into the Comédie Française. They were lodged originally at the former acting troupe's original location. After the Revolution, in 1799, the government provided for the troupe to move into its legendary location, Palais-Royal's Salle Richelieu. Molière, the company's founder, collapsed on stage here while performing in "*Le Malade Imaginaire*," and died several hours later. The chair onto which he collapsed is still on display, along with several busts of famous actors crafted by equally famous sculptors. Visconti's *Fontaine de Molière* is only a few steps from where Molière died at no. 40. Today, the Comédie Française also has locations at the Théâtre du Vieux-Colombier and the Studio-Théâtre.

*Ⓜ Palais Royal-Musée du Louvre. **i** Visits not available; you have to get tickets to one of the shows to see the Salle Richelieu. Ⓢ Spectacles €6-47. Cheapest tickets are available minutes before the show, so try going on a weeknight Spectacle start times vary.*

FONTAINE DES INNOCENTS — HISTORIC MONUMENT

Pl. des Innocents

Built to commemorate King Henri II's entry into Paris in 1549, Lescot's fountain was heavily influenced by the Renaissance Italian work done for Francis I at Fontainebleau. What is perhaps more interesting is the story of what happened to the Fountain after it was built; today, the Fontaine des Innocents is the lone remnant of the Église and Cimetière des Sts-Innocents, which once bordered Les Halles. In 1787, the cemetery of Saint-Innocent was demolished to rid the area around the church of the smell of rotting corpses. The corpses were moved to the Catacombs. Originally built with only three facades, the fountain received a face-lift when it was moved after the destruction of the cemetery to its new location at the place des Innocents; Augustin Pajou added a fourth facade. Today, cruddy benches are available as a post for your enjoyment of the Fountain's aesthetic beauty, but don't try climbing on it. In such a crowded area, you will get flic'd (a verb for encountering the French police, otherwise known as "*les flics*").

Ⓜ Châtelet.

EGLISE ST-GERMAIN L'AUXERROIS

CHURCH

2 pl. du Louvre   ☎01 42 60 13 96 ▪www.saintgermainauxerrois.cef.fr

The Church boasts an unsavory, yet juicy, historical vignette. On August 24, 1572, the church's bell sounded the signal for the St. Bartholomew's Day Massacre. The street along which the Church sits is named for one of the Massacre's first victims, Admiral de Coligny, who fell at the hands of a foot soldier of the Duc de Guise moments after the bell's sounding. Thousands of Huguenots were hacked to death by a mob of Catholics and the troops of the counter-reformist Duc de Guise, while King Charles IX shot at the survivors from the palace window. Today, visitors are allowed inside the Church to view the violet windows or listen to Sunday evening vespers before mass. Having undergone several different renovations over the years, the church combines Roman, Gothic, and Renaissance architectural and decor styles. Don't miss the super throwback 15th-century wooden statue of Saint-Germain.

✦ ⓜLouvre-Rivoli. Located behind the Louvre, along rue de l'Amiral de Coligny. ⓢ Free. ⓩ Open M-T 8am-7pm, W 8am-8:30pm, Th-F 8am-7pm, Su 9am-8pm.

BIBLIOTHÈQUE NATIONALE: SITE RICHELIEU

✦ MUSEUM, LIBRARY

During renovations entrance at 5 Rue Vivienne   ☎01 53 79 59 59 ▪www.bnf.fr

Site Richelieu was the main branch of the Bibliothèque Nationale de France (National Library of France) until 1998, when most of the collection was moved to the Site Mitterrand in the 13ème. Now, the heavily secured Site Richelieu (between bag checks and an uncommon number of security guards by French standards, they've got it covered) houses various valuable wares: stamps, coins, photographic art, medals, maps, and manuscripts. Getting access to the reading rooms upstairs is notoriously difficult, so for the average tourist, it makes sense to just stick to the exhibits. The **Galerie Mazarin** and **Galerie de Photographie** host excellent temporary exhibits of books, prints, lithographs, and photographs taken from outside artists, as well as its permanent collection. While the Site Richelieu is normally thought of as a coin collection, don't be too quick to stereotype it as a traditional museum; exhibits are often a bit more risqué, like a summer 2010 exhibit featuring the exclusively nude artwork and film of Bettina Rheims and Serge Bramly. Upstairs, the Cabinet des Médailles displays coins, medallions, and objets d'art confiscated during the French Revolution; the National Library's collection of coins and other metal wares numbers over 600,000. The Cabinet des Médailles is on deck for some major renovations from 2010-2017, so don't count on seeing more than what the Library has to offer in its temporary exhibits for the time being.

✦ ⓜBourse, Pyramides. ⓘ French tours of the former reading room, La Salle Labrouste, 1st Tu of the month 2:30pm, €7. ⓢ Admission depends on the exhibit but is typically €7, students €5, under 18 free. ⓩ Galleries open only when there are exhibits Tu-Sa 10am-7pm, Su noon-7pm.

BOURSE DE COMMERCE

HISTORIC MONUMENT

2 Rue de Viarmes   ☎01 55 65 55 65 ▪www.ccip.fr

Today, the Bourse du Commerce is Paris's main commodities trading building. While its modern-day suit-and-tie uniformed business people are a bit dull, the building's history is far from boring. In the late 15th century, a convent of repentant sinners, headed by King Charles VIII's confessor, Jean Tisseran, occupied the site. Catherine de Médicis threw them out in 1572, when a horoscope convinced her that she should stop construction of her home at the Tuileries and build her palace at the Bourse instead. Louis XV later replaced the structure with a grain market, which it remained until 1889, when it was transformed into the commodities market that it is today. The iron-and-glass cupola, built in 1782 by architects Jacques-Guillaume Legrand and Jacques Molinos, was much admired at the time across the world, notably by then U.S. Ambassador Thomas Jefferson. It forms a tremendous skylight, allowing sunlight to flood onto the ceiling's

frescoes. Occasional exhibits; check the website or call in advance for info.
⇄ Ⓜ Louvre-Rivoli. $ Free. ⏰ Open M-F 9am-5:30pm.

GALÉRIES ET PASSAGES — NEIGHBORHOOD

Back in the 19th century, Paris's 15 *passages* were the world's first shopping malls. The second quarter of the 19th century saw the dawn of haute bourgeois consumer culture; in order to satisfy and nurture this growing demand, entrepreneurs started building *passages* in alleys all over central Paris. Americans appropriated and corrupted this innovation, coming up with the bright idea turned social problem, the super mall. Surely the pioneers of Paris' *passages* had no idea that Americans would expand on their idea, only to have France appropriate the bastard child of the *passages*, the super mall, across the nation. Today the galleries that surround the Palais-Royal are the most famous in Paris. The *passages* house upscale clothing boutiques, cafes, gift shops (several sell antique postcards), antique bookstores, and tons of Indian restaurants.
⇄ Ⓜ Palais-Royal.

the marais

There's more to see in the Marais than strutting fashionistas and strolling rabbis. A unique mix of historic and new, the area boasts an impressive list of quirky and worthwhile sights. The eastern section of the arrondissement harbors a labyrinth of old, quaint streets, a smattering of churches, and some of Paris's most beautiful *hôtels particuliers*, or mansions (particularly around the **Place des Vosges**). The Centre Pompidou, the undisputed main attraction of the Marais, breaks up the beige monotony in the western part of the arrondissement. Though the Pompidou, quite like a spoiled child, tends to attract the most attention, there are a number of other museums that are less touristy and just as entertaining. The underrated Musée Carnavalet visually portrays the history of Paris, while the Musée de la Chasse tells the story of the animals that died here. Even if you aren't the museum-going type, **Vieille du Temple** and **Rue des Rosiers** are great streets to explore.

✓ CENTRE POMPIDOU — COMPLEX

Pl. Georges-Pompidou, rue Beaubourg ☎01 44 78 12 33 www.centrepompidou.fr

Erected in Beaubourg, a former slum *quartier* whose high rate of tuberculosis earned it classification as an *îlot insalubre* (unhealthy block) in the 1930s, the Pompidou was and still is considered alternately an architectural breakthrough and a monstrosity. Pioneered in the '70s by architects Richard Rogers, Gianfranco Franchini, and Renzo Piano at the commission of President Pompidou, the design features a network of yellow electrical tubes, green water pipes, and blue ventilation ducts along the exterior of the building. The range of functions that the center serves are as varied as its colors—a sort of cultural theme park of an ultra-modern exhibition, performance, and research space. It most famously hosts the **Musée National d'Art Moderne.** The **Salle Garance** houses an adventurous film series, and the **Bibliothèque Publique d'Information** (*entrance on rue de Renard*) is a free, non-circulating library with Wi-Fi, which is almost always packed with students. Located in a separate building is the **Institut de la Recherche et de la Coordination Acoustique/Musique (IRCAM),** an institute and laboratory for the development of new technologies. The Pompidou was engineered to accommodate 5000 visitors a day, but the center now attracts over 20,000, making it more popular than the Louvre. The spectacular view from the top of the escalators, which can be reached only by purchasing a museum ticket or by dining at the rooftop restaurant, **Georges,** is well worth the lengthy ascent. From there, look out across at the Parisian skyline and observe the cobblestone square out front, filled with artists, musicians, punks, and passersby.

The **Musée National d'Art Moderne** is the Centre Pompidou's main attraction. While its collection spans the 20th century, the art from the last 50 years is particularly brilliant. It features everything from Philip Guston's uncomfortably adorable hooded figures to Eva Hesse's uncomfortably anthropomorphic sculptures. Those looking for a less provocative experience will want to see Cai Guo-Qang's *Bon Voyage*, an airplane made of wicker and vine hanging from the ceiling and studded with objects confiscated from passengers' carry-on luggage at the Tokyo airport. A large part of its contemporary display is now devoted to work by women artists in a much-needed exhibition called elles@centrepompidou. On the museum's second level, early-20th-century heavyweights like Duchamp and Picasso hold court. Most of the works were contributed by the artists themselves or by their estates; Joan Miró and Wassily Kandinsky's wife are among the museum's founders.

✢ ⓜRambuteau or ⓜHôtel de Ville. RER: Châtelet-Les Halles. ⓢ Library and forum free. Museum admission to permanent collection and exhibits €12, under 26 €9, EU citizens under 25 and under 18 free. 1st Su of month free for all visitors. Visitors' guides available in bookshop. ⌚ Center open M 11am-10pm, W-Su 11am-10pm. Museum open M 11am-9pm, W 11am-9pm, Th 11am-11pm, F-Su 11am-9pm. Last entry 1 hr. before close. Library open M noon-10pm, W-F noon-10pm, Sa-Su 11am-10pm.

▧ MUSÉE CARNAVALET
◆ MUSEUM

23 rue de Sévigné   ☎01 44 59 58 58 🖳www.carnavalet.paris.fr

Housed in Mme. de Sévigné's beautiful 16th-century *hôtel particulier* and the neighboring Hôtel Le Peletier de Saint-Fargeau, this meticulously arranged museum traces Paris's history from its origins to the present. The chronologically-themed rooms follows the city's evolution from Caesar's Roman conquest to Mitterrand's Grands Projets. The museum goes to great lengths to avoid didacticism—the city's urban development is conveyed through paintings, artifacts, and historical reconstructions rather than a tiresome timeline with a few grainy photographs. Highlights include Proust's fully reconstructed bedroom, a piece of the Bastille prison wall, and Sévigné's interior decor itself. The **Wendel Ballroom**, painted by Jose-Maria Sert, and the **Charles Le Brun ceilings** in rooms 19 and 20 are also worth the trip. Of course, Madame didn't neglect the exterior of her opulent abode; the courtyard gardens feature symmetrically designed bushes and bright pink flowers and are a lovely place to relax after perusing the collections. The museum also regularly hosts special exhibits, featuring the work of cartoonists, sculptors, and photographers.

✢ ⓜChemin Vert. Take rue St-Gilles, which turns into rue de Parc Royal, and turn left on rue de Sévigné. *i* Credit card min. €15. ⓢ Free. Special exhibits €7, under 26 €3.50, seniors €5, under 14 free. ⌚ Open Tu-Su 10am-6pm. Last entry 5:15pm.

▧ MUSÉE DE LA CHASSE ET DE LA NATURE
MUSEUM

62 rue des Archives   ☎01 48 87 40 36 🖳www.chassenature.org

The collection may be quirky, but it's one of the few in Paris that is sure to elicit some sort of response—whether that be fascination or disgust. Housed in the Hôtel de Guénégaud, the only private mansion built by François Mansart that still exists, the recently opened Musée de la Chasse et de la Nature displays hunting-themed art, weaponry, and stuffed animals from Africa, America, and Asia. It's dead animals from start to finish—a giant polar bear, a ceiling covered with owl heads, a snappy fox, antler-shaped chandeliers—all elegantly arranged in lavish rooms. The Trophy Room is an impressive arrangement of deceased beasts—lions, cheetahs, bison, a rhino—while the Salle des Armes tells the story of how they were shot. Animal-rights activists and pet lovers would be wise to avoid, though the museum does manage to create an aesthetic experience. The multimedia exhibit on the myth of

the marais

the unicorn is especially noteworthy, as is the interactive display of bird calls.

⌖ Ⓜ Rambateau. $ €6, ages 18-25 and seniors €4.50, under 18 free. 1st Su of each month free. ⏰ Open Tu-Su 11am-6pm.

a peck of picasso

Ever wonder how Pablo Picasso came up with masterpieces such as *Guernica* and *Three Musicians*? Well if you want to see some of his preliminary artwork and many more pieces, then The **Musée National Picasso** in Paris is for you! This museum dedicated to Picasso stands in the Hôtel Salé, which is located in the Marais, one of the most historic districts of the city and houses more than a thousand of his paintings, sculptures, and drawings. The Hôtel Salé was built in the mid 17th century and started being converted to a museum only 2 years after Picasso's death in 1975, when the French state decided to make a museum to present his art. (Fun fact: France obtained his pieces after his death by excusing his family from paying taxes.) The museum was officially opened to the public ten years later, in 1985, and also houses some work of Matisse and Cézanne. For only €8.50, you can go in and peruse all of his art, but get there early, as the museum closes at 5 pm. You don't want to stay overnight and get caught in a Dan Brown novel.

👍 PLACES DES VOSGES — SQUARE

Paris's oldest and most harmonious public square has served many generations of the city's residents, from the knights who clanged swords in medieval tournaments to the hipsters who swap bottles during picnics in the park today. The **central park** (sq. Louis XIII), with its manicured trees and four elegant fountains, is surrounded by beautiful 17th-century Renaissance mansions. The **Palais de Tournelles** was originally built by Henri II, but his wife Catherine de Médici had it destroyed after Henri died there in a jousting tournament in 1563. Henri IV later ordered the construction of a new public square, in what was the first European example of royal city planning. During the Revolution, the statue of Louis XIII in the center of the park was destroyed in a fit of anti-monarchical sentiment (the current statue is a replica), and in 1800 the park was renamed pl. des Vosges in honor of the first French department to pay its taxes.

Today, the park is constantly full of frolicking families, cutesy couples, and snooty French teenagers. All 36 of the buildings lining the square were constructed by Baptiste de Cerceau in the same architectural style; look for the pink brick, slate-covered roofs, and street level arcades. The largest of these townhouses, which forms the square's main entrance, was the king's pavilion; opposite is the smaller pavilion of the queen. Originally intended for merchants, the **Place Royale** was a historic home of the city's nobility, including **Madame de Sevigné** (who was born at no. 1bis) and **Cardinal Richelieu** (who lived at no. 21 when he wasn't busy mad-dogging musketeers). In the 18th century, **Molière, Racine,** and **Voltaire** filled the grand parlors with their *bons mots*, and **Mozart** played a concert here at the age of seven. The arcades around the perimeter of pl. des Vosges form an elegant promenade that is rich with window-shopping opportunities, swanky galleries and cafes, and plaques that mark the homes of famous residents. French poet **Théophile Gautier** and writer **Alphonse Daudet** lived at no. 8., and **Victor Hugo** lived at no. 6, which now features a museum dedicated to his life and work. The corner door at the right of the south face of the place (between no. 5 and 7) leads into the garden of the **Hôtel de Sully**.

✦ ⓂChemin Vert or ⓂSt-Paul.

🖾 FAIT AND CAUSE　　　　　　　　　　　　　　　　　GALLERY

58 rue Quincampoix　　　　　　　　　☎01 42 74 26 36 ▩www.sophot.com

Dedicated to increasing humanist and humanitarian consciousness through documentary photography and other media, this gallery draws large crowds with its award-winning exhibits. Past featured artists have included Jacob Riis, Jane Evelyn Atwood, and Robert Doisneau.

✦ ⓂRambuteau or ⓂÉtienne -Marcel.　🕐 Open Tu-Sa 1:30-6:30pm.

LA MAISON EUROPÉENNE DE LA PHOTOGRAPHIE　✦♿ MUSEUM, GALLERY

5-7 rue de Fourcy　　　　　　　　　☎01 44 78 75 00 ▩www.mep-fr.org

Contrary to what most Facebook profile pictures suggest, photographic display is an artform. Located in the Hôtel Hénault de Cantobre, La Maison hosts both works from its permanent collection and temporary exhibits featuring international and contemporary photography. The Hôtel also houses rotating galleries, an excellent library, and a *vidéothèque* with almost 900 films by photographers.

✦ ⓂSt-Paul or ⓂPont Marie.　*i* Credit card min. €10. For tours call ☎01 44 78 75 30. ⓢ €6.50, under 26 and seniors €3.50, under 8 and W after 5pm free. 🕐Open W-Su 11am-8pm. Last entry 7:30pm.

MAISON DE VICTOR HUGO　　　　　　　　　　　✦♿ HISTORIC HOME

6 pl. des Vosges　　　　　　　☎01 42 72 10 16 ▩www.musee-hugo.paris.fr

Dedicated to the father of the French Romantics and housed in the building where he lived from 1832 to 1848, the museum displays Hugo memorabilia, including little-known paintings by his family and the desk where he wrote standing up. On the first floor, one room is devoted to paintings of scenes from *Les Misérables*, another to *Notre Dame de Paris*, and a third to other featured plays and works. Upstairs are Hugo's apartments, a recreation of the bedroom where Hugo died, and the *chambre chinoise*, which reveals Hugo's flamboyant interior decorating skills and just how much of a romantic he was.

✦ ⓂChemin Vert, ⓂSt.Paul, or ⓂBastille.　*i* Credit card min. €15. ⓢ Permanent collection free; special exhibits around €7-8, seniors €5, under 26 €3.50-4. Audio tour €5. 🕐 Open Tu-Su 10am-6pm. Last entry 5:40pm.

MUSÉE COGNACQ-JAY　　　　　　　　　　　　　　　MUSEUM

8 rue Elzévir　　　　　　　　　　☎01 40 27 07 21 ▩cognacq-jay.paris.fr

Like many of the excessively rich, department store founder Ernest Cognacq and his energetic wife Marie-Louise Jay were prolific philanthropists and collectors. Upon their deaths, they generously bequeathed the bulk of their fortune to the city of Paris to fund the construction of the quiet Musée Cognacq-Jay, which now displays mostly 18th-century art. The museum is housed in the 16th-century Hôtel Donon, a work of art in and of itself that is notable for the austere purity of its lines, exemplified by its lack of external sculpted decoration. The museum's five floors house Enlightenment art and furniture, including minor works by Rembrandt, Rubens, Greuze, La Tour, and Fragonard. The house also features interior designs by Natoire, Van Loo, and Boucher as well as a bucolic collection of German porcelain sculpture.

✦ ⓂSt-Paul. Walk up rue Pavée and take a left on rue des Francs-Bourgeois and a right on rue Elzévir. ⓢ Free. 🕐 Open Tu-Su 10am-6pm. Last entry 5:30pm. Garden open from mid-May to mid-Sept 10am-12:45pm and 4-5:35pm.

MUSÉE D'ART ET D'HISTOIRE DU JUDAÏSME　　　　✦♿ MUSEUM

71 rue de Temple　　　　　　　　　☎01 53 01 86 60 ▩www.mahj.org

Housed in the grand Hôtel de St-Aignan—once a tenement for Jews fleeing Eastern Europe—this museum displays a history of Jews in Europe and North Africa with a focus on communal traditions throughout the Diaspora; expect to learn a lot about Hanukkah and circumcision. Modern testimonials on Jewish identity are interspersed with exquisite ancient relics. Highlights include a number of Chagall and Modigliani paintings, Lissitzky lithographs, and art collections looted by the Nazis from Jewish homes. There is also a notable selection of letters and articles concerning Captain Alfred Dreyfus, the French Jew accused of treason and espionage in the greatest socio-political controversy of the late 19th century.

⚲ Ⓜ*Rambuteau*. *i Credit card min. €12.* Ⓢ *€6.80, ages 18-26 €4.50, under 18, art and art history students free; includes an excellent English audio tour. Special exhibits €5.50, ages 18-26 €4. Combined ticket €8.50/6. Guided tours €9/6.50.* ⏰ *Open M-F 11am-6pm, Su 10am-6pm. Last entry at 5:30pm.*

IGOR STRAVINSKY FOUNTAIN
FOUNTAIN

pl. Igor Stravinsky

This novel installation features irreverent and multi-chromatic mobile sculptures by Niki de St-Phalle and Jean Tinguely. The whimsical elephants, lips, mermaids, and bowler hats are inspired by Stravinsky's works and have been known to squirt water at unsuspecting bystanders. While the fountain's colorful quirkiness is in keeping with the Centre Pompidou, it stands in contrast to the nearby historic rue Brisemiche and Église de St-Merri.

⚲ Ⓜ*Hôtel de Ville. Adjacent to the Centre Pompidou on rue de Renard.*

17 RUE BEAUTREILLIS
MEMORIAL

Jim Morrison perished here, in his bathtub, on the third floor, (allegedly) when his heart stopped. There is no commemorative plaque, and today the building houses a massage parlor. His grave at the Cimetière Père Lachaise is a better memorial.

⚲ Ⓜ*Bastille or* Ⓜ*St. Paul.*

RUE DES ROSIERS
NEIGHBORHOOD

The pulsing heart of the Jewish community of the Marais, rue des Rosiers is packed with kosher shops, *bucheries*, bakeries, and falafel counters. Until the 13th century, Paris's Jewish population lived around Notre Dame, but when Philippe-Auguste expelled them from the city limits, many families moved to the Marais. During WWII, many who had fled to France to escape the pogroms of Eastern Europe were murdered by the Nazis. Assisted by French police, Nazi soldiers stormed the Marais and hauled Jewish families to the **Vélodrome d'Hiver,** an indoor cycling stadium. Here, French Jews awaited deportation to work camps like Drancy, in a northeastern suburb of Paris, or to camps farther east in Poland and Germany. The **Mémorial de la Déportation** commemorates these victims. In the 1960s, new waves of North African Sephardim Jews fleeing Algeria moved into the area. Today, the Marais's Jewish community is thriving and sports two synagogues (at 25 rue des Rosiers and 10 rue Pavée) designed by Art Nouveau architect Hector Guimard. The mix of Mediterranean and Eastern European Jewish cultures gives the area a unique flavor, with homemade kugel and the best falafel in Paris served side by side.

⚲ Ⓜ*St-Paul. 4 blocks east of Beaubourg.*

RUE VIEILLE DU TEMPLE AND RUE STE-CROIX DE LA BRETTONERIE
NEIGHBORHOOD

The intersection of rue Vieille du Temple and rue Ste-Croix de la Brettonerie is always hot. The epicenter of Paris's thriving GLBT community, these streets boast beautiful boys in tight pants and super-stylish girls who can't have them. The crowd here consists of variations on fabulous. Dashing intellectuals frequent **La Belle Hortense,** a wine bar on the corner; loving couples share gelato at Amorino; trendy and aloof students hang out at the local bars; and women batting for all teams come for some of the best shopping in the city. Especially on weekends, this is the place to see (and be seen in) an outfit from one of the many surrounding boutiques.

✦ Ⓜ St-Paul or Ⓜ Hôtel de Ville.

HÔTEL DE VILLE
♿ GOVERNMENT BUILDING

Information office, 29 rue de Rivoli ☎01 42 76 43 43, 01 42 76 50 49

As the constant stream of tourists and their flashing cameras will attest, the Hôtel de Ville is the most extravagant and picture-worthy non-palace edifice in Paris. The present structure is the second incarnation of the original edifice, which was built in medieval times and, during the 14th-15th centuries, served as a meeting hall for merchants who controlled traffic on the Seine. In 1533, King François I appointed Domenica da Cortona, known as Boccador, to expand and renovate the structure into a city hall worthy of the metropolis; the result was an elaborate mansion built in the Renaissance style of the Loire Valley châteaux. On May 24, 1871, the Communards, per usual, doused the building with gasoline and set it on fire. The blaze lasted a full eight days and spared nothing but the building's frame. Undaunted, the Third Republic built a virtually identical structure on the ruins, with a few significant changes. For one, the Republicans integrated statues of their own heroes into the facade: historian Jules Michelet graces the right side of the building, while author Eugène Sue surveys the rue de Rivoli. They also installed crystal chandeliers, gilded every interior surface, and created a Hall of Mirrors that rivals the original at Versailles. When Manet, Monet, Renoir, and Cézanne offered their services, they were all turned down in favor of the didactic artists whose work decorates the Salon des Lettres, the Salon des Arts, the Salon des Sciences, and the Salon Laurens. Originally called pl. de Grève, pl. Hôtel de Ville is additionally famous for its vital contribution to the French language. Poised on a marshy embankment *(grève)* of the Seine, the medieval square served as a meeting ground for angry workers, giving France the useful and ever necessary phrase *en grève* (on strike). In 1610, Henri IV's assassin was quartered alive here by four horses bolting in opposite directions.

Today, place de Hôtel de Ville almost never sleeps: strikers continue to gather here, and the square occasionally hosts concerts, special TV broadcasts, and light shows. Every major French sporting event—Rolland Garros, the Tour de France, and any game the Bleus ever play—is projected onto a jumbo screen in the *place*. The information office holds exhibits on Paris in the lobby off the rue de Lobau.

✦ Ⓜ Hôtel de Ville. 🕐 Open when there is an exhibit M-Sa 9am-7pm; otherwise 9am-6pm. Group tours available with advance reservations; call for available dates. Special exhibit entry on rue de Lobau.

MUSÉE DE LA POUPÉE
⊛ MUSEUM

Impasse Berthaud ☎01 42 72 73 11 🖥www.museedelapoupeeparis.com

This small museum, nestled in a cul-de-sac, is the ultimate fantasy fulfillment for those who still play with Ken and Barbie on occasion. The first rooms are devoted to a permanent collection of dolls from 1805 to the present, while the rest of the museum hosts more specialized exhibits such as "Baby Boom" and "Dream with Barbie." The museum also hosts special events, including puppet shows *(W 2:30pm; €7-11)*, appraisals of antique dolls *(W 11am; €12)*, and "torch visits" in the dark *(1 Th per month; €10)*. Kids will probably like it, though grown-ups may find it creepy. The attached shop sells antique dolls and performs restorations.

✦ Ⓜ Rambateau. Ⓢ €8, under 25 and seniors €5, ages 3-11 and handicapped €3. Free 2nd F of each month 10am-noon. 🕐 Open Tu-Su 10am-6pm. Last entry 5:30pm.

HÔTEL DE SULLY
MONUMENT

62 rue St-Antoine ☎01 44 61 20 00

Built in 1624, the Hôtel de Sully was commissioned by the Duc de Sully, minister to

Henri IV and king of sass. Often cuckolded by his young wife, Sully would say when giving her money, *"Voici tant pour la maison, tant pour vous, et tant pour vos amants"* ("Here's some for the house, some for you, and some for your lovers"). The classical composition of the building is adorned with elaborate sculpted decoration representing the elements and the seasons. The inner courtyard accommodates fatigued tourists with benches, shade, and a formal garden. The building houses both an annex of the **Musée de Jeu de Paume** and the **Centre d'Information des Monuments Nationaux,** which distributes free maps and brochures on Paris monuments and museums. The back garden contains an entrance into the pl. des Vosges.

⚹ Ⓜ*St-Paul.* 🕿 *Centre d'Information des Monuments Nationaux open M-Th 9am-12:45pm and 2-6pm, F 9am-12:45pm and 2-5pm.*

GALERIE EMMANUEL PERROTIN
⬗ GALLERY

76 rue Turenne and 10 impasse St-Claude   ☎01 42 16 79 79 ▣www.galerieperrotin.com

A celebrated visionary in the art world, Perrotin first made waves with his "ambitious" Miami gallery. Situated in a courtyard building once occupied by the directors of the Bastille prison, the Miami gallery's Parisian counterpart features artists from around the world and displays everything from installation art to sculpture. The collection is big enough to be a small museum.

⚹ Ⓜ*St-Sebastien Froissart.* Ⓢ *Free.* 🕿 *Open Tu-Sa 11am-7pm.*

GALERIE THULLIER
⬗ GALLERY

13 rue de Thorigny   ☎01 42 77 33 24 ▣www.galeriethuillier.com

Despite being one of the city's most active galleries—over 1,500 pieces of art are featured here each year at 21 annual expositions across two sizable shop fronts—Galerie Thullier still manages to feel intimate. The gallery thrives commercially by displaying a variety of media and styles as well as both temporary and permanent artists.

⚹ Ⓜ*St-Sébastien-Froissart.* 🕿 *Open M-Sa 1-7pm.*

HÔTEL DE SENS
MONUMENT

1 Rue du Figuier   ☎01 42 78 14 60

One of the city's few surviving examples of medieval residential architecture, the Hôtel de Sens was built in 1474 for Tristan de Salazar, the Archbishop of Sens. Its military features are indicative of the violence of the era: the turrets were designed to survey the streets outside, and the square tower served as a dungeon. An enormous arched and Gothic entrance—complete with chutes for pouring boiling water on invaders—makes the mansion all the more intimidating. While enemies found it hard to penetrate the *hôtel*, lovers had an easier time. As the former residence of Henri IV's first wife Marguerite de Valois, infamously known as Queen Margot, the Hôtel de Sens has witnessed some of Paris's most scandalous romantic escapades. In 1606, the 55-year-old queen drove up to the door of her home and witnessed her two current lovers arguing out front. One reached for the lady's carriage door; the other shot him dead. Unfazed, the queen demanded the execution of the offender, which she watched from a window the next day. The *hôtel* now houses the **Bibliothèque Forney,** a reference library for the fine arts open to the public, and a beautiful courtyard with an ornately designed garden.

⚹ Ⓜ*Pont Marie.* Ⓢ *Special exhibits €4, under 26 and seniors €2.* 🕿 *Open Tu 1:30-7:30pm, W-Th 10am-7:30pm, F-Sa 1:30-7:30pm. Special exhibits are held 4 times a year; call for schedule.*

HÔTEL DE BEAUVAIS
MONUMENT

68 Rue François-Miron   ☎01 48 87 74 31

The Hôtel de Beauvais was built in 1654 for Catherine Bellier, the not-so-attractive wife of merchant Pierre de Beauvais and the chambermaid/intimate of Anne d'Autriche. One of history's most successful cougars, the 40-year-old Mme. Bellier is perhaps best known for taking the virginity of the queen's son, the 16-year-old Louis XIV; this being France, the queen felt deeply indebted to Bellier for her services and subsequently promoted her husband to royal advisor. In 1660, Anne d'Autriche and Cardinal Mazarin watched the entry of Louis XIV and his bride, the Spanish princess Marie-Thérèse, into Paris from the balcony of the *hôtel*. A century later, Mozart played his first piano recital here as a guest of the Bavarian ambassador. Restored in 1967 and home to the Administrative Court of Appeals since 1995, it is only open to the public through the tours given by Paris Historique.

✠ ⓂHôtel de Ville. *i* Paris Historique at 44-46 Rue François Miron.⌚ Open M-Sa 11am-6pm, Su 2-5pm.

ÉGLISE ST-GERVAIS-ST-PROTAIS   CHURCH
Pl. St. Gervais

St-Gervais-St-Protais was named after Gervase and Protase, two Romans martyred during Nero's reign. The Classical facade, flamboyant Gothic vaulting, stained glass, and a Baroque wooden Christ carved by Préault all constitute this working convent (penguin sightings more than possible). The exterior of the church dates back to the 15th century, while the parish was built in the 6th century and is thought to be the oldest on the Right Bank.

✠ ⓂHôtel de Ville. On Rue François-Miron. ⌚ Gregorian chant Tu-Sa 7am, Su 8am. Vespers Tu-Sa 6pm, Su 6:30pm. Mass Tu-Sa 6:30pm, high mass Su 11am.

TOUR ST-JACQUES   TOWER
Rue de Rivoli

A lone erect structure in its own park, this flamboyant Gothic tower is the only remnant of the 16th-century **Église Saint-Jacques-la-Boucherie.** The 52m tower's meteorological station and the statue of Blaise Pascal at its base commemorate his experiments on the weight of air, performed here in 1648. The tower also marks Haussmann's *grande croisée* of rue de Rivoli and the bd. Sébastopol, the intersection of his east-west and north-south axes for the city.

✠ ⓂHôtel de Ville. 2 blocks west of the Hôtel de Ville.

MÉMORIAL DE LA SHOAH   ♿ MEMORIAL
17 rue Geoffroy l'Asnier   ☎01 42 77 44 72 🖳www.memorialdelashoah.org

Opened in 2005, the Mémorial de la Shoah (the Memorial of the Holocaust) functions as a museum, resource center, and archives whose formal mission is to form a bridge between Holocaust survivors and subsequent generations. Beautifully conceived and intensely moving, the museum accomplishes much more. Visitors enter into a small courtyard that features a series of monuments: the memorial to the Unknown Jewish Martyr; a large bronze cylinder resembling the chimney of a gas chamber that bears the names of the major concentration camps; and the Wall of Names, inscribed with the names of the 76,000 Jews, including 11,000 children, deported from France during the Nazi regime. Inside, there is an extensive series of exhibits recounting the deportation itself as well as the somber but beautiful black marble crypt, shaped in the Star of David. In a dark room lit by a single flame, the crypt symbolizes the tomb of the six million Jews who died without a proper burial and contains the ashes of martyrs taken from the death camps and from the ruins of the Warsaw Ghetto.

✠ ⓂPont Marie or ⓂSt-Paul. Ⓢ Free. ⌚ Open M-W 10am-6pm, Th 10am-10pm, F 10am-6pm, Su 10am-6pm. Tours Su 3pm or upon request. English tours every 2nd Su of the month.

NATIONAL ARCHIVES   MUSEUM
60 Rue des Francs-Bourgeois   ☎01 40 27 62 18 🖳www.archivesdefrance.culture.gouv.fr

The most famous documents of the National Archives are on display in the Musée de l'Histoire de France, ensconced in the plush 18th-century **Hôtel de Soubise.** Two to three annual rotating exhibits feature such transformative treatises as the

Treaty of Westphalia, the Edict of Nantes, and the Declaration of the Rights of Man as well as Marie-Antoinette's last letter, letters between Benjamin Franklin and George Washington, and a note from Napoleon to his beloved empress Josephine. Louis XVI's entry for July 14, 1789, the day the Bastille was stormed, reads simply "*Rien*" ("nothing")—referring to the hunt that day at Versailles, far from the riots in Paris. Also open to visitors are the apartments of the Princess de Soubise, which are sculpted with mythological motifs and feature works by Boucher. Call for information on current exhibits, as well as occasional performances by foreign dance companies. The Archives' second location at **Hôtel de Rohan** (*87 rue Vieille-du-Temple*), is currently closed but is still worth a glance from the outside.

✦ ⓂRambuteau. Ⓢ *€3, ages 18-25 and seniors €2.30, under 18 free. Su €2.30 for all.* ⓩ *Open M 10am-12:30pm and 2-5:30pm, W-F 10am-12:30pm and 2-5:30pm, Sa-Su 2-5:30pm.*

HÔTEL DE LAMOIGNON ✎ LIBRARY
22 Rue Malher ☎01 44 59 29 60

Built in 1584 for Henri II's daughter, Diane de France, the Hôtel de Lamoignon is one of the finest *hôtels particuliers* in the Marais. The facade's Colossal style was copied later in the Louvre. Now the site of the **Bibliothèque Historique de la Ville de Paris,** a non-circulating library of Parisian history with 800,000 volumes, Lamoignon also hosts rotating art exhibits portraying Paris. The quiet courtyard on the rue des Francs-Bourgeois is great for picnicking, sunbathing or canoodling.

✦ ⓂSt-Paul. Ⓢ *Temporary exhibits €4, students and seniors €2, under 8 free.* ⓩ *Exhibition hall open Tu-W 11am-7pm, Th 11am-9pm, F-Su 11am-7pm. Bibliothèque open M-Sa 9am-6pm.*

MUSÉE DE JEU DE PAUME ♿ MUSEUM
62 rue St-Antoine ☎01 42 74 47 75, 01 47 03 12 52 💻www.jeudepaume.org

Located in the Hôtel de Sully on the lower left-hand of the courtyard, this is an annex of the main Musée de Jeu de Paume at pl. de Concorde. It shows only temporary photo exhibitions, but they are usually well worth the visit. Check the website for current showings.

✦ ⓂSt. Paul. Ⓢ *€5, seniors and under 25 €2.50. Admission to both Concorde and Sully €8/4.* ⓩ *Open Tu-F noon-7pm, Sa-Su 10am-7pm. Call for tours.*

CONSERVATOIRE NATIONAL DES ARTS ET MÉTIERS ♿ MUSEUM
60 rue Réaumur ☎01 53 01 82 00 💻www.arts-et-metiers.net

Formerly the Abbey St-Martin-des-Champs, this flamboyant Gothic structure became the Conservatoire National des Arts et Métiers in 1794. Its curators originally hoped to showcase the finest in French industry, but today the structure itself is more impressive than the stuff it contains; the original collection of over 80,000 scientific and mechanical objects and nearly 15,000 detailed scientific drawings is now displayed in the informative, but rather dry, **Musée des Arts et Métiers.** In the remaining exhibits, follow the evolution of scientific instruments, materials, construction, communication, energy, mechanics, and transportation—from Gramme's "dynamo" to Ader's flying machine, the windmill to the iPod. The Conservatoire's innovative design ideas don't stop once you leave the museum; ⓂArts et Métiers services the area, which is entirely covered in copper tiling in an homage to the museum and its collection. A theater of automatons—full of princesses, magicians, and acrobats—turns on for performances Wednesday and Sunday at 2, 3, and 4pm and Thursday at 5pm. Entrance to the first-floor exhibition space is free, as is the Merovingian-era former chapel that houses historical scientific instruments and a 1/16-size copper model of the Statue of Liberty.

✦ ⓂArts et Métiers or ⓂRéaumur-Sébastopol. Ⓢ *€6.50, students €4.50, under 18 free. Special exhibits €6/4/free. Combined ticket €8/6/3. Audio tour €5.* ⓩ *Open Tu-W 10am-6pm, Thu 10am-9:30pm, F-Su 10am-6pm. Daily guided visits in French.*

ÉGLISE ST-PAUL

99 rue St-Antoine

CHURCH

☎01 42 72 30 32

Dating from 1627, when King Louis XIII laid its first stone, the Église St-Paul is an imposing fixture on the colorful rue St-Antoine. Its large dome—a trademark of Jesuit architecture—is visible from afar but hidden by ornamentation on the facade. Paintings inside the dome depict four French kings: Clovis, Charlemagne, Robert the Pious, and St-Louis. The embalmed hearts of Louis XIII and Louis XIV were kept here in vermeil (ruby red) boxes before they were destroyed during the Revolution. The church's Baroque interior is graced with three 17th-century paintings of the life of St-Louis and Eugène Delacroix's dramatic *Christ in the Garden of Olives* (1826). A work by Lebrun is also on display. The holy-water vessels were gifts from Victor Hugo.

✝ Ⓜ*St-Paul.* Ⓢ *Free tours in French at 3pm every 2nd Su of the month or upon request.* ☒ *Open M-F 9am-8pm, Sa 9am-7:30pm, Su 9am-8:30pm. Mass M 7pm, Tu-F 9am, 7pm, Sa 6pm, Su 9:30, 11am, 7pm.*

latin quarter and st-germain

Sights, sights, sights, and more sights. There's more to see in the fifth and sixth than there is time to do it in. With that being said, there are a few things that you can't miss. The **Museums of the Middle Ages** (Musée de Cluny) and the **National Delacroix Museum** are two of the finest selections in Paris. The **Jardin de Luxembourg** is magnificent, and, alongside the Tuileries, one of the finest chill spots Paris has to offer. If you're the artsy type, you can't miss the slew of galleries in the **Odéon/Mabillon** area.

PANTHÉON

Place du Panthéon

HISTORICAL MONUMENT, CRYPT

☎01 44 32 18 04 🖳http://pantheon.monuments-nationaux.fr

Among Paris's most majestic and grandiose structures, the multi-faceted Panthéon is the former stomping ground and final resting place of many great Frenchmen and women of days past. In the 1760s, Louis XV recovered from a serious illness, and, having vowed to transform the basilica of Ste-Genevieve to something bigger if he survived, followed up on his promise. Originally designed to be the enlarged version of the Abbey of Ste-Genevieve, it was decided during the early stages of the French Revolution to guard the massive structure as a secular mausoleum. Some of France's greatest citizens are buried in the Panthéon's crypt, including Marie and Pierre Curie, politician Jean Jaurès, Braille inventor Louis Braille, Voltaire, Jean-Jacques Rousseau, Émile Zola, and Victor Hugo. Now that's a list. There's something here for everybody; if you ever took a high-school French class, you'll enjoy paying homage to Antoine de St-Exupéry, writer of "Le Petit Prince." Alexandre Dumas became the crypt's most recent addition, following his November 2002 interment. Compte de Mirabeau, a great Revolutionary orator, received the first nomination for a chunk of real estate at the Panthéon. However, the government expelled his ashes one year later when the public discovered his counter-Revolutionary correspondence with Louis XVI. Beyond the "ooh, look who's buried here," appeal of the crypt, the Panthéon's other main attraction is a famous science experiment any respectable nerd will have heard of: Foucault's Pendulum. The pendulum's plane of oscillation stays fixed as the Earth rotates around it, confirming the Earth's rotation. While you might be struck by the pendulum's oscillation, don't step in its path. The Earth's not gonna stop for ya.

✝ Ⓜ*Cardinal Lemoine.* ℹ *Dome visits Apr-Oct Dutch-, English-, French-, German-, Russian-, and Spanish-language.* Ⓢ *€7.50, ages 18-25 €4.80, under 18 and 1st Su of the month Oct-Mar free.* ☒ *Open daily Apr-Sept 10am-6:30pm; Oct-Mar 10am-6pm. Last entry 45min. before close.*

LE JARDIN DU LUXEMBOURG

GARDEN

Main entrance on bd. St-Michel

"There is nothing more charming, which invites one more enticingly to idleness, reverie, and young love, than a soft spring morning or a beautiful summer dusk at the Jardin du Luxembourg," wrote Léon Daudet in a fit of sentimentality in 1928. The gardens were once a residential area in Roman Paris, the site of a medieval monastery, and later the home of 17th-century French royalty, when Marie de Médicis hired architect Jean-François-Thérèse for the task of landscaping the garden's roughly 55 acres of prime Latin Quarter real estate in 1612. Revolutionaries liberated the gardens in the late 18th century and transformed them into a lush public park.

Today, Latin Quarter Parisians flock to Le Jardin de Luxembourg to sunbathe, stroll, flirt, drink, inhale cigarettes, and read by the rose gardens and central pool. The acres are patchworked by lawns of Wimbledon-esque precision, symmetrical pathways, and sculptures; taking in the garden can be a daunting task. Visitors saunter through the park's sandy paths, passing sculptures of France's queens, poets, and heroes. Nerds and chess phenoms challenge the local band of aged chess masters to a game under shady chestnut trees. If you have kids, they can sail toy boats in the fountain, ride ponies, and see the *grand guignol*, or puppet show. Tennis courts in the garden generally fill up pretty quickly; you'll have a long wait to stretch out your muscles before showing off the skill set to passing French hotties. Undoubtedly the best, and most sought-after, spot in the garden is the **Fontaine des Médicis,** just east of the Palais, a vine-covered grotto complete with a murky fish pond and Baroque fountain sculptures. You might have to wait a few minutes, or hours, to get one of the coveted chairs bordering the Fontaine. Do not step on the portions of grass that bear a small divider from the walkways. There are tons of cops roaming the Garden at all times, so chances are you will get caught, *gueuled* (that's French for stank-faced), and, possibly, if you are so unlucky as to draw a supercop, fined. A more beautiful rest stop does not exist in Paris. The **Palais du Luxembourg,** located within the park and built in 1615 for Marie de Médicis, is now home to the **French Senate** and thus closed to the public. During WWII, the palace was used by the Nazis as headquarters for the Luftwaffe.

✳ Ⓜ Odéon or RER: Luxembourg. *i* Guided tours in French Apr-Oct 1st W of each month 9:30am. Tours start at pl. André Honorat behind the observatory. ⌚ Open daily.

MUSÉE NATIONAL DU MOYEN AGE

MUSEUM

6 pl. Paul Painlevé ☎01 53 73 78 00 ▧www.musee-moyenage.fr

Located on a site originally occupied by first-to-third-century Gallo-Roman baths and the 15th-century Hotel of the Abbots of Cluny, the Musée National du Moyen Age sits on one of the few prime pieces of historical real estate in Paris. In 1843, the state converted the *hôtel* that stands here today into a medieval museum; post-WWII excavations unearthed the baths. The museum showcases an unusually wide variety of art in its collection and attracts lots of Italian and Japanese tourist groups. While the baths host some Medieval and Roman sculpture, the *hôtel* features a magnificent tapestry exhibit, an expansive ivory collection (the second biggest in Paris, next to the Louvre's), and a number of examples of Gothic sculpture. Plenty of artwork is devoted to everyday life in medieval times.

The museum's collection includes art from Paris's most important medieval religious structures: Ste-Chapelle, Notre Dame, and St-Denis. Panels of brilliant stained glass from Ste-Chapelle are found on the ground floor. The **Galerie des Rois** contains sculptures from Notre Dame—including a series of marble heads of the kings of Judah, severed during the Revolution. The museum's medieval jewelry collection carries daggers; it looks like jewelry has only acquired a recreational purpose in recent times. A series of allegorical tapestries, titled **"La**

Dame à la Licorne" (The Lady at the Unicorn), are among the most remarkable and most famous pieces in the museum. Claiming a room all their own, the woven masterpieces depict the five senses. If they look familiar to you, it may because you've seen them before—they deck the halls of the Gryffindor common room in the *Harry Potter* films. The complete cycle comprises the centerpiece of the museum's collection of 15th- and 16th-century Belgian weaving.

The grounds are divided into several sections, including the **Forest of the Unicorn,** which contains uncultivated wild plants, **Le Jardin Céleste** (The Heavenly Garden) dedicated to the Virgin Mary, **Le Jardin d'Amour** (The Garden of Love) which features plants used for medicinal and aromatic purposes, and **Le Tapis de Mille Fleurs** (Carpet of a Thousand Flowers) inspired by the *mille fleurs* tapestries. The museum also sponsors chamber music concerts during the summer.

⚑ ⓂCluny-La Sorbonne. *i* Audio tour included. Ⓢ €8.50, ages 18-25 €6.50. Free 1st Su of the month (audio tour €1). ⓩ Open M 9:15am-5:45pm, and W-Su 9:15am-5:45pm. Last entry 30min before close.

▨ SHAKESPEARE AND CO. BOOKSTORE
⚐ BOOKSTORE

37 rue de la Bûcherie ☎01 43 25 40 93 ▣www.shakespeareco.org

Sylvia Beach's original Shakespeare and Co., at 8 rue Dupuytren (later at 12 rue de l'Odéon) is legendary among Parisian Anglophones and American literature nerds alike. The alcoholic expat crew of writers gathered here in the '20s; Hemingway described the bookstore in *A Moveable Feast.* The shop is most famous for publishing James Joyce's *Ulysses* in 1922, which was initially deemed too obscene to print in England and America. According to (hardly believable) local legend, the location at Odéon closed when one of the clerks refused to sell a German officer the last copy of Joyce's *Finnegan's Wake.* George Whitman—unrelated to Walt—opened the current rag-tag bookstore located on the shores of the Seine in 1951. Shakespeare hosts poetry readings, free Sunday afternoon tea parties *(4pm),* a semiannual literary festival, and other funky events throughout the year; check the website for more info. Some of the "tumbleweeds"—a.k.a. young writers who work as employees in the store for a few hours a day—can be a bit brisk. Just remember that, in their eyes, they're the future of the humanities as we know them. No traces of the Lost Generation remain, but there are plenty of lost boys and girls who call its burlap couches home. You're free to grab a book off the shelves, camp out, and start reading. This isn't your run-of-the-mill money-machine bookstore; they're in it for the love of the game.

⚑ ⓂSt-Michel. ⓩ Open daily 10am-11pm.

▨ ÉGLISE ST-GERMAIN-DES-PRÉS
CHURCH

3 pl. St-Germain-des-Prés ☎01 55 42 81 33 ▣www.eglise-sgp.org

The Église St-Germain-des-Prés is the oldest church in Paris, and it shows. The church is the last remnant of what was once the Abbey of St-Germain-des-Prés, a formidable center of Catholic intellectual life until it was disbanded during the Revolution. In the sixth century, King Childebert I commissioned a church on this site to hold relics he had looted from the Holy Land in Jerusalem. The rest of the church's history reads like an architectural Book of Job. Sacked by the Normans and rebuilt three times, the present-day church dates from the reconstructions performed in the 11th century under the rule of Robert the Pious. On June 30, 1789, revolutionaries seized the church two weeks before the storming of the Bastille. In 1794, the 15 tons of gunpowder that had been stored in the abbey exploded. The ensuing fire devastated the church's artwork and monastic library. Haussmann tore down the remains of the abbey when he extended rue de Rennes to the front of the church and created pl. St-Germain-des-Prés. Completely refurbished in the 19th century, the interior does its best to compensate for the building's modest exterior. Especially striking are the frescoes depicting the life of Jesus and the fantastic mosaic-adorned chapels of Ste-Marguerite and Francis-Xavier, located on opposite ends of the transept. In the second chapel—on the right after the apse—a stone marks the interred heart of René Descartes. Here, visitors can also find an altar dedicated to the victims of the September 1792 massacre in which 186 refractory priests were slaughtered in the courtyard. The information window at the entrance has a schedule of the church's frequent punk and hip-hop concerts.

⚡ Ⓜ St-Germain-des-Prés. ⏰ *Open daily 8am-7:45pm. Info office open M 2:30-6:45pm, Tu-F 10:30am-noon and 2:30-6:45pm, Sa 3-6:45pm.*

🏛 PONT DES ARTS   HISTORIC MONUMENT
Across from the Institut de France

Located in between l'Institut de France and the Court of the Palais du Louvre, the Pont des Arts is one of the most beautiful bridges in Paris, with delicate iron-work and unparalleled views of the Seine. The masterpiece was originally built as a toll bridge in 1803 and was the first bridge to be made of iron. On the day it opened, 65,000 Parisians paid to walk across it. In the 1970s, it showed signs of extreme weakness and was rebuilt in the early 1980s; thirty years out, it's safe to bet on the sturdiness of this bridge. Today, the bridge is free, still crowded, and a perfect place for a picnic dinner, a view of the sunset, and a little romance (if you're cool with VPDA, or Very Public Displays of Affection). A fantastic spot that acts as a point of convergence of Paris's usual suspects: students, camera-flicking tourists, and locals going about their daily lives.

🏛 RUE MOUFFETARD   HISTORIC NEIGHBORHOOD

The *5ème's* rue Mouffetard hosts one of Paris's oldest and liveliest street mar-kets, in addition to stretches of both cheap and expensive food vendors. The stretch up rue Mouffetard, past Pl. de la Contrescarpe, and onto rue Descartes and rue de la Montagne Ste-Geneviève makes for a pleasant and entertaining Latin Quarter stroll, attracting a mix of fast-walking, cigarette-inhaling Parisians and lost, sidewalk-blocking travelers. Along Mouffetard, there are a few restaurants (read: there is nothing but restaurants). Hemingway lived off Mouffetard on 74 rue du Cardinal Lemoine.

⚡ Ⓜ Cardinal Lemoine, Ⓜ Place Monge, or Ⓜ Censier Daubenton.

🏛 LA FONTAINE DE ST-SULPICE   ♿ HISTORIC MONUMENT
Pl. St-Sulpice

Situated smack dab in the middle of the pl. St-Sulpice adjacent to the church, the Fountain of St-Sulpice is one of the most beautiful and grandiose of its kind. Constructed in 1847, the fountain was originally named "La Fontaine des Quatre Points Cardinaux" by its sculptor Louis Tullius Joachim Visconti, in honor of the then-bishops Bossuet, Fenélon, Massillon, and Fléchier. Humorously, none of the men ever became cardinals, making the monument's name obsolete and leading to its renaming as the Fontaine de St-Sulpice. Anyway, it's big, beautiful, and ironic. What more could you ask for?

⚡ Ⓜ St-Sulpice.

🏛 MUSÉE DELACROIX   ✒ MUSEUM
6 rue de Furstemberg   ☎ 01 44 41 86 50 💻 www.musee-delacroix.fr

The Musée Delacroix combines the personal and scholarly perspectives of 18th-century Romanticist painter Eugène Delacroix, the artistic master behind the famous *Liberty Leading the People* (1830). The museum is situated in the modest, refurbished, three-room apartment and atelier where Delacroix lived and worked for much of his life. Watercolors, engravings, letters to Théophile Gautier and George Sand, sketches for his work in the Église St-Sulpice, and souvenirs from his journey to Morocco constitute the permanent holdings. Temporary exhibits

sights

broadcast new developments in Delacroix scholarship. There is a tranquil enclosed garden near the atelier equipped with Delacroix's original palettes and studies.

 # Ⓜ St-Germain-des-Prés or Ⓜ Mabillon. i Free same-day entry with a Louvre ticket. $ €5, under 18 and students free. ⏰ Open June-Aug M 9:30am-5pm, W-F 9:30am-5:30pm; Sept-May M 9:30am-5pm, W-Su 9:30am-5pm. Last entry 30min. before close.

PLACE ST-MICHEL ♿ HISTORIC NEIGHBORHOOD

The Latin Quarter meets the Seine at Place St-Michel. The *place* is heavily frequented by tourists for the food options that pack onto rue St-Séverin and rue de la Huchette. Historically speaking, this is where the 1871 Paris Commune and the 1968 student uprising, two of Paris's most extreme examples of citizen uprising, began. Today, tourists, pigeons, and street performers crowd the place around the Fontaine St-Michel, constructed by Gabriel Davioud with the help of eight other sculptors. The honoree of the sculpture was itself a hotly contested topic; in 1858, a plan to represent Napoleon drew such ire from the supporters of Louis-Napoleon that all parties involved agreed on the more universally satisfying image of St-Michel defeating the devil. Several branches of the Gibert Joseph/Jeune bookstore fan out along bd. St-Michel, while lesser known antiquarian booksellers and university presses surround the place, ready to indulge a range of literary tastes, from the touristy and superfluous to the arcane and dry. Watch your belongings, as pickpockets like to operate in this busy part of town.

 # Ⓜ St-Michel.

frenchism

If you hear a few familiar words while in Paris, even though you don't speak French, don't be alarmed; the adoption of English words here is both a common and **controversial phenomenon.** *Le hamburger, le jogging,* and *le weekend* are all words that French-speakers use regularly. As the digital age introduced words like *podcast, email,* and *Wi-Fi,* French has struggled to keep up with English in the creation of new terminology. Most French people find it easiest to simply say "podcast" or "Wi-Fi" (pronounced **wee-fee**), but French cultural purists feel that this is an outrage. Enlisting French linguists at the **Académie Française**, nationalists associated with the Ministry of Culture have started a movement to invent new French words for the influx of new ideas. Podcast becomes *diffusion pour baladeur* and Wi-Fi, *acces sans fil a l'internet.* It's a valiant crusade, but Wi-Fi is just so much easier to say!

LA SORBONNE UNIVERSITY

45-47 rue des Écoles

France's most famous place of higher learning was founded in 1257 by theologist Robert de Sorbonne as a dormitory for poor theology students. The smartly located Sorbonne has since diversified its curriculum and earned a place among the world's most celebrated universities. Its sheer age makes American celebrations of its university bicentennials (or, you know, America in general) seem quite insignificant. Soon after its founding, the Sorbonne became the administrative basis for the University of Paris and the site of France's first printing house in 1470. Protest and sedition are peppered throughout the Sorbonne's very long history; back in 1336, the university sided with England during the Hundred Years' War. Today, the French government has solved that problem and officially controls the Sorbonne, having incorporated the university into its extensive, convoluted, and much-disdained public education system. Of the University of Paris's 13 campuses, "the Sorbonne" comprises four: Paris I, Paris III, Paris IV, and Paris V. Students studying at Paris IV take classes at the original 13th-century complex to which historical references refer. Befitting its elite status, the Sorbonne remains closed to the public through 2011, when the Chapelle de la Sorbonne might re-open after restoration. Cafes, students, and all the wonderful things that result from mixing cafes with students (PDA, nerds, self-importance, etc.) are in the nearby pl. de la Sorbonne, making it a favorite people-watching and chilling destination.

⚑ Ⓜ*Cluny-La Sorbonne or RER: Luxembourg.* *i* *Closed to the public.*

COLLÈGE DE FRANCE
UNIVERSITY

11 pl. Marcelin-Berthelot ☎01 44 27 11 47 🖳www.college-de-france.fr

Founded by François I in 1530 as a Sorbonne substitute, the Collège de France lies behind its more prestigious and well-known counterpart. The humanist motto *Doce Omnia* ("Teach Everything") is emblazoned in mosaics in the interior courtyard; its original mission was to mirror the College of Three Languages, a Belgian college founded earlier in the 16th century by Jérôme de Busleyden, designed to revive the study of the classics through a curriculum centered on Greek, Latin, and Hebrew. Originally, the "Collège Royal" consisted of only six lecturers. Courses at the college have since been given by such luminaries as Claude Lévi-Strauss, Michel Foucault, and Pierre Bourdieu. Lecture schedules are posted around the courtyard.

⚑ Ⓜ*Maubert-Mutualité.* Ⓢ *Free.* 🕐 *Courses Oct-May. Reception Sept-July M-F 9am-6pm.*

ÉGLISE ST-ÉTIENNE DU MONT
CHURCH

30 rue Descartes ☎01 43 54 11 79

The smaller and less frequented Église St-Étienne once vied with the Panthéon for cryptic fame. Ste-Geneviève, the patron saint of Paris, is buried in the crypt of the nearby **Abbaye-Sainte-Geneviève.** As visitors started flocking to pay homage to Geneviève, chapels were built to satisfy the demand until the 16th century, and construction on St-Étienne Du Mont began. In the 17th and 18th centuries, the church was critical of Paris's religious (read: Catholic) community; it was from here that the processions of the hunt of Ste-Geneviève proceeded. The church has the French Revolution to blame for its disintegrated status—during the Revolution, it was closed and turned into a "Temple for Brotherly Piety." Mathematician Blaise Pascal and dramatist Jean Racine are buried there today. The structure's atypical facade blends Gothic windows, an ancient belfry, and a Renaissance dome and nave. Inside, the church's unique central attraction still inspires awe. Sculpted from stone and flanked by spectacular spiral staircases, the choir screen is among the last of its kind in Paris. To the right of the nave, check out a Herculean Samson holding up the wood-carved pulpit.

⚑ Ⓜ*Cardinal Lemoine.* Ⓢ *Free.* 🕐 *Open M noon-7:30pm, Tu-F 8:45am-7:30pm, Sa-Su 8:45am-noon and 2-7:45pm. Mass M 6:45pm, Tu-F 12:15, 6:45pm, Sa 9, 11am, 6:45pm, Su 6:45pm.*

ÉGLISE SAINT-SÉVERIN
CHURCH

3 rue des Prêtres ☎01 43 54 49 31 🖳www.saint-severin.com

An often-slept-on attraction of the fifth arrondissement, this church isn't much in comparison to Paris's overwhelming cathedrals, but it does have a few visit-worthy characteristics. St-Séverin was a hermit who prayed and lived on the modern-day site of the church. Upon his death, a basilica was constructed on the former land of his hermit activities. After this basilica was destroyed by Vikings in the 11th century, construction on the modern-day church began. Surprisingly (sarcasm), it took hundreds of years to build the church, and most of its features turned out to be characteristic of the 15th century. The church boasts seven stained-glass windows around the ambulatory, fashioned by Jean René Bazaine, honoring the seven sacraments of the Catholic religion and a fine collection of gargoyle sculptures on the church's facade. A great spot for meditation or prayer.

✦ ⓂSt-Michel. Ⓢ Free. ☪ Open daily 11am-7:30pm.

ÉCOLE NORMALE SUPÉRIEURE
UNIVERSITY

45 rue d'Ulm
☎ 01 44 32 30 00 🖥www.ens.fr

Nerd alert! France's premier university, the École Normale Supérieure, is situated right near the Sorbonne. As one of the Grands Écoles, a system of elite schools that are the equivalent of an Ivy League university, the École Normale Supérieure is considered more prestigious within France than, say, the Sorbonne. Normale Sup'—as its students, the *normaliens*, call it—has programs in literature, philosophy, and the natural sciences. During the school year *(Oct-May)*, you can hang out around the school's campus, but not in it, and catch a glimpse of the nation's future (and current) elite. The school's graduates include Michel Foucault, Louis Pasteur, and Jean-Paul Sartre.

✦ ⓂCluny-La Sorbonne. *i* Closed to the public.

MOSQUÉE DE PARIS
❋ MUSEUM, MOSQUE

2bis pl. du puits de l'Ermite
☎01 43 31 38 20 🖥www.la-mosquee.com

The Grande Mosquée de Paris was built in 1920 to honor the contributions of North African countries in WWI. While the construction was financed by France, it was carried out by natives of the countries it was to honor. This is probably why its construction avoided decades of delays; it was consecrated in 1926. During WWII, the mosque served as a strong point for the Arab resistance against the Nazi invasion. While tourists are more than welcome at the mosque, understand that you're entering a religious space. While prayer and worship spaces are closed to the public, all visitors are welcome to wonder at the 33m tall minaret, relax in the exquisite *hammam's* steam baths, or sip mint tea at the soothing cafe. Dress appropriately: bare shoulders and legs are discouraged, especially for women. It's OK to take your clothes off (most of them, at least) in the steam bath.

✦ ⓂCensier Daubenton. *i* Hammam (steam bath) for men and women. Ⓢ Guided tour €3, students €2. Hammam €15. 10min. massage €10, 30min. €30. Bikini wax €11. ☪ Open Th 9am-noon and 2-6pm, Sa-Su 9am-noon and 2-6pm. Hammam open for men Tu 10am-9pm, Su 10am-9pm; M, W-Th, and Sa 10am-9pm, F 2-9pm.

ARÈNES DE LUTÈCE
⦅ᵖⵟ⦆ PARK, HISTORIC MONUMENT

At the intersection of rue de Navarre and rue des Arènes

Once an outdoor theater, the Arènes de Lutèce now serves as a glorified sandpit used for pickup games of soccer or *boules*, while its dilapidated arena seating shelters various acts of adolescent delinquency (drinking and smoking peculiarly stinky "cigarettes"). Enter the sandpit at your own risk. The little ones stubbornly refuse to stop playing, ever. Romans built the theater in the first century CE to accommodate 10,000 spectators, but their arena suffered severe damage during the third-century invasions of the barbarian hordes. Similar to the remains of oval amphitheaters in Rome and southern France, the ruins were unearthed in 1869 and restored in 1917; all the seats are modern additions.

✦ ⓂPlace Monge. ☪ Open in summer M-F 8am-9:30pm, Sa-Su 9am-9:30pm; in winter M-F 8am-5:30pm, Sa-Su 9am-5:30pm.

MUSÉE D'HISTOIRE NATURELLE
MUSEUM ❷

57 rue Cuvier
☎01 40 79 30 00 🖥www.mnhn.fr

Three science museums constitute the Museum of Natural History, all situated within the **Jardin des Plantes**. The four-floor **Grande Galérie d'Evolution** is definitely the best out of the three; while not striking in and of itself, it looks better alongside its positively horrible comrades. The exhibit illustrates evolution with a series of stuffed animals (Curious George not included) and numerous multimedia tools. A section of the permanent exhibit is dedicated to human interaction with the environment, with displays on farming and sustainable development as well as a slightly alarming world population counter estimating future figures. This part of the exhibit smartly connects man's evolution and modifications of the world to his further evolution, all in a very accessible, non-science-test format. Next door, the **Musée de Minéralogie** displays rubies, sapphires, and other minerals—nothing exciting. The **Galeries d'Anatomie Comparée et de Paléontologie** are at the other end of the garden. Inside is a ghastly cavalcade of femurs, ribcages, and vertebrae from prehistoric animals. Despite some snazzy new placards, the place doesn't seem to have changed much since it opened in 1898; it's almost more notable as a museum of 19th-century grotesquerie than as a catalog of anatomy.

✦ ⓜ*Jussieu.* ⓢ *Grande Galerie de l'Evolution €7, students under 26 and ages 4-13 €5. Musée de Minéralogie €8, students under 26 €6. Galéries d'Anatomie Comparée et de Paléontologie €7, students €5, under 4 free. 2-day passes for the 3 museums and the ménagerie €20; valid for 1 entry at each museum Sa or Su.* ⓩ *Grande Galerie de l'Evolution open M 10am-6pm, W-Su 10am-6pm. Musée de Minéralogie open daily 10am-6pm. Galéries d'Anatomie Comparée et de Paléontologie open M-F 10am-5pm, Sa-Su 10am-6pm. Last entry for all museums 45min. before close.*

CAFÉ DE FLORE
172 bd. St-Germain

✎ HISTORIC CAFE
☎01 45 48 55 26

Sartre composed *Being and Nothingness*, and allegedly the very concept of Existentialism, while taking most of his meals here during World War II; Apollinaire, Camus, Artaud, Picasso, Breton, Trotsky, and Thurber all sipped brew here too. Legend has it that when Sartre dined here, he and his friends (with benefits, if you're talking de Beauvoir) camped out on the opposite side of the cafe as communist Marguerite Duras and company. In the contemporary feud between Café de Flore and Les Deux Magots, Flore reportedly snags more intellectuals by offering an annual well-respected literary prize, Le Prix de Flore. The Art Deco seating upstairs is the coolest (check out Sartre and de Beauvoir's booth on the left).

✦ ⓜ*St-Germain de Prés.* ⓩ *Open daily 7:30am-1:30am.*

LES DEUX MAGOTS
6 pl. St-Germain-des-Prés

♨ HISTORIC CAFE
☎01 45 48 55 25

This cozy cafe behind high hedges has been a home to Parisian and expat writers since 1885, including Mallarmé, Hemingway, and some guy named Picasso. The cafe is now favored mostly by Left Bank residents and tourists who like to be seen; haute couture is the norm, so if you don't know how to mix sailor and '80s styles into sailor-'80s chic, prepare to be shown up. The cafe is named for 2 Chinese porcelain figures (the originals are still inside), not for fly larvae.

✦ ⓜ*St-Germain-des-Prés.* ⓩ *Open daily 7:30am-1am.*

ODÉON
NEIGHBORHOOD

Odéon is one of the most picturesque and memorable areas in the 6*ème*. The diametrically opposed **boulevard Saint-Germain** is just steps away. Buzzing cafes, cinemas, retail boutiques, and chatting locals at the outdoor seating are the norm here. The neighborhood has a touch of historical swagger as well. The **Relais Odéon** is a fantastic example of architecture and decoration in the Belle Époque style. The **Mazarin passageway** winds its way to the apartment where a clandestine Revolution-era press published Jean-Paul Marat's *L'Ami du Peuple*. Just to the south of bd. St-Germain is the **Carrefour de l'Odéon**, a favorite Parisian hangout filled with sidewalk bistros and cafes that are a bit calmer than their counterparts on the bd. St-Germain, perhaps because their denizens are thinking and scribbling.

✦ ⓜ*Odéon.*

ÉGLISE ST-SULPICE
♿ CHURCH

50 rue Vaugirard ☏01 42 34 59 60 ✉www.paroisse-saint-sulpice-paris.org

The Neoclassical facade of Église St-Sulpice dominates the large square bearing its name, where children and street vendors gather around the meditative fountain. The church was designed by Servadoni in 1733, and, in classic French fashion, its Neoclassical facade was never finished. Today, it is in the middle of large-scale exterior renovations (or completions, maybe?). Despite its many practical complications, the church boasts a few unique attractions. A set of badly faded Delacroix frescoes, *Jacob Wrestling with the Angel* and *Heliodorus Driven from the Temple*, in the first chapel on the right are deeply moving. Jean-Baptiste Pigalle's similarly faded *Virgin and Child* is in a chapel in the rear of the building. A fantastically monumental organ (five keyboards!) is used in frequent concerts; check the bulletin at the front of the church for more information. Unfortunately, the poorly lit interior of the church provides an unbecoming setting for the church's artistic stronger points.

♯ Ⓜ St-Sulpice or Ⓜ Mabillon. 🕯 Open daily 7:30am-7:30pm.

BOULEVARD ST-GERMAIN
NEIGHBORHOOD

One of the centerpieces of Haussmann's Parisian Renewal Project in the mid-19th century, bd. St-Germain is best known as a former literati hangout for expat and Parisian Existentialists. Today, the bd. St-Germain is torn between nostalgia for its storied intellectual past and shameless deference to all things fashionable. Each of these aspects is intimately connected to the throngs of tourists that tread its spotless sidewalks every day. The boulevard is home to scores of cafes and designer boutiques where expensive coffee and long lines of Japanese tourists outside Louis Vuitton are *de rigeur*.

♯ Ⓜ St-Germain-des-Prés.

ÉCOLE NATIONALE SUPÉRIEURE DES BEAUX-ARTS
◉ UNIVERSITY

14 rue Bonaparte ☏01 47 03 50 00 ✉www.ensba.fr

Napoleon founded France's most acclaimed art school in 1811 just across the Seine from the Louvre, and it quickly became the coveted cradle of Parisian art. Its current building, the Palais des Études, was finished in 1838 and counts such greats as Gustave Moreau and Claude Monet among its alumni. Unfortunately, the public is not permitted to freely tour the building. The best shot at a glimpse of the lifeblood of the École des Beaux-Arts is the nearby **exhibition hall** at 13 quai Malaquais; here, you can get a free look at the painting and photography of the new generation of Parisian artists.

♯ Ⓜ St-Germain-des-Prés. *i* Tours by reservation; call ahead. Ⓢ Tours €4, students €2.50. 🕯 2 "open days" per year, when the public is allowed to wander through the workshops and classrooms of the school. Call for schedule and info. Exhibition hill open Tu-Su 1-7pm.

PALAIS DE L'INSTITUT DE FRANCE
MONUMENT

pl. de l'Institut

The Palais de l'Institut de France broods over the Seine from beneath its famous black-and-gold dome. Designed by royal architect Le Vau, one of Louis XIV's preferred architects, the building has been used as both a school (1688-1793) and a prison (1793-1805). The beautiful building is now most notably home to the **Académie Française**, devoted to the patronage and protection of the arts, letters, and sciences. The *académiciens*, modestly self-titled "The Immortals," wear snazzy green jackets and even carry swords, which come in very handy in their attempts to regulate the French language against its illegitimate offspring (that would be *verlan*, a form of speech popular among young people in France). The Palais is not open to the public, but peek inside the courtyard to the right to catch a glimpse of Cardinal Mazarin's funeral sculpture and maybe even a green jacket or two. The grounds are frequently open to "historians" for historical seminars and conferences—i.e., you.

✠ Ⓜ*Pont Neuf.* *i* *Check Pariscope or Figaroscope for listings of frequent seminars, lectures, and openings. A schedule is also available from just inside the gates in the office on the left.*

MUSÉE ZADKINE
➦ MUSEUM

100bis Rue d'Assas ☎01 55 42 77 20 ▣www.paris.fr/musees/zadkine

Installed in 1982 in the former house and studio of Russian sculptor Ossip Zadkine (1890-1967), the pleasantly tourist-free Musée Zadkine houses a collection of his work, along with contemporary art exhibits. What makes this museum, willed to the city of Paris by Zadkine's wife, worth going to? While most artists, and certainly sculptors, tend to stick to one style, Zadkine worked in 12 different styles, from Primitivism to Neoclassicism to Cubism, and the museum's collection represents all 12 of his creative periods. Zadkine's tremendous artistic flexibility is the collection's greatest strength; visitors pore over his classical masterpiece *L'hommage à Apollinaire,* then immerse themselves in his more modern, emotionally raw *Maquette du Moment de la Ville Detruite.* The tiny, forested garden, realized by landscape painter Gilles Clément, is a welcome retreat from the busier northern part of the 6*ème.*

✠ Ⓜ*Vavin.* Ⓢ *€4, reduced €3, under 18 €2.* ⌚ *Open Tu-Sa 10am-6pm.*

MUSÉE DE LA MONNAIE
♿ MUSEUM

11 quai de Conti ☎01 40 46 55 35 ▣www.monnaiedeparis.fr

Housed in the Hôtel des Monnaies, a mint until 1973, the Musée de la Monnaie (Currency Museum) is not just for coin collectors. Displays in this small museum document the political and economic histories of French coinage, from Roman times to the present, from enormous medieval Gallic coins to the unassuming euro. There is also a large set of old-school machinery that was formerly used in the manufacturing of coins, at the hotel and elsewhere. While the museum does have some appeal, it's generally pretty empty or filled with older folks. Coin collectors, nerds, and proponents of the gold standard should enjoy the display nonetheless.

✠ Ⓜ*Pont Neuf.* *i* *Guided visits available for individuals and groups. Call ahead for info.* Ⓢ *Free.* ⌚ *Open Tu-F 11am-5:30pm, Sa-Su noon-5:30pm.*

GALERIE LOEVENBRUCK
GALLERY

6 rue Jacques Callot ☎01 53 10 85 68 ▣www.loevenbruck.com

An outstanding gallery, specializing in loosely political, Dada- and Pop-inspired, avant-garde, and contemporary sculpture, video, photography, and painting—most of it with a careless sense of humor. Art subjects range from donkeys to clothed pornography.

✠ Ⓜ*Mabillon.* ⌚ *Open Sept-July Tu-Sa 11am-7pm.*

GALERIE KAMEL MENNOUR
GALLERY

60 rue Mazarine ☎01 56 24 03 63 ▣www.kamelmennour.com

A hip gallery with a young and (you guessed it) hip staff. It exhibits prized work by artists you've probably never heard of and some of the best photography, video, and painting that abstract up-and-comers have to offer. All things non-traditional come to the surface here: abstract sculpture, painting, watercolor, and mixed media.

✠ Ⓜ*Mabillon,* Ⓜ*Odéon.* ⌚ *Open Tu-Sa 11am-7pm.*

GALERIE SEINE 51
GALLERY

51 rue de Seine ☎01 43 26 91 10 ▣www.seine51.com

With one of the most far-out collections of contemporary art on the Left Bank, including occasional pink walls and astroturf, Seine 51 is an amusing foray into experimental art. Street and nude photography are the norm; exhibits range from Pop-inspired installations, photography, and furniture to works in standard mediums.

✠ Ⓜ*Mabillon.* ⌚ *Open M 2-6pm, Tu-Sa 11am-1pm and 2:30-7pm.*

GALERIE LOFT

GALLERY

3bis rue des Beaux-Arts ☎01 46 33 06 87 🖥www.galerieloeb.com

Featuring extremely avant-garde Chinese art, this is a unique selection amongst the rest of the often monotonous rest of the galleries in the St-Germain/Odéon area.

[M]Pont Neuf. ⏰ Open Tu-Sa 10am-6:30pm.

CLAUDE BERNARD

GALLERY

7-9 rue des Beaux-Arts ☎01 43 26 97 07 🖥www.claude-bernard.com

Founded in 1957, Claude Bernard is perhaps one the most prestigious galleries of rue des Beaux-Arts. Originally designed to hold contemporary sculpture, the gallery now plays home to contemporary photography, painting, sculpture, and mixed media. It has showcased such famous artists as Dubuffet, Balthus, David Levine, and Henri Cartier-Bresson.

[M]St-Germain de Prés. ⏰ Open Tu-Sa 9:30am-12:30pm and 2:30-6:30pm.

MUSÉE DU LUXEMBOURG

♿ MUSEUM

19 rue Vaugirard

The Musée du Luxembourg is housed in the historic Palais du Luxembourg, and offers rotating art exhibitions featuring everything from classical to contemporary artists. The museum has recently exhibited the celebrated *oeuvres* of Maurice de Vlaminck and Giuseppe Arcimboldo. While the curators are generally on point, this is easily one of the biggest museum rip-offs in Paris. Unless you're really into the exhibition in question, steer clear and check out the Delacroix or Zadkine Museums for a much cheaper, less touristed, and introspective museum experience.

[M]Odéon. $ €11, ages 10-25 €9. Audio tours available for €3.50 in English, French, Spanish, German, Italian, and Dutch.. ⏰ Open M 10:30am-10pm, Tu-Th 10:30am-7pm, F-Sa 10:30am-10pm, Su 9am-7pm.

invalides

Visit this arrondissement more than once if you can. Unsurprisingly, the Tour Eiffel towers over all of the *7ème* attractions, but the posh neighborhood also hosts the French national government, a number of embassies, and an astonishing concentration of famous museums. Be sure to stop by the Musée de Rodin and Musée d'Orsay.

EIFFEL TOWER

♿ TOWER

No address needed. You can see it from anywhere. ☎01 44 11 23 23 🖥www.tour-eiffel.fr

In 1937, Gustave Eiffel remarked on his construction, "I ought to be jealous of that tower; she is more famous than I am." The city of Paris as a whole could share the same lament. A true French synecdoche, the Eiffel Tower has come to stand for Paris itself. Gustave Eiffel designed it to be the tallest structure in the world, intended to surpass the ancient Egyptian pyramids in size and notoriety. Parisians, per usual, were not impressed; the same city-dwellers who cringed at the thought of skyscrapers mumbled disapprovingly before construction had even begun. Critics called it, perhaps not unfairly, the "metal asparagus," and a Parisian Tower of Babel. Writer Guy de Maupassant thought it was so hideous that he ate lunch every day at its ground-floor restaurant—the only place in Paris where you can't actually see the Eiffel Tower.

When the tower was inaugurated in March 1889 as the centerpiece of the World's Fair, Parisians forgot their earlier displeasure. Nearly two million people ascended the engineering miracle during the event. Throughout its history, the tower has been more than an aesthetic controversy and photo backdrop. In WWI, it functioned as a radio-telegraphic center that intercepted enemy messages, includ-

sights

ing the one that led to the arrest of Mata Hari, the Danish dancer accused of being a German spy. Since the expo, over 150 million Parisians and tourists have made it the most visited paid monument in the world. A Parisian icon represented on everything from postcards to underwear to umbrellas, Eiffel's wonder still comes under fire from some who see it as Maupassant did: a metal monstrosity overrun with overly tanned tourists, cheap trinkets, and false promises of cliché romance.

Still, at 324m—just a tad shorter than New York City's Chrysler Building—the tower is a tremendous feat of design and engineering, though wind does cause it to occasionally sway 6 to 7cm. Though arguably ugly, it will still take your breath away with its sheer size, especially up close. The top floor and its unparalleled view deserve a visit. And despite the 7,000 tons of metal and 2.5 million rivets that hold together its 12,000 parts, the tower appears light and airy. Its distinctive bronze color is repainted every seven years and is graduated from a lighter tone at the summit to a darker one at the base to highlight the monument's elegant line of perspective.

The cheapest way to ascend the tower is by walking up the first two floors; the third floor is only accessible by elevator. Waiting until nightfall to make your ascent cuts down the line and ups the glamour. At the top, captioned aerial photographs help you locate other famous landmarks. On a clear day it is possible to see Chartres, 88km away. From dusk until 2am *(Sept-May 1am)*, the tower sparkles with light for 10min. on the hour.

⌗ Ⓜ*Bir-Hakeim or* Ⓜ*Trocadéro.* Ⓢ *Elevator to 2nd fl. €8.10, ages 12-24 €6.40, ages 4-11 and handicapped €4, under 3 free; elevator to top €13.10/11.50/9/free; stair entrance to 2nd fl. €4.50/3.50/3/free.* ✪ *Open daily from mid-June to Aug elevator 9am-12:45am (last access 11pm), stairs 9am-12:45am (last access midnight); from Sept to mid-June elevator 9:30am-11:45pm (last access 11pm), stairs 9:30am-6:30pm (last access 6pm).*

▨ CHAMPS DE MARS
                                                ♿ PARK

Lined with more lovers than trees, the expansive lawn that stretches from the École Militaire to the Eiffel Tower is called Champs de Mars (Field of Mars). Close to the neighborhood's military monuments and museums, it has historically lived up to the Roman god of war for whom it was named. In the days of Napoleon's empire, the field was used as a drill ground for the adjacent École Militiare, and in 1780 Charles Montgolfier launched the first hydrogen balloon from its grassy fields. During the Revolution, the park was the site of civilian massacres and political demonstrations. In 2000, a glass monument to international peace was erected at the end of the Champs in quiet defiance of the École Militaire across the way. Named the Mur pou la Paix (Wall for Peace), the structure consists of two large glass walls covered from top to bottom with the word "peace" written in 32 languages. Viewed through the monument's walls, École Militaire appears to have the word "peace" scrawled all over it.

⌗ Ⓜ*La Motte Picquet-Grenelle or* Ⓜ*École Militaire.*

▨ MUSÉE DE RODIN
                                          ➥♿(ⁱ) MUSEUM

79 rue de Varenne   ☎01 44 18 61 10 🖳www.musee-rodin.fr

According to Parisians in the know, this museum is one of the best in Paris. During his lifetime (1840-1917), Rodin was among the country's most controversial artists and was considered by many as the sculptor of Impressionism. Today, the art world considers him the father of modern sculpture and applauds him for imbuing stone with an unmatched level of psychological complexity. Today, some of Auguste Rodin's most notable pieces are showcased here in the former Hôtel Biron, an elegant 18th-century building where he lived and worked at the end of his life. A hotbed of artistic breakthroughs, Rodin's neighbors in the hôtel included Isadora Duncan, Cocteau, Matisse, and Rilke.

The *hôtel*'s remarkable garden embeds some of Rodin's most famous works among rose bushes and fountains, including the piece nearly all visitors go to the

invalides

museum to see: *Le Penseur (The Thinker)*, which is situated on the right side of the garden as you enter. Originally entitled *The Poet*, the piece was meant to depict Dante pondering his great epic poem, *The Divine Comedy*. Across the garden, a miniature of this contemplative man can be seen atop *La Porte de L'Enfer (The Gate of Hell)*, which portrays the hellish cast of characters from *The Inferno*, the first third of *La Commedia Divina*. The overpowering sculpture is 6m high, 4m wide, 1m deep, and intricately detailed; viewing machines placed in front of it allow visitors to look more closely at the anguished faces of souls damned to purgatory. Originally commissioned as the entrance doors for the new École des Arts Décoratifs, *The Gate of Hell* was never finished. In response to his critics, the humble master of French sculpture asked, "Were the cathedrals ever finished?" Near *Le Penseur* stands the sculpture of a haughty, slightly hunched man in robes: Balzac. Commissioned in 1891 by the Société des Gens de Lettres, the sculpture took years for Rodin to design in an attempt to convey the great writer accurately—made more difficult by the fact that he was already dead. The amount of time it took Rodin to complete the project caused a rift to erupt between the sculptor and the Société, and after years of battle Rodin cancelled the commission and kept the statue himself. Later in his life, he noted, "Nothing that I made satisfied me as much, because nothing had cost me as much; nothing else sums up so profoundly that which I believe to be the secret law of my art."

After thoroughly exploring the gardens, enter the hotel for another concentrated dose of artistic mastery. Many of Rodin's sculptures were based on characters or scenes from *The Inferno*. *Le Baiser*, for example, tells the story of Francesca da Rimini, who fell in love with her brother-in-law, Paolo Malatesta. Parallel to Dante's compassionate portrayal of Francesca in Canto V of *The Inferno*, Rodin's depiction shows the lovers in a moment of passion right before Rimini's husband discovered and killed them. Adultery has never looked so good.

In addition to Rodin's masterpieces, the hotel's walls are casually adorned with works by Renoir, Munch, Van Gogh, Géricault, and Steichen. The museum also houses several works by Camille Claudel, Rodin's muse, collaborator, and lover. Claudel's striking *L'Age Mûr* has been read as her response to Rodin's decision to leave her for another woman; the powerfully moving ensemble shows an angel of death dragging a man away from his pleading lover. Many, however, claim that it was Claudel who left Rodin, and it has recently been argued that she was also responsible for some of Rodin's most celebrated works. Either way, her talent for capturing the essence of romance is undeniable—if you liked Rodin's *Le Baiser*, spend some time in front of Claudel's *La Valse*, a union of staggering complexity and beauty.

✦ Ⓜ*Varenne*. *i* *Temporary exhibits housed in the chapel, to your right as you enter. Touch tours for the blind and educational tours available (*☎ 01 44 18 61 24*).* Ⓢ *Museum €6, ages 18-25 €5, EU citizens under 26 free, under 18 free. Exhibition €7/5/5/free. Joint ticket €10/7/5/free. Garden €1/1/free/free. Free 1st Su of the month. Audio tours in 7 languages €4 each for permanent and temporary exhibits, combined ticket €6.* ◷ *Open Tu-Su Apr-Sept 9:30am-5:45pm; Oct-Mar 9:30am-4:45pm. Last entry 30min. before close. Gardens open Tu-Su Apr-Sept 9:30am-6:45pm; Oct-Mar 9:30am-5pm.*

🖼 MUSÉE D'ORSAY   ✈⛟ MUSEUM

62 rue de Lille   ☎01 40 49 48 14 🖥www.musee-orsay.com

Aesthetic taste is fickle. When a handful of artists were rejected from the Louvre salon in the 19th century, they opened an exhibition across the way, prompting both the scorn of stick-up-their-arses Académiciens and the rise of Impressionism. Today, people line up at the Musée d'Orsay to see this collection of groundbreaking rejects, which were considered so scandalous at the time. Established in 1982 in a dramatically lit former railway station, the collection includes paintings, sculpture, decorative arts, and photography dating from 1848 to WWI.

The museum building is a story in itself. Built for the 1900 World's Fair, the

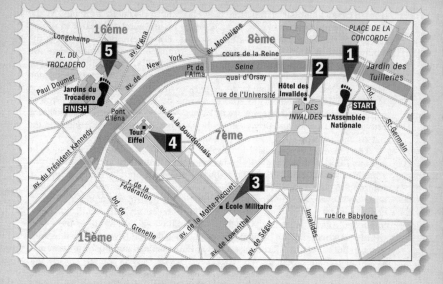

the best of the 7ème

Let's see...you're in Paris. You have one afternoon to walk around and see as much as you possibly can. You're going to the *7ème*. Hands down, you won't find more famous stuff per mile anywhere else in paris.

1. L'ASSEMBLÉE NATIONALE. The French National Assembly houses the lower house of the French Parliament

2. HÔTEL DES INVALIDES. You would probably get sick a little more often if you know the ambulance would bring you here. Formerly a home for injured soldiers (invalids, if you will) Hôtel des Invalides is Napolean's final resting place.

3. ÉCOLE MILITAIRE. Napolean's *alma mater.* Do you really need another reason to go?

4. TOUR EIFFEL. Granted you can see this from anywhere, but if you're on a stroll through the 7*ème*, you should probably check out the Eiffel Tower.

5. JARDINS DU TROCADERO. Pretty flowers—yay!

WALKING TOUR

Let's Go

Gare d'Orsay's industrial function was carefully masked by architect Victor Laloux behind glass, stucco, and a 370-room luxury hotel, so as not to offend the eye of the 7ème's sophisticated residents. For several decades, it was the main departure point for southwest-bound trains, but newer trains were too long for its platforms, and it closed in 1939. After WWII, the station served as the main French repatriation center, receiving thousands of concentration camp survivors. Orson Welles filmed *The Trial* here in 1962. Twenty four years later, Musée d'Orsay opened in the station as one of Mitterrand's Grands Projets, gathering works from the **Louvre, Jeu de Paume, Palais de Tokyo, Musée de Luxembourg,** provincial museums, and private collections to add to the original collection the Louvre had refused.

The museum is organized chronologically from the ground floor up. The ground floor is dedicated to Pre-Impressionist paintings and sculpture and contains the two scandalous works that started it all, both by Manet. *Olympia*, rumored to be a common whore whose confrontational gaze and nudity caused a stir, and *Déjeuner sur l'Herbe*, which shockingly portrayed a naked woman accompanied by fully clothed men. Back in the 19th century, scenes like that never happened. (Or at least not publicly.) The detailed section study of the Opéra Garnier is situated in the back of the room and is definitely worth a visit as well. The top floor includes all the big names in Impressionist and Post-Impressionist art: Monet, Manet, Seurat, Van Gogh, and Degas. Degas's famed dancers and prostitutes are a particular highlight. In addition, the balconies offer supreme views of the Seine and the jungle of sculptures in the garden below. Beyond the permanent collection, seven temporary exhibition spaces, called *dossiers*, are scattered throughout the building. Call or pick up a free copy of *Nouvelles du Musée d'Orsay* for current installations. The museum also hosts conferences, special tours (including children's tours), and concerts. Because this is one of the most popular museums in Paris, we recommend that you visit on Sunday mornings or Thursday evenings to avoid the masses.

✢ ⓂSolférino. Access to visitors at entrance A off the square at 1 rue de la Légion d'Honneur. Ⓢ €8, ages 18-25 €5.50, under 18 and EU citizens 18-26 free (free tickets directly at museum entrance). 🕐 Open Tu-W 9:30am-6pm, Th 9:30am-9:45pm, F-Su 9:30am-6pm. Visitors asked to leave starting at 5:30pm (Th 9:15pm).

🖼 MUSÉE DE QUAI BRANLY
27, 37, 51 quai Branly

♥♿❄ MUSEUM
☎01 56 61 70 00 🖳www.quaibranly.fr

During their country's long period of colonial expansion, restless Frenchmen traveled to foreign lands in search of the exotic and brought everything from artifacts to people to systems of thought back home with them. The Musée de Quai Branly showcases a stunning 300,000 of these questionably acquired works. Representing a wide range of African, Asian, Oceanic, and American civilizations, the story of a colonizer, adventurer, and/or traveler lurks behind each object; each artifact doubles as an expression of his or her sensibilities, doubts, prejudices, and wonder. The collection remains controversial in the art world due to its positioning of once-ethnographic items as aesthetic objects, but it nonetheless opens a window onto another way of life and sparks a timely discussion on France's relation to foreign cultures. Hidden enclaves, video screens, and interactive displays bring the pieces to life, underlining the museum's commitment to cultural dialogue. Designed by Jean Nouvel, the massive and wildly inventive building is ensconced behind a looming glass shield designed to deflect traffic noise and is surrounded by a lush jungle. Once inside, visitors are greeted by a stark white, winding ramp—the beginning of the "fresh approach" that Branly promises. The Garden Gallery (admission separate) hosts special exhibits that include rotating pieces from the permanent collection as well as loans from other museums. Quai

Branly also hosts consortiums, workshops, and lectures in art history, philosophy, and anthropology, along with concerts, dance performances, cinema, and theater, establishing itself as a diverse and rich source of cultural growth.

✦ ⓂAlma-Marceau. Ⓢ €9.50, teachers and EU citizens ages 18-25 free. ⌚ Open Tu-W 11am-7pm, Th-Sa 11am-9pm, Su 11am-7pm.

🏛 LA PAGODE
CINEMA, HISTORIC SITE

57bis rue de Babylone   ☎01 45 55 48 48 🖥www.etoile-cinemas.com

Some men buy flowers. Others build pagodas. A Japanese temple built in 1895 by Bon Marché department store magnate M. Morin as a gift to his wife, La Pagode endures as an artifact of the Orientalist craze that swept France in the 19th century. When Mme. Morin left her husband for his associate's son just prior to WWI (a pagoda just wasn't enough), the building became the scene of Sino-Japanese soirees despite tensions between the two countries. La Pagode opened its doors to the public in 1931 and was transformed into a cinema, cafe, and frequent haunt of Gloria Swanson. The theater closed during the Nazi occupation, re-opened in 1945, and closed again in 1998 due to a lack of funding, despite having been declared a historic monument by the Ministry of Culture in 1982. It was re-opened under private ownership in November 2000. The two-screen cinema continues to draw hipsters and older crowds to screenings of smaller, independent films. The cafe in the bamboo garden outside is particularly pleasant.

✦ ⓂSt-François-Savier. 𝒊 Reduced prices M and W nights. Ⓢ Tickets €7, students and under 18 reduced prices. ⌚ Cafe open daily between shows.

ÉCOLE MILITAIRE
♿ GOVERNMENT SITE

1 pl. Joffre

Demonstrating the link between sex, war, and power once again, Louis XV founded the École Militaire in 1751 at the urging of his mistress, Mme. de Pompadour, who hoped to make officers of "poor gentlemen." In 1784, 15-year-old Napoleon Bonaparte enrolled. A few weeks later, he presented administrators with a comprehensive plan for the school's reorganization, and by the time he graduated three years later, he was a lieutenant in the artillery. Teachers foretold he would "go far in favorable circumstances." Little did they know. Louis XVI turned the building into a barracks for the Swiss Guard, but it was converted back into a military school in 1848. Today, the extensive structure serves as the living quarters of the Chief of the National Army and additionally houses the Ministry of Defense and a variety of schools for advanced military studies, such as the Institute for Higher Studies of National Defense, the Center for Higher Studies of the Military, the Inter-Army College of Defense, and the School of Reserve Specialist Officers of State.

✦ ⓂÉcole Militaire.

AMERICAN CHURCH IN PARIS
CHURCH

65 quai d'Orsay   ☎01 40 62 05 00 🖥www.acparis.org

The self-proclaimed international, inter-dominational, English-speaking, Protestant congregation has just as many services as it does titles. In addition to the expected religious stuff, the church is also an informal meeting ground for expats in Paris and provides useful information on job and apartment listings and language courses. The simple Gothic structure surrounds a pretty courtyard and sometimes echoes with the sound of chamber music.

✦ ⓂInvalides. At the corner of Quai d'Orsay and Rue H. Moissan.

UNESCO
♿ HISTORIC SITE

7 pl. de Fontenoy   ☎01 45 68 05 16 🖥www.unesco.org

If Napoleon had imagined the least fitting neighbor to the École Militaire, he would have dreamed up UNESCO (United Nations Educational, Scientific, and Cultural Organization). A stark contrast to the grand, gilded building across the way, this modern, Y-shaped, glass-and-concrete structure was constructed in 1958 as a major international monument to represent its 188 member nations. In what may possibly epitomize one of the UN's many problems, the architect's design attempted to please everyone and doesn't satisfy anyone. UNESCO's building has little personality save its pleasant garden, the work of three compromising architects: American Marcel Breuer, Italian Luigi Nervi, and Frenchman Bernard Zehrfuss. Meant to foster science and culture throughout the world, the organization hosts various exhibitions. Ignore the intimidating, institutional exterior; guards will obligingly let you in.

✣ ⓂSégur. *i* Bring a form of identification. Map of the building available at the information desk to your left, beyond the elevators after you enter. Ⓢ Free. Ⓩ Open M-F 9am-12:30pm and 2:30-6pm. Bookshop open M-F 9am-noon and 2:30-5:15pm. Exhibits open M-F 9am-6pm.

INVALIDES
▰ Historic Building

Situated at the center of the 7ème, the gold-leaf dome of the Hôtel des Invalides glimmers conspicuously rain or shine, adding a touch of bling to the Parisian skyline. Most visitors assume that the building's history is just as scintillating, but Invalides has always led a life of seriousness and importance. Originally founded by Louis XVI in 1671 as a home for disabled soldiers, it is now the headquarters of the military governor of Paris and continues to serve, on a small scale, as a military hospital. Stretching from the building to the Pont Alexandre III is the tree-lined **Esplanade des Invalides** (not to be confused with the Champs de Mars). The Musée de l'Armée, Musée des Plans-Reliefs, Musée des Deux Guerres Mondiales, and Musée de l'Ordre de la Libération are housed within the Invalides museum complex, as is **Napoleon's tomb,** which lies in the adjoining Église St-Louis. To the left of the Tourville entrance, the Jardin de l'Intendant is strewn with benches and impeccably groomed trees and bushes, a topiary testament to the army's detail-oriented (read: anal) mentality. A ditch lined with captured foreign cannon runs around the Invalides area where a moat used to be, making it impossible to leave by any means beyond the two official entrances. Be aware that certain areas are blocked to tourists, out of respect for the privacy of the war veterans who still live in the hospital.

✣ ⓂInvalides. Ⓢ €9; under 18, EU citizens 18-25, after 5pm free.

QUAI VOLTAIRE
♿ NEIGHBORHOOD

Though the Quai Voltaire is known for its beautiful views of the monuments along the Seine, this street boasts an artistic heritage more distinguished than any other pretty block in the city. Voltaire spent his last days at no. 27. The hotel at no. 19 served as a temporary home to Baudelaire while he wrote *Les Fleurs du Mal (Flowers of Evil)* from 1856 to 1858, to Richard Wagner as he composed *Die Meistersinger* between 1861 and 1862, and to Oscar Wilde during his exile. The studios of Eugène Delacroix and Jean Auguste Dominique Ingres were located at no. 9-11, followed by Jean-Baptiste-Camille Corot. The Russian ballet dancer Rudolf Nureyev lived at no. 23 from 1981 until his death in 1993. Finally, though more a patron than an artist himself, former President Chirac and his wife Bernadette lived briefly at no. 1 after leaving the Palais d'Élysée.

✣ ⓂRue de Bac. Along the Seine between Pont Royal and Pont du Carrousel. Walk up rue du Bac to the river.

MUSÉE DES EGOUTS DE PARIS
◉ MUSEUM, SEWER

Pont de l'Alma ☎01 53 68 27 81 ✉visite-des-egouts@paris.fr

If you stop to think about it—"I'm paying to go see sewers"—you might hold on to those €3. And make no mistake; you are paying more for the symbolic subversion of walking with feces rushing underfoot while everyone else skips around beautiful Paris (suckers) than for a high-quality museum. Some of the posters look like something out of a high-school civics project, and at times the museum smells, well, like shit. Still, it is kind of cool to see the literal underbelly of the city, and the guided tours provide food for thought (already digested of course). For example, there are twice as many rats as people in Paris, and they eat three times their body weight in waste.

⇆ ⓂAlma-Marceau. Opposite 93 Quai d'Orsay. $ €4.30, students €3.50, under 5 free. ⏰ Open in summer M-W 11am-5pm, Sa-Su 11am-5pm; in winter M-W 11am-4pm, Sa-Su 11am-4pm.

underground paris: sewers

Below the streets of Paris lie approximately **2,100 kilometers** of sewer tunnels, a system which has existed in theory since 1850, although the very first Parisian sewers were in fact built at the beginning of the 13th century. Oddly enough, for as long as there have been sewers, there have been people who want to tour them. Don't ask us why, but tourists flocked for years to **ride along the waste** in boats or suspended carts; the unsanitary tours persisted until around 1970. Today there are several new options for the **sewer-loving tourist**. Guided sewer tours, now along raised walkways that run throughout the tunnels, are still popular, as is the new *Musée des Égouts de Paris,* or **Paris Sewer Museum.** Visitors who are interested in public works, engineering, or perhaps Victor Hugo's *Les Miserables,* are all likely to enjoy a visit to this odd museum, located beneath the Quai d'Orsay on the Left Bank. Just watch where you step.

MUSÉE DE L'ARMÉE

🎫 MUSEUM

129 rue de Grenelle ☎01 44 42 37 64 💻www.invalides.org

If you like guns, then you'll love the Musée de l'Armée. Celebrating the French military, it lies in two wings on opposite sides of the Invalides' main cobblestone courtyard, the Cour d'Honneur. The West Wing (Aile Occident) is filled almost exclusively with French armor from medieval times onward, including the breastplates of France's more powerful kings; there is also a variety of Asian metalwork. The East Wing (Aile Orient) is better rounded, with uniforms, maps, royal ordinances, medals, and portraits in addition to armor, focusing on the 17th, 18th, and 19th centuries. Beautiful sets of Chinese and Japanese armor provide a fascinating contrast with the Western displays. Meanwhile, Napoleon Bonaparte's body rests in a tomb here, with his military victories represented all around. The **Musée des Deux Guerres Mondiales, Musée des Plans-Reliefs,** and the **Musée de l 'Ordre de la Libération** are also housed at Invalides.

⇆ ⓂInvalides or ⓂSt-François-Xavier. $ Admission to all museums €9, students under 26 €7, EU citizens and under 18 free; after 5pm and late on Tu €7. ⏰ Open Apr-Sept M 10am-6pm, Tu 10am-9pm, W-Su 10am-6pm; Oct-Mar daily 10am-5pm. Closed 1st M of each month.

MUSÉE MAILLOL

🎫♿ MUSEUM

61 rue de Grenelle ☎01 42 22 59 58 💻www.museemaillol.com

When obsession with the female nude takes the form of sculpture, we're less prone to think of it as sexual neurosis. But Aristide Maillol's work on naked women is nothing less than a fetish. In an arrondissement with some of the best art museums in Paris, the Musée Maillol holds its own, showing the sculptor, artist, and painter's many models of the human—mostly female—form. At age 15, Dina Vierney met Maillol and became his muse, eventually finding her own passion as a collector of modern art.

The museum's permanent collection combines the careers of these two (art) lovers; it includes Maillol's work as well as pieces by Matisse, Kandinsky, Gauguin, Redon, Poliakoff, and Couturier, among others. Opened in 1995, the museum has chosen to display its permanent collection in a series of excellent temporary exhibitions.

⚲ ⓂRue du Bac. Ⓢ €11, ages 11-25 and handicapped €9, under 11 free. ⌚ Open Tu-Th 10:30am-7pm, F 10:30am-9:30pm, Sa-Su 10:30am-7pm. Last entry 45min. before close.

MUSÉE DE LÉGION D'HONNEUR ♿ MUSEUM
2 rue de la Légion d'Honneur ☎01 40 62 84 94 ✉musee@legiondhonneur.fr

Created in 1802 by Napoleon Bonaparte, membership to the Légion d'Honneur has symbolized talent, courage, and dedication to France. This relatively small museum features medals, costumes, and various artifacts of war in a surprisingly interactive display. One of the collection's prize pieces is Napoleon's Collier de la Légion d'Honneur, made by Biennais in gold and enamel, which he wore at his coronation and is often figured with when painted in imperial costume.

⚲ ⓂSolférino. ⓘ Handicapped entrance at 1 rue de Solférino. Ⓢ Free. ⌚ Open Tu-Su 1-6pm.

walk, walk fashion baby

As the home of major luxury fashion flagships such as Chanel and Yves Saint-Laurent, Paris takes its couture to the extreme. With the **Fédération française de la couture** (French Fashion Federation) running biannual fashion weeks at the Carrousel du Louvre, the fashion industry in Paris mostly centers on the Rue du Faubourg Saint-Honoré, where anyone wearing a T-shirt and jeans may be heckled and stoned. But France's sartorial history provides some even stranger insight into the country's fashion evolution.

- **NOT SO AMERICAN.** The actual origin of supposedly all-American denim is Nîmes, located in the south of France. Levi Strauss actually imported the unique fabric from the city, which also explains blue jeans' other name—"de Nîmes."

- **THE BANE OF A MILLION WOMEN.** In the 1940s, two Frenchmen became rivals in their quest to claim the bikini as their invention. Jacques Heim first introduced his skimpy two-piece swimsuit design in public, calling it l'Atome. But when Louis Reard hired a skywriter to scrawl his term "Bikini" over the skies of the French Riviera, Heim got shafted, and generations of body image issues began.

- **PRETTY PROPAGANDA.** When Louis XIV reigned over the French court, he became so obsessed with the idea of France as the revolutionary fashion arbiter that he would send life-sized dolls dressed in the most up-to-date gowns to other European courts. It remains unclear whether they were as effective as today's Bratz dolls.

- **FASHION DICTATORSHIP.** The tradition of French rulers manipulating the country's fashion industry runs deep. When Napoleon came into power in the early 19th century, he barred textile imports from England and single-handedly rejuvenated the Valenciennes lace industry, reintroducing *tulle* and *batiste* into popular trends, particularly women's dress. But in typical totalitarian style, Napoleon took it a step farther and forbade women in his court to wear the same dress twice for public appearances, in an ongoing effort to stimulate the fashion industry.

sights

champs-élysées

There's a reason that the 8*eme* remains Paris' most touristed arrondissement, long after the Champs-Élysées ceased to be posh. The area harbors more architectural beauty, historical significance, and shopping opportunities than almost any other area in the city, and remains an exhilarating—if hectic—place to spend a day. Champs-Élysées also hosts a variety of art museums in its northern corners; they are often located in *hotels particuliers*, where they were once part of the private collections.

🏛 ARC DE TRIOMPHE   ♿ ✎ HISTORIC MONUMENT

Pl. de l'Etoile   ▣www.arc-de-triomphe.monuments-nationaux.fr

The highest point between the **Louvre** and the **Grande Arche de la Defense,** the Arc de Triomphe offers a stunning view down the Champs-Élysées to the **Tuileries** and Louvre. Plans for the monument were first conceived by the architect Charles Francois Ribar in 1758, who envisioned an unparalleled tribute to France's military prowess—in the form of a giant, bejeweled elephant. Fortunately for France, the construction of the monument was not undertaken until 1806, when Napoleon conceived a less bizarre landmark modeled after the triumphal arches of victorious Roman emperors like Constantine and Titus. Napoleon was exiled before the arch was completed, and Louis XVIII took over its construction in 1823. He dedicated the arch to the French military's recent intervention in Spain and its commander, the Duc d'Angouleme, and placed its design in the hands of Jean-Francois-Therese Chalgrin. The Arc de Triomphe was consecrated in 1836; in honor of the emperor that conceived of its design, the names of Napoleon's generals and battles are engraved inside. The arch has been a magnet for various triumphant armies ever since. After the Prussians marched through the Arc in 1871, the mortified Parisians purified the ground beneath it with fire. On July 14, 1919, the Arc provided the backdrop for an Allied victory parade headed by Ferdinand Foch. After years under Germany's brutal occupation during WWII, a sympathetic Allied army ensured that a French general would be the first to drive under the Arc in the liberation of Paris.

Today, the arch is dedicated to all French army soldiers and veterans. The **Tomb of the Unknown Soldier,** illuminated by an eternal flame, is situated under the arch, and was added to the structure on November 11, 1920. The memorial honors the 1.5 million Frenchmen who died during WWI. Visitors can climb up to the terrace observation deck for a brilliant view of the **Historic Axis** from the Arc de Triomphe du Carrousel and the **Louvre Pyramid** at one end to the **Grande Arche de la Défense** at the other. There is also a permanent exhibit, "Between Wars and Peace," which reads like the Arc's autobiography.

✝ Ⓜ*Charles de Gaulle-l'Etoile.* *i* *Expect long waits daily, although you can escape the crowds if you go before noon. You will kill yourself (and face a hefty fine) trying to dodge the 10-lane merry-go-round of cars around the arch, so use the pedestrian underpass on the right side of the Champs-Élysées facing the arch. Tickets sold in the pedestrian underpass before going up to the ground level.* Ⓢ *Admission €9, ages 18-25 €5.50, under 18 and EU citizens 18-25 free.* ☼ *Open daily Apr-Sept 10am-11pm; Oct-Mar 10am-10:30pm. Last entry 30min. before close.*

AVENUE DES CHAMPS-ÉLYSÉES   ✎ SHOPPING DISTRICT

from pl. Charles de Gaulle-Etoile southeast to pl. de la Concorde

Radiating from the huge rotary surrounding the Arc de Triomphe, the Champs-Élysées seems to be a magnificent celebration of pomp and the elite's fortuitous circumstance. As you ford the swarms of tourists and walk slowly along the avenue, however, you'll quickly realize that its legendary elegance, for better or for worse, is fading away. Constructed in 1616 when Marie de Médicis ploughed the Cours-la-Reine through the fields and marshland west of the Louvre, the Avenue remained an unkempt thoroughfare until the early 19th century, when the

champs-élysées

city finally invested in sidewalks and installed gas lighting. It quickly became the center of Parisian opulence and maintained a high density of flashy mansions and exclusive cafes well into the early 20th. More recently, the Champs has undergone a bizarre kind of democratization, as commercialization dilutes its former glamour. Shops along the avenue now range from designer fashion boutiques to car dealerships to low-budget tchotchke shops; the colossal **Louis Vuitton** flagship emporium stands across from an even larger Monoprix, a low-budget all-purpose store. Overpriced cafes compete with fast-food outlets for the patronage of tourists, while glitzy nightclubs and multiplex cinemas draw large crowds well into the evening.

Despite its slip in sophistication, the Champs continues to be known as the most beautiful street in the world. In 1860, Louis Vuitton spearheaded a committee to maintain the avenue's luxury, and it still strives to do so today, installing wider sidewalks and trying to prevent certain shops from moving in—H&M was refused a bid in 2007 but eventually won out. With rents as high as €1.25 million a year for 1,000 sq. m. of space, the Champs is the second richest street in the world (New York's 5th Avenue is number one, if you really want to know). The Avenue also continues to play host to most major French events: on **Bastille Day,** the largest parade in Europe takes place on this street, as does the final stretch of the **Tour de France.** And while the Champs itself may be deteriorating, many of its side streets, like **Avenue Montaigne,** have picked up the slack and ooze class in their own right.

✠ ⓂCharles de Gaulle.

FOUQUET'S
🍴 RESTAURANT, HISTORIC MONUMENT

99 Ave. des Champs-Élysées ☎ 01 47 23 70 60

A remnant from glamour days past, Fouquet's is a testament to the Champs' former glory and a designated historical monument. This outrageously expensive cafe/restaurant was once a favorite haunt of French film stars; these days, it has more celebrities in its picture frames than its seats. The somewhat over-the-top red-awninged eatery, which has been open since 1899, hosts the annual César awards.

✠ ⓂGeorge V. Ⓢ Appetizers from €30.

GRAND PALAIS
🍴⛄ PALACE

3 Ave. du Général Eisenhower ☎ 01 44 13 17 17 🖳www.grandpalais.fr

Designed for the 1900 World's Fair, the Grand Palais and the accompanying Petit Palais across the street were lauded as exemplary works of Art Nouveau architecture. Today, most of the Grand Palais is occupied by the **Palais de la Découverte,** a children's science museum; it is most beautiful at night, when the statues are backlit and the glass dome glows from within. The complex also hosts 2 temporary exhibit spaces in the **Galeries Nationales;** the main space at 3 av. du Général Eisenhower boasts four special expositions a year, and the other gallery around the corner changes its exhibits seasonally. Make sure an exhibit's going on before you visit, as the Palais is closed between shows.

✠ ⓂChamps-Élysées-Clemenceau. Ⓢ €11, students €8. For special exhibits, admission varies; expect €7-15 and €5-8 for students, free for art students. Audioguide availability depends on exhibit, €5. ⚐ Open M-Tu, Th-Su 10am-8m, W 10am-10pm. Last entry 45min. before closing.

PETIT PALAIS
🍴⛄ MUSEUM

av. Winston Churchill ☎ 01 53 43 40 00 🖳www.petitpalais.paris.fr

Also known as the Musée des Beaux-Arts de la Ville de Paris, the Petit Palais showcases a hodgepodge of European art that includes 19th-century sculpture, 17th-century portraiture, Renaissance objets d'arts, and ancient Greek relics, as well as the largest public collection of Christian Orthodox icons in France. Themed displays include 19th-century Impressionist works (think Monet and Cézanne) and

17th-century Flemish and Dutch masterpieces (including Rubens and Rembrandt). The beautiful exotic garden displays more of the Palais' grandiose architecture.

⚑ Ⓜ*Champs-Élysées-Clemenceau* or *Franklin D. Roosevelt. Follow av. Winston Churchill towards the river; the museum is on your left.* ⓘ *Credit card min. €15.* Ⓢ *Permanent collection free. Special exhibits €9, ages 14-27 €4.50, seniors €6, under 14 free. Audio tour €4.* ◲ *Open Tu-Su 10am-6pm, Tu open until 8pm for special exhibits. Last entry 15min. before close.*

PALAIS DE LA ÉLYSÉES
⬦❋ HISTORIC BUILDING

55 Rue du Faubourg Saint-Honoré
☎ 01 42 92 81 00

Built in 1718, the palais was once home to Louis XV's celebrated mistress Madame de Pompadour; the building's sheer size suggests that Louis was compensating for something. Later, Napoleon lived here with Josephine, who recognized that affairs are better outside palace walls. In 1848, the National Assembly officially declared Élysées the presidential residence. Napoleon III remodeled the Classical style a bit with the help of architect Joseph-Eugène Delacroix. For the French, it remains a symbol of the Republic. Entrance requires a personal invitation or a daring break-in. Beware though; guards pace around the corner of av. de Marigny and rue du Faubourg St-Honoré to protect it.

⚑ Ⓜ*Champs-Élysées-Clemenceau.*

THÉÂTRE DES CHAMPS-ÉLYSÉES
⬦❋ THEATER

15 Ave. Montaigne
☎ 01 49 52 50 50 ▧www.theatrechampselysees.fr

Built by the Perret brothers in 1912 with bas-reliefs by Bourdelle, the Théâtre des Champs-Élysées is best known for staging the scandalous premiere of Stravinsky's ballet *Le Sacre du Printemps (The Rite of Spring)*. The score, conducted by Pierre Monteux, was dissonant and arhythmic, and Vaslav Nijinsky's choreography had the dancers dressed in feathers and rags, hopping about pigeon-toed to evoke primitivism. The spectacle provoked the most famous riot in music history; the audience jeered and shouted so loudly that the dancers couldn't hear the orchestra. Today, the theater has three theatrical spaces that host operatic, orchestral, and dance performances; it is also home to the Orchestre National de France and Orchestre Lamoureux.

⚑ Ⓜ*Alma-Marceau.* ⓘ *Student rates available.* Ⓢ *Vary by show, see website.* ◲ *Showtimes vary by day, see website.*

PLACE DE LA CONCORDE
HISTORIC MONUMENT

Pl. de la Concorde

In the center of Paris's largest and most infamous public square, the 3,300 year-old Obélisque de Luxor stands at a monumental 72 ft. The spot was originally occupied by a statue of Louis XV (whom the square was originally named after) that was destroyed in 1748 by an angry mob. King Louis-Philippe, anxious to avoid revolutionary rancor, opted for a less contentious symbol: the 220-ton red granite, hieroglyphic-covered obelisk presented to Charles X from the Viceroy of Egypt in 1829. The obelisk, which dates back to the 13th century BC, recalls the royal accomplishments of Ramses II and wasn't erected until 1836. Gilded images on the sides of the obelisk recount its 2-year trip to Paris in a custom-built boat. Today, it forms the axis of what many refer to as the "royal perspective"—a spectacular view of Paris from the **the Louvre** in which the Place de la Concorde, the **Arc de Triomphe**, and the **Grande Arche de la Défense** appear to form a straight line through the center of the city. The view serves as a physical timeline of the Paris's history, from the reign of Louis XIV to the Revolution to Napoleon's reign, and finally, all the way to the celebration of commerce.

Constructed by Louis XV in honor of, well, himself, the Place de la Concorde quickly became ground zero for all public grievances against the monarchy. During the Reign of Terror, the complex of buildings was renamed place de la Révolution, and 1,343 aristocrats were guillotined there in less than a year. Louis XVI met his end near the statue that symbolizes the French town of Brest, and the obelisk marks the spot where Marie-Antoinette, Charlotte Corday (Marat's assassin), Lavoisier, Danton, and Robespierre lost their heads. Flanking either side of Concorde's intersection with the wide **Champs-Élysées** are reproductions of Guillaume Coustou's **Cheveaux de Marly:** Also known as *Africans Mastering the Numidian Horses*, the original sculptures are now in the Louvre to protect them from pollution. The *place* is ringed by eight large **statues** representing France's major cities: Brest, Bordeaux, Lille, Lyon, Marseille, Nantes, Rouen, and Strasbourg. At night, the Concorde's dynamic ambience begins to soften, and the obelisk, fountains, and lamps are dramatically illuminated. On **Bastille Day,** a military parade led by the President of the Republic marches through Concorde (usually around 10am) and down the Champs-Élysées to the Arc de Triomphe, and an impressive fireworks display lights up the sky over the *place* at night. At the end of July, the **Tour de France** finalists pull through Concorde and into the home stretch on the Champs-Élysées. Tourists be warned: between the Concorde's monumental scale, lack of crosswalks and heavy traffic, crossing the street here is impossible at best, fatal at worst.

✣ ⓜ*Concorde.*

MADELEINE
CHURCH

pl. de la Madeleine　　　　☎ 01 44 51 69 00 ▣ www.eglise-lamadeleine.com

Mirrored by the Assemblée Nationale across the Seine, the Madeleine was begun in 1763 by Louis XV, who modeled it after a Greco-Roman temple. Construction of the church was halted during the Revolution, when the Cult of Reason proposed transforming the building into a bank, a theater, or a courthouse—anything but a church. When Napoleon came to power, he unsurprisingly wanted to dedicate the building to his prestigious army, declaring it the "Temple of Glory of the Grand Army." Louis XVIII finally restored the church to its original purpose, and construction was finally completed in 1842. Even among Parisian churches, the Madeleine really stands out, distinguished by her gigantic pediment, four ceiling domes, fifty-two 66 ft. exterior Corinthian columns, and a curious altarpiece adorned by an immense sculpture of the ascension of Mary Magdalene, the church's namesake. The reliefs on the impressive bronze doors depict the 10 Commandments. While the church is worth a visit because of its immensity, there isn't much else to see, though there are frequent chamber and music concerts. Today, clothing and food shops line the square surrounding Madeleine. Marcel Proust spent most of his childhood nearby at 9 bd. Malesherbes, which might explain his penchant for his aunt Léonie's madeleines with tea. You, too, can enjoy a sweet treat at the world-famous Fauchon, 24-30 pl. de la Madeleine, behind the church.

✣ ⓜ*Madeleine.* ⓩ *Open daily 9am-7pm. Regular organ and chamber concerts; contact the church for a schedule and come to the church or call Virgin or FNAC for tickets (commission fee). Mass M-F 12:30pm and 6:30 at the nearby chapel; Sa 6pm; Su 9:30, 11am, and 7pm with organ and choir.*

CHAPELLE EXPIATOIRE
CHURCH

29 rue Pasquier　　　　　　　　　　　　　　☎ 01 44 32 18 00

Pl. Louis XVI is composed of the immense Chapelle Expiatoire, monuments to Marie-Antoinette and Louis XVI, and a lovely, quiet park that is excellent for picnicking. During the Revolution, when burial sites were in high demand, lime-filled trenches were dug here to accommodate hundreds of bodies. Louis XVIII had his brother's and sister-in-law's remains removed to St-Denis in 1815, and there are no graves remaining, despite rumors of Marat's assassin Charlotte Corday being buried here. Statues of the expiatory king and queen stand inside the Chapelle, symbolically guarding a tomb-shaped altar. Their touching final letters are engraved in French on the base of the sculptures.

➤ Ⓜ*Madeleine, Havre-Caumartin, or St.-Lazare. Chapel inside pl. Louis XVI, just below bd. Haussmann.* ℹ *English-language pamphlets available at entrance.* $ *€5, ages 18-25 €3.50, under 18 and EU Citizens 18-25 free.* ⏰ *Open Th-Sa 1-5pm. 45min. tours in French available 1:30 and 3:30pm some Sa of the month.*

PARC MONCEAU
⛅ PARK

58 Bld. de Courcelles

The signs say *"Pelouse interdite"* (keep off the lawn), but on sunny days, everyone pretends to be illiterate. Protected from the chaos of the city by gold-tipped, wrought-iron gates, the Parc Monceau is an expansive urban oasis especially popular with families. There's plenty of shade, courtesy of the largest tree in Paris: an oriental *platane*, 7m thick and two centuries old. The park was designed by painter Carmontelle for the Duc d'Orléans and completed by Haussmann in 1862. A number of architectural oddities—covered bridges, Dutch windmills, Roman ruins, and roller rinks—make this a kids' romping ground as well as a formal garden. As it is slightly out of the way, it tends to be locals only.

➤ Ⓜ*Monceau or Courcelles.* ⏰ *Open daily Apr-Oct 7am-10pm, Nov-Mar 7am-8pm. Last entry 15min. before close.*

CATHÉDRALE ALEXANDRE-NEVSKY
CATHEDRAL

12 rue Daru ☎ 01 42 27 37 34

Known as the Église Russe, this gold, five-domed cathedral is Paris's primary Russian Orthodox church and Russian cultural center. The spectacular, recently restored interior, lavishly decorated in religious icons, was painted by artists from St-Petersburg in gold, reds, blues, and greens in classic Byzantine style. An altar at the back of the church on the right dates from 1289, and is thought to have been (ahem) liberated from another church during the Napoleonic Wars; it was given to the Alexandre-Nevsky by the Menier family (famous chocolatiers). The Virgin Mary icon to its right was a gift from a cavalier regiment of the Russian Imperial Guard. Dress for a Russian winter; no shorts or uncovered shoulders are allowed inside.

➤ Ⓜ*Ternes.* ⏰ *Open Tu, F, Su 3-5pm. Services in French and Russian Sa 6-8pm, Su 10am-12:30pm.*

MUSÉE JACQUEMART-ANDRÉ
🎟 MUSEUM

158 bd. Haussmann ☎ 01 45 62 11 59 💻 www.musee-jacquemart-andre.com

Nélie Jacquemart's passion for art and her husband Edouard André's wealth were combined to create this extensive collection, which is housed in their gorgeous late-19th century home. During the couple's lifetime, Parisian high society admired their extravagant, double-corniced marble and iron staircase; however, only very special guests got a glimpse of their precious collection of English, Flemish, French, and Italian Renaissance artwork, which included a *Madonna and Child* by Botticelli, *St-George and the Dragon* by Ucello, and *Pilgrims at Emmaeus* by Rembrandt. Today, you can wander through the mansion—a sight in itself, with its wealth of gold embellishments, towering windows, and marble columns—and peruse a collection worthy of the most prestigious museums. The couple imported the magnificent fresco on the upper level, set above a walled indoor garden, from Italy. The courtyard offers a nice view of the museum's facade, and more importantly, benches where you can rest before moving on.

➤ Ⓜ*Miromesnil.* $ *€11, students and ages 7-17 €8.50, under 7 and 2nd child free. English audio tour included.* ⏰ *Open M 10am-9:30pm, T-Su 10am-6pm. Last entry 30min. before close.*

PALAIS DE LA DÉCOUVERTE
🎟♿❄ MUSEUM

av. Franklin D. Roosevelt, in the Grand Palais ☎ 01 56 43 20 20 💻 www.palais-decouverte.fr

Kids tear around the Palais's interactive science exhibits, and it may be hard not to join them—nothing brings out your inner child like buttons that start model comets on their celestial trajectories, spinning seats that demonstrate angular motion, and displays of creepy-crawlies. What's more, adults and children alike are likely to learn a surprising amount about the physics, chemistry, astronomy, geology, and biology. The temporary exhibits (4 per year) are usually crowd-pleasers; the most recent, entitled "Dinosaur Diet" featured real-sized animated dinosaurs. The planetarium has four shows *(11:30am, 2, 3:15, 4:30pm)* per day; arrive early during school vacation periods.

⇟ [M]Franklin D. Roosevelt or [M]Champs-Élysées-Clemenceau. [$] €7, students, seniors, and under 18 €4.50, under 5 free. Planetarium €3.50. ⏰ Open Tu-Sa 9:30am-6pm, Su 10am-7pm. Last entry 30mins. before close.

PINACOTHEQUE

🎟❄ MUSEUM

28 pl. de la Madeleine ☎ 01 42 68 02 01 💻 www.pinacotheque.com

Opened in 2007, this for-profit museum garnered a fair share of suspicion from the oh-so-altruistic art world. Since then, the anxiety of cultural enthusiasts has been somewhat quelled; La Pinacotheque has consistently put on quality shows. With 2,000 sq. m. of floor space, the museum organizes large exhibitions dedicated to one or a few artists, with aims of giving a fresh look at old names. Most recently, it gathered more than 250 works by Edvard Munch, selected to highlight the difference between his general work and his iconic masterpiece *The Scream*; easily-distracted museum-goers may enjoy the opportunity to look closely at one artist's *oeuvre*.

⇟ [M]Madeleine. [i] Audioguides available for download online. [$] €10, ages 12-25 and students €8. ⏰ Open M-Tu, W 10:30am-9:30pm, Th-Su 10:30am-6:30pm. Last entry 45min. before close.

MUSÉE CERNUSCHI

♿🎟 MUSEUM

7 av. Velasquez ☎ 01 53 96 21 50 💻 www.cernuschi.paris.fr

France's second-largest museum of Asian art lies just outside of the beautiful Parc Monceau. Between 1871 and 1873, Italian banker Henri Cernuschi gathered this assortment of ancient to 18th-century Asian art during a trip around the world. Transporting his collection back home must have been a feat in itself; the museum's most notable piece is giant, three-ton Japanese buddha. The permanent collection is mostly from China, and is organized in chronological order with pedagogical plaques from the Wei-Sui dynasties to the Qing dynasty, including excellent Tang pottery pieces. The Henri Cernuschi Memorial Room is in the basement.

⇟ [M]Villiers or [M]Monceau. Just outside the gates of Parc Monceau. [i] Credit card over €15. [$] Admission to permanent collection free; special exhibits €7, seniors €5.50, under 26 €3.50. ⏰ Open Tu-Su 10am-6pm.

MUSÉE NISSIM DE CAMONDO

♿🎟 MUSEUM

63 rue de Monceau ☎ 01 53 89 06 50

This museum was dedicated by a wealthy Turkish banker to the Musée des Arts Décoratifs, in memory of his son who died in WWI. The extensive collection of is mostly comprised of 18th-century decorative arts, and includes Chinese vases, Savonnerie carpets, and magnificent sets of Sévres porcelain. The museum also explains life in a grand mansion at the turn of the century through its pristinely preserved sitting rooms, bedrooms, bathrooms, and kitchen.

⇟ [M]Villiers or [M]Monceau. [$] €7, ages 18-25 €5, under 18, EU citizens, and residents free. English-language audio tour included. ⏰ Open W-Su 10am-5:30pm. Closed national holidays and Aug. 15.

opéra

OPÉRA NATIONAL DE PARIS/OPÉRA GARNIER

Pl. de l'Opéra

☎ 08 92 89 90 90 ◼ www.operadeparis.fr

● ⊗ THEATER

Formerly known as the Opéra National de Paris before the creation of the Opéra Bastille in 1989, this splendid historic structure is now better known as Opéra Garnier. Architect Garnier was extensively inspired by his studies in Greece, Turkey, and Rome, and it definitely shows; the Opéra's wondrous frescos and dazzling stone and marble designs regularly leave visitors speechless. That being said, visiting the Opéra is a roll of the dice. The building is periodically closed due to performances or set construction, and these interruptions are rarely listed on the website. We also advise that you take one of the guided tours, as the guides are all extremely knowledgeable. You might get a tour guide with a nearly incomprehensible French accent, so try to schedule this visit later in your stay when you're well accustomed to English à la frog.

✣ Ⓜ *Opera.* Ⓢ *€9, under 25 €5. Guided visit €12, 12 and under €6, over 60 €10, students €9, big families €30.* ⌚ *10am-4:30pm; may be closed on performance days, so check the website.*

NOTRE DAME DE LORETTE

18bis Rue de Châteaudun

☎ 01 48 78 92 72 ◼ www.notredamedelorette.org

CHURCH

Constructed between 1823 and 1836 by architect Hippolyte Le Bas, Notre Dame de Lorette is a remarkably ornate neoclassical church in an otherwise average residential neighborhood. At the time of its construction, it pushed the limits of socially acceptable extravagance and even compelled a cadre of church officials, journalists, and other *Parisiens* to disapprove of its borderline-vulgar extravagance. The four massive and intricately carved pillars that support the church's blackening entrance will remind you of the Parthenon; splendid frescoes adorn the ceilings of each of the four chapels, and portray the Virgin Mary and the four principal sacraments (baptism, eucharist, wedding, and ailing, for those not in the know) in detail. Though a must-see for lovers of art and architecture, Notre Dame de Lorette remains an active neighborhood church, so try to avoid Mass times unless, of course, you want to go for Mass. Given some serious disrepair, the future of the church's renovation is up in the air. Catch it while it's still here.

✣ Ⓜ *Notre-Dame-de-Lorette.* ⌚ *Reception M-F 2:30-6:30pm, Sa 5:00-6:30pm. Open for visitors 9am-6pm daily.*

CAFE DE LA PAIX

12 bd. des Capucines

☎ 01 40 07 36 36 ◼ cafedelapaix.fr

● HISTORIC RESTAURANT

A trip to Cafe de la Paix should be less about eating (you'll be getting severely ripped off), and more about witnessing a Parisian institution steeped in more than a century of history. Constructed by Charles Garnier, the same guy who designed the National Opera, Cafe de la Paix was the regular haunt of an impressive list of celebrities; Emile Zola, Guy de Maupassant, and Salvador Dali all wined and dined at the establishment. Beware though; prices are comically high (for the record, we would only pay €26 for a cheeseburger in apocalyptic situations). Stop by at breakfast for a reasonable tartine and butter combo *(€4),* or grab a coffee mid-afternoon *(€12)* after your visit to the Opera Garnier. The decor is fabulous, and any visitor can't help but feel a bit more important and innovative after they've dined here.

✣ Ⓜ *Opéra.* Ⓢ *Entrées €16-68.* ⌚ *Open M-Sa 9am-6pm.*

PIGALLE

● NEIGHBORHOOD

Like seedy strip clubs, sex shops, fake Gucci, and pigeon shit? Then the Quartier Pigalle is for you. Named after French sculptor Jean-Baptiste Pigalle (who per-

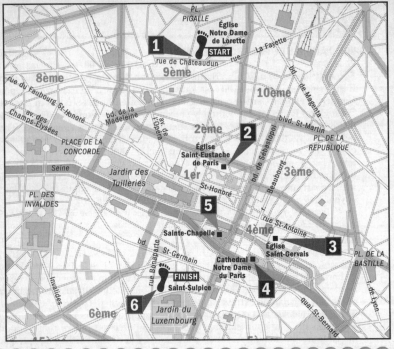

the churches of **paris**

"PARIS IS WELL WORTH A MASS." These famous words of Henri IV probably have a little something to do with the fact that anywhere you turn in Paris, you see a church. Seriously, try it—we dare you.

1. ÉGLISE NOTRE DAME DE LORETTE. Once lauded as one of Paris's most ornate and extravagant churches, Notre Dame de Lorette looks more like something you'd find in Rome than in Paris.

2. ÉGLISE SAINT-EUSTACHE DE PARIS. Something's fishy about Église Saint-Eustache—its history. Located in Les Halles, the original funding for Saint-Eustache came from taxes collected from sales of fish in a nearby market.

3. ÉGLISE SAINT-GERVAIS. Tracing its history back to the 4th century, Saint-Gervais once served as the seat of the brotherhood of wine merchants. You can't make this stuff up.

4. CATHEDRALE NOTRE DAME DE PARIS. We know, we know—Notre Dame is the *crème de la crème.* You really don't need us to tell you why.

5. SAINTE-CHAPELLE. Notre Dame isn't the only church on Île de la Cité, and we'd be remiss in our duties if we didn't send you to Sainte-Chapelle. The ceiling and the stained glass will blow your mind.

6. SAINT-SULPICE Nobody ever remembers the guy who comes in second. Saint-Sulpice is only slightly smaller than Notre Dame, but doesn't get any of the press and it's a shame, because it's a sight to behold.

WALKING TOUR

Let's Go
.com

petually rolls in his grave), this neighborhood is so nasty it's internationally famous. Sketchy old guys with stained shirts and way-too-small pants stumble after tired, scantily-clad women, and an overwhelming colony of pigeons have begun a hostile takeover of the area. If you aren't accustomed to the grimier things in life, you might get sick to your stomach even before you exit the Pigalle Metro stop. It is absolutely in no way a good idea to come here at night, whether you're a man or a woman, or together. Women, beware of sexual deviants, and guys, beware of getting roped into one of the cabarets or strip clubs. Stories of being forced—like, physically, by burly bouncers—into coughing up €100 for a drink are commonplace. The area does boast a few cool spots: famous cabarets like **Folies Bergère, Moulin Rouge,** and **Folies Pigalle** are all stationed here, as well as Elysee Montmartre, a rock/hip-hop/soul/alternative concert venue that always has something cool happening. Music gear is sold at several outlets a minute or so south of Pigalle place.

[M] Pigalle.

MUSÉE GUSTAVE MOREAU MUSEUM

14 rue de La Rochefoucauld ☎ 01 48 74 38 50 🖥 www.musee-moreau.fr

Provided that its workers aren't on strike (this appears to be a recreational activity in France), the Musée Gustave Moreau is one of the finest and most intimate museums that Paris has to offer. Located within spitting distance of the Opéra district, the Museum offers the premier collection of Moreau paintings, sculptures, and drawings on the site of the eccentric artist's home in the 9th arrondissement. The first floor of the museum is the sight of Moreau's dining room, boudoir, bed rooms, and office, richly decorated in 19th-century style. The second and third floors, bridged by a uniquely shaped, beautiful spiral staircase, showcase the diverse artistic tones and masterpieces of the multi-talented and faceted Moreau. While small, this museum is best taken in at leisure; the paintings and sculptures require all the brainpower that the average Muggle might have for a wizard like Moreau's many *chefs d'oeuvre*.

[M] Trinité. Make a right on rue St-Lazare and then a left onto rue de La Rochefoucauld. $ €5, under 26 and Su €3, under 18 and 1st Su of the month free. ⏰ Open M, W-Su 10am-12:45pm and 2-5:15pm.

canal st-martin and surrounds

It seems that the number of sketchballs and number of cool sights in a given neighborhood are inversely related. While the *10ème* doesn't offer much in the way of landmarks or museums, there are a few quick sights that you might want to check out; **Le Marché Saint-Quentin** could take a bit longer.

LE MARCHÉ SAINT-QUENTIN ♿ HISTORIC SIGHT, MONUMENT

Corner of rue de Chabrol and bd. Magenta

The largest covered market in Paris, Le Marché St-Quentin was constructed in 1865 and renovated in 1982. A series of huge windows allow the sun to pour in and keep the complex warm, even in winter. Come here for the finest cheeses, fish, and meats, or just experience the delicious mix of aromas and mingle with veteran foodies who spend their days browsing for the finest permutation of Camembert. There's a bistro in the middle of the market for those who can't wait until they get home to chow down on their produce.

[M]Gard de l'Est. ⏰ Open M-Sa 8:30am-1pm and 4pm-7:30pm, Su 8:30am-1pm.

PORTE ST-DENIS AND ST-MARTIN MONUMENT

bd. St. Denis

The grand Porte St-Denis looms triumphantly at the end of rue du Faubourg St-Denis. Built in 1672 to celebrate the victories of Louis XIV in Flanders and the Rhineland, the gate imitates the Arch of Titus in Rome. The site of the arch was once a medieval entrance to the city; today it serves as a traffic rotary and a gathering place for pigeons and loiterers alike. In the words of André Breton, "*C'est très belle et très inutile*" ("It's very beautiful and very useless"). On July 28, 1830, revolutionaries scrambled to the top and rained cobblestones on the monarchist troops below. The Porte St-Martin at the end of Rue du Faubourg St-Martin, constructed in 1674, is a variation on a similar theme, with more subdued architecture on a smaller scale. On the bd. St-Martin side, a Herculean Louis XIV dominates the facade, wearing nothing but a wig and a smile.

✝ Ⓜ*Strasbourg-St-Denis.* Ⓢ *Free.*

PORTE ST-MARTIN
MONUMENT

bd. St. Denis at rue du Faubourg St-Martin

This one is a bit less ornate and impressive. The arch was similarly designed and erected at the order of the reticent, self-deprecating Louis XIV, in honor of his victories on the Rhine and in Franche-Comté. Built in 1674, it replaced a medieval gate in the city walls built by Charles V. The arch has a distinctly more modern look; the sculpture's facade is engraved with non-representative, patterned engravings. The four symmetrically aligned sculptures were contributed by four different sculptors. Worth checking out, but not as impressive as Porte St-Denis.

✝ Ⓜ*Strasbourg-Saint-Denis. Facing the Porte St-Denis, take a right and continue down Bld. Saint-Denis. The Porte St-Martin will appear unmistakably on your left.* Ⓢ *Free.*

bastille

There are few monumental ones that still exist in this neighborhood, aside from the **place de la Bastille.** Still, the symbolic historical value of the arrondissement remains, and the lively neighborhood provides many of its own contemporary diversions. The 12*ème* boasts giant monoliths of modern architecture, like the **Opéra Bastille** and the **Palais Omnisports.** Most of the construction is commercial, fitting the working-class background of the area, but a bit of old-fashioned charm can be seen in the funky **Viaduc des Arts** near the Bastille. There are generally more hospitals than museums in the neighborhood, but in October 2007 the arrondissement welcomed a new museum, the **Cité Nationale de l'Histoire de l'Immigration,** which is a must-see if only for its present relevance. It is housed in the **Palais de la Porte Dorée** along with the aquarium; if you make it there, hop on over to the nearby **Bois de Vincennes** for the impressive château and grounds.

🏛 MALHIA KENT
WORKSHOP

19 av. Daumesnil
☎01 53 44 76 76 🖳www.malhia.com

Fulfilling every Project Runway fantasy, this workshop gives an up-close, behind-the-scenes look at fashion. Artisans weave gorgeously intricate fabrics that become *haute couture* for houses like Dior and Chanel. Also gives you a chance to buy clothing—mostly jackets and blazers—before a label is attached and the price skyrockets.

✝ Ⓜ*Gare de Lyon.* Ⓢ *Usually €75-300.* 🕐 *Open M-F 9am-7pm.*

PLACE DE LA BASTILLE
SQUARE

This bustling intersection is where the Bastille Prison housed many a criminal before the "Storming of Bastille" and its subsequent physical deterioration during the French Revolution. The Revolutionaries wiped out all traces of the history they made. Though the revolutionary spirit has been largely lost, today a similar fervor manifests itself nightly in fits of drunken revelry, most marked on **Bastille Day.** At the center of the square is a monument of winged Mercury holding a torch of freedom, symbolizing France's movement toward democracy.

✝ Ⓜ*Bastille.*

BASTILLE PRISON

Visitors to the prison subsist on symbolic value alone—it's one of the most popular sights in Paris that doesn't actually exist. On July 14, 1789, an angry Parisian mob stormed this bastion of royal tyranny, sparking the French Revolution. They only liberated a dozen or so prisoners, but who's counting? Two days later, the Assemblée Nationale ordered the prison demolished. Today, all that remains is the ground plan of the fortress, still visible as a line of paving-stones in the place de la Bastille.

The proletariat masses couldn't have chosen a better symbol to destroy. The prison was originally commissioned by Charles V to safeguard the eastern entrance to Paris; strapped for cash, Charles "recruited" a press-gang of passing civilians to lay the stones for the fortress. Construction was completed by the end of the 14th century, and the Bastille's formidable towers rose 100 ft above the city. After serving as the royal treasury under Henri IV, the building was turned into a state prison by Louis XIII. Internment there, generally reserved for heretics and political dissidents, was the king's business, and as a result it was often arbitrary. But it was hardly the hell-hole that the Revolutionaries who tore it down imagined it to be. Bastille's titled inmates were allowed to furnish their suites, use fresh linens, bring their own servants, and receive guests; the Cardinal de Rohan famously held a dinner party for 20 in his cell. Notable prisoners included the 🎭**Mysterious Man in the Iron Mask** (made famous by writer Alexandre Dumas), the Comte de Mirabeau, Voltaire (twice), and the Marquis de Sade, who wrote his notorious novel *Justine* here.

On the day of the "storm," the Revolutionary militants, having ransacked the Invalides for weapons, turned to the Bastille for munitions. Surrounded by an armed rabble, too short on food to entertain the luxury of a siege, and unsure of the loyalty of the Swiss mercenaries who defended the prison, the Bastille's governor surrendered. His head was severed with a pocket knife and paraded through the streets on a pike. Despite the gruesome details, the storming of the Bastille has come to symbolize the triumph of liberty over tyranny. Its first anniversary was cause for great celebration in revolutionary Paris. Since the late 19th century, July 14 has been the official state holiday of the French Republic. It is a time of glorious firework displays and copious amounts of alcohol, with festivities concentrated in the pl. de la Bastille.

⚑ Ⓜ*Bastille.*

OPÉRA DE BASTILLE

130 rue de Lyon

☏08 92 89 90 90 ▣ www.operadeparis.fr

⛵ & THEATER

President Mitterand made a bold move when he plunked the Opéra Bastille down in this working-class neighborhood, though the Opéra did later employ almost 1,000 people. The largest theater in the world, the building was engineered by Uruguayan architect Carlos Ott, and opened on July 14, 1989 (the bicentennial of the Revolution) amidst some very Parisian protests over its unattractive and overall clunky design. The "People's Opera" has been not so fondly referred to as ugly, an airport, and a huge toilet, due to its uncanny resemblance to the coin-operated *pissoirs* on the streets of Paris. Yet the opera has not struck a completely sour note and has helped renew local interest in the arts. The guided tour offers a behind-the-scenes view of the colossal theater. The immense granite and glass auditorium, which seats 2,703, comprises only 5% of the building's surface area. The rest of the building houses exact replicas of the stage (for rehearsal purposes) and workshops for both the Bastille and Garnier operas.

⚑ Ⓜ*Bastille. Look for the words "Billeterie" on the building.* ℹ *Guided French tours (1hr) almost every day usually at 1pm or 5pm. Call 01 40 01 19 70 for schedule. For wheelchair access, call*

bastille

2 weeks ahead 01 40 01 18 50. Tickets €5-200. 💲 *€11, over 60 and students €9, under 18 €6. Tickets can be purchased by internet, mail, phone (M-Th 9am-6pm, Sa 9am-1pm), or in person (M-Sa 10:30am-6:30pm). Rush tickets 15min. before show for students under 25 and seniors.* ⏰ *Open M-Sa 10:30am-6:30pm.*

JULY COLUMN TOWER

Towering above the always-busy place de la Bastille, this light-catching column commemorates a group of French freedom fighters—though, somewhat illogically, not those who stormed the Bastille. Topped by the conspicuous gold cupid with the shiny bum, the pillar was erected by King Louis-Philippe in 1831 to pay hommage to Republicans who had died in the *Trois Glorieuses*, three-days of street fighting that engulfed Paris in July of 1830. Victims of the Revolution of 1848 were subsequently buried here, along with two mummified Egyptian pharaohs (we're not sure what their involvement was). The column is closed the public.

🧭 *ⓂBastille. In the center of pl. de la Bastille.*

CITÉ NATIONALE DE L'HISTOIRE DE L'IMMIGRATION — 🎫♿ MUSEUM

293 Ave. Daumesnil — ☎01 53 59 58 60 💻www.histoire-immigration.fr

It is both appropriate and ironic that the recently opened museum on immigration is housed in the Palais de la Porte Dorée, which was built during France's colonial expansion and thus features not-so-politically-correct friezes of "native culture" (read: savages) on its outside walls. The museum inside, however, is a much-needed and much-anticipated commemoration of the tumultuous history of immigration in France, an issue that remains heated today. Presented chronologically, the permanent collection traces the arrival and subsequent attempts at integration of immigrants in France, from 1830 to today. Videos, testimonials, photos, and factual displays provide a surprisingly balanced account of both France's experience and the experiences of the immigrants themselves.

🧭 *ⓂPorte Dorée. In the Palais de la Porte Dorée. On the western edge of the Bois de Vincennes.* 💲 *Admission €3, ages 18-26 €2, under 18, handicapped visitors, EU citizens and 1st Su of every month free. During exhibits €5/3.50. Audioguide included. Cité and Aquarium €6, during exhibits €7.* ⏰ *Open Tu-F 10am-5:30pm, Sa-Su 10am-7pm. Last entry 45min. before close.*

RUE DE LA ROQUETTE — NEIGHBORHOOD

Though a bit quieter than its neighbor, the ever bubbling **Rue de Lappe,** but still lively, this winding street has some unostentatious treasures. The 17th-century byway was once home to poet **Paul Verlaine,** who lived at no. 17. The street is now lined with off-beat cafes, bars, independent boutiques, an avant-garde church, and countless restaurants serving everything from Italian to Thai food. The charming **Sq. de la Roquette** is an ideal way to end a stroll along this multi-faceted street.

🧭 *ⓂBastille or ⓂVoltaire.*

LA GALERIE AKIÉ ARICHI — 🎫 ART GALLERY

26 rue Keller — ☎09 51 46 51 14 💻galeriearichi.com

A small gallery committed to the work of international artists, many of whom employ nails, silkscreen, and other industrial methods. The gallery's little dog is as friendly as the owner.

🧭 *ⓂBastille.* ⏰ *Open Tu-Sa 2:30-7pm.*

VIADUC DES ARTS AND PROMENADE PLANTÉE — PARK

9-129 Ave. Daumesnil — ☎01 44 75 80 66 💻www.viaducdesarts.fr

Paris's swankier artists have set up shop under the heavy archways of the **Viaduc des Arts,** a former old railway viaduct and current hive of creative activity. The buildings numerous *ateliers* (studios) house artisans who make everything from *haute couture* fabric to hand-painted porcelain to futuristic furniture. Restorators of all kinds are parked here as well; bring your oil painting, 12th-century book, grandmother's linen, or childhood dollhouse, and they'll return it good as new. Interspersed among the stores are gallery spaces, many of which are rented by a new artist each month. As of this writing, Jean Paul Gautier's gallery is located at no. 30 Rue du Faubourg St-Antoine. High above the avenue, on the "roof" of the viaduct, runs the lovely **Promenade Plantée,** which is decorated with rose covered gazebos. It's an ideal spot in Paris for a Sunday afternoon run or stroll.

✠ ⓜBastille. The viaduct extends from rue de Lyon to rue de Charenton. Entrances to the Promenade are at Ledru Rollin, Hector Malot, and bd. Diderot. ⌚ Park opens M-F 8am, Sa-Su 9am; closing hours vary, around 5:30pm in winter and 9:30pm in summer. Stores open M-Sa; hours vary, with many taking a 2hr. lunch break at noon.

the bottom dwellers

Imagine walking through the Catacombs in Paris. It's nighttime, dark underneath the streets of Paris, and the beam of light emitting from your flashlight is flickering, signaling that it is almost out of battery. You have a few options:

- **BRAVE THE DARKNESS AND CONTINUE EXPLORING**
- **RUN**
- **WHY ARE YOU STILL READING THESE OPTIONS? AREN'T YOU SUPPOSED TO BE RUNNING?**

Running is your best and smartest bet, as the underground tunnels of Paris house more than 6 million bodies and about as many ghosts. These catacombs run for more than 150 miles underground and came about after the Romans carved out a lot of limestone in the quarry underneath Paris to use it for building materials. In the late 18th century, when the French realized that their cemeteries were getting full, citizens suggested that they bury the dead in the underground tunnels, the Catacombs. When the cemetery opened to the public around the middle of the 19th century, some feathers were ruffled, especially superstitious ones. Apparently some crazies believed that disturbing the dead was a no-no. Those who dare to venture down into the abyss are greeted with stares from stacks of bones and skulls on either side of them, sometimes up to 6 ft high. Thirty generations of families are forever stored underneath Paris and will inhabit the Catacombs for more generations to come.

bastille

ART UP DECO ✒ GALLERY
39-41 Ave. Dumesnil ☎01 46 28 80 23 ▯www.artupdeco.com

A gallery designed for amateur collectors, the pieces here comes in standardized sizes, and are stacked against each other warehouse style (*€60-1,500*). Over 100 contemporary artists show pieces here, improving chances that the work of a future master will catch your eye.

✠ ⓜGare de Lyon. ⌚ Open Tu-Sa 11am-7pm, Su 2-7pm.

ITHEMBA ✒ SHOWROOM
67 Ave. Daumesnil ☎01 44 75 88 88 ▯www.ithemba.fr

A colorful, funky showroom filled with sparkling beads and light bulbs, Ithemba has upped its street cred since 2003 and committed itself to the fight against HIV/AIDS in Africa. Over 60 artists design lightbulbs and shades, which are then handmade by HIV/AIDS victims in South Africa and Swaziland, then shipped back to Paris and sold here.

✠ ⓜGare de Lyon. ⌚ Open M-Sa 11am-7pm.

AQUARIUM TROPICAL

♿ MUSEUM

293 Ave. Daumesnil ☎01 44 74 84 80 🖥www.aquarium-portedoree.fr

This tropical aquarium was originally conceived as part of the 1931 Colonial Exposition to display exotic fauna from the French colonies. Now it simply celebrates animal diversity, and showcases over 5,000 creatures representing 300 species from all over the world. The hands-down highlight is the perpetually dozing alligators of all sizes.

[M]Porte Dorée. In Palais de la Porte Dorée, on the western edge of the Bois de Vincennes. $ *€4.50, ages 18-26 €3, under 18, and first Su of the month free. During exhibition periods €5.70/4.20. Cité and Aquarium €6, during exhibits €7.* ⏰ *Open T-F 10am-5:30pm, Sa-Su 10am-7pm. Ticket office closes 45min. before close.*

BERCY QUARTER

PARK

The Bercy Quarter is renowned for its clunky, bureaucratic buildings, beginning with the **Mitterrand's Ministère des Finances** building, a modern monolith to match the similarly block-like **Bibliothèque** across the river. Any of the many new cafes and brasseries along the **rue de Bercy** offer a great view of the mammoth grass-and-glass **Palais Omnisports** concert and sports complex. Each of its sloping sides is covered in green grass; local youth and the occasional tourist periodically try to climb up, but we've never seen someone do it successfully. The **Parc de Bercy** is not quite the tranquil getaway some visitors may seek, but it's still a popular hangout for locals. A lovelier site is the **Yitzhak Rabin Garden** at the eastern edges of the park, which offers rose arbors, grape vines, an herb garden, and a playground dedicated to the Nobel Prize-winning Prime Minister of Israel. To top off this bizarre, 21st-century, rapidly built-up neighborhood, Frank Gehry added a psychedelic building of his own to no. 51 rue de Bercy, which now houses the **Cinémathèque Française.** To one side of the park is what used to be Paris's wine depot; the rows of former wine storage buildings have now been converted into a Club Med. The **Cour St-Émilion** is a hot spot for tourists and locals during warmer weather.

[M]Bercy. East of the Gare de Lyon.

butte-aux-cailles and chinatown

There are no monuments in the 13*ème* to speak of, and that's to its credit. Diverse, residential, and pleasantly odd, the neighborhoods here retain the daily rhythm of Parisian life, and remain uninterrupted by the troops of pear-shaped tourists in matching fanny packs that plague the more pristine arrondissements. Though short on medieval cathedrals, hidden gems from Paris's more recent legacy of mass immigration and perturbed Bo-Bos (i.e., Bohemian Bourgeosie) are scattered throughout the area. Adventurous wanderers will enjoy getting lost in the quirky and sprawling Chinatown, and the formerly working class Butte-aux-Cailles neighborhood harbors a thriving street-art culture.

QUARTIER DE LA BUTTE-AUX-CAILLES

NEIGHBORHOOD

Intersection of Rue de la Butte-aux-Cailles and Rue 5 diamants

Once a working class neighborhood, the Quartier de la Butte-aux-Cailles was home to the *soixantes-huitards*, the activists who nearly paralyzed the city during the 1968 riots. Permutations of the district's original counter-culture remain alive and well; dreadlocks are the hairstyle of choice, and the fashionably disaffected tag walls with subversive graffiti, armed with guitars at all times. Funky restaurants like **Chez Gladines** and the co-operative **Le Temps des Cerises** line the cobbled streets, and attract a boisterous, artsy crowd. **L'Eglise de St.**

Anne, which stands on the corner of rue Bobillot and rue de Tolbiac, boasts a gorgeous stain-glass collection that refracts the afternoon sun into red, blue, and purple light.

✣ Ⓜ*Corvisart. Exit onto Bld. Blanqui and then turn onto Rue 5 diamants, which will intersect with Rue de la Butte-aux-Cailles.*

QUARTIER CHINOIS
NEIGHBORHOOD

Just south of rue de Tolbiac

Spread out over four metro stops just south of rue de Tolbiac, Paris's Chinatown is home to a significant population of Cambodian, Chinese, Thai, and Vietnamese immigrants. Signs change from French to Asian languages, and restaurants advertise steamed dumplings in lieu of *magret de canard*. Non-residents roam the streets looking for the best Asian cuisine Paris has to offer.

✣ Ⓜ*Porte d'Ivry, Porte de Choisy, Tolbiac and Maison Blanche are near Chinatown.*

BIBLIOTHEQUE NATIONALE DE FRANCE: SITE FRANCOIS MITTERRAND
🐾👤 LIBRARY

11 quai Francois Mauriac　　　　　　　☎01 53 79 59 59 ▨www.bnf.fr

With its wide windows and towering steel frame, the library is an imposing piece of architecture worthy of the 13 million volumes it houses. Highlights of the collection include **Gutenberg Bibles** and first editions from the Middle Ages and are displayed in rotation the Galerie des Donateurs. The exhibit can be accessed for free. Scholars hunker down beneath the vaulted ceiling of the library's imposing reading room, or lounge on the extensive deck, surveying the Seine with cigarettes in hand.

✣ Ⓜ*Quai de la Gare.* Ⓢ *Day pass to reading rooms €3.30. 15-day pass €20. Annual membership €35, students €18. Tours €3.* 🕓 *Open M 2-7pm, Tu-Sa 10am-7pm, Su 1pm-7pm. Tours Tu-F 2pm, Sa-Su 3pm.*

EGLISE DE ST. ANNE DE LA BUTTE-AUX-CAILLES
👤 CHURCH

189 Rue de Tolbiac　　　　　☎01 45 89 34 73 ▨www.paroissesainteanne-paris.fr

Though this church is neither as grand nor as famous as the Notre Dame, its exceptionally gorgeous stained glass windows make it worth a visit. Instead of depicting religious figures, the windows refract light through a series of intricate patterns, sending a shock of kaleidoscoped light into the white marble interior of the church. Visitors are welcome to sit in the quiet pews.

✣ Ⓜ*Tolbiac.* 𝒊 *Mass M 7 pm, Tu 9am and 7pm, W 9am and noon, Th 9am and 7 pm, F 9am and noon, Sa 9am. Wheelchair-accessible entrance 11 Rue Martin Bernard.* 🕓 *Open M-F 10am-noon and 4-6:45pm, Sa 10am-noon and 4-6pm.*

montparnasse

CIMETIÈRE MONTPARNASSE
CEMETERY

3 bd. Edgar Quinet　　　　　　　　　　　　　☎01 44 10 86 50

Opened in 1824, Cimetière Montparnasse is the prestigious final resting place of countless famed Frenchmen and an escape from the touristy hustle and bustle of Montparnasse. Be sure to stop at the security station at the **Bld. Quinet** entrance for a map marking the resting places of the cemetery's celebrities. The map reads like a *Who's Who?* of French greatness: Charles Baudelaire, Alfred Dreyfuss, Guy de Maupassant, Samuel Beckett, Jean-Paul Sartre and Simone de Beauvoir (the two are buried together). The presence of these great minds is surely enough to make any humanities buff shed a tear, and the graves continue to be lovingly adorned with cigarette butts, beer bottles, metro tickets, and personal statements of gratitude in several languages. The rest of the cemetery, however, leaves a bit to be desired. The broken windows, bright green trash receptacles, and candy-cane-striped "Do Not Enter" signs detract from the solemn beauty. Local residents have co-opted the grounds for their own purposes; kids play tag, older kids from the *banlieues* bum cigarettes off tourists, and locals drink excessively. Nonetheless, the cemetery showcases some delightful architecture, an impressive list of tenants, and relatively few tourists.

⚹ Ⓜ *Edgar Quinet, opposite the Square Delambre.* Ⓢ *Free.* ◷ *Open 24hr.*

FONDATION CARTIER POUR L'ART CONTEMPORAIN
⬥& MUSEUM

261 bd. Raspail ☎01 42 18 56 50 ▣www.fondation.cartier.com

With a spectacularly sunny, industrial-deco first floor and a cooler basement level home to audiovisual displays, this terrific contemporary museum showcases a series of non-sequitur exhibits that add a little edge to Paris's vibrant art scene. In years past, the Cartier has hosted several Japanese artists, including Hiroshi Sugimoto, Takashi Murakami, and Daido Moriyama, and avant-garde exhibits on graffiti and rock and roll. The innovative, quirky displays push the limits of visitors' interaction with art. Half the fun is in watching how visitors react to the unconventional displays; older folks generally have a blank, "what the hell is going on?" look on their faces as they walk through.

⚹ Ⓜ *Raspail or Denfert Rochereau.* Ⓢ *€7.50, students and unemployed €5, under 18 free.* ◷ *Open Tu 11am-10pm, W-Su 11am-8pm.*

CITÉ UNIVERSITAIRE
& UNIVERSITY

17 bd. Jourdan ☎01 44 16 64 00 ▣www.ciup.fr

Built in the 1920s to nurture cultural exchange between students from around the world, the Cité Universitaire teaches students of over 140 different nationalities. The university's architecture is pretty impressive—the roof of Le Corbusier's Pavilion Suisse housed anti-aircraft guns during WWII—but the best thing to do here is grab a drink at the Maison's café, and head out to the back deck, where students blend languages, bend accents, and study a whole lot of nothing. There's always at least one soccer game and one picnic happening on the big lawn. The Cité welcomes merrymakers of all ages; many a wannabe student has attempted to relive college years here, only to pay the price of admission in cigarette giveaways to students doubling as professional moochers. Whether you're a student yourself or an aging Boomer looking for your personal Hot Tub Time Machine, this is a great place to make some new friends.

⚹ ⓂPorte D'Orléans. RER Cité Universitaire. *i Guided tours first Su of the month 3pm.* Ⓢ *Free entrance. Guided tours €8, students €3, residents free.* ◷ *Reception open M-F 8am-1pm and 2-7:45pm, Sa 11am-2pm. Grounds open daily 7am-10pm.*

CATACOMBS
⬥ HISTORIC LANDMARK

1 Ave. du Colonel Henri Roi-Tanguy ☎01 43 22 47 63 ▣www.catacombes-de-paris.fr

The Catacombs were originally the sight of some of Paris's stone mines, but were converted into an ossuary (i.e. place to keep bones) in 1785 due to the stench arising from overcrowded cemeteries in Paris. A journey into these tunnels is not for visitors with disabilities or the light of heart—it's a 45min. excursion, and there are no bathrooms, so we recommend that all middle-aged men double down on their Maxiflow early, and handle business before you descend into the abyss. The visitor enters down a winding spiral staircase, and soon thereafter, is greeted by a welcoming sign: "Stop, here is the Empire of Death." The visuals are quite unlike anything you've ever seen before. Morbid graffiti lines the walls, and the view of hundreds of thousands of bones makes you feel, well, quite insignificant in the grander scheme of things. Try to arrive before the opening at 10am; nestled twice as deep below ground as the metro, the Catacombs offer a refreshing respite from the midday heat in the summer, and hoards of tourists form extremely long lines in an attempt to get out of the beating sun. The visitor's passage is well-signed, so don't worry about getting lost. Try trailing behind the group a little for the ultimate creepy experience; you won't be disappointed.

⚑ Ⓜ *Denfert Rochereau. Cross av. Roi-Tanguy with lion on your left.* Ⓢ *€7, over 60 €5.50, ages 14-26 €3.50, under 14 free.* ☼ *Open Tu-Su 10am-4pm.*

TOUR MONTPARNASSE ♿ TOWER
33 ave. du Maine ☎01 45 38 52 56

Built in 1969, this modern tower stands 59 stories tall and makes Paris look uncommonly small. The elevator is allegedly the fastest one in Europe, and spits you out to a mandatory photo line on the 56th floor. After being shoved in front of a fake city skyline and forced to smile for a picture that you probably don't want, you're finally allowed up to the 59th floor to take in the real, slightly more breathtaking view. From this obnoxiously lofty modern skyscraper, you can properly take in the beauty, uniformity, and meticulous planning behind Paris' historic streets. Thankfully, the city ruled that similar eyesores could not be constructed in Paris's downtown shortly after this one was built; the city's distinctive style is definitely here to stay. The Tour has a cafe, which provides a wildly overpriced selection of prepackaged food. The view can be a little much on hot summer days but is nonetheless cool for those who aren't afraid of outdoor, non-enclosed heights.

⚑ Ⓜ *Montparnasse-Bienvenue. Entrance on rue de l'Arrivée.* ☼ *Open M-Th Su 9:30am-10:30pm, F-Sa 9:30am-11pm. Last entry 30min. before close.*

MUSÉE BOURDELLE 🢒 MUSEUM
16 rue Antoine Bourdelle ☎01 49 54 73 73 🖳www.paris.org/Musees/Bourdelle

No, this is not a museum of whorehouses, you dirty, dirty traveler—you're thinking of *bor*delle. The Musée *Bour*delle is tucked away on the rue Bourdelle, delightfully close to Montparnasse Bienvenue. Despite its convenient location for tourists, there are few of them here; thanks to the tranquil block on which the museum is located, you might be so lucky as to forget you're anywhere near major tourist attractions. For the 🖳**philistines** among us, Antoine Bourdelle was a French sculptor whose work was extremely influential in the early 1920s; this museum is located at the site of his former home and workshop. Start your visit in the **Salle des Platres,** the first main room to the left of the entrance. An informational video walks visitors through the process of constructing a sculpture employed by Bourdelle and his peers. Some of the museum's most beautiful offerings, including the gigantic *Aphrodite ou La Naissance de la Beauté*, and a commanding sculpture of an American soldier, are dedicated to the memory of the United States' aid in WWI. The quiet central garden is also decorated with colossal sculptures, and both Bourdelle's original *atelier* (workshop) and bedroom have been preserved. Make sure to speak to the history experts stationed throughout the museum. They can give you the details necessary to enrich your Bourdelle experience.

⚑ Ⓜ*Montparnasse Bienvenue. Take ave. du Maine heading away from bd. Montparnasse, and it will be on your left.* Ⓢ *€7, teachers €5, ages 14-26 €3.50, under 13 free.* ☼ *Open Tu-Su 10am-6pm. Last entry 5:45pm.*

MÉMORIAL DE LA LIBÉRATION DE PARIS MEMORIAL
23 allée de la 2ème D.B., Jardin Atlantique ☎01 40 64 39 44

Opened in 1994 for the 50th anniversary of the liberation of Paris from Nazi control, the memorial is comprised of the **Mémorial du Maréchal LeClerc** and the **Musée Jean Moulin,** named after two celebrated WWII heroes. LeClerc led the first Allied

division to liberate Paris from German control in 1944, and Moulin founded the National Council of Resistance, collaborating with de Gaulle to overthrow the German occupation from the inside. The museum contains a wealth of newspaper clippings, radio segments, slideshows, and old guns and uniforms from the period. Savvy multi-taskers are likely to be thrilled by the dazzling 13-superscreen slideshow upstairs. The image of tanks barreling through empty Parisian streets and American soldiers receiving hugs from tearful Parisians will choke up even the most cynical of visitors. The Memorial's visual exhibits are certainly cool, but we necessarily don't recommend visiting the Memorial unless you have a background in the history or are willing to devote the time necessary to understand the historical narrative laid out here.

✚ Ⓜ*Montparnasse-Bienvenue. Follow signs for the Memorial Leclerc from Metro stop to the Memorial.* Ⓢ *Admission to the permanent collection is free; admission to rotating exhibits €4, seniors and handicapped €3, under 26 €2, under 13 free.* ☼ *Open Tu-Su 10am-6pm.*

PARC ANDRÉ CITROEN
⊛& PARK

Inaugurated on the scene of a former Citroen automobile company plant in 1992, the Parc was designed by an ensemble of architects, under the direction of Clément and Alain Provost. The park spans 13 hectares, and boasts two greenhouses, a 250m long pool, ping pong tables, basketball courts, a hot air balloon station, and an unintended skate park for the fashionably disaffected young males of Paris. In the summer, sunbathers, screaming children, and curled old men are permanent fixtures on the park's benches and manicured lawns. If you really feel the need to tweet or blog about how awesome the park is, bring your laptop and take advantage of one its three Wi-Fi areas.

✚ Ⓜ*Balard.* Ⓢ *Guided tours leave from the Jardin Noir, between rue Balard and rue St-Charles;*

€3-6. Balloon takes off every 15min. from 9am-6:30pm daily, except in the case of inclement weather. M-F €10, ages 12-17 €9, ages 3-11 €5; Sa-Su and holidays €12/€10/€6. Residents of Paris under 3 ride free. ② *Park open in summer M-F 8am-9:30pm, Sa-Su 9am-9:30pm; in winter M-F 8am-5:45pm, Sa-Su 9am-5:45pm.*

INSTITUT PASTEUR
⬤ RESEARCH INSTITUTE

25 rue du Docteur Doux ☎For group visits, 01.45.68.82.83 ▤www.pasteur.fr

You probably learned about this guy in middle school bio. An extremely influential scientist in the late 19th century, Louis Pasteur's breakthroughs in pasteurization (gee, wonder who that was named after?), crystallization, vaccination, and the nature of germs guaranteed him a halo-ed spot in the history books and a street named after him in almost every French city. Today, Pasteur's legacy is manifested in this research institute—which uncovered the AIDS virus in 1983—and commemorated in the public museum, which is housed in Pasteur's former laboratory and renovated home. If you're a nerd, or have a ▤nurse/doctor fetish, your trip here will be pretty exciting. You're in France now; there are plenty of good-looking doctors. The museum has preserved Pasteur's test tubes and instruments for public viewing in the actual laboratory where he pasteurized, germinated, etc. Non-science people, much of this stuff will likely float over your head. But the richness of the decor and masonry in Pasteur's home, and even a few of Pasteur's own artistic creations (yes, he painted too!) should get pretty much everybody going. Don't leave before seeing the basement tomb where Pasteur is buried; it's a magnificent marble masterpiece, decorated with detailed mosaics commemorating his many awesome discoveries.

✚ Ⓜ *Balard.* Ⓢ *€7, students €3.* ② *Open Sept-July M-F 2-5:30pm. Audio tour guide is advisable (€5/€2.50), unless you're with a group. Call ahead at least a couple of months for a group tour.*

passy and auteuil

With streets named after Theopold Gautier, Benjamin Franklin, George Sand, and other illustrious figures, the 16*ème* echoes with previous eras of high culture. Remnants of these periods are now housed in the Quarter's many museums. Fans of *Last Tango in Paris* can wander onto the Bir-Hakeim bridge where scenes were shot, and Honoré de Balzac's devotees can lovingly touch the desk where he wrote. Though packed with tourists, Trocadero and its surroundings feature wonderful views of the Eiffel Tower and boast a bustling center of street art, not to mention the graves of some of Paris's most notable residents.

▨ CIMETIÈRE DE PASSY
CEMETERY

2 rue du Commandant-Schloesing ☎01 53 70 40 80

Opened in 1820, this cemetery is home to some of Paris's most notable deceased, including the Givenchy family, Claude Debussy, Berthe Morisot, and Èdouard Manet. The idiosyncrasies and enduring rivalries of these figures continue even in death; the graves here look more like little mansions than tombstones. The tomb of the Russian artist Marie Bashkirtseff is a recreation of her studio, and stands at an impressive 40 ft. Morisot and Manet are buried in a more modest tomb together. We suspect that Morisot's husband would not have approved. Well-groomed and quiet, the graveyard is more of a shadowy garden, with a wonderful view of the Eiffel Tower.

✚ Ⓜ*Trocadero, veer right on ave. Paul Doumer.* Ⓢ *Free.* ② *Open Mar 16-Nov 5 M-F 8am-6pm, Sa 8:30am-6pm, Su and public holidays 9am-6pm; Nov 6-Mar 15 M-F 8am-5:30pm, Sa 8:30am-5:30pm, Su and public holidays 9am-5:30pm. Last entry 30min. before close. Conservation office open M-F 8:30am-12:30pm and 2-5pm.*

MUSÉE D'ART MODERNE DE LA VILLE DE PARIS — MUSEUM

11 ave. du President Wilson ☎01 53 67 40 00 🖥mam.paris.fr

Though smaller than the Centre Pompidou, the Musee D'art Moderne de la Ville de Paris is less crowded and just as enjoyable. Rooms are organized according to artistic movement, and include Fauvism, Cubism, Realism, and abstraction. Exhibits additionally showcase the works of major figures like Mondrian, Picasso, and Duchamp. Graffiti lines the wall, pulling the museum in a deliberate contemporary artistic discourse. During the summer, the museum cafe opens up to a gorgeous terrace with a river view.

 # [M]Iena. Cross the street to ave. du President Wilson, walk down with the Seine at your right. $ Admission to permanent exhibits free. ⏰ Open Tu-Su 10am-6pm. Last entry 5:45pm. Special exhibits open Th 10am-10pm.

MUSÉE DU VIN — MUSEUM

rue des Eaux ☎01 45 25 70 89 🖥www.museeduvinparis.com

Formerly a 15th-century monastery, the Musée du Vin's underground vaults display a number of wine-related objects that the building's devout former residents may not have approved of. Exhibits explain the life cycle of a bottle of wine in great detail. The highlight of the trip is the glass of wine available for purchase at the end of the tour, though you could always save that €10 to buy 10 bottles of your own somewhere else. The adjoining restaurant provides lunch and dinner.

 # [M]Passy. Go down the stairs, turn right onto pl. Albioni, and then right on rue des Eaux; museum tucked away at the end of the street. $ Unguided tour and 1 glass of wine €12, students, seniors, handicapped €10. ⏰ Open Tu-Su 10am-6pm.

JARDINS DU TROCADERO — PARK

The ultimate tourist hub, the gardens provide the perfect "I've been to Paris" photo opp, with one of the clearest views of the Eiffel Tower. The sprawling, sloping lawns and fountain are great for a picnic or watching the many street performers working for your spare change.

 # [M]Trocadero.

MUSÉE NATIONAL DES ARTS ASIATIQUES (MUSÉE GUIMET) — MUSEUM

6 pl. d'Iena ☎01 56 52 53 00 🖥www.museeguimet.fr

The Musée Guimet houses one of the largest collections of Asian art outside of the Orient. Over 45,000 works from 17 different countries occupy the five-floor labyrinth of rooms. Free audio guides enhance the museum experience, explaining the significance of select objects.

 # [M]Iena. $ Admission to permanent collection €7.50, under 18, handicapped and unemployed, EU residents 18-25 free. ⏰ Open M 10am-6pm, W-Su 10am-6pm. Last entry 5:45pm.

MUSÉE MARMOTTAN MONET — MUSEUM

2 rue Louis Boilly ☎01 44 96 50 33 🖥www.marmottan.com

With paneled floors, high ceilings and large glass windows, the Musée Marmottan Monet feel as airy and light as the landscapes portrayed in the Impressionist paintings it houses. Gold detail, intricate molding, and luxurious furniture recreate the atmosphere of another era. The lowest floor is devoted exclusively to one of the most important collections of Claude Monet's work in the world. The series looks well past the haystacks to his lesser known pieces, and explores the breadth of his *oeuvre*. Random biographical objects are also on display; Monet's spectacles, tinged green, sit in a glass box, as does one of his many palettes, still colored with dry paint. A number of works by Berthe Morisot, the only well-known female Impressionist painter, also enrich the collection.

 # [M]Muette, walk through the Jardin de Ranelagh on Avenue Jardin de Ranelagh. The museum

is on the right on rue Louis-Boilly. $ *€9, groups of 10, under 25 and under 8 €5.* ⏰ *Open Tu-Su 11am-6pm. Last entry at 5:30pm.*

MAISON DE BALZAC
🎫 MUSEUM

47 rue Raynouard ☎01 55 74 41 80 💻www.balzac.paris.fr

When he wasn't sleeping his way through Paris, Honoré de Balzac hid from the world in this three-story house, where he wrote most of *La Comédie Humaine*. Today, the house features drafts of his most famous work and various paintings, sculptures, and books related to his life. Visitors can also see the heavy-set desk where he worked. If you've never read Balzac, check out the select quotes lining the walls for a quick introduction to his style. If you have no interest at all in this literary figure, benches scattered amongst bushy trees and Wi-Fi make the accompanying garden a beautiful and practical place to sit.

➔ *ⓂPassy or ⓂLa Muette.* ℹ *Call ahead for guided tours.* $ *Permanent collection free. Temporary exhibits €4.* ⏰ *Open Tu-Sun 10am-6pm. Last entry 5:30pm. Library open M-F 12:30-5:30pm, Sa 10:30am-5:30pm.*

STATUE OF LIBERTY
STATUE

Îles des Cygnes

One of the many replicas of the Statue of Liberty worldwide, this Parisian version faces toward the original in New York Harbor. Standing tall on the man-made Île de Cygnes, the statue can be seen from the Pont Bir-Hakeim where *Last Tango in Paris* was shot. A peaceful walk down the Allée de Cygnes past runners and lovers will yield a close-up view.

➔ *ⓂPassy. Walk down rue d'Albioni toward the Seine, cross av. du President Kennedy to the Pont Bir-Hakeim. Turn right onto Allée de Cygnes if you want a closer look.*

PALAIS DE TOKYO
🎫 MUSEUM

13 ave. du President Wilson ☎01 47 23 54 01 💻www.palaisdetokyo.com

Housing both the Musée d'Art Moderne de la Ville de Paris as well as the Site de Creation Contemporaine, this neoclassical palace is devoted to art. The west wing is perhaps the trendier side, with arcade games, photo booths, and graphic T-shirts. The Site de Creation Contemporaine showcases some of today's hottest artists. There is also an adjoining restaurant, Tokyo Eat.

➔ *ⓂIena.* ℹ *Closed May 1.* $ *€6, seniors, under 25, and groups of 10 or more €4.50, artists and art students €1.* ⏰ *Open Tu-Su 12pm-12am.*

PLACE DU TROCADERO
SQUARE

One of the most bustling hubs in the 16th, Place du Trocadero offers one of the best views of the Eiffel Tower. Street artists dance to a mélange of hip-hop and pop, vendors push their wares on foot, and angsty youth mill about with skateboards. The nearby cafe **Carette** has some of the best hot chocolate in Paris *(€7)*.

➔ *ⓂTrocadero.*

MUSÉE DE LA MODE ET DU COSTUME
🎫 MUSEUM

10 ave. Pierre, 1er de Serbie, entrance on place Rochambeau ☎01 56 52 86 00 💻

There's no denying it—the French dress to impress. This museum elegantly displays the history of fashion from the 18th to 20th century. With 30,000 outfits, 70,000 accessories, and not much space in which to show them, the museum organizes its exhibits by century and rotates them more swiftly than a Lady Gaga costume change.

➔ *ⓂIena. Walk down ave. Pierre 1er de Serbice. Entrance is on the right side of the street.* $ *€7, students and seniors €5.50.* ⏰ *Open Tu-Su 10am-6pm. Last entry 5:30pm.*

batignolles

There's a reason the 17ème isn't a go-to tourist destination. Sights in the traditional sense are few and far between here, but the mostly residential neighborhood and its juxtaposition of bourgeois and working-class Paris is still worth exploring. The lively **Village Batignolles** is a highlight; stretching from **Bld. de Batignolles** to **place du Dr. Félix Lobligeois,** the area is lined with hip cafes and populated by locals who believe in afternoon drinking. During warmer months, **rue de Levis** turns into an open-air market, and the local groceries and boutiques park their carts of bananas and hang their canopies of frilly skirts outside to tempt passerby.

SQUARE DES BATIGNOLLES   SQUARE

Formerly a hamlet for workers, and then a storage sight for illicit ammunition, Square des Batignolles is now an English-style park where the trees grow wild, unfettered by neurotic French trimmings and metal bars. Monet once sat here to paint the Gare St-Lazare train tracks, before heading over to a favorite cafe at 11 rue de Batignolles. Today, less illustrious but just as ambitious artists line its winding paths, watching the local joggers go by. The gently flowing river and pooling lake make the park an idyllic respite from the bustle of the city.

✦ Ⓜ*Brochant. Walk down rue Brochant. Cross place de Charles Fillion* Ⓢ *Free.* ⏰ *Open M-F 8am-9:30pm, Sa-Su and holidays 9am-9:30pm.*

CIMETIÈRE DE BATIGNOLLES   CEMETERY
8 rue St-Just   ☎01 53 06 38 68

Cemeteries are known for being creepy; this one does nothing to reverse that reputation. Mossy tombstones, unkempt streets, and a lingering smell of pee make for an unsettling cemetery-going experience; we'd bring Buffy along if we were you, just in case. If you can stand the heebie jeebies, verse poet Paul Verlaine and, fittingly, surrealist authors André Breton and Benjamin Peret are among its notable interred.

✦ Ⓜ*Port de Clichy. Walk north along avenue Port de Clichy and turn right onto avenue du Cimetière des Batignolles.* ℹ *Request free map inside.* ⏰ *Open Mar 16-Nov 5 M-F 8am-6pm, Sa 8:30am-6pm, Su and holidays 9am-6pm. Nov 6-Mar 15 M-F 8am-5:30pm, Sa 8:30am-5:30pm, Su and holidays 9am-5:30pm. Conservation Bureau open M-F 8am-noon and 2-5:30pm. Last entry 5:15pm.*

CITÉ DES FLEURS   NEIGHBORHOOD

This row of lavish private homes and gardens in an otherwise working class neighborhood encapsulates the socioeconomic contradictions of the 17ème. Owners are required to plant at least three flowering trees in their gardens, resulting in an uncommonly pretty drive. If you're in the area, it can be a pleasant respite.

✦ Ⓜ*Brochant. Walk up avenue de Clichy. Turn right onto Cité des Fleurs.*

MUSÉE DE JEAN-JACQUES HENNER   MUSEUM
43 avenue de Villiers   ☎01 47 63 42 73 🖥 www.musee-henner.fr

Known for the two big e's in painting---eroticism and exoticism---Jean-Jacques Henner's work is displayed here in one of its most important collections. If you're not a big fan of his work, you might consider skipping the museum.

✦ Ⓜ*Malherbes.* Ⓢ *Tickets €5, students €3.* ⏰ *Open M and W-Su 11am-6pm, first Th of every month 11am-9pm.*

buttes chaumont

Sights in Buttes are pretty much limited to the **Parc des Buttes** and the unique **Parc de la Villette,** a former meatpacking district that provided Paris with much of its beef before the advent of the refrigerated truck. In 1979, the slaughterhouses were replaced with an artistic park, and *voilà.* Architect Bernard Tschumi's three-part vision took 461 teams from 41 different countries to complete.

▨ PARC DES BUTTES-CHAUMONT   ♿ PARK

This awe-inspiring neighborhood park shrewdly uses impressive manmade topography to make visitors feel like you're in Atlantis, or maybe some kind of movie. Napoleon III commissioned the park in 1862 to quell his homesickness for London's Hyde Park, where he spent a good deal of time in exile. Construction of the park was directed by designer Adolphe Alphand, whose main triumph was the park's central hill, with its breathtaking exposed crags. The park's area has been a well-trafficked part of Paris since the 13th century, but before Napoleon III, it was famous for very different reasons. Once the site of a gibbet (an iron cage filled with the rotting corpses of criminals), a dumping ground for dead horses, a haven for worms, and a gypsum quarry (the source of "plaster of Paris"), the modern-day Parc des Buttes-Chaumont has come a long way. Today's visitors walk the winding paths surrounded by lush greenery and hills and enjoy a great view of the 19*ème,* 20*ème,* and the rest of Paris from the Roman temple at the top of the cliffs. The lower rungs of the park provide a lovely and shaded respite on a warm summer's afternoon. Families, rebellious teens, and runners constitute the park's main demographics.

⚐ Ⓜ*Buttes-Chaumont.* Ⓢ *Free.* ⌚ *Open daily May-Sept 7am-10:15pm; Oct-Apr 7am-8:15pm.*

▨ CITÉ DES SCIENCES ET DE L'INDUSTRIE   ♨♿ MUSEUM

30 av. Corentin Cariou   ☎01 40 05 12 12 ▣www.cite-sciences.fr

If any structure in Paris has ADHD, it's the Cité des Sciences et de l'Industrie; to call it a multi-purpose complex would be an understatement. The Cité houses the fabulous **Explora Science Museum,** one of the top destinations for the children of Paris. Highlights include a magnificent planetarium, a movie theater, a library, a massive cyber cafe, and an aquarium. The whole structure is an architectural tour de force. Outside of the Cité is the enormous **Géode,** a mirrored sphere that essentially looks like a gigantic disco ball but somehow doubles as the Cité complex's second movie theater; the 1,000-sq.-m surface provides ample screen space. To the right of the Géode, the *Argonaute* details the history of submarines, from the days of Jules Verne to present-day nuclear-powered subs. If the *Argonaute* looks like a real naval submarine, that's because it is. The exhibit is fantastic, but will cost you a little extra. At Level 1 in the Cité, you'll find consultation areas for jobs and health; while not exactly a fun outing with the kids, this stuff can be useful if you're looking for a job or wondering how to stay healthy during your time in Paris.

⚐ Ⓜ*Porte de la Villette.* *i Admission includes English or French audio tours.* Ⓢ *Formule summer (access to all aspects of the Cité) €21, reduced €19. Explora and Planetarium €11, under 25 €8. Argonaute €3. Cinaxe €4.80. Explora and Géode €17.50, reduced €14, under 7 €9.* ⌚ *Open M-Sa 9:30am-6pm, Su 9:30am-7pm. Argonaute open Tu-Sa 10am-5:30pm, Su 10am-6:30pm. Cinaxe open Tu-Su 11am-1pm and 2-5pm; showings every 15min.*

PARC DE LA VILLETTE   ♿ PARK

211 av. Jean Jaurès   ☎01 40 03 75 75 ▣www.villette.com, www.fnac.com for tickets

Cut in the middle by canals de l'Ourcq and Ste-Denis, Parc de la Villette separates the Cité des Sciences from the Cité de la Musique. Put simply, the park is a mega-entertainment center. The steel-and-glass **Grande Halle** dominates the center of the complex and features concerts, films, plays, and unfathomably long lines. But the unabashedly modern park is perhaps more famous for its assortment of 26 uniquely shaped red buildings called "follies." What's so crazy about these follies? Well, you could start with their red-is-always-in "cutting-edge" architectural style, or with the fact that the contents of the follies range from Le Quick Burger Stands to themed playgrounds to jazz clubs. Located before the Grande Halle, the information Villette folly distributes free maps and brochures of the expansive park. During July and August, La Villette hosts a free open-air film festival. Finally, the **Promenade des Jardins** links several thematic gardens, including the **Garden of Dunes and Wind,** reminiscent of a seashore, the **Garden of Childhood Fears,** which winds through a wooded grove resonant with spooky sounds, and the roller coaster Dragon Garden.

⚐ ⓂPorte de Pantin. 🕐 *Info office open M-Sa 9:30am-6:30pm. Garden open Sa-Su 3-7pm.*

CITÉ DE LA MUSIQUE
◆ MUSEUM

221 av. Jean Jaurès ☎01 44 84 44 84 🖳www.citedelamusique.fr

Constructed by architect Christian de Portzamparc and opened in 1995, the Cité de la Musique's stunning glass ceilings and loops of curved steel house an impressive complex of musical venues and materials. Though nominally a music museum, the institute also includes two concert halls, conference rooms, practice rooms, and over 70,000 books, documents, music journals, and photographs. The museum is mostly geared toward classical-music lovers; visitors don headphones that tune in to musical excerpts and describe the pieces constituting the museum's vast collection of over 900 antique instruments, sculptures, and paintings. The Cité de la Musique's two performance spaces—the 900-seat Salle des Concerts and the 230-seat Amphithéâtre—host an eclectic range of concerts, ranging from rock to jazz to classical.

⚐ ⓂPorte de Pantin. *i Extra charges may apply for temporary exhibits.* ⑤ *Museum €8, under 18 €4. 1hr. French-language tour €10, under 18 €8.* 🕐 *Info center open Tu-Sa noon-6pm, Su 10am-6pm. Musée de la Musique open Tu-Sa noon-6pm, Su 10am-6pm; last entry 5:15pm. Médiathèque open Tu-Sa noon-6pm, Su 1-6pm.*

montmartre

One of Paris's most storied neighborhoods, Montmartre was once home to lots of famous artists. Today, the **Place du Tertre**, a former artist hangout, is dominated by drunk portraitists instead. From the hills of Montmartre to the seedy underworld of Pigalle, there's plenty to see here and plenty of English spoken.

▨ HALLE ST-PIERRE
◆ MUSEUM

2 rue Ronsard ☎ 01 42 51 10 49 🖳www.hallesaintpierre.org

Halle St-Pierre is a one-of-a-kind abstract art museum located right down the street from the basilica. Exhibits are constantly rotating, so the museum is naturally hard to pin down. The art on display tends to be a bit far out. One of Halle St-Pierre's more recent exhibits was on "Art Brut Japonais," or Japanese Outsider Art; during our visit, a standout among the many mind-bending works there was a series of dirty pairs of underwear or, as the French call them, slips (luckily they didn't smell). Halle St-Pierre also houses rentable workshops, a top-notch bookstore, and a constantly crowded cafe. The museum section is not closed off, so the soft din of cafe chatter accompanies any museum visit.

⚐ ⓂAnvers, ⓂAbesses. ⑤ *€7.50, students €6.* 🕐 *Open Aug M-F noon-6pm; Sept-July daily 10am-6pm.*

CIMETIÈRE MONTMARTRE
CEMETERY

20 ave. Rachel
☎01 53 42 36 30

A particularly vast cemetery, Montmartre was built belowground on the site of a former quarry and stretches across a significant portion of the 18th arrondissement. It is now the resting place of multiple famous people: painter Edgar Degas, artist Gustave Moreau, writer Émile Zola, saxophone inventor Adolphe Sax, and ballet dancer Marie Taglioni are among the long-term residents. Fans leave ballet shoes on Taglioni's grave and coins, notes, etc. at some of the other famous gravestones. The cemetery itself is in disrepair; several graves have broken windows, and could use some maintenance and cleaning. The mischievous crowd of the Red Light District is surely to thank for this.

⚡ Ⓜ*Place de Clichy.* Ⓢ *Free.* Ⓔ *Open Nov. 6-May 15 M-F 8am-5:30pm, Sa 8:30am-5:30pm, Su 9am-5:30pm; March 16-Nov. 5 M-F 8am-6pm, Sa 8:30am-6pm, Su 9am-6pm.*

BASILIQUE DU SACRÉ-COEUR
   ♿ CHURCH

35 rue du Chevalier-de-la-Barre   ☎01 53 41 89 00 ✉www.sacre-coeur-montmartre.fr

Situated 129m above sea level, the steps of the Basilique offer what is possibly the best view in the whole city. This splendid basilica first underwent construction in 1870. Its purpose? To serve as a spiritual bulwark for France and the Catholic religion, under the weight of a pending military loss and German occupation. The basilica was initially meant to be an assertion of conservative, Catholic power, commissioned by the National Assembly. Today, the Basilica sees over 10 million visitors per year and is accompanied by an attendant list of tourist traps; outside the basilica, beware of men trying to "give you" a bracelet or other tourist trinkets, because they'll start to yell emphatically that you have to pay them once you don't. The cathedral itself is home to two souvenir shops. The museum has some interesting artistic and architectural features; its slightly muted Roman-Byzantine architecture was a reaction against the perceived excess at the recently constructed Opera Garnier.

⚡ Ⓜ*Lamarck-Caulaincourt.* Ⓢ *Free.* Ⓔ *Basilica open daily 6am-11pm. Mass M-F 11:15am, 6:30pm, 10pm, Sa 10pm, Su 11am, 6pm, 10pm.*

PLACE DU TERTRE
NEIGHBORHOOD

rue Norvins

On the lovely, constantly bustling Place du Tertre, artists set up their easels to showcase their old works and draw portraits of tourists. The very existence of this square recalls a different time for the Montmartre neighborhood, when painters like Picasso and Salvador Dalí lived here and revolutionized 20th-century art. Today, street artists—many of them drunk and drinking—chef up quick portraits of tourists; kids squirm uncomfortably, posing in front of hundreds of passersby as their parents assure them that they'll thank them later (maybe?). Several of the cafes surrounding the square have terraces in the middle of the *place* that offer a gluttonous people-watching experience.

⚡ Ⓜ*Anvers or* Ⓜ*Abesses.*

MUSÉE MONTMARTRE
☞ MUSEUM

12 rue Cortot
☎01 49 25 89 37

Located on the site of the former home of Claude de La Rose (Molière's successor), and in the building that housed the ateliers of Van Gogh and Renoir, the Musee Montmartre is dedicated entirely to the fascinating history of the 18*ème*. Exhibits intertwine the rich histories of individual neighborhoods within the arrondissement: those of the Vignes, the Basilique Sacré-Coeur, several of the artists who worked in the neighborhood, and the Lapin Agile, among others.

The museum tells many eccentric stories; we for one didn't know that the name for Le Lapin Agile came about when a picture of a rabbit escaping from a pan was painted on its outer walls. The museum is small, the staff is unnecessarily nitpicky with its guests, and the rooms can get a bit musty, but this is nonetheless a good place to start before you continue touring Montmartre. Don't forget to check out the beautiful view of Paris from the museum's garden on your way in or out.

✠ Ⓜ Anvers Ⓜ Lamarck-Caulaincourt. Ⓢ €8, reduced price €6, students aged 12-26 €4, under 12 free. 🕐 Open July-Aug Tu-Th 11am-6pm, Fri-Su 11am-7pm; Sept-June Tu-Su 11am-6pm.

LES VIGNES
HISTORIC SIGHT

rue des Saules

All the way back in the 16th century, the primary occupation of the residents of Montmartre was owning and operating vineyards. In 1933, Paris decided to plant ceremonial vines on a plot of land on the Butte Montmartre. The wine was never all that good. In the words of one very unflattering 17th-century saying: "It's Montmartre wine of which you drink a pint and piss out a quart." Access to the public is forbidden (by the looks of the vines, it's closed to vineyard workers as well!), except during the Celebration of the Harvest of Montmartre, held annually in the fall. The grapes from the rather unkempt vines are pressed into wine in the basement of the 18th arrondissement's Mairie.

✠ Ⓜ Lamarck-Caulaincourt, right across the street from the Lapin Agile. 🕐 Closed to public, except during the Fete des Vendanges; see 🖥 www.fetedesvendangesdemontmartre.com for scheduling information.

LE BATEAU LAVOIR
HISTORIC MONUMENT

11bis pl. Émile Godeau

This house is known principally for being the home/workshop of many famous early-20th-century painters and writers. The name of the house (The Washing Boat) was coined because, on stormy days, the poorly built shacks on the pl. Émile Godeau (then pl. Ravignan) shook and swayed about in the wind and stormy weather, reminding residents of washing boats on the Seine. This house's list of residents/occupants is impressive: Picasso, Gertrude Stein, Henri Matisse, and Max Jacob all lived or hung around the Bateau Lavoir. A fire in the 1970s completely burned the house's inside, leaving only its facade standing. It was rebuilt and divided into 25 artist workshops. It is always closed to the public, but you can feel the history that emanates from it if you stand outside or peer in.

✠ Ⓜ Abbesses. 𝒊 Closed to public.

belleville and père lachaise

🏛 CIMETIÈRE DU PÈRE LACHAISE
CEMETERY

16 rue du Repos
☎ 01 55 25 82 10

One of the most prestigious cemeteries in Paris, the Cimetière du Père Lachaise is the byproduct of innovative public-health codes and 19th-century public-ity stunts. Cemeteries were banned inside Paris in 1786 after the closure of the Saints Innocents Cemetery (Cimetière des Innocents); the cemetery was located on the fringe of Les Halles food market, and local officials came to realize that this (shockingly) presented a health hazard. Père Lachaise, in the east of the city, was the biggest of the new cemeteries outside of the city's center, the others being Montmartre and Montparnasse. As any tourist who has visited the 20th arrondissement knows all too well, the 20ème is far removed from the heart of Paris, and the cemetery didn't attract many burials immediately after its creation. In a savvy marketing move, administrators made a grand spectacle of moving the remains of two renowned Frenchmen, Molière and La Fontaine, to Père Lachaise. The strategy worked. Thousands of burials occurred at Lachaise over the next few years, and the cemetery now holds over 300,000 bodies and many more cremated remains. Today the well-manicured lawns and winding paths of the Cimetière du Père Lachaise have become the final resting place for many French and foreign legends. The cemetery's over-occupied graves house the likes of Balzac, Delacroix, La Fontaine, Haussmann, Molière, and Proust. Expat honorees include Modigliani, Stein, Wilde, and, most visited of all the graves at Lachaise, Jim Morrison.

You'll notice that many of the tombs in this landscaped grove strive to remind visitors of the dead's worldly accomplishments. The tomb of French Romantic painter **Théodore Géricault** bears a reproduction of his *Raft of the Medusa*, with the original painting now housed in the Louvre. On **Frédéric Chopin's** tomb sits his muse Calliope, sculpted beautifully in white marble. Although **Oscar Wilde** died destitute and unable to afford such an extravagant design, an American admirer added bejeweled Egyptian figurines to his grave in 1912. The sculpture was defaced in 1961, prompting false rumors that the cemetery director, finding a part of the sculpture's anatomy to be out of proportion, removed the offending jewels of the Nile and kept them as a paperweight. Despite an interdiction to kiss the tomb, dozens of lipstick marks from adoring fans cover Wilde's grave today. **Baron Haussmann**, responsible for Paris's large boulevards, originally wanted to destroy Père Lachaise as part of his urban renewal project; having relented, he now occupies one of the cemetery's mausoleums.

Upon entering the cemetery, you might feel a distinctly bohemian vibe. Well, that's because The Doors's former lead singer, **Jim Morrison**, holds permanent real estate here at Lachaise. Apparently the crooner remains popular even in death. Honored with the most visited, though rather modest, grave in the cemetery, Morrison's final resting place is annually mobbed by hundreds of thousands of visitors. Admirers bearing beer, flowers, joints, poetry, Doors T-shirts, bandannas, jackets, and more surround the resting place of their idol daily.

While over a million people are buried at Père Lachaise, only 100,000 tombs exist. This discrepancy arises from the old practice of burying the poor in mass graves. To make room for new generations of the dead, corpses are removed from these unmarked plots at regular intervals. Even with such purges, however, Père Lachaise's 44 hectares are close to bursting; hence, the government digs up any grave unvisited in 10 years and transports the remains to a different cemetery. To avoid being disinterred, those who die alone hire professional "mourners" before their death to ensure against getting moved somewhere else.

The monuments marking collective deaths remain the most emotionally moving sites in Père Lachaise. The **Mur des Fédérés** (Wall of the Federals) has become a pilgrimage site for left-wingers. In May 1871, a group of Communards, sensing their reign's imminent end, murdered the Archbishop of Paris, who had been their hostage since the beginning of the Commune. They dragged his corpse to their stronghold in Père Lachaise and tossed it in a ditch. Four days later, the victorious Versaillais found the body. In retaliation, they lined up 147 Fédérés against the cemetery's eastern wall before shooting and burying them on the spot. Since 1871, the Mur des Fédérés has been a rallying point for the French left, which recalls the massacre's anniversary every

Pentecost. Near the wall, other monuments remember **WWII Resistance fighters** and **Nazi concentration-camp victims.** The cemetery's northeast corner provokes greater solemnity than the well-manicured central plots' grand sarcophogi, so take playful activities elsewhere.

✝ ⓂPère Lachaise or ⓂGambetta. *i* Free maps at the Bureau de Conservation near Porte du Repos; ask for directions at guard booths near the main entrances. Free 2½hr. guided tour from Apr to mid-Nov Sa 2:30pm. For more info on "theme" tours, call ☎01 49 57 94 37. ⓢ Open from mid-Mar to early Nov M-F 8am-6pm, Sa 8:30am-6pm, Su 9am-6pm; from Nov to mid-Mar M-F 8am-5:30pm, Sa 8:30am-5:30pm, Su 9am-5:30pm. Last entry 15min. before close.

PARC DE BELLEVILLE
                         ♿ PARK
27 rue Piat

A park on a hill with an urban twist, Parc de Belleville is in fact a series of terraces connected by stairs and footpaths. In between the paths, the abundant stretches of greenery beckon sunbathers, PDAs, and nature types. From its high vantage point, the park offers spectacular views of Parisian landmarks, including the Eiffel Tower and the Panthéon. The park features ping-pong tables, an open-air theatre, and a playground for kids. Shrieking children clamor around the park's playground near the entrance, while parents rest their weary legs on nearby benches. Dotted by flowers, napping couples, and gangs of youths (nonviolent, if a bit too energetic) in the summer, the serene oasis seems curiously far removed from the city at night. The park's low fences make it easy to hop into, so it becomes a center for adolescent deviance at night.

✝ ⓂPyrénées. ⓢ Free. ◷ Open daily dawn-dusk.

FOOD

Say goodbye to foot-long subs and that sticky pre-sliced cheese they sell at Costco—you're not in Kansas anymore. The preparation and consumption of food are integral to French daily life; while world-famous chefs and their three-star prices are a valued Parisian institution, you don't have to pay their prices for excellent cuisine. Bistros and cafes provide a more informal, expensive option. Even more casual are brasseries, which foster a lively and irreverant atmosphere. The least expensive option is usually a crêperie, a restaurant specializing in thin Breton pancakes filled with meats, vegetables, cheeses, chocolates, or fruits; crêperies might be hotspots for yuppie brunches and awkward first dates in the US, but you can often eat a crêpe here for less than you'd pay at the great Golden Arches. The offerings of specialty food shops, including *boulangeries* (bakeries), *patisseries* (pastry shops), and *chocolatiers* (chocolate shops), provide delicious and inexpensive picnic supplies. A number of cheap kebab and falafel stands around town also serve some scrumptious cheap fare. Bon appetit!

greatest hits

- **IT DOESN'T GET MORE FRENCH THAN THIS:** The hip and modern **Page 35** serves as a restaurant, crêperie, and art gallery, and embodies the Marais' zany mix of refinement and funk.

- **THE MARKET OF RED CHILDREN:** Okay, so the **Marché des Enfants Rouges** shouldn't be translated literally. If you want to feast on a cheap and fresh collection of international cuisine, though, this open air market is the place to go.

- **BEST QUICKIE YOU'LL EVER HAVE:** Famed French chef Christian Constant opened **Les Cocottes** in an attempt to provide upscale cuisine to the masses at cheap prices with fast service. He succeeds extravagantly.

- **HE'S CHUCK BASS: Ladurée** bakery is now so famous that a long-suffering intern for Gossip Girl was flown here to buy some of their macaroons, so that Chuck could offer his heart to Blair properly.

- **WORTH EVERY PENNY:** After dining at **Le Troquet,** one of our researchers came back with this verdict: "if you have to eat at sweaty kebab take-out spots for a week, or even two weeks, to afford this, just do it." Sha-zam.

student life

Nom nom nom—Parisian cuisine is excellent. You'll be hard-pressed to find a block without a bistro or crêperie. We'll leave it to you to figure out how to ask for your snails on the side, but the best eats in Paris are most definitely in the 8*ème*. Although generally known as the glamorous part of the city, you can definitely find affordable places to grab a bite here.

île de la cité and île st-louis

The islands are dotted with traditional dimly lit French restaurants, ideal for the couples who walk hand in hand down the *quais*. But the old heart of Paris is now the tourist center of Paris, and a romantic meal here comes at a price. Expect to pay more than you would for an equivalent meal on the mainland—or just settle for some ice cream. Île St-Louis is perhaps the best place in Paris to stop for a crêpe or a cool treat while strolling along the Seine. And until you're rolling in dough, or dating someone who is, a snack will have to do.

BERTHILLON — ICE CREAM ❶

31 rue St-Louis-en-l'Île — ☎01 43 54 31 61

You just can't leave Paris without having a bit of this ice cream. The family-run institution has been doing brilliant marketing work since 1954, but it's not all false advertising; Berthillon delivers with dozens of flavors that cater to your every craving. If you can't stand the epic lines, you can get pints of the same stuff at nearby stores.

‡ [M]Pont Neuf. [$] Single scoop €2.20, 2 scoops €3.40, 3 scoops €4.80. ⏰ Open from Sept to mid-July W-Su 10am-8pm. Closed 2 weeks in Feb and Apr.

CAFÉ MED — RESTAURANT, CRÊPERIE ❷

77 rue St-Louis-en-l'Île — ☎01 43 29 73 17

There may not be doctors in attendance, but they'll fill that hole in your stomach and won't charge you an arm and a leg for your visit. One of the cheapest and most charming options on the isle. The three-course menu at €10 is an astonishing deal.

‡ [M]Pont Marie. [$] 3-course menus at €10, €10.50, €14, €20. Weekend special tea €6. ⏰ Open M-F 11am-3:30pm and 7-10:30pm, Sa-Su 11am-10:30pm.

BRASSERIE DE L'ISLE ST-LOUIS — BRASSERIE ❷

55 quai de Bourbon — ☎01 43 54 02 59

An old-fashioned brasserie that manages to feel just a tad bit inauthentic, with red-checkered napkins and closely packed wooden tables. This island institution is known for regional specialties like southern *cassoulet* (a casserole dish of meat and beans; €18), which keep the Frenchmen coming. Outdoor *quai* seating with a view of the Panthéon makes up for the number of tourists dining here.

‡Pont Marie. [$] Entrees €6-10. Plats €17-45. Desserts €7-11. ⏰ Open daily noon-11pm.

AUBERGE DE LA REINE BLANCHE — TRADITIONAL ❸

30 rue St-Louis-en-l'Île — ☎01 46 33 07 87

Miniature wooden chairs, bronze pans, and peasant dolls decorate the shelves, walls, and corners as subdued customers enjoy two- to three-course meals. Standard French dishes and simple salads are featured on the menu.

‡ [M]Pont Marie. i Menu available in English. [$] 2-course lunch €15.50, dinner €19.50; 3 courses €19.50/25. Plat €12/15. ⏰ Open daily noon-2:30pm and 6-10:30pm.

LA PETITE SCIERIE

● SPECIALTY STORE ❺

60 rue St-Louis-en-l'Île

☎01 55 42 14 88 ■www.laPetitescierie.fr

Committed to true French artisanship, Cathérine Duoy makes all products by hand, schlepping around the animal fat herself on a local farm. Her high-quality specialties have been sold on the isle for the last 25 years, and can be tasted on little baguettes with a shot of wine. The traditional *foie-gras* (180g €32; 320g €60) need not be refrigerated for two years.

✦ ⓂPont Marie. 🕘 *Open Jan-Nov M 11am-7pm, Th-Su 11am-7pm; Dec daily 11am-7pm.*

AMORINO

● GELATO ❷

47 rue St-Louis-en-l'Île

☎01 44 07 48 08 ■www.amorino.com

Seducing the child in you, Amorino does gelato right. Serves exceedingly rich concoctions in much more generous portions than Berthillon. Sizes go up all the way to *grandissimo*. Approach with caution; it's a lot to handle.

✦ ⓂPont Marie. ⑤ *Small gelato €3.50, medium €4.50, large €6.50, giant €7.50, huge €9.* 🕘 *Open in summer M-Th 11:30am-11pm, F-Sa 11:30am-midnight, Su 11:30am-11pm.*

LES FOUS DE L'ÎLE

●((•))⅄❄ BISTRO ❸

33 rue des Deux Ponts

☎01 43 25 76 67 ■www.lesfousdelile.com

This quirky neighborhood bistro boasts a menu with the workings of a French feast. Playing on some inside joke about chickens, the restaurant is completely decorated with poultry parapharnelia.

✦ ⓂPont Marie. 🕘 *Open daily noon-11pm.*

MA SALLE À MANGER

●⅄⌂ TRADITIONAL ❸

26 pl. Dauphine

☎01 43 29 52 34

A no-fuss, lovable restaurant tucked away at the edge of the square. Traditional dishes with the occasional Italian or Spanish influence served by the occasionally Italian or Spanish waitstaff.

✦ ⓂPont Neuf. *i Reservations necessary for Su evenings.* ⑤ *Plats €14. 2-course meal €18. 3-course meal €23. €3 supplement for dinner.* 🕘 *Open M-Sa noon-2:30pm and 7:30-10:30pm, Su noon-2:30pm.*

QUAI QUAI

●⅄⌂ TRADITIONAL ❸

74 quai des Orfèvres

☎01 46 33 69 75

Exuding glamorous grit, the food here is good but served in the kind of portions skinny people like and hungry travelers don't. The trendy, underground location is tourist-free, but you'll be paying for the peace and quiet.

✦ ⓂPont Neuf. ⑤ *Entrées €8-15.50. Plat du jour €12. Plats €18-27. Desserts €7.50-12. Lunch 2-course formule €16, 3 course €20.50.* 🕘 *Open Tu-F noon-2:30pm and 7:30-11pm, Sa 4-11:30pm.*

LE CAVEAU DU PALAIS

●⅄⌂ TRADITIONAL ❷

17-19 pl. Dauphine

☎01 43 26 04 28 ■caveaudupalais@wanadoo.fr

A mostly older, local clientele enjoys a meat-heavy menu, happily forgetting the dangers of arteriosclerosis in an elegant dining room. Rich French food is slightly more expensive but high on quality.

✦ ⓂPont Neuf. ⑤ *Entrees €9-19. Plats €19-50. Desserts €9-10.* 🕘 *Open M-Sa 12:15-2:15pm and 7:15-10:15pm, Su 12:15-2pm and 7:15-10pm.*

LE PETIT PLATEAU

●⅄⌂ CAFE ❶

1 quai aux Fleurs

☎01 44 07 61 86

Le Petit Plateau is not in plain view of the Notre Dame, so most tourists naturally skip over this cute *salon de thé*. It has a light lunch fare and a dessert selection at a price Parisians would pay.

✦ ⓂCité ⑤ *Quiches and salad €8.50. Tartines and salad €10-11. Soup €6.50-8.50. Salads €10-11.* 🕘 *Open M-Sa 10am-6pm.*

île de la cité and île st-louis

BRUSCHET CAFFE

CAFE ❷

20 pl. Dauphine

☎01 44 07 28 17

A *cafe de luxe* with reasonably priced, light lunch fare (€12). Menu is fairly limited and generally unimpressive, but it's the cheapest option around the square. ⚲Pont Neuf. ⌚ *Open daily 10am-7pm.*

châtelet-les halles

Food in the Châtelet area is unabashedly overpriced and often touristy. Nonetheless, there are a few classics that you simply have to visit—Angelina comes to mind—and a couple neighborhood options with unique dining experiences that are not to be missed.

▧ LE PÈRE FOUETTARD

TRADITIONAL ❸

9 rue Pierre Lescot

☎01 42 33 74 17

Boasting a cozy interior dining room and a heated terrace that stays open year-round, Fouettard serves up tasty traditional French cuisine at slightly elevated prices. If you can bear to pass up the ambiance of a cafe meal, it's better to sit inside; you'll be closer to the bar. Rich wood walls, ceilings and floors are decorated with wine bottles basically wherever they fit. Meals on the terrace are by candlelight at night; how romantic! The location is fantastic, in the midst of the Châtelet-Les Halles neighborhood.

⚲ Ⓜ*Etienne Marcel.* Ⓢ *Formules midi €14.90-19.90. Salads €13.90-14.50. Plats €12.50-23.50.* ⌚ *Open daily 7:30pm-2am.*

ANGELINA

TEA HOUSE ❸

226 rue de Rivoli

☎01 42 60 82 00

A hot chocolate at Angelina will make you feel like Eloise at the Plaza. Located right across from the Jardin des Tuileries, this *salon de thé* has been around since 1903; bright frescoes, mirrored walls, and white tablecloths have immortalized Angelina's status as a Paris classic. There's always a long line outside of Angelina; expect to wait 20-30 minutes to get a table. The wait can obviously get out of hand at peak times (weekends during the summer). The hot chocolate (€7.50) is to die for, even in the heat of the summer. In order to cut down on the line, all food items are available for take-out, but there's often a line for that as well.

⚲ Ⓜ*Tuileries.* Ⓢ *Salads €17-19. Patisseries €5.90-8.90. Tea and coffee €4-7.50.* ⌚ *Open daily 9am-7pm.*

ASSIETTE AVEYRONNAISE

TRADITIONAL ❷

14 rue Coquillière

☎01 42 36 51 60

A neighborhood favorite; Parisians come from all corners of the city for the delicious traditional *saucisse aligot* (a sausage engulfed by a mix of mashed potatoes and cheeses), and they won't hesitate to initiate newcomers to the house's best dishes. A half-plate of the house specialty will leave most guests incapable of continuing onto the *millefeuille*, the house's dessert specialty. The restaurant's dining room is no-frills and brightly lit, while the terrace (heated when necessary) unspectacularly looks out on the entrance to a parking garage. The service is extremely friendly despite being insanely busy with the droves of regulars.

⚲ Ⓜ*Les Halles.* Ⓢ *Entrées €7.20. Plats €13.80. Formules €18.50, €23.80, €28.30.* ⌚ *Open Tu-Su noon-2:30pm and 7:30-midnight.*

BIOBOA

CAFE, ORGANIC ❷

3 rue Danielle Casanova

☎01 42 61 17 67

A small, affordable lunch spot *à la americaine*, ideal for a light lunch. The "food

food

spa" serves up soups, salads, paninis, and desserts to be eaten at one of the restaurant's few tables, looking out onto rue Casanova from the window-side bar, or for take-out (a very rare find in France!). Plenty of fashion-conscious types nibble on paninis and sip on smoothies here for lunch, but big appetites should opt for something a bit more substantial.

✚ ⓂPyramides. Ⓢ Smoothies €5.50-6.50. Entrées €5-7.20; plats €9-16. ☼ Open M-Sa 11am-6pm.

dining with strangers

Do you find yourself feeling hungry and lonely on a Sunday night in Paris? Then you should head to Jim Haynes's home and grab dinner with him and about 70 other strangers. Haynes, once a very important and influential figure in the UK underground scene in the '60s, has hosted a dinner party every Sunday night for the past 30 years with no plans of stopping. Everyone is welcome, but reservations must be made on his website, ▧www.jim-haynes.com. Spots are first-come, first-served, and only the first 60 to 70 people will be accepted. Guests from all over the globe will range from the semi-famous Parisian to an average Joe from Scotland. The menu is different every night, ranging from Indian food, to Greek, or even Japanese. Donations are suggested, usually around €25, and gladly accepted by Haynes, who donates the proceeds to a charity. More than 120,000 guests have been in his studio since the tradition started, and more will continue to go every Sunday night. If you ever want to meet that Lebanese master pianist you've read about, chances are they'll be at Jim's place.

LE COUP D'ETAT

✦☕ CAFE, BRASSERIE ❷

164 Rue Saint-Honoré

☎01 42 60 27 66

Perfectly located for a coffee or meal before or after your Louvre visit, Le Coup d'Etat looks out on the famous museum, if you're well placed on the terrace. Food is tasty and not ridiculously expensive, but nothing special: just traditional French cuisine. Le Coup d'Etat hopes there would never be a coup d'etat, because it would instantly lose all of its tourist customers.

✚ ⓂLouvre-Rivoli. Ⓢ Entrées €7-13. Plats €13-18. Desserts €6. ☼ Open daily 7am-2am.

AU CHIEN QUI FUME

✦ SEAFOOD, TRADITIONAL ❹

33 rue du Pont Neuf

☎01 42 92 00 24 ▧www.auchienquifume.com

Au Chien Qui Fume has been a staple of the Parisian dining scene since 1740. Chefs arrange mouth-watering seafood platters at the oyster bar (tantalizingly visible from the street). The seafood is fresh from the market the same day. A traditionally decorated dining room and terrace portray the unmistakable class of this establishment, which is arguably Paris' number one for oysters and seafood. The crowd tends to be pretty old or touristy; the former just trying to revisit the "good old days" and escape the dreadfully multicultural modern Paris, the latter falling into a particularly delicious tourist trap.

✚ ⓂLes Halles. Ⓢ Menus €24.90, €32.98, €37.90. Plats €17.50-29.60. ☼ Open daily noon-2am.

AU P'TIT GORGEON

✦🍷 BRASSERIE ❶

76 rue de Richelieu

☎01 42 86 13 19

You'll feel right at home at this small brasserie; family pictures and jovial regulars are fixtures. Frequented by businessmen and neighborhood regulars alike, and hopefully a few tourists (that's you). The food is rich and tasty, perfect for a reasonably priced midday retreat to replenish the energy tanks. The owner and waitress at lunch somehow keeps her wits about her in dealing with an often demanding crowd. Nothing fancy, but it will get you from one point to another, leave a good taste and an ever better impression.

[M]Quatre Septembre. [$] Sandwiches €3.20-6.50. Entrées €4.50-6.50. Plats €12.50-14. Grands plateaux €13. ⏰ M-Sa noon-2pm and 7pm-9pm.

LES NOCES DE JEANNETTE

🍴🍸 TRADTIONAL ❷

9 rue d'Amboise ☎ 01 42 96 36 89 💻www.lesnocesdejeannette.com

Boasting five dining rooms (a couple are almost always used for private occasions) each with a slightly different feel, Les Noces de Jeannette is a good deal for a high end dining experience. In the Bistrot Côté Ciné, for example,'50s and '60s movie posters hang from the walls, while the Bistrot Côté Opéra is decorated with opera posters and advertisements. Menus will please the traditionalists among our readers; nothing new for the relatively conservative and business-minded 2nd arrondissement. If there's a place to try the classically French dish *Andouillette*, it's here. Let's just say it's a very... specific taste. Ask your waiter what's inside after you enjoy it.

[M]Richelieu Druout. [$]Menu Jeannette €28. Entrées €8. Plats €18. Desserts €8. Wine by the bottle €25-85. ⏰ Open daily noon-2pm and 7-10pm.

AU VIEUX COMPTOIR

🍴🍸 WINE BAR ❸

17 rue des Lavandières Sainte-Opportune ☎01 45 08 53 08 💻www.au-vieux-comptoir.com

Located smack dab in the middle of the Saint-Germain l'Auxerrois neighborhood right off rue de Rivoli, Au Vieux Comptoir proposes a wide selection of wines and traditional cuisine. This is a good spot for a delicious glass of wine and appetizer before dinner, or for a full meal. Classy bar-goers enjoy spirits alongside dining families. Ingredients are fresh from their respective regions (meats from Alsace and Basque regions). Wine choices are copious and span a wide price range; wine bottles for take-out are available at discounted prices.

[M]Chatelet. [$] Formule lunch €13. Entrées €10-15, plats €16-25. Wine by the bottle €22-166. ⏰ Open M-Sa 10am-midnight.

LA BOURSE OU LA VIE

🍴 TRADITIONAL ❸

12 rue Vivienne ☎01 42 60 08 83

A great date spot for those seeking to fire up a romance in the city of lights, one of life's greatest existential questions, La Bourse ou La Vie? (Money or Life?) comes in the form of a charming small dining room with lots of bright colors, and unfortunately thin metal chairs that only get comfortable about halfway through your meal. In the summer time, the front window lets in a delicious waft of air, creating a truly heavenly forum for after-dinner conversations. The options are tasty, but somewhat predictable takes on traditional gastronomy: steak au poivre, foie gras, etc.

[M]Bourse. [$] Plats €15-23.50. Desserts €5-6. ⏰ Open M-F noon-3pm and 7-10pm.

MUSCADE

🍴 TEA HOUSE ❷

36 rue de Montpensier ☎01 42 97 51 36

Mixing Mediterranean and British tea traditions, La Muscade is located in the northwest corner of the Palais Royal. A less-frills (but still a few, nonetheless) version of the neighborhood's older, more prestigious tea salons. The indoors tea room boasts an unpretentious black-and-white checkered floor, black-and-white chairs, and a black menu chalkboard with white writing on it (imagine that!). Something about black and white must get you in the mood for tea, because it sure is delicious at Muscade. The only tough part is picking between the 23 tea options. Given its prime location in the courtyard of the Palais Royal and its high quality, you might want to make a reservation.

✚ ⓂPyramides. Ⓢ Pastries €7. Tea €5.50. ⌚ Open Tu-Sa 10am-10:30pm, Su 10am-7pm. Tea served daily 3-7pm.

LE GRAND COLBERT
2 rue Vivienne

✒ TRADITIONAL ❹

☎01 42 86 87 88 ▣www.legrandcolbert.fr

Waiters dressed to the nines, tall ceilings, and a beautiful dining room add a touch of old-school French class to this popular restaurant which specializes in fish and, to a lesser extent, meat dishes. While the prices are a bit steep, you get your money's worth (if that's even possible when food is this expensive) if you forget about your wallet and slip into the refined mood at Le Grand Colbert. From 3-6pm in the afternoon, the establishment doubles as a tea salon.

✚ ⓂPyramides. ⓘ Formule Lunch €29.50, Formule dinner €23.50-€38. Hot drink and pastry €12-14. Entrees €10-24. Plats €18-35. ⌚ Open daily noon-1am. Tea served 3-6pm.

the marais

Though at times it can feel like eating in the 4ème is less about food and more about how you look eating it, there are a number of quality restaurants here, specializing in everything from regional French cuisine to New Age fusion. This is not the cheapest place to lunch, but if you're ready for a bit of a splurge, your appetite will be more than sated here, even if your bank account is not. Satisfy them both with the unbeatable lunchtime menus, or by grabbing a sandwich from Le Gay Choc or a falafel on rue des Rosiers for €5. If you decide on dinner, make sure you make a reservation at the hotter venues. Dozens of charming bistros line rue St-Martin, and kosher food stands and restaurants are located around rue du Vertbois and rue Volta.

▨ CHEZ JANOU
2 rue Roger Verlomme

✒✿☕ BISTRO ❷

☎01 42 72 28 41 ▣www.chezjanou.com

The food is so good here it inspires desert-island hypotheticals: if you were stranded on a desert island, would you bring an endless supply of Chez Janou's *magret de canard* or the best lover you've ever had? It's a tough one. Tucked into a quiet corner of the 3ème, this Provençale bistro serves affordable ambrosia to a mixed crowd of enthusiasts. The chocolate mousse *(€6.60)* is brought in an enormous self-serve bowl, though Parisians count on self-control. Over 80 kinds of pastis.

✚ ⓂChemin-Vert. ⓘ Reservations always recommended, as this local favorite is packed every night of the week. Ⓢ Entrées start at €8.50; plats start at €14 . ⌚ Open daily noon-midnight. Kitchen M-F noon-3pm and 7:45pm-midnight, Sa-Su noon-4pm and 7:45pm-midnight.

▨ ROBERT AND LOUISE
64 rue Vieille du Temple

✒ TRADITIONAL ❷

☎01 42 78 55 89 ▣www.robertetlouise.com

Defined by a firm belief that chicken is for pansies (let's not even talk about vegetarians), Robert and Louise offers a menu that's wholeheartedly carnivorous—we're talking veal kidneys, steak, prime rib, and lamb chops. The only concession to white meat is their *confit de canard*. Juicy slabs are grilled in the open wood-fire oven and then served up on cutting boards. There's a definite homey vibe here; you'll feel like you've been given shelter by a generous French family who found you abandoned and shivering when they were coming back from a hunt.

✚ ⓂSt-Paul or ⓂFiles du Calvaire. Ⓢ Entrées €5-16. Plats €8-18. Desserts €5-6. ⌚ Open Tu-Su noon-2:30pm and 7-11pm. Reservations recommended.

the marais

404

69 rue des Gravilliers

❄ ☙ ❄ ◿ MAGHREB ❸

☎01 42 74 57 81 ▣www.404-resto.com

A plain stone facade masks this hot restaurant of the moment—a sophisticated family-owned Maghreb restaurant specializing in mouthwatering couscous (€15-24) and *tagines* (€15-19). The romantic, rich decor of deep-red curtains and dark carved wood makes for mood dining, day or night. Seating in the airy, casual terrace in the back during lunchtime is particularly pleasant.

⧗ Ⓜ*Arts et Métiers.* *i* *Brunch berbère (€21) Sa-Su noon-4pm. Dinner reservations are a must.* Ⓢ *Lunch menu (M-F only) €17.* 🕗 *Open M-F noon-2:30pm and 8pm-midnight, Sa-Su noon-4pm and 8pm-midnight.*

PAGE 35

4 rue du Parc Royal

◣ CRÊPERIE ❷

☎01 44 54 35 35 ▣www.restaurant-page35.com

Owned by a triad of very accommodating gentlemen, this hip, modern art gallery-restaurant-crêperie sums up the spirit of the Marais with its extensive menu of light, fresh, and creative fare. Hordes of tourists come for the beautifully presented buckwheat crêpes (€10-15), French favorites (confit de canard; €15) and salads (€10-16). The dessert crêpes are fantastic; try the melt-in-your-mouth *crêpe au salidou* (made with salted butter caramel; €7.50). Theophile Gautier once lived in this historic storefront.

⧗ *Chemin Vert.* Ⓢ *Flash your Let's Go for a free Kir.* 🕗 *Open Tu-F 11:30am-3pm and 7-11:00pm, Sa-Su 11:30am-11pm.*

GEORGES

Centre Pompidou, 6th fl.

◣ CAFE, UPSCALE ❸

☎01 44 78 47 99

Cafe Georges is almost more impressive than the museum—almost. Between its steel design, aluminum and spleen-shaped party rooms, and pastel accents, the interior of the cafe itself is a true artistic experience only surpassed by the Parisian skyline; the view from the rooftop terrace is unbeatable. Dinner here may be unaffordable (plats €16-40), but you'll have a better (and cheaper) time drinking a glass of wine or champagne (€8-12). The menu was designed by Dior menswear creator Hedi Slimane, so dress to impress.

⧗ Ⓜ*Rambuteau* or Ⓜ*Hôtel de Ville. Enter via the center or, after hours, the elevator to the left of the Pompidou's main entrance.* *i* *Reservations suggested for dinner.* Ⓢ *Entrées €12-28, Plats €16-40.* 🕗 *Open M and W-Su noon-2am.*

food

MARCHÉ DES ENFANTS ROUGES

39 rue de Bretagne

The oldest covered market in Paris, the Marché des Enfants Rouges originally earned its seemingly politically incorrect name ("market of the red children"?) by providing shelter for orphans. The market is now a famous foodie paradise of hidden restaurants and chaotic stands. Comb through an eclectic selection of produce, cheese, bread, and wine, not to mention Japanese, Middle Eastern, Afro-Caribbean, and every other variety of ethnic cuisine. Parisians often duck in for lunch at one of the wooden tables, which are heated in the winter. The wine bar in the upper right-hand corner, L'Estaminet, is airy and relaxed and offers some cheap glasses (€3-3.50) and bottles (€5-25).

✦ ⓂFilles du Calvaire or ⓂArts et Métiers. ⓈWine €3-3.50. ⌚ Open Tu-Th 9am-2pm and 4-8pm, F-Sa 9am-8pm, Su 9am-2pm.

PALAIS DES THÉS

TEA SHOP ❹

64 rue Vieille du Temple　　　　☎01 48 87 80 60 ▣ www.palaisdesthes.com

Selling organic teas collected by the owners from 20 countries in Asia, Africa, and South America, the Palais has become a worthy rival of long-standing local tea fave, **Mariage Frères,** and as an added bonus fosters a less colonial vibe; all teas are fair trade, and the owners regulate estate working conditions. They may not have a *salon de thé,* but they do have over 200 teas, beautiful teapots (€40-165), and a welcoming, racially diverse staff eager to send you home with the perfect tea. Occasional free samples.

✦ ⓂSt-Paul. 𝒊 4 other locations around the city. Ⓢ Tea €3.50-120 per 100g. ⌚ Open M-Sa 10am-8pm.

EQUINOX

TRADITIONAL ❷

35 rue des Rosiers　　　　☎01 40 41 95 03

After the falafel storm on rue des Rosiers, Equinox comes as a welcome respite. Traditional French fare and a few crowd-pleasers (ahem, pasta and salads) are served in a warmly lit, charming stone dining room. For the price of three falafel specials, the three-course lunch or dinner meal comes at an unbeatable €15.

✦ ⓂSt-Paul or ⓂHôtel de Ville. Ⓢ Entrees €7-14.50. Plats €12-17. ⌚ Open daily Sa noon-3pm.

L'AS DU FALAFEL

FALAFEL ❶

34 rue des Rosiers　　　　☎01 48 87 63 60

Allegedly proclaimed "the best falafel in the world" by Lenny Kravitz and more modestly dubbed "the best in Paris" by its shouting employees, this kosher stand has become a landmark. Patrons line up outside for the famous "falafel special" (€5)—which, by the time you factor the balls in, is too big to fit in your mouth. Grab a fork if you're eating out.

✦ ⓂSt-Paul or ⓂHôtel de Ville. Ⓢ Falafel special €5. Shawarma €7. ⌚ Open in summer M-Th noon-midnight, F noon-7pm, Su noon-midnight; in winter M-Th noon-midnight, F noon-5pm, Su noon-midnight.

LE GAY CHOC

BAKERY ❶

17 rue des Archives and 45 Ste-Croix-de-la-Bretonnerie　☎01 48 87 56 88 ▣www.legaychoc.fr

A *boulangerie* with flair, and amazingly delicious goodies to eat. Le Gay Choc takes the idea of food as foreplay literally. Creative concoctions include honey and almond muesli loaf (€2-3), gooey *fondant au chocolat* (€2), and melt-in-your-mouth cookies (€1). Employees joke that you have to be 18 or older to see the *pain magique* (€2), which is shaped like a penis, naturally. The only Marais *boulangerie* open on Sunday.

✦ ⓂHôtel de Ville. Ⓢ Loaves of bread €2-3. Cookies €1. ⌚ Open M 8am-8pm and W-Su 8am-8pm.

the marais

www.letsgo.com ℗ **141**

CAVES ST-GILLES

♦ TAPAS, WINE ❸

4 rue St-Gilles   ☎01 48 87 22 62 ▪www.caves-saint-gilles.fr

A Spanish-style bistro outfitted with a mosaic tile floor, small wooden tables, checkered tablecloths, and a flamenco playlist. The menu is all *vino* and generous, filling portions of tapas *(€5.50-19)*. The multilingual staff speaks French, Spanish, and English.

⚐ Ⓜ*Chemin Vert.* Ⓢ *Tapas €5.50-19.* ⏱ *Open daily 8am-1:30am. Kitchen open noon-3pm and 7:30pm-midnight or whenever the lively crowd dies down.*

TAXI JAUNE

❋ TRADITIONAL ❸

13 rue Chapon   ☎01 42 76 00 40

A casual and convivial atmosphere as temporarily intimate as a taxicab draws a devoted crowd who delight in the creative and original dishes. Menu changes regularly according to the seasonal produce and the owner's whim.

⚐ *Arts et Métiers.* *i* *Reservations strongly recommended.* Ⓢ *Entrées €6-13. Plats €10.50-25. 2-course lunch menu €14.50.* ⏱ *Open M-F 8:30am-midnight. Kitchen open noon-2:30pm and 8-11pm. Closed 3 weeks in Aug and winter holidays.*

AU PETIT FER À CHEVAL

♦❋ TRADITIONAL ❷

30 rue Vieille du Temple   ☎01 42 72 47 47 ▪www.cafeine.com

A small oasis of chèvre, kir, and Gauloises, graced by a low-key (but never boring) crowd of locals and expats. Tucked away behind the bar are a few wooden tables where you can order traditional French dishes. The *tarte tatin* is a house specialty *(€8)*.

⚐ Ⓜ*Hôtel de Ville* or Ⓜ*St-Paul. From* Ⓜ*St-Paul, go with the traffic on rue de Rivoli and turn right; the restaurant will be on your right.* Ⓢ *Plats €6.50-20. Salads €9-13.* ⏱ *Open daily 8-2am. Kitchen open noon-1:30am.*

PAIN VIN FROMAGE

♦ TRADITIONAL ❸

3 rue Geoffrey L'Angevin   ☎01 42 74 07 52 ▪painvinfromage.com

A cozy and rustic Parisian classic with heartily comforting fare. *Fondues (€14-16), raclettes (€13.50-19),* and *croûtes compagnards (grilled breads with toppings; €11-19.50)* are accompanied by a winning wine list.

⚐ Ⓜ*Rambuteau* or Ⓜ*Hôtel de Ville.* *i* *Reservations recommended.* Ⓢ *Dishes €4-19.50.* ⏱ *Open daily 7-11:30pm.*

CRU

♦❋ RESTAURANT, BAR ❹

7 rue Charlemagne   ☎01 40 27 81 84 ▪www.restaurantcru.fr

Cru is a minimalist restaurant/bar in every sense, with a simple decor and not much in the way of cooking. The vegetables, meat, and fish here are expertly pureed, chopped, and sliced—and are always raw. The *plat/verre* deal *(€8; 6-8:30pm)* served at the bar and terrace is light on the *plat*, but it's a good way to get some food with a glass of wine. Courtyard is particularly pleasant.

⚐ Ⓜ*St. Paul.* Ⓢ *Plat du jour with coffee €14. Lunch special €19.* ⏱ *Open Tu-Sa noon-11pm, Su noon-6pm.*

FUXIA

♦ CAFE, ITALIAN, CHAIN ❸

50 rue Francois Miron   ☎01 42 72 22 74 ▪www.fuxia.fr

This rustic-chic cafe-restaurant-caterer whips up Italian food that would make even fat mothers in Tuscany proud. Inventive pastas with veggies, fresh cheese, meat, or seafood *(€9.50-17)* are all made with the freshest of ingredients and a little va-va-voom. Deliciously huge salads are also available *(€10-15);* for the less calorie-conscious, decadent Italian delicacies include panna cotta, tiramisu, and *crostata al cioccolata (chocolate tarte; €7).* Fuxia also sells imported olive oils, wines, and pastas.

⚐ Ⓜ*St-Paul. Rue F. Miron branches off the south side of rue de Rivoli and toward the river.* *i*

6 other locations around Paris. $ Plats €13.50-17. ⏰ Open M-F noon-3pm and 7-11:30pm, Sa-Su noon-11:30pm.

BREAKFAST IN AMERICA

AMERICAN [2]

4 rue Malher ☎01 42 72 40 21 💻www.breakfast-in-america.com

BIA promises to be one thing: "An American diner in Paris." It delivers. From the shiny red booths to the delicious fries, shakes, bottomless mug o' joe, and the expected post-meal tips, it doesn't get more American than this. This is still Paris, of course, so the whole diner thing is classed up a bit. The delicious brunch includes an omelet or meat and eggs, a stack of pancakes, a muffin, a brownie, or a doughnut and yogurt, plus an espresso or bottomless mug o' joe with OJ *(€15).*

 # [M]St-Paul. i Breakfast served all day M-Sa. Also at 17 rue des Écoles, ☎01 43 54 50 28. $ Milkshakes €5. Burgers and sandwiches €9-12. Student formule of burger, fries, and drink €8. ⏰ Open daily 8:30am-11pm.

PINK FLAMINGO

PIZZA [2]

105 rue Vieille du Temple ☎01 42 71 28 20 💻 www.pinkflamingopizza.com

This new kid on the block bakes up gourmet pizzas with organic flour and entirely fresh ingredients. Ambitious topping combos include bacon and banana chutney *(L'Obama; €14.50)* and eggplants, red peppers, and hummus *(L'Aphrodite; €13).*

 # [M]Rambateau or [M]St-Sebastien-Froissant. i Credit card min. €15. $ Pizzas €10.50-16. ⏰ Open M-F noon-3pm and 7-11:30pm, Sa-Su noon-4pm and 7-11:30pm.

LA PERLA

MEXICAN [2]

26 rue Francois Miron ☎01 42 77 59 40 💻 www.cafepacifico-laperla.com

An airy, colorful restaurant-bar that gives away free baskets of nachos but makes you pay for their specialty tequilas *(€7.90-30).* Traditional and modern Mexican food served non-stop, or, more accurately, between frozen margaritas *(€9.40).*

 # [M]St-Paul. Rue F. Miron branches off the south side of rue de Rivoli and toward the river. i Happy hour M-F 5-8pm. $ Nachos and quesadillas €6.30. Beef taco €10.70. ⏰ Open M-Sa noon-2am, Su noon-midnight.

CHEZ HANNA

FALAFEL [1]

54 rue des Rosiers ☎01 42 74 74 99

In the fierce falafel battle on rue des Rosiers, Hanna is a bit of a sore loser but better loved by locals because of it. Whether their falafel is better than L'As du Falafel's is a matter of taste, but it's definitely a more pleasant place to eat.

 # [M]St-Paul or [M]Hôtel de Ville. $ Hummus €4.50. Frites €2.50. Falafel €5. ⏰ Open Tu-Su noon-midnight.

CURIEUX SPAGHETTI BAR

ITALIAN [2]

14 rue St-Merri ☎01 42 72 75 97 💻www.curieuxspag.com

A rainbow-themed restaurant and bar where the walls are multicolored, and the patrons feast on generous helpings of spaghetti, risotto, or gnocchi *(€12-16).* A techno and hip-hop soundtrack sizzles in the background.

 # [M]Rambuteau or [M]Hôtel de Ville. i Happy hour 5-8pm, drinks come with a free snack pizza. $ Lunch formule €11.50. Buffet brunch (reserve 48hr. ahead) Sa-Su noon-4pm (€26). ⏰ Open M-Th noon-2am, F-Sa noon-4am, Su noon-2am. Kitchen open noon-midnight.

PETIT BOFINGER

BISTRO [3]

6 rue de la Bastille ☎01 42 72 05 23 💻www.flobrasseries.com

The classic Parisian bistro experience: typically French cuisine in a refined atmosphere with uptight diners. But there's a reason Petit Bofinger attracts those with upturned noses: the worth-the-splurge *prix-fixe* menu *(€19.50-26.50)* includes wine and all the greatest hits of fine French cooking. Across the street, the original Bofinger attracts an even older crowd dressed to the nines.

 # [M]Bastille. $ Entrées €7-20. Plats €16-25. Desserts €6-8. ⏰ Open daily noon-3pm and 7pm-midnight.

LE DÔME BASTILLE

🍴🍸 BISTRO, SEAFOOD [3]

2 rue de la Bastille ☎01 48 04 88 44

This elegant restaurant steams, grills, and bakes just about every type of fish for its refined patrons. Expect light, simple dishes of fresh *poisson*, like their *dorade* grilled with thyme *(€23)*. Also serves a variety of desserts, such as *tarte fine aux pommes (€7-8).*

⇆ [M]Bastille. $ Entrees €8.50-11. Plats €20-28. Desserts €7.50-8.50. ⏰ Open daily 12:15-2pm and 7:15-10:30pm.

about those snails...

If you're traveling to France, you're sure to get plenty of opinions on eating *escargot,* or snails. Lord knows why, but the snails have been eaten in this area since Ancient Roman times; today, the French are the leading consumers of snails in the world, and devour **40,000 tons** of them per year! A newly-developed (and slightly disturbing) industry, snail-breeding, became necessary when experts discovered that the diet of snails is not always agreeable to the human stomach. Since they eat mainly **decayed matter** and **wild leaves,** snails' stomach contents can occasionally be **toxic**. That's right; eating slimy creepy crawlers can be bad for you. The risks that come with consuming snails can be counterbalanced by removing their stomachs, keeping the snails in isolation for 2 weeks before consumption, feeding them only human-safe materials, or simply buying the snails from a trusted breeder. If you're thinking about a little **snail snack,** look for escargot prepared *"à la Bourguignone,"* with garlic, butter, and spices, or perhaps a *Feuilleté aux escargots*—snails in flaky pastry!

CAFE HUGO

🍴 CAFE [3]

22 pl. des Vosges ☎01 42 72 64 04 💻www.cafehugo.com

Named after the famous Romantic writer, this cafe gets Hugo's spirit right—it's all classic with a colorful flair. The only place on the pl. des Vosges to concede to affordability, and thus the only place whose patrons are under 60. The food is less remarkable than the atmosphere.

⇆ [M]Chemin-Vert, [M]St. Paul or [M]Bastille. $ Cold drinks €3.50-4.40. Plats €11.30-38. ⏰ Open daily 8am-2am.

BREIZH CAFÉ

🍴🍸☀ CAFE [2]

109 rue Vielle du Temple ☎01 42 74 13 77 💻www.breizhcafe.com

A rare find in many ways, this relaxed Breton crêperie is full of surprises. In a city full of duds, Breizh makes inexpensive and inventive crêpes with the highest quality ingredients (organic veggies, raw milk and cheeses, and normand sausage). In this extravagant and edgy quartier, Breizh offers a relaxed, welcoming, and understated atmosphere.

⇆ [M]Filles du Calvaire. i Reservations recommended during peak hours. $ Galettes €4-11. Crêpes €3.50-7.50. ⏰ Open W-Sa noon-11pm, Su noon-10pm.

ROYAL BAR

🍪 CAFE [1]

19 rue du Parc Royal ☎01 42 72 33 03

The walls at Royal Bar are lined with (tasteful) paintings of naked women and photos of Picasso, the artist who loved them; it's no surprise that people come here for dessert. The menu features delicious, homemade pastries *(€6-7)* and a decadent *chocolat chaud* or *glacé* with a small pot of *chantilly (whipped cream,*

€5-6). Be warned that the place can get quirky; the friendly owner runs it more like a hobby than a business.

⌗ *ⓂChemin-Vert. 💲 Wine €5. ⏰ Hours vary—and the owner insists upon it—but usually open daily about 10am-7pm.*

CAFÉ DES MUSÉES
💳❄ CAFE ❸

49 rue de Turenne ☎01 42 72 96 17

Part bar, part cafe, and part bistro, Café de Musées may be undergoing something of an identity crisis, but it draws a diverse crowd as a result; enjoy your *entrée* with businessmen finishing the workday, students with tattered backpacks, old couples enjoying morning coffee, and families out to dinner. The dishes here are mostly French with a creative twist.

⌗ *Chemin Vert. 💲 Entrées €5.50-15. Plats €12-23. ⏰ Open daily 8am-midnight; Kitchen open noon-3pm and 9-11pm.*

MARIAGE FRÈRES
💳 TEA SHOP ❸

30 and 35 rue du Bourg-Tibourg ☎01 42 72 28 11 💻www.mariagefreres.com

Started by two brothers who thought British tea was shoddy, this *salon de thé* has become a French institution in which white-suited waiters and sophisticated clientele invoke the colonial days. The establishment offers 500 varieties of tea *(€7-15 per 100g)* and an in-house book detailing the history and uses of each. It also sells a wide variety of books and tea kettles.

⌗ *ⓂHôtel de Ville. ℹ 5 other locations around the city. 💲 Plats €23-26. ⏰ Open daily 10am-7:30pm.*

BUBBLES
💳 DIET BAR ❶

4 rue Malher ☎01 40 29 42 41 💻 www.bubbles-dietbar.com

This "diet bar" is best known for its deliciously sweet smoothies *(banana, cocoa, and Nutella €4.50)* and its creative fruit juice concoctions *(orange, carrot, and ginger €4.50)*. The very attractive waiters and waitresses swear by the fresh soups and salads *(€4-7)* and hot dishes *(€7.50-10.60)*, but you might want to take their success stories with a grain of salt.

⌗ *ⓂSt-Paul. 💲 Soups and salads €4-7. Entrées €7.50-10.60. ⏰ Open M-Sa 9:30am-8pm.*

JADIS ET GOURMANDE
💳 CHOCOLATIER ❸

39 rue des Archives ☎01 48 04 08 03

As if it weren't the Marais's Willy Wonka's already, Jadis et Gourmande takes chocolate beyond the realm of delicious and into the realm of edible art, sculpting chocolate into everything from Eiffel Towers to pencils. Typical conformist squares with nuts and other toppings are available for shape purists. Custom-order chocolate messages are also available.

⌗ *ⓂRambuteau. ℹ 4 other locations. 💲 Chocolate objects €2.40-25. Chocolate €7.30 per 100g. ⏰ Open M-Sa 10am-7:30pm, Su 11:30am-7pm.*

MY BERRY
💳📶 FROZEN YOGURT ❶

25 Vieille du Temple ☎01 42 74 54 48 💻www.myberry.fr

It looks like the non-fat frozen yogurt craze has finally hopped the Pond. Based on the New York/LA shop Pinkberry, the yogurt at My Berry is just as delicious; light, tangy, and perfect with one of the many toppings. Mango, strawberry, kiwi, pineapple, granola, chocolate chips, almonds, and coconut are just some of the options. The perfect afternoon snack if you're willing to brave the lines on a hot day.

⌗ *ⓂHôtel de Ville. ℹ Credit card min. €15. 💲 Petit €2.80; moyen €3.50, with 3 toppings €5.90; grand €4.50/€7; special XXL €8/€12. Each topping €0.95. Smoothies €4.90-6.50. ⏰ Open in summer daily noon-midnight.*

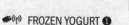

latin quarter and st-germain

The rule with food in these neighborhoods is not to eat on **rue de la Huchette** or at a cafe with English menus on one of the main boulevards. You'll leave with higher cholesterol and a lighter wallet. Venture inland a bit to find a host of terrific selections. The Comptoir Méditerranée is a great cheap lunch option, Così is a convenient cheap eat at any time of day, and Le Foyer Vietnam provides a nice switch from heavy traditional French cuisine.

SAVANNAH CAFÉ
27 rue Descartes   ☎01 43 29 45 77 ▣www.savannahcafe.fr   LEBANESE ❷

Owned by the friendly and omnipresent Richard Sahlani, this cheerful, tiny, yellow-walled restaurant serves a large selection of very tasty Lebanese food. Limited terrace seating is available as well. Try the noodles stuffed with spinach and ricotta cheese in a basil cream sauce *(€14)*. Yum.

⚤ Ⓜ*Cardinal Lemoine.* Ⓢ *Entrees €8-13.50. Pasta €14. Plats €14-16. Desserts €6-7.50.* ⓩ *Open M-Sa 7-11pm.*

COMPTOIR MÉDITERRANÉE
42 rue du Cardinal Lemoine   ☎01 43 25 29 08 ▣www.savannahcafe.fr   LEBANESE ❶

Savannah Café's little sister, Comptoir Méditerranée, is run by the same welcoming owner. A bit more of a deli than restaurant, Comptoir Méditerranée serves fresh and colorful Lebanese dishes, which can be easily ordered to go or consumed in the airy, if informal, dining room. The house lemonade incorporates a unique melange of spices and is not to be missed *(€2.20)*. Neither is the delicious baklava *(€1.30...or €2.60, because you'll want 2.)*

⚤ Ⓜ*Cardinal Lemoine.* Ⓢ *Sandwiches €4.40.* ⓩ *Open M-Sa 11am-10pm.*

COSÌ
54 rue de Seine   ☎01 46 33 35 36   SANDWICHES ❶

Find yourself in the touristy region of Paris and yearning for a high-quality, non-artery-clogging, cheap meal option? Così's got ya covered. Enormous, tasty, reasonably priced sandwiches are served up after being freshly toasted in the restaurant's brick oven. Above the register hangs a sign that boasts about Così's great clients and rotten staff; contrary to this comical message, the staff somehow remains friendly and smiling after a long day of dealing with tourists. This is the original Così that inspired the now-popular American chain. Upstairs dining room offers nice views of the crowded, happening rue de Seine.

⚤ Ⓜ*Mabillon.* Ⓢ *Sandwiches €5.50-8.50. Salads €4-8. Formules €9.50, €10.50, €11.50.* ⓩ *Open daily, noon-11pm.*

LE FOYER DE VIETNAM
80 rue Monge   ☎01 45 35 32 54   VIETNAMESE ❶

It's easy to miss this local favorite, whose meager decor foreshadows its meager prices. We suggest that you look for the crowds—Le Foyer de Vietnam is always packed, though it manages to keep hungry patrons waiting for only a few minutes tops. Portions are large but not unmanageable; try one of this hole in the wall's delicious meat- and spice-laced soups, followed by the duck with bananas *(€8.50)*. Wash it all down with the delicious and ambiguously titled Saigon Beer *(€2.60)*. Unconventional desserts prevail; ever heard of lychees in syrup *(€2.50)* for dessert? The restaurant appeals to everybody except tourists, offering student discounts on certain menu choices.

⚤ Ⓜ*Monge.* Ⓢ *Menus €9.20, students €7.50. Entrees €3.80-7.50. Plats €6.50-9.20.* ⓩ *Open M-Sa noon-2pm and 7-10pm.*

food

LE GRENIER DE NOTRE-DAME

🕊 TRADITIONAL, VEGAN ❷

18 rue de la Bûcherie

☎01 43 29 98 29

A meditative array of sunflowers, small eco-friendly lamps, and plants decorate this upscale cafe's patio and interior. A popular spot for vegans and splurging students conveniently located off the bustling rue de la Huchette, Le Grenier gives vegetarian specialties a French spin. Revolutionizing what it means to have "greens" as a main course, the autumn salad *(€16)* combines chestnuts, endives, feta, ginger, hazelnuts, honey, olives, and oranges. Overkill? Don't speak until you taste it. Known to veggie circles as one of the top vegetarian gastronomic spots in Paris.

✢ ⓂSt-Michel. Ⓢ Soups €6.60-6.80. Entrees €6.30-7. Plats €15.50-18. Salads €14.50-16.50. Desserts €5.50. Ⓒ Open M-Th noon-2pm and 7-10:30pm, F-Sa noon-2pm and 7-11pm, Su noon-2pm and 7-10:30pm.

L'HEURE GOURMANDE

🕊 TEA HOUSE ❷

22 Passage Dauphine

☎01 46 34 00 40

Tucked away on the quiet, largely residential Passage Dauphine, this classy and understated *salon de thé* boasts a quiet terrace and upstairs balcony that overlooks a beautiful side street. Cuisine-wise, selections range from salad to ice cream. While they don't go together well, the salads and ice creams are equally mouthwatering.

✢ ⓂOdéon. Ⓢ Cakes €4.50-6.50. Tartines €13-14. Salads €13-14. Teas €5-6. Ⓒ Open M-Sa 11:30am-7:30pm, Su noon-7pm.

CAFÉ DELMAS

🥐 CRÊPERIE, CAFE ❸

2-4 pl. de la Contre Escarpe

☎01 43 26 51 26

Two venues in one, Delmas is the place to while away the hours (stylishly) in a happening part of town. A modern crêperie and cafe on the stylish pl. Contre Escarpe, Delmas's menu boasts a wide variety of choices, from stylish cocktails to traditional cuisines to crêpes. Don't sit inside; the painted library in the back corner is a rather tragic decorative decision.

✢ ⓂCardinal Lemoine. Ⓢ Sweet crêpes €3.50-8.50. Salads €13.50-18. Plats €16-24.50. Ⓒ Open M-Th and Su 7:30am-2am, F-Sa 7:30am-5am. Happy hour 7-9pm.

CASA PEPE

🍽🍷 TAPAS, SPANISH ❸

5 rue Mouffetard

☎01 44 27 01 85 ✉ www.lacasapepa.com

The exterior of this charming Spanish restaurant on the tourist-frequented Rue Mouffetard is decorated with pictures of past soirees and pictures of Pepe himself with various Spanish athletes and celebrities. Every night, there's a guitar serenade that generally persuades the clientele to get down on the floor. Food is pricey, flavorful, and copious.

✢ ⓂCardinal Lemoine. Ⓢ Menus €20-22. Paellas €14-29. Tapas €15-17. Ⓒ Open daily noon-midnight.

JARDIN DES PATES

🍽🍷 ITALIAN ❷

4 rue Lacépède

☎01 43 31 50 71

Ideally located around the corner from the Jardin des Plantes, the Jardin des Pates combines a relaxed atmosphere and a lovely terrace with tasty, inventive, and fruity pasta dishes. Bright white plant-decorated walls and tiled floors evoke a yogi kitchen vibe. Selections are unconventional to say the least, like the avocado and melon sorbet *(€6)*. Sweet tooths, be warned that there is a somewhat paltry selection of desserts; for those with normal appetites, a meal here should do the trick.

✢ ⓂJussieu. Ⓢ Entrees €4.50-10. Pasta €9.50-14. Desserts €5.50-6.50. Wines €17-77. Ⓒ Open daily noon-2:30pm and 7-11pm.

AMORE MIO

♦✌ ITALIAN ❷

13 rue Linné

☎01 45 35 83 95 ▣www.amoremio.fr

A cheap Italian restaurant that cooks up simple dishes and offers tasty home-made desserts. The terrace is luxuriously large and shady on hot days; a familial vibe pervades the dark wood dining rooms. If you're lucky and pay in cash, your waiter might do a disappearing coin magic trick at the table; don't worry, he gives you back your money.

� ⓂJussieu. Ⓢ Entrees €7.30-15.50. Salads €12.90. Pizzas €10-13.50. Wines €16.50-69. ◷ Open daily noon-2:45pm and 7-10:45pm.

LE PERRAUDIN

♦♨ TRADITIONAL ❸

157 rue St-Jacques   ☎01 46 33 15 75 ▣www.restaurant-perraudin.com

Simple and elegant, Le Perraudin has a deep-red exterior decorated with old French ads and posters, a lovely, intimate garden seating option, and red-and-white checkered tablecloths; the setting is traditional and very relaxed. The restaurant offers a nice selection of traditional Parisian favor-ites: we recommend the *tête de veau* and *boeuf bourguignon*, with some *ile flottante* to finish off. Vegetarians and (God forbid) vegans should probably stay away.

✦ RER: Luxembourg Ⓢ Menu €30. Entrees €5.70-17.40. Plats €16-29. Desserts €5.50-11. ◷ Open daily noon-2:30pm and 7-10:30pm.

GÉRARD MULOT

⬤ PATISSERIE ❷

76 rue de Seine

☎01 43 26 85 77

A wide selection of succulent French pastries. Selections range from mundane croissants to flan to marzipan, and are laced with any kind of fruit imaginable. Widely recognized by locals as one of Paris' finest patisseries.

✦ ⓂOdéon. Ⓢ Macaroons €3. Tarts €3.50. Cakes €6.50. ◷ Open M-Tu 6:45am-8pm, Th-Sa 6:45am-8pm.

LE PETIT MABILLON

♦♨ TRADITIONAL, PASTA ❷

6 rue de Mabillon

☎08 99 69 80 00

Le Petit Mabillon specializes in fresh, homemade pasta, but successfully dabbles in traditional French cuisine. A small five-table terrace is lovely on beautiful nights, but the rustic, exposed-wood and brick dining room promises an equally lovely soiree. The owner chats it up with customers regularly, so sharpen up your French before heading to lunch or dinner here.

✦ ⓂMabillon. Ⓢ Entrees €4.30-9.50. Pasta €10.50-11. Meats €12-13.50. Menu €15.80. ◷ Open M 7-11pm, Tu-Su noon-11pm.

GUEN-MAÏ

♦ VEGAN, EPICERIE ❶

6 rue Cardinale

☎01 43 26 03 24

This healthy-living oasis might have more appeal for vegetarians and vegans than for carnivores (though they do have fish); anyone who craves seitan and soy will find a little slice of macrobiotic heaven here. Also a lunch restaurant, this is a great alternative to yet another heavy traditional French meal; flush out the butter, oil, and richness with one of Guen's homemade vegetarian op-tions. The all-natural food products are made completely in-house. The lunch counter quadruples as a *salon de thé*, food market, bookstore, and vitamin boutique.

✦ ⓂMabillon. Ⓢ Lunch menu entrees €3-5. Plats €7-12.50. Desserts €5. ◷ Open M-Sa 9:30am-8:30pm.

LE BISTROT D'HENRI

♦✌ TRADITIONAL ❷

16 rue Princesse

☎01 46 33 51 12

This Left Bank bistro's offerings are fashioned with the freshest, albeit heavy, ingredients. The outdoors is unmistakably covered in travel-guide recommendations, while the interior portion is a dimly lit small dining room. Let's Go just had to hop on the bandwagon. Around the corner is Le Machon d'Henri *(8 rue Guisarde* ☎ *01 43 29 08 70)*, with the same menu in a smaller, white-stone alcove.

⌗ ⓂMabillon. Ⓢ Entrees €7-15. Plats €14-23. Wines €21-38. ⌚ Open M-Sa noon-2:30pm and 7-11:30pm.

LE COMPTOIR DU RELAIS

9 carrefour de l'Odéon

🍽⍦ BISTRO ❷
☎01 44 27 07 97

A tourist trap that Let's Go still recommends, Le Comptoir has a menu that's diverse and surprisingly sharp on all accounts. The young local crowd is the highlight of this experience; fashionable and self-conscious types unabashedly use the Comptoir's sparkly clean wine glasses as mirrors while they scoff at the poorly clad commoners walking by. The place is always super crowded, so don't expect to be seated immediately if you come at peak lunch and dinner hours. While Le Comptoir is admittedly pretty pricey, the lunch *formules* are definitely a bit more affordable.

⌗ ⓂOdéon. Ⓢ Entrees €7.10-16.50. Salads €13.40-17.80. Beer €4.80-9.40. Plats €14.90-27. Lunch formules €16.90-21.50. ⌚ Open M-Th noon-midnight, F-Sa noon-2am, Su noon-midnight.

for crêpes sake

What is it about crêpes that everybody loves so much? They seem to be deliciously justifiable at any time of day: the satisfaction of a breakfast craving for those with a sweet tooth, a postprandial snack, a light meal, or, better yet, an indulgent snack once night life has wound down.

For Americans, they're like pancakes, but somehow a touch better. Be wary, however, of patronizing the first crêpe shop that's kind to you. Wandering throughout any Parisian neighborhood, one will find at least a handful of small crêperies. Try to survey them at a popular time (late afternoon, or later in the evening) so that you can tell whether the establishment is up to standard. See for the French, crêpes have been around since the mid 19th century (when they were introduced to the palette of the upper classes), and they're at this point a staple of the cuisine française.

That means that if there's a line of locals, or, if the seats are full of locals, it's a go. Many crêperies appreciate unsuspecting American customers a bit too much (i.e., as their entire patronage). If the spot is empty, it might be because they toss precooked crêpes in a microwave, put in a somewhat meager helping of Nutella and banana (which is the best combo), or generally lack pride in their crêpe making process. The best ones you can find are freshly wrought from a mix of eggs, flour, milk and butter, stuffed with your choice of filling, and handed to you by someone who exudes love of the game, folded into a triangle, and exploding with filling, a precocious visual portent of its lusciousness. Grab some napkins and a table or a park bench, and watch the world pass. Two of the most reputed crêperies in Paris happen to have the same street number: Josselin, 67 rue du Montparnasse in the 14th arrondissement, and Crêperie Bretonne, 67 rue de Charonne, 12th arrondissement. Crêpes tend to be best in the 14th near Montparnasse; many people argue that this neighborhood owes its excellence to being the location of a train stop from Brittany, whose immigrants introduced the Breton crêpe to Paris.

MARCHÉ BIOLOGIQUE 🛒 MARKET

Bld. Raspail between Cherche-Midi and Rennes

Under the leafy shelter of bd. Raspail, French New Age marketers peddle everything from seven-grain bread to olives and tofu patties. The selection caters to, but is not limited by, its largely vegan clientele; fish, meat and cheese are available en masse.

⇌ Ⓜ Rennes. ⏰ Open T, F, Su 9am-2pm.

invalides

The chic *7ème* is low on budget options, but there are a number of quality restaurants that are worth shelling out the extra euro. **Rue Saint-Dominique, rue Cler,** and **rue de Grenelle** feature some of the best gourmet bakeries in Paris, and the steaming baguettes and pastries make for an ideal picnic by the nearby Eiffel Tower.

🍴 LE SAC À DOS 💳🍸 TRADITIONAL [3]

47 rue de Bourgogne ☎01 45 55 15 35 💻www.le-sac-a-dos.fr

A neighborhood favorite, this intimate restaurant does French dining right—excellent food, good wine, and fresh bread cut to order. The standing red lamps and old books on mahogany shelves make Le Sac à Dos feel more like a living room than a restaurant, and the chummy proprietor's hearty jokes and attentive service really make the experience; don't be surprised if he (jokingly) asks for some of your wine. The *midi* and *soir formule* *(€16)* will give you the most bang for your buck.

⇌ Ⓜ Varenne. $ Burger and fries €14. Desserts €5. ⏰ Open M-Sa noon-2:30pm and 7-10:30pm.

🍴 LES COCOTTES 💳 TRADITIONAL [2]

135 rue St.-Dominique ☎01 45 50 10 31

Christian Constant, a famed Parisian chef, realized that not everyone wants to pay their left arm and right leg for a good meal. Then he opened Les Cocottes. The fourth of his restaurants on the street, the food is just as delicious and half the price. Unsurprisingly, the house specialty is the *cocottes* *(€12-17)*, cast-iron skillets filled with pig's feet and pigeon or fresh vegetables. The decor is a sophisticated take on an American diner, with high upholstered stools at the tall tables, where you can get in and out pretty fast. The best quickie you'll ever have.

⇌ Ⓜ École Militaire or Ⓜ La Tour-Maubourg. $ Mousseline d'artichaut €16. Salads €10-12. Mousse au chocolate €7. ⏰ Open M-Sa noon-4pm and 7-11pm. Closed on Su without reservation.

🍴 LA GRANDE ÉPICERIE DE PARIS 💳 SUPERMARKET, SPECIALITY SHOP [4]

38 rue de Sèvres

If a skinny, chic, Chanel-toting Frenchwoman took on supermarket form, she would become La Grande Épicerie. In addition to its near-obscene bottled water and wine display (€30 for water? seriously?), this celebrated gourmet food store features all things dried, canned, smoked, and freshly baked in itsy-bitsy packets. The butcher actually has a thin twirled mustache. We thought only cartoon French people looked like that. Most items here are overpriced, so it's better to treat La Grande Épicerie de Paris as a fascinating anthropological sample than a supermarket. You might want to avoid the American food section, which showcases such treasured "traditional" cuisine as marshmallows, brownie mix, and Hershey's syrup. The market's refined local patrons cluck their tongues disapprovingly as they walk down the aisle; it's kind of embarrassing.

✻ Ⓜ*Vaneau.* Ⓢ *Water €30; this place is way too expensive for you.* ☒ *Open M-Sa 8:30am-9pm.*

BARTHÉLÉMY

51 rue de Grenelle

✻ SPECIALTY SHOP ❸

☎01 45 48 56 75

A cheese lover's dream. Every type of cheese imaginable is stacked in this small *fromagerie* from top shelf to bottom, and it has the smell to prove it. A little lamb statue sits innocently by the door, as if to say, "You're welcome." A small selection of chocolate and pastries is sold as well. As quintessentially French as Barthélémy's may be, the proprietress does not seem to view her shop as a tourist attraction and gets a little flippy if you start taking pictures, so be sure to remain respectful.

✻ Ⓜ*Rue de Bac.* Ⓢ *Boulamour raisins €6.50.* ☒ *Open Tu-F 8:30am-1pm and 4-7:15pm, Sa 8:30am-1:30pm and 3-7pm.*

CAFÉ DES LETTRES

53 rue de Verneuil

✻⚭♿♁ CAFE ❸

☎01 42 22 52 17

Close to the Musée d'Orsay, this Scandinavian restaurant offers a refreshing, if sacrilegious, change from the required dishes on most French menus; try the *oeur de rumsteak facon strogonoff* (€22). The inner courtyard is dotted with statues, and fosters a relaxing atmosphere.

✻ Ⓜ*Solférino.* Ⓢ *Rumble d'aubergines et chevre €9. Duo gambas et St-Jacques €26. Formule €18.50.* ☒ *Open June M-F noon-2:30pm and 8-10:30pm, Sa-Su noon-7pm; July-May M-F noon-2:30pm and 8-10:30pm.*

DEBAUVE ET GALLAIS

30 rue des Sts-Pères

✻ CHOCOLATIER, TEA SHOP ❸

☎01 45 48 54 67 ▤www.debauve-et-gallais.com

Chocolate is an ancient vice. Marie Antoinette, Louis XVIII, Charles X, and Louis-Phillippe all apparently favored it dark and unsweetened, and Debauve de Gallais was not one to disappoint them. Founded in 1800, this *chocolatier* and tea shop was once an official producer for the kings and queens of France. The local institution continues to produce chocolates without additives, dyes, or sweeteners. Prices are steep, but it's worth the splurge.

✻ Ⓜ*St-Germain-des-Prés* or Ⓜ*Sèvres-Babylone.* Ⓢ *Chocolate nougat €10. Amandas (chocolate with almonds) €3.90.* ☒ *Open M-Sa 9am-7pm.*

AU PIED DE FOUET

45 rue de Babylone

✻❄ CAFE ❷

☎01 47 05 12 27 ▤www.aupieddefouet.com

One of the cheaper options in the otherwise pricey 7ème, this pleasant cafe has good, simple food at a fair price. The iconic red-checkered table cloths add a typically French feel; the loft seating makes it feel like a wood cabin.

✻ Ⓜ*Vaneau.* *i* *Other locations at 3 rue St-Benoit, 6ème (☎01 42 96 59 10) and 96 rue Oberkampf, 11ème (☎01 48 06 46 98).* Ⓢ *Plats €10.70. Filet de merlon à la crème d'estregon €10.90. Fondant au chocolate €3.* ☒ *Open Sept-July M-Sa noon-2:30pm and 7-11pm.*

STÉPHANE SECCO

20 rue Jean-Nicot

✻ SPECIALTY SHOP ❷

☎01 43 17 35 20

Formerly the popular Poujaran, this beautiful *boulangerie-pâtisserie* has changed ownership and only gotten better; Parisians are talking about its macaroons, and the baskets of apples, stacked jars of honey, and wide range of salads, quiches, and tarts make this a great place to stock up before picnicking at the nearby Champs de Mars.

✻ Ⓜ*La Tour-Maubourg.* *i* *Another location at 25 bd. de Grenelle, 15ème.* Ⓢ *Macaroons €1-2.* ☒ *Open Tu-Sa 8am-8:30pm.*

invalides

LOTUS BLANC

✈ ✤ VIETNAMESE ❷

45 rue de Bourgogne

☎01 45 55 18 89

This small restaurant has been serving authentic Vietnamese dishes for over 30 years. The steamed specialties prove you don't have to trek down to Chinatown to get good Asian food; try the prawn *siu mai* or pork balls *(€7)*. The restaurant is situated below street level, and its oppressive stone walls make it feel like a Parisian cave.

✦ Ⓜ*Varenne.* Ⓢ *Express midi €11.90. Entree, plat, and rice €13.90.* ⏰ *Open M-Sa noon-2:30pm and 7:30-11pm.*

CAFÉ DU MARCHÉ

✈ ✤ ✤ ✤ CAFE ❷

38 rue Cler

☎01 47 05 51 27

On the quaint, cobbestoned rue Cler, this cafe has a jovial atmosphere. A popular spot for tourists, it loses much of its French feel and could do a better job with the food. The drinks are delicious, though *(cocktails €5.50)*.

✦ Ⓜ*École Militaire.* Ⓢ *Salads €9.50. Plats €10.50.* ⏰ *Open M-Sa 7am-midnight. Kitchen open 11am-11pm.*

champs-élysées

Once the center of Paris' most glamorous dining and world-class cuisine, the 8*ème's* culinary importance is on the decline, but its prices are not. There are still plenty of extravagant establishments, particularly south of the Champs-Élysées, but few of them merit the small investment required to eat there. The best affordable restaurants are on side streets around **rue la Boétie, rue des Colisées,** and **place de Dublin.**

🔲 TY YANN

✈ CRÊPERIE ❶

10 rue de Constantinople

☎01 40 08 00 17

The ever-smiling Breton chef and owner, M. Yann, cheerfully prepares outstanding and relatively inexpensive *galettes (€7.50-10.50)* and crêpes in a tiny, unassuming restaurant; the walls are decorated with his mother's pastoral paintings. Creative concoctions include La Vannetaise *(sausage sauteed in cognac, Emmental cheese, and onions; €10).* Create your own crêpe *(€6.40-7.20)* for lunch.

✦ Ⓜ*Europe.* ℹ *Credit card min. €12.* Ⓢ *Crêpes €7.50-10.50.* ⏰ *Open M-F noon-2:30pm and 7:30-10:30pm, Sa 7:30-10:30pm.*

🔲 LADURÉE

✈ TEA HOUSE ❷

16 rue Royale

☎01 42 60 21 79 🖳 www.laduree.com

Opened in 1862, Ladurée started off as a modest bakery; it has since become so famous that a Gossip Girl employee was flown over to buy macaroons here, so that Chuck could offer his heart to Blair properly. On a more typical day though, the Rococo decor of this tea salon attracts a jarring mix of well-groomed shoppers and tourists in sneakers. One of the first Parisian *salons de thé,* Ladurée shows its age but remains a must-see (and taste). Along with the infamous mini macaroons arranged in high pyramids in the window *(16 different varieties; €1.50),* this spot offers little that hasn't been soaked in vanilla or caramel. Dine in the salon or queue up an orgasm to go.

✦ Ⓜ*Concorde.* Ⓢ *Macaroons €1.50 each.* ⏰ *Open M-Th 8:30am-7:30pm, F-Sa 8:30am-8pm, Su 10am-7pm. Also at 75 av. des Champs-Elysées,* ☎ *01 40 75 08 75.*

THABTHIM SIAM

✈ THAI ❷

28 rue de Moscou

☎01 43 87 62 56

A Thai favorite where locals come for their curry fix. With embroidered tapestries, silk-draped chairs, and bronze statues, Thabthim Siam is an intimate

food

place to enjoy dinner for two. The rotating menu allows patrons to sample a wide range of Thai cuisine. As good as pad thai is, try some of their more exotic options—you'll be happy you did.

[M]Rome. $ Entrées €8. Plats €13-17. 2-course lunch menu with drink €14. ⏰ Open M-Sa noon-2pm and 7-10:30pm.

MOOD JAPANESE ❷

114 av. des Champs-Elysées and 1 rue Washington ☎01 42 89 98 89 💻 www.mood-paris.fr

Like the Asian woman's nipple that greets you at the door (don't get too excited; it's only a photograph), Mood is a matter of personal taste, and you may or may not think the restaurant warrants all the fuss. The sensuous mélange of Western decor and delicate Japanese accents reflects the fusion cuisine. The prix-fixe lunch *(€16.50-20.72)* might be the only affordable way to finagle your way into the surprisingly beige upper dining room.

[M]George V. ℹ Live music and DJ in the evenings. $ Entrées €9-17.50. Plates €16.50-35. Cocktails €18. ⏰ Restaurant open M noon-2:30pm, Tu-Th noon-2:30pm and 7pm-2am, F noon-2:30pm and 7pm-4am, Sa 7pm-4am, Su noon-2:30pm and 7pm-2am. Bar open M-Th and Su 5pm-2am, F-Sa 5pm-4am. Reservations recommended for the restaurant, required for the lounge.

FAUCHON MARKET ❸

26-30, pl. de la Madeleine ☎01 47 42 60 11 💻 www.fauchon.com

A Mecca of gourmet food, Parisians (and tourists) travel from far and wide for Fauchon's coffee, jams, teas, caviar, wine, chocolate, and other fancy culinary fare. Occupying two separate storefronts on pl. de la Madeleine alone, this traiteur, pâtisserie, épicerie, and charcuterie serves heaping portions at reasonable prices. Never fear—browsing is *a la mode.* You might succumb to the many tins of yummy though.

[M]Madeleine. ⏰ Épicerie and confiserie open M-Sa 9am-8pm. Boulangerie (bakery) open 8am-9pm, eat-in 8am-6pm. Traiteur and pâtisserie open 8am-9pm. Tea room open 9am-7pm.

FOUQUET'S CAFE ❺

99 Ave. des Champs-Élysées ☎01 47 23 50 00

Restaurants can only dream of this kind of fame. The sumptuous, red velvet-covered café once welcomed the likes of Chaplin, Churchill, Roosevelt, and Jackie Onassis. But as its gilded interior suggests, all that glitters is not gold. Today, Fouquet's is owned by a hotel and dining conglomerate, and the only celebrity spottings you'll see are the framed pictures on the wall. Still, it's an experience of quintessential old-time Parisian glamour, easy on the eyes and devastating for the bank account *(starters run upwards of €30)*. Best to buy a coffee *(€8)* and see and be seen.

[M]George V. $Plates €20-55. ⏰Open daily 8am-2am. Food served all day in the cafe. Restaurant open daily 7:30-10am, noon-3pm, and 7pm-midnight in the restaurant.

opéra

The Opéra district has a few classic food spots—**Chartrier** and **Saveurs et Coincidences** are particular favorites—but the area definitely suffered from the loss of one-of-a-kind restaurant Chez Haynes in 2009. Most of the high-quality, affordable options in the district are located in the St. Georges area.

SAVEURS ET COINCIDENCES FINE DINING ❸

6 rue de Trévise ☎01 42 46 62 23 💻www.saveursetcoincidences.com

Saveurs et Coincidences maintains a small, charming dining room; in the summertime, a few tables are set up outdoors and the front windows are flung open, letting the air waft in. Recently purchased by expert chef Jean-Pierre

Coroyer—a former semi-finalist in a national gastronomical competition—the new Saveurs et Coincidences combines traditional French cuisine with Japanese, Italian, and other global favors for a succulent and entirely unique collection of entrees. Ingredients are ridiculously fresh. According to the chef, the restaurant doesn't even have a fridge; ingredients are ordered and received from suppliers in the mornings, then sliced, diced and stewed the same day. This process costs Coroyer a good deal of returns, but he proudly declares that he isn't interested in ripping off his customers. It certainly shows in his prices which are incredibly lower than those at most cafes. The lunch formules are such a deal, it should be illegal; an entree, plat, dessert, and coffee combo is only €17.

✦ Ⓜ *Grands Boulevards.* Ⓢ *Entrees €8.60. Plats €14.20. Desserts €7.50. Formules midi €17, €12.50, €10.40.*

🏠 CHARTRIER
🍴♥ TRADITIONAL ❷

7 rue du Faubourg Montmartre   ☎47 70 86 29 ▣www.restaurant-chartrier.com

Chartriet has served French traditional cuisine, en masse, since 1896, and remains a unique experience that is not to be missed. Think Cheesecake Factory meets Friendly's family vibe, without the plethoric portions (portions are a good size here, just not disgustingly huge). We recommend the *tête de veau (that 's sheep's head; €11.80)*, and then some classic *profiteroles au chocolat chaud* for dessert *(€4)*. If you go alone, you'll be seated with somebody you don't know, which can either be a fantastic experience or a boring, very awkward one. Waiters provide rapid service and are patient with Americans, but only to a point; know what you want to order, because they've got their hands full. If you want to be guaranteed a table, we recommend getting here early—the line stretches about 200m around the block by 7:30pm.

✦ Ⓜ *Grands Boulevards.* Ⓢ *Entrées €2-10.30. Plats €8.50-12.20. Desserts €2.20-4.50. Wine €6.50-34.00.* ☪ *Open daily 11:30am-10pm.*

🏠 NO STRESS CAFE
● AMERICAN ❸

24 rue Clauzel   ☎48 78 00 27

No Stress Cafe adds an American twist to the cafe experience, and fosters an appropriately relaxed, American atmosphere (hence the name). The inside seating option has a Starbucks-meets-Cheers vibe, while the terrace hits you with a multi-colored bright table configuration. This is, unfortunately, a pretty expensive joint—the stress definitely hits when you get the bill. The giant salad menu should do well for vegetarians.

✦ Ⓜ *St. Georges.* Ⓢ*Plats €13.50-€17.50. Woks €15-18. Salads €14-€15.50. Desserts €7.50-€8.50.* ☪ *Open Tu-Su 11am-2am.*

KASTOORI
➤ INDIAN ❷

4 pl. Gustave Toudouze   ☎47 70 86 29

Kastoori offers tasty, hearty Indian fare at a collection of tables on the lovely Place Toudouze; the indoor seating area is cozier, with plush chairs and couches in a small dining room that doubles as the kitchen. Pricewise, Kastoori is a steal during the lunch hour *(thali du jour tasting plate €10)*. There are also plenty of veggie plates for the granola types among you. Waiters are quick to put their cigarettes down to replenish your carafe. Unfortunately, no alcohol is served here; we consider this to be a human rights violation.

✦ Ⓜ *Saint-Georges.* Ⓢ *At lunch (entrée, plat, naan) €10. Menu (entrée, plat, naan, coffee) €17. Desserts €5. Plats €7-13.* ☪ *Open Tu-Sa 11am-2:30pm and 7-11pm.*

COMME PAR HASARD
● TAKE-OUT ❶

48 rue Notre Dame de Lorette   ☎06 28 25 51 23

Comme Par Hasard is a small sandwich shop that offers affordable options, ideal

food

for take-out or a quick bite outside on the terrace (or inside the claustrophobic dining room). The sandwiches certainly aren't your standard *boulangerie jambon beurre* or *crudite salade tomate* that any student in Paris is all too familiar with. Try the "Pignon" sandwich with fig butter, smoked duck, and tomatoes for a flavorful, cheap midday belly-filler *(€5.10)*. The tarts and desserts are also tasty *(€2-4.60)*.

⚡ Ⓜ St. Georges. Ⓢ *Salads €4-6.70. Sandwiches €3.90-5.10. Plats €6.60-8.50. Desserts €2-4.60.*

LE SELECT

🍴 CAFE ❸

37 rue des Martyrs

☎01 53 20 00 67

This neighborhood favorite serves exceptional cafe fare to residents, and sports an exceptional terrace overlooking the bustling rue des Martyrs. Sip that latte outside and watch local schoolchildren terrorize pedestrians, frazzled parents try to discipline said children, and rebellious tweens saunter home with baguettes in hand for dinner. If people watching isn't really your scene, booths are available inside for families, and tables run along the sides of the restaurant around the fully stocked bar. The food is quite tasty; salads are prepared with fresh veggies, and the cuts of steak are thick and juicy.

⚡ Ⓜ Saint Georges. Ⓢ *Entrées and salades €8-15. Dinner formule €27. Lunch formule €14. Plats €9-19. Bottles of wine €18-36.* ⏰ *Open M-Su 7am-11pm.*

LE BRIGADIER

🍴🍸 CAFE, BRASSERIE

12, rue Blanche

☎ 01 48 74 87 16

A collection of small children and unbearably cute English spaniels run through this small and deliciously airy cafe; cat lovers are rumored to not be allowed on the premises. Nestled in a residential area of the *9ème*, Le Brigadier offers a relaxed vibe and reasonably cheap menu that make it a favorite with young local families. The "traditional" cuisine here is a bit uninspired; the house wine needs to breathe a little *(€3)*, and the panaché is made with Sprite *(€4)*. But really, when you need a stiff drink these are very minor details.

⚡ Ⓜ Saint-Georges. Ⓢ *Appetizers €7-14. Plats €19. Dinner formule €19. Wine by the bottles €21-31. Shots €6.50-9. Cocktails €4-7.* ⏰ *No official hours, but open for lunch M-F, dinner Tu-Sa.*

canal st-martin and surrounds

The 10ème has a few all-star food spots, and both just happen to be located on the Canal St-Martin. Stay away from the brasseries on the main boulevards, and make the trip down to the canal (specifically its side streets) to find great deals on great grub.

🍽 LE CAMBODGE ✦ CAMBODIAN ❶

10 Ave. Richerand ☎01 44 84 37 70 🌐www.lecambodge.fr

Le Cambodge doesn't take reservations, and Parisians of all shapes and sizes regularly wait up to 2hr for a table. You'd think Lady Gaga was in town; by the time the restaurant opens, the line at the door is already 20 ft. long. We recommend that you arrive 30min or so before opening time, so as to secure a table on the terrace or in the more secluded dining room—and avoid wandering around the 10ème at night. Incredibly, Le Cambodge is not overrated. This is some of the best Asian food in Paris, and the plentiful main courses will only run you back €9.50-13.

♯ ⓂRépublique. ⓢ Entrées €3-10.50. Main courses €9.50-13. Vegetarian plates €8.50-11.50. Desserts €4.50-5.50. 🕐 Hours can vary day to day, giving locals a legup on early opening notices. Generally, however, Open M-Sa noon-2pm and 8-11:30pm.

🍽 LA CANTINE DE QUENTIN ✦ MARKET, DELI ❸

52 rue Bichat ☎01 42 02 40 32

Foodies rejoice at this cozy, unique food spot right next to the Canal St-Martin. A market of many talents, La Cantine de Quentin serves as an epicerie, restaurant, and wine cave. The restaurant bit is only open for lunch, but the selections are divine. You can also buy a picnic basket loaded with cheeses, breads, meats, and wine (€20-27) and eat dinner along the Canal St. Martin. Quentin's epicerie also boasts the finest *foie gras*, pâté, and pre-cooked plates. The wines are (of course) mostly French and extend far beyond your average streamlined Carrefour selection.

♯ ⓂJacques Bonsergent or ⓂRépublique. ⓢ Lunch formule €14. Brunch menu €25. Beers €4-5. Champagne €8-9. 🕐 Boutique open daily 10am-7:30pm. Restaurant open daily noon-3:30pm.

POOJA ✦ INDIAN ❸

91 Passage Brady ☎01 48 24 00 83 🌐www.poojarestaurant.com

Indian cuisine in Paris is generally quite bad compared to what Americans—and certainly Brits—are used to, but if you really need your mango lhassi fix, the best place to go is Passage Brady. Ideally situated at the border between the 10ème and Opéra, just about every storefront on this street belongs to an Indian grocery store or restaurant. Pooja is one of the best. In order to maintain its prime real estate, the restaurant routinely smacks down the omnipresent competition that surrounds it. The food is good, but beware: the decor is just plain bad. Green astroturf carpets the terrace, and the windows have suffered from the enormous biological curry footprint inherent to Passage Brady. Aesthetically sensitive foodies should stay away.

♯ ⓂStrasbourg-St-Denis. ⓢ Lunch menu €12. Main courses €12-14.50. 🕐 Open daily noon-3pm and 7-11pm.

LE FLASH ✦ MOROCCAN ❸

10 rue Lucien Sampaix ☎01 42 45 03 30

Within walking distance of ⓂRépublique, Le Flash chefs up Tunisian and Moroccan specialties, kosher-style. Seriously. This eccentric fusion of traditions comes with slightly elevated prices, but the dinners here are reliably tasty, and always blessed by the Beth-Din of Paris. Observant Jews understand that this is quite the rarity in Paris.

♯ ⓂRépublique or ⓂJacques Bonsergent. ⓢ Plats €16-35. Sandwiches €8 (lunch only). 🕐 Open M-F 11:30am-3:30pm.

bastille

With as many kebab stands as people, Bastille swells with fast-food joints. But the diverse neighborhood also boasts a number of classy restaurants with an ethnic touch, many of which are cheaper than those in the more central *arrondissements*. The most popular haunts line the bustling **rues de Charonne, Keller, de Lappe,** and **Oberkampf.** In terms of food, the 12*ème* is a generally affordable *arrondissement*, where casual establishments serve a variety of cuisines, from North African to Middle Eastern to traditional French. Most of the better places are on side streets, scattered throughout the neighborhood. On **rue du Faubourg St-Antoine** there's a slew of nice but overpriced restaurants competing with cheap fast food spots; the **Viaduc des Arts** hosts a couple of classy terrace cafes where designers take up residence.

🏛 L'EBAUCHOIR

☞ BISTRO ❸

45 rue de Citeaux　　　　　　　　　☎01 43 42 49 31 🖳www.lebauchoir.com

Colorful restaurant packed with colorful people. Serves only European meats and fish with a creative twist. Notable wine menu.

✤ Ⓜ*Faidherbe-Chaligny.* **i** *Credit card min. €25.* Ⓢ *Lunch formules €12-22.50. Entrees €8-15. Plats €17.25. Desserts €8.* 🕓 *Open M 8pm-11pm, Tu-Th noon-2:30pm and 8-11pm, F-Sa noon-2:30pm and 7:30-11pm.*

🏛 CAFÉ DE L'INDUSTRIE

☞🍴 CAFE ❷

15-17 rue St-Sabin　　　　　　　　　　　　　　　☎01 47 00 13 53

There's a reason that podunk cafes specialize in coffee, but the menu at this one will make you forget it. Funky 20-somethings retreat to this bustling and shady spot and enjoy the extensive, fairly priced menu. The 3-course formule is a steal (€10.50); the chocolate cake is nothing short of divine (€3).

✤ Ⓜ*Breguet-Sabin.* Ⓢ *Plats €8-14. Desserts €2.50-6.* 🕓 *Open daily 10am-2am.*

🏛 LE BAR À SOUPES

☞🍴 SOUP BAR ❶

33 rue de Charonne　　　　　　　　☎01 43 57 53 79 🖳www.lebarasoupes.com

It may not have the most personality in the world, but it does have some of the best soups in Paris. The chef is committed to combos, like leeks and curry or zucchini and ginger. The salad and dessert selection is less spectacular.

✤ Ⓜ*Ledru-Rollin* or Ⓜ*Bastille.* Ⓢ *Soups €5-6. Formule midi includes soup, bread roll, salad, dessert or cheese plate, wine, iced tea, or coffee. Take away available.* 🕓 *Open M-Sa noon-3pm and 6:30-11pm.*

🏛 PAUSE CAFÉ

☞🍴⛱ CAFE ❶

41 rue de Charonne　　　　　　　　　　　　　　　☎01 48 06 80 33

Hipster glasses are an unofficial pre-req for working here. An alternative and lively crowd gathers on the large outdoor terrace and peruses the slightly uninspired menu; the daily chalkboard specials are more interesting. Run-down chic, but cool enough to be featured in the film *Chacun Cherche Son Chat.*

✤ Ⓜ*Ledru-Rollin* Ⓢ *Entrees €5-10.* 🕓 *Open M-Sa 8am-2am, kitchen open noon-midnight. Su 9:30am-8pm, kitchen open noon-5pm.*

🏛 LA BAGUE DE KENZA

☞ PASTRY SHOP, ALGERIAN ❶

106 rue St-Maur　　　　　　　　　　　　　　　　☎01 43 14 93 15

Parisians make pilgrimages to buy their own sweet bit from pyramids of Algerian pastries—most of which are built up from nuts, butter, honey, and/or dried fruits (€1.70-3). Fluffy or dense Algerian bread comes in all variety of fried flavors (€2.10-3.50).

✤ Ⓜ*Rue Saint-Maur* or Ⓜ*Paramentier.* **i** *Credit card min. €16.* Ⓢ *€1.70-€3.50.* 🕓 *Open M-Th 9am-10pm, F 2-10pm, Sa-Su 9am-10pm.*

bastille

L'EMPREINTE
TRADITIONAL ❸
54 Ave. Daumensil
☎01 43 47 25 59 ⬛www.lempreinte.fr

A domesticated jungle theme extends from the overgrown potted plants to the food; traditional French dishes are given an exotic twist.

⌗ Ⓜ Gare de Lyon. *i* Credit card min. €15. ⓈSalads €11-12. Plats €13.50-15.50. Formules €12.80-13.80 ⓏOpen M-Sa 7am-11pm. Kitchen open noon-2:30pm and 7-10:30pm.

LE CHEVAL DE TROIE
TURKISH ❷
71 rue de Charenton
☎01 43 44 24 44 ⬛www.chevaltroie.com

A festive Oriental restaurant specializing in grilled meat platters. Savory Turkish food served right up with Orientalist fantasies. Traditional Arabic music jingles and clatters in the background.

⌗ ⓂLedru-Rollin or ⓂBastille. Ⓢ Mezzes €6.50-12.50. Plats €12-15.80. Ⓩ Open M-Sa noon-2:30pm and 7-11:30pm. Oriental dancers on Sa nights.

MORRY'S BAGELS & TOASTS
BAGELS ❶
1 rue de Charonne
☎01 48 07 03 03

Trust the French to make bagels fancy; bold statements like the Magret de Canard *(bagel with guacamole, cream cheese and sundried tomatoes; €5.80)* and the Foie Gras *(€5.90)* are daring but delicious.

⌗ ⓂBastille. Ⓢ Bagels w/coleslaw €3-5.90. Desserts €1.50-3.35 Ⓩ Open M-Sa 8:30am-7:30pm.

LES P'TITES INDÉCISES
BISTRO ❷
2 rue des 3 Bornes
☎01 43 57 26 00

Opting for brighter colors and daring dishes, this vaguely tropical bistro defies the expectations of a typical French cafe. Rebel *plats* include gnocchi with a truffle sauce (€12.90) and lamb marinated with honey and rosemary (€15.90).

⌗ ⓂParmentier. Ⓩ Open M-F 8am-2am, Su 9am-1am.

CHEZ PAUL
BISTRO ❸
13 rue de Charonne
☎01 47 00 34 57 ⬛www.chezpaul.com

Chez Paul is as charming and warm as bistros tend to be, with mustard walls and a touch of class, farm-style. Don't let the obscenely long list of entrees distract you from delicious mains like pepper steak with cognac (€19.50).

⌗ ⓂBastille. Ⓢ Entrees €5.70-24. Plats €16-28. Ⓩ Open daily noon-3pm and 7pm-midnight.

CAFÉ CHARBON
CAFE/BAR ❶
109 rue Oberkampf
☎01 43 57 55 13

Still riding on its *fin de siecle* dance-hall days, this restaurant and bar continues to pack a steady crowd into its beautiful interior. Soaring ceilings and burnished mirrors make for some run-down glamour.

⌗ ⓂParamentier or ⓂMénilmontant. Ⓢ Espresso €1.95. Wine €2.90-€4.20. Beer €2.80-€3.60. Ⓩ Open M-W 9am-2am, Th 9am-4am, Sa-Su 9am-2am. Kitchen open noon-3pm and 8pm-midnight.

LE BISTROT DU PEINTRE
CAFE, BISTRO ❷
116 ave. Ledru-Rollin
☎01 47 00 34 39 ⬛www.bistrotdupeintre.com

The classy, artsy bistro sticks to its Art Nouveau roots, and maintains its faded dark wood paneling, curvy mirrors, ornate floral tiles, and ivy-covered facade with care. An outdoor table here is just the place for the sociable clientele to watch the 11*ème* whirl, clang, and honk by.

⌗ ⓂLedru-Rollin. Ⓢ Entrees €5.20-12.30. Ⓩ Open daily 7am-2am. Kitchen open noon-midnight.

RESTAURANT ASSOCE
TURKISH ❷
48bis rue St-Maur
☎01 43 55 73 82

One of the classiest eat in/eat out ethnic restaurants around. The extensive list of hot and cold entrees (€4.10-8.40) are a tempting way to warm up before the main course.

⌗ ⓂSt-Maur. Ⓢ Grilled plates €11-12.50. Ⓩ Open M-Sa noon-3pm and 6:30-11:30pm.

food

BABYLONE

21 rue Daval

📧 FALAFEL, SHAWARMA ❷
☎01 47 00 55 02

Distracted by the neon lights, snazzy music, and trendy atmosphere, you might forget that you're overpaying for Middle Eastern fast food. Still, if you're tired of the semi-sketchy and hole-in-the-wall places that usually sell falafel here, this upscale joint might be a welcome upgrade.

✦ Ⓜ*Bastille.* Ⓢ *Entrees €4.60. Shawarma plates €8.60-10. Falafel plates €8.60-9.50.* 🕐 *Open M 11am-3pm, Tu-F 11am-3pm and 6:30pm-midnight, Sa 11am-midnight.*

L'OGA

8 rue JP Timbaud

📧🍷 TRADITIONAL ❸
☎01 43 57 60 15 📧www.loga-resto.com

A leather-and-lace interior with red-and-black tables and mismatched antiques wed punk and old elegance for a kinky-posh mix. Le Brunch by L'Oga every Su with 3 *assiettes* to choose from Anglaise, Asie and Terroir (€24-26).

✦ Ⓜ*Parmentier.* Ⓢ *Entrees. €9. Plats €19.* 🕐 *Open Tu-Sa 8pm-2am, Su noon-6pm.*

AMERICAN BISTROT

74 rue de la Folie Méricourt

📧 AMERICAN FOOD ❷
☎09 81 86 99 72

A half-hearted stylish upgrade on a diner, with the prices to match. They serve up the classics like cheeseburgers (€12.50-15.50), sandwiches and bagels (€12-13.5). Strawberry and banana milkshakes (€6) are given a French feel and are dressed up with fancy names.

✦ Ⓜ*Oberkampf.* Ⓢ *Burgers starting at €12.50.* 🕐 *Open M-Th noon-3pm and 7-11pm, F-Sa noon-3pm and 7-11:30pm, Su noon-4pm.*

SARL CHISTOL

18 rue Daval

📧 BAR/RESTAURANT ❶
☎01 48 05 28 72

It looks and feels like a bar, but for six hours a day it masquerades as a restaurant. Menu is limited to the absolute French favorites (no need to get ambitious) like magret de canard, salmon filet, beef tartare, and roasted chicken.

✦ Ⓜ*Bastille.* Ⓢ *Plat du jour €9.50.* 🕐 *Open daily 10am-2am. Kitchen open noon-3pm and 8-11pm.*

MARCHÉ BASTILLE

on Bld. Richard-Lenoir from pl. de la Bastille north to rue St-Sabin

MARKET❷

Weave through stalls stacked high with produce, cheese, exotic mushrooms, bread, fish, meat, flowers, second-hand clothing, and housewares with a mob of Parisians. The choices are seemingly endless in the sea of items stretching from Richard Lenoir to Bastille.

✦ Ⓜ*Bastille.* 🕐 *Open Th 7am-2:20pm and Su 7am-3pm.*

MARCHÉ BEAUVAU ST-ANTOINE

on Pl. d'Aligre between rue de Charenton and rue Crozatier

MARKET❷

We don't know if local vendors sentimentally chose to set up shop in pl. d'Aligre because of its (verbal) proximity to Algeria, but it sure feels like they did; the market here is like a quick trip to a Middle Eastern souk. Halal butcher shops, florists and delis frame the line of stalls staffed by shouting men.

✦ Ⓜ*Ledru-Rollin, runs all along rue d'Aligre.* 🕐 *Produce market open Tu-Th 8am-1pm and 4-7:30pm, F-Sa 8am-1pm and 4-8pm, Su 8am-1pm.*

MARCHÉ POPINCOURT

on Bld. Richard-Lenoir between rue Oberkampf and rue JP Timbaud

MARKET❷

A less famous market in the 11*ème* with fresh, well-priced fruits, vegetables, meat and fish. The occasional vendor spices things up, selling essentials like socks, sunglasses, shoes, shirts, and underwear.

✦ Ⓜ*Oberkampf.* 🕐 *Tu and F 7am-2:30pm.*

bastille

butte-aux-cailles and chinatown

Unbeknownst to many a tourist, the 13ème is a haven for funky, fun and affordable restaurants. Bump elbows with locals over papier-mached tables in the crowded Butte-Aux-Cailles, or enjoy the unfathomable delights of Chinatown's many Asian restaurants. Eating on a budget never tasted better, especially in Paris.

CHEZ GLADINES
BRASSERIE ❷

30 rue des 5 Diamants
☎01 45 80 70 10

This no-fuss restaurant specializing in Southwest and Basques cuisine is a neighborhood institution. Rowdy patrons and starving students ignore the neighbors' pleas to keep it down, and continue to consume endless amounts of wine over huge salads (€7.60-€9.80). Come early to avoid long lines.

✦ Ⓜ Place d'Italie. Ⓢ Entrées €10-€15. ☾ Open M-Tu noon-3pm and 7pm-midnight, W-Sa noon-3pm and 7pm-1am, Sa noon-4pm and 7pm-1am, Su noon-4pm.

MUSSUWAM
AFRICAN ❷

33 Bld. Arago
☎01 45 35 93 67 ◨ mussuwam.fr

The new kid on the block, Mussuwam offers Senegalese cuisine in an area dominated by southern French restaurants. Creole music, chocolate brown walls, and a colorful decor creates an ethnic feel. Fresh juices (€5) are a highlight of the tropical menu.

✦ Ⓜ Les Gobelins. Ⓢ Plat du jour €15. ☾ Open M-Sa noon-3pm and 7-11:30pm, Su 11am-3pm.

TANG FRERES
SUPERMARKET ❸

48 Ave. d'Ivry
☎01 45 70 80 00

This commercial complex features a bakery, charcuterie, fish counter, flower shop, and grocery store. The mouth-watering smell will hit you like a bus. A good place to stock up on cheap Asian beer (Singha €1) and bags of nuts (€1.30-6). The instant noodle selection spreads an entire aisle.

✦ Ⓜ Port d'Ivry. ℹ Look out for number 44, and go down the stairs. ☾ Open M-Sa 10am-8:30pm.

LA BUTTE AUX CAILLES CRÊPERIE
CRÊPERIE ❷

33 rue Bobillot
☎01 45 80 07 07 ◨ creperie.labutteauxcailles@wanadoo.fr

Quieter than the surrounding neighborhood restaurants, La Butte aux Cailles Crêperie is like a calm retreat into a Southern enclave. The wide range of salty, sweet, and flambé gourmet crêpes (€5-8) are delicious, if somewhat forgettable. The award-winning cider is a different story (€3). You'll leave drunk and satisfied.

✦ Ⓜ Place d'Italie. Ⓢ Crêpes €5-8. ☾ Open Tu-Sa noon-2:15pm and 7-10:15pm, M 7-10:15pm.

LES TEMPS DES CERISES
TRADITIONAL ❷

18-20 rue de la Butte-aux-Cailles
☎01 45 89 69 48

Another popular option on rue de la Butte-aux-Cailles, the restaurant is a co-operative workers' society of production and more succinctly, a neighborhood fixture. The menu is extensive and the atmosphere is convivial, waiters are more apt to treat you like a friend than a customer.

✦ Ⓜ Place d'Italie. Ⓢ Plat du jour €7.50 (inside) €10 (outside). Entrees €7.50-€17. ☾ Open M-F 11:45am-2:10pm and 7:15-11:45pm. Sa 7:15-11:45 pm.

LE SAMSON
TRADITIONAL, MEDITERRANEAN ❷

9 rue Jean-Marie Jego
☎01 45 89 09 23

Run by a Franco-Greek owner, the restaurant offers reasonably priced options and generous portions. It attracts a slightly older, but local crowd.

✦ Ⓜ Place d'Italie, follow rue Samson off of rue de la Butte-aux-Cailles. ℹ Kids menu €11. Menu €18.50. ☾ Open daily noon-2:30pm and 7-11:30pm.

food

montparnasse

LE TROQUET

21 rue François Bonvin

✍♔ SPANISH, FUSION ❸
☏01 45 66 89 00

This place is worth budgeting for; if you have to eat at sweaty kebab take-out spots for a week, or even two weeks, to afford this, just do it. The food is simply sublime, and the prices are extremely reasonable given the quality. Original recipes developed under the supervision of master chef Christian Ethebest have their origins in traditional Basque cuisine, specifically from the Béarn region. Unlike some other super-gourmet restaurants you may have indulged in, the portions here are hearty. We recommend the caviar *d'aubergine* or the Basque *charcuterie* platter, which are both to die for. For main courses, go with the *joue de cochon* in red-wine sauce. The desserts are beyond tasty too. Menus change every three weeks, but the aforementioned items tend to make frequent comebacks. The service here is super professional and friendly. Could be tough for visitors with disabilities, since the dining room is very small and tightly packed. Expect long waits.

♯ Ⓜ *Sevres Lecourbe, off of Boulevard Garibaldi.* Ⓞ *Dinner formule €32. Tasting plate €40.50. Wine €23-77.50 per bottle. Midi entrée, plat or plat-dessert combo €26.* ⌂ *Tu-Sa 12:30-2pm and 7:30-11pm.*

ATELIER AUBRAC

51 Bld. Garibaldi

✍♿♔ TRADITIONAL ❷
☏01 45 66 96 78 ✉www.atelieraubrac.com/fr

Located a convenient stone's throw away from the Sevres-Lecourbe Metro stop on Boulevard Beaugirard, Atelier Aubrac is undoubtedly one of the cheapest high-quality restaurants in Paris. A newcomer to the Parisian fine dining scene, the restaurant serves up traditional meat-heavy French cuisine; what sets it apart is that all the meat comes from the mountainous region of Auvergne. Card-holding PETA members should be aware that this is not an animal rights-conscious establishment—on its Facebook page, the restaurant posts photos of animals that were sacrificed for customers' enjoyment. *Plats du jour* rotate, but certain staples always grace the menu. The icy fresh tomato, mozzarella, basil, and pesto appetizer cleans out your palate for the main course, and the chicken in *foie gras* sauce with rice is fantastic. Finish it off with a bowl of *fromage blanc aux fruits rouges*. If he has the time, the owner will clarify the menu, especially if you don't speak French and need some explanation in English. Reserve ahead for dinner, as Aubrac is catching on like wildfire.

♯ Ⓜ *Sevres Lecourbe.* Ⓞ *Entree plat or plat dessert €15, entree, plat, dessert combo €18, soir formules €22-28.50.* ⌂ *Open M-F 12-2:30pm and 7-10:30pm, Sa 7-10:30pm.*

LE DIX VINS

57 rue Falguiere

✍♿♔ TRADITIONAL
☏01 43 20 91 77

Located on a side street uphill on Bld. Pasteur from the Metro stop, Le Dix Vins serves up terrific traditional French cuisine at a reasonable price. This is undoubtedly a fine dining experience. In 2010, the restaurant won a prize from the prestigious *Confrerie Gastronomique de la Marmite d'Or* for its cuisine. Located on a quiet street, the restaurant's front windows open up on warm days, and air wafts through the two tightly packed dining rooms. The food is divine, but when we visited the chef told us to write down a few recommendations. For starters, try the artichoke hearts with *foie de veau*, then order the *filets de rougets à la Normande* for your first course. For dessert, the chef proposes the tartin de poires with a scoop of vanilla ice cream. The menu switches up periodically, but don't hesitate to ask the gregarious waiter for more suggestions. Technically wheelchair accessible, but it could be a bit tricky space-wise.

♯ Ⓜ *Pasteur.*

TANDOORI

10 rue de l'Arrivée

A trip to Tandoori will leave you incredibly full and mildly amused. The table-cloths and carafes are curry-stained, and the dining room has a funky, musky smell to it, which, unfortunately smells nothing like curry. We advise sitting outside if the weather permits. The beer selections are quite limited to the comically generically-titled *bierre indienne* (€6). The food, however, is pretty good. Despite some grossly over-buttered (and nearly inedible) *naan*, the meat and vegetables were tasty and rich. The lunch formule of entrée-plat or plat-dessert is priced very reasonably (€10 M-F, €12 Sa). There's a nice selection of vegetarian options.

‡ Ⓜ*Montparnasse Bienvenue.* Ⓢ*Entrees €6-20. Plats €10-20. Desserts €6-8. Drinks €6-8.* 🕑*Open M-Sa noon-2:30pm and 7-11pm.*

AU ROI DU CAFÉ

🍴🍷 CAFE, TRADITIONAL ❷
☎01 47 34 48 50

59 rue Lecource

Au Roi du Café is a cheap neighborhood hotspot and perfect for drinks or a casual, delicious meal. Service can be a bit slow at peak meal times, and certain glasses could stand, shall we say, a bit more time in the dishwasher. But plenty of locals dine, drink and suck down their fair share of cigarettes here, and you can definitely see why. Cocktails are served with a delicious and complimentary tasting plate of fresh marinated olives. The salads are copious, and the vegetables are very fresh. Simple, tasty, fresh, and well-presented French café fare. The drinks are reasonably priced (*cocktails €7, beers €4-8*), especially during happy hour (*cocktails, pints €5*)

‡ Ⓜ*Sevre Lecourbe, about two blocks down rue Lecourbe after its intersection with Bld. Garibaldi.* Ⓢ *Salads €9. Plats €10. Midi plat cafe €11.* 🕑 *M-Sa 6:30am-midnight, Su 6:30am-5pm.*

SAMAYA

🍴 LEBANESE ❷
☎01 53 95 03 81

21 Bld. de Grenelle

Just finished up at the Eiffel Tower or need to fuel up for the long line? Walk down to Samaya for a tasty, heaping serving of homemade Lebanese food. Take-out and eat-in options are available. The owner doubles as the only waiter, so while service certainly isn't slow, it can have some momentary lags. The dining room is very spacious, a definite rarity in Paris. Plates are garnished with a fresh salad. Meat is tasty and much less fatty than the options you'll find in other Mediterranean food spots. Samaya's a winner through and through. Wheelchair-accessible.

‡ Ⓜ*Bir-Hakeim.*

LE FILIPPO

🍴🍷 ITALIAN ❷
☎01 43 06 19 73

54 rue Cambronne

Located a short walk away from the Cambronne Metro stop, Le Filippo provides a reasonably priced bougie Italian food and a pleasant dining experience, if you can stand the brisk service smaller parties tend to get. The pasta dishes come in highly generous servings (*pasta with pesto €12*), which makes sense if you're on a budget. If you're not, choose from classic Italian fare and wines.

‡ Ⓜ*Cambronne. Walk up Bld. Garibaldi to its intersection with rue de la Croix Nivert, then take a sharp left down rue Cambronne past the Hotel Ibis Paris. Le Filippo is about 3-4 blocks down* Ⓢ *Entrees €7-15. Plats €10-22. Formule €16.*

TY BREIZ

🍴♿ CRÊPERIE ❶

52 Bld. de Vaugirard

☎01 43 20 83 72 ▪www.tybreizcreperieparis.fr

The menu boasts that this crêperie was elected the "best crêpe" in Paris. This is certainly a lofty claim, and while it's impossible to choose amongst all of Paris' delicious crêpes, Ty Breiz has got to be up there. Ty Breiz serves up Breton crêpes, and reinforces its down-home image with clogs and dark wooden walls. The crêpes are deliciously well-buttered; for salty crêpes, go with the filling La Savoyarde (€11.10), while for sweet crêpes try the chocolate specialité maison, a crêpe graced by the house's delicious dark chocolate concoction (€6.50).

🍴 Ⓜ *Pasteur, about two blocks down Boulevard Pasteur at its intersection with boulevard de Vaugirard.* Ⓢ *Kirs €4.30-8.10. Sweet crêpes €3.70-10.60. Salty crêpes €3.70-11.10.* ⏰ *Open T-Sa 11:45am-2:45pm and 7-11pm.*

passy and auteuil

Like everything in the 16ème, most dining options are on the pricier side, but the food is of the highest quality. If you're willing to spend a little more, the splurge is definitely worth it. Budget-friendly ethnic restaurants are clustered on **rue Lauriston**.

🏮 LES FILAOS
5 rue Guy de Maupassant

🍽 AFRICAN ❸

☎01 45 04 94 53 🖳www.lesfilaos.com

The first joint in Paris to specialize in Mauritian cuisine, Les Filaos provides an ethnic touch to the 16th restaurant scene. Delicious punches (€5) are made fresh behind the straw hut bar. Curries (€15-16) can be made as spicy as you like and are topped off with fresh fruit for dessert. Octopus is an island specialty. Saturday night features live Mauritian dancers.

🍴 Ⓜ*Rue de la Pompe.* 𝒾 *Prixe-fixe lunch €19.50, dinner €30.* ⏰ *Open Tu-Su noon-2:30pm and 7-10:30pm.*

🏮 LE SCHEFFER
22 rue Scheffer

🍽 BISTRO ❷

☎01 47 27 81 11

With red-checkered tablecloths, walls papered with posters, and an almost entirely local clientele, Le Scheffer is as authentic as French bistros get. Slightly tipsy diners chat loudly over the din of clattering plates and shouting waiters. Plats include fois de veau with honey vinegar (€15) and beef haddock (€15).

🍴 Ⓜ*Trocadero.* Ⓢ *Entrees €15-20.* ⏰ *Open M-Sa noon-2:30pm and 7:30-10:30pm.*

ROSIMAR
26 rue Poussin

🍽 SPANISH ❸

☎01 45 27 74 91

If Rosimar were a person, she'd be your grandma—you know, the one who's had work done, wears Coco Chanel, and likes to serve your friends cocktails. The floor-to-ceiling mirrors and pink-and-white decor give the place a feminine touch for a moneyed and elderly clientele. While this may not be the most happening spot, it does serve up some of the best Spanish food in Paris. The paella for two (€23) is a house specialty.

🍴 Ⓜ*Michel-Ange Auteil. Walk up rue Girodet to rue Poussin.* 𝒾 *Paella €23.* ⏰ *Open daily noon-2:30pm and 7pm-10pm.*

batignolles

If residents had to make a pilgrimage into central Paris every time they wanted a good meal, no one would live in the 17ème. Thankfully, good restaurants are a dime a dozen here, and the diverse population that lives here make for a wide array of choices, from ethnic to French to vegetarian.

🏮 BATIGNOLLES ORGANIC PRODUCE MARKET
Bld. de Batignolles

MARKET ❷

Stretching across Bld. de Batignolles every Saturday morning, the Batignolles

Organic Produce Market is a delectable jumble of sporadically-singing shoppers, hats, bottles of apple cider, scarves, loaves of bread, and obscenely large hunks of cheese, not to mention organic fruits and vegetables. Construct a gourmet picnic lunch with ease and schlep it to the nearby Square des Batignolles on a fine day. Prices vary widely.

✦ ⓂRome. *On the traffic divider along bd. des Batignolles, border of 8ème and 17ème.* Ⓢ *Sugar crêpes €1.70. Box of strawberries €6. Organic wool sweaters €45.* ⌚ *Open Sa 9am-2pm.*

▨ LE MANOIR
((•)) CAFE ❷

7 rue des Moines   ☎01 46 27 54 51

A true neighborhood favorite, Le Manoir is popular with the kind of cool, fun Parisians you'd want to hang out with. Local parents meet their children in front of the cafe's red awning to pick them up after school. The waiters here are so friendly you'd think there was a catch. When a certain intrepid Let's Go researcher left her computer in her nearby apartment, the young waitress offered to watch her drink for her while she ran home to get it. The menu is comprised of local standards and is particularly well-known for its salads (€11).

✦ ⓂBrochant. *i* Wi-Fi included. Ⓢ *Plats €13. Two-course menu midi €12. Salmon tartare €13.20.* ⌚ *Open daily 7:30am-2am.*

LA FOURNÉE D'AUGUSTINE
TRADITIONAL ❶

31 rue des Batignolles   ☎01 43 87 88 41

It's no mystery why La Fournée d'Augustine won Paris' medaille d'or in 2004. Luring in customers with the delicious aroma of freshly baked pastries, this boulangerie is everything you thought Paris would smell like: butter, chocolate, and heaven in general. The wide selection of desserts is reasonably priced (cakes €4; pain au chocolat €0.80). Fresh sandwiches (€3-4) and other lunch options are also available. The storefront can be hard to spot, so look for the white, wooden tiles painted with lilacs, and follow the smell.

✦ ⓂRome. Ⓢ *Donuts €0.60. Loaf of brioche €4.60.* ⌚ *Open M-Sa 7:30am-8pm.*

AU VIEUX LOGIS
🍴♿♻♨ BISTRO ❷

68 rue des Dames   ☎01 43 87 72 27

This standard French bistro serves standard French fare on standard red checkered tablecloths in a pleasant atmosphere and would be utterly forgettable if not for its absolutely delicious food and generous portions. No wonder there are so many regulars.

✦ ⓂRome. Ⓢ *Plat du jour €10. Plats €12-16. 2-course lunch menu €12.* ⌚ *Open M-Sa noon-3pm and 7-11pm.*

LE PATIO PROVENCAL
♨ TRADITIONAL ❷

116 rue des Dames   ☎01 42 93 73 73 www.patioprovencal.fr

Airy and cool with a trickling fountain inside, this restaurant tricks you into thinking you're outside. The menu features standard cuisine from the South of France, but the stone walls, black wooden benches, and sprigs of lavender recreate a peaceful Southern atmosphere.

✦ ⓂVilliers. *Follow rue de Levis away from the intersection and turn right on rue des Dames.* Ⓢ *Glass of wine €3. Greek salad entree €8.50. Confit de canard roti €16.* ⌚ *Open M-Sa noon-2:30pm and 7-11pm.*

JOY IN FOOD
♿♨♨ VEGETARIAN ❷

2 rue Truffaut   ☎01 43 87 96 79

In Paris, a vegetarian establishment is about as rare as obesity. This macrobiotic restaurant boasts an exclusively veggie menu, though a limited one, in what looks like your French mother's kitchen.

✦ ⓂPlace de Clichy. Ⓢ *Plats €9. Apple crumble €4.* ⌚ *Open M-F noon-2:30pm.*

food

3 PIECES CUISINE

TRADITIONAL ❷

25 rue de Cheroy

☎01 44 90 85 10

Moving away from the precious options on the rue Batignolles, this cafe provides a more funky, laid-back atmosphere. The menu is limited to cheeseburgers, tartines, and salads, but the portions are huge. Young crowds of locals and English-speaking tourists play Chinese checkers and French trivia games over brunch (*€10*).

 # Ⓜ Villiers or Ⓜ Rome. [$] Cheeseburger €12. Lexies croque €8. Salads €9. ⏰ Open M-F 8:30am-2am, Sa-Su 9:30am-2am. Kitchen open daily noon-3pm and 8-10:30pm.

BATIGNOLLES COVERED MARKET

♿ MARKET ❷

96bis rue Lemercier

Large selection of fresh produce, meat, cheese, and wine for weekday grocery shopping. Also sells ready-made Senegalese food.

 # Ⓜ Brochant. Entrances also on rue Brochant, 5 rue Fourneyron. ⏰ Open Tu-F 8:30am-1pm and 4-8pm, Sa 8:30am-8pm, Su 8:30am-2pm.

ETOILE DU KASHMIR

INDIAN ❸

1 rue des Batignolles

☎01 45 22 44 70

Specializing in Indian and Pakistani cuisine, the restaurant serves up a number of classics. The plain, cheese, and garlic naan are a specialty and reasonably priced *(€1.50)*, though prices can go up from there; we thought it was a sign that most of the customers were drinking Evian instead of tap water. Glowing decor features white tablecloths and engraved wood paneling. Many vegetarian options. If you want it spicy, say so; otherwise expect a fairly tasteless meal.

*# Ⓜ Rome. **i** Discount on takeout. [$] Menu express midi €7.50. Chicken tika masala €11.50. Vegetarian formule option €15. ⏰ Open M-Sa noon-3pm and 6:30-11:30pm, Su 6:30-11:30pm.*

buttes chaumont

✓ LAO SIAM

🍷 VIETNAMESE ❸

48 rue de Belleville

☎01 40 40 09 68

While most of the dishes here are cheap, Lao Siam sneaks a few more euro from your wallet by charging separately for rice *(€2.20)*. The decor is nothing fancy. Paper napkins leave no room for pretension; old-fashioned miniature figures mix awkwardly alongside their younger anime-influenced compatriots. But the food speaks louder than the decor, and the place is generally packed. The *filet du poisson* with "hip-hop" sauce *(€8.80)* is not to be missed. Lots of very tasty and salty duck selections.

 # Ⓜ Belleville. [$] Plats €6.80-22. Entrees €7-10.80. Wine bottles €11-55. Beer €3.50. ⏰ Open daily noon-3pm and 7-11pm.

✓ L'ATLANTIDE

🍷 NORTH AFRICAN ❷

7 av. Laumière

☎01 42 45 09 81 🖥www.latlantide.fr

A relatively hard-to-find type of restaurant in Paris, L'Atlantide practices true North African *gastronomie*, using meats and spices coming directly from the mountains of North Africa. If you can stand a lot of Oriental-rug patterning (rugs, tablecloths, and waiters' aprons are all coordinated), you'll get a nice hearty plate of couscous you won't forget.

 # Ⓜ Laumière. [$] Entrees €5.50-10. Couscous €11-19.50. Plats €13-19.50. Vins €12.50-22.50. ⏰ Open M-F 7-10:30pm, Sa-Su 12-2:30pm and 7-10:30pm.

LA KASKAD' CAFÉ
💵 CAFE ❹

2 pl. Armand-Carrel ☎01 40 40 08 10

Just outside the Parc des Buttes-Chaumont, La Kaskad' nets its fair share of unsuspecting—and suspecting—visitors. Their spacious wrap-around terrace is a perfect place to relax after a stroll in the Parc des Buttes-Chaumont. Varied, American-friendly cuisine includes palatial sundaes *(€7.50-9)*. You know what you're getting into, but you'll be properly fed and ready to get into the Buttes.

🚏 ⓂLaumière. $ Entrees €4.90-12.90. Plats €12.90-18.90. Lunch formule €14.90. ⏰ Open daily 7:30am-2am.

LA BOULANGERIE PAR VÉRONIQUE MAUCLER
💵 BOULANGERIE, PATISSERIE ❶

83 rue de Crimée ☎01 42 40 64 55

Baking its divine bread in one of only four remaining wood-fired ovens in France, Maucler uses only organic ingredients in her creations. This cozy neighborhood boulangerie doesn't stick to the often-narrow boulangerie formula; it serves a pretty cheap Sunday brunch. For €11, those who enjoy the continental breakfast side of brunch can sample the numerous homemade breads, pastries, and jam, washed down by fresh OJ and coffee or hot chocolate. No right-minded person can walk by this place and turn down one of the shrewdly placed mini-cakes and patisseries.

🚏 ⓂLaumière. $ Baguette traditionelle €1.30. Flavored brioche €9.80-10.40. Patisseries €2.20-5.10. ⏰ Open M 8am-8pm, Th-Su 8am-8pm.

PIZZA AND PASTA
💵🍸 ITALIAN ❷

36 av. Jean Jaurès

This restaurant may be too small to have a listed phone number, but don't be fooled by appearances; despite this hole in the wall's comically unassuming moniker, you won't find a better deal on quality homemade Sicilian or Italian food in Paris. The interior looks more like a convent cafeteria than a restaurant, but plenty of regular customers enjoy the restaurant's cozy terrace on av. Jean Jaurès. The food is truly splendid; fresh Sicilian selections make you feel like a house guest in Sicily.

🚏 ⓂJaurès. $ Appetizers €3.50-9. Pasta €5.50-8.50. Meats €10-13.50. Pizzas €7-16.50. Carafe of wine €3.

food

montmartre

👍 REFUGE DES FONDUS
💳🍸 FONDUE ❷

17 rue des 3 Frères ☎01 42 55 22 65

The best thing about Refuge des Fondus is its originality. A self-proclaimed refuge from one of the most touristy areas in Paris, this restaurant serves its customers one of two selections—meat or cheese fondue—and wine in baby bottles at two long communal tables. The quality of the wine isn't great—perhaps because it's served in a baby bottle. Happy customers have scribbled their gratitude all over the restaurant's chalkboard walls. The help is convivial, as are (hopefully) your tablemates. You'll either leave shaking your head in amazement or, if you're more traditionally inclined, in disgust. But, in any case, you'll leave shaking your head, and that's saying something for a restaurant in the heart of a tourist machine.

🚏 ⓂAnvers, ⓂPigalle, or ⓂAbesses. $ Menu €18. ⏰ Open daily 7pm-2am.

BODEGA

54 rue Ordener

This fantastic small restaurant and bar is the Ritz of budget eating. The owner and bartender is very friendly, and frequently chats with his customers; if you're seated by the large open window, don't be surprised if he co-opts your party to help him pass plates of food to his customers outside on the terrace. The prices are rock-bottom, the portions are large, and the ingredients are fresh. Everything is served with a smile.

✠ Ⓜ Marcadet-Poissonniers. *Located down rue Ordener; turn left facing the Mairie and it will be on your left.* Ⓢ *Sandwiches €3.90-4.50. Salads €5-7. Plats du jour €5-9.* ⏰ *Open Tu-Su noon-2am.*

LE CARAJAS

BRAZILIAN ❸

24 rue des 3 Frères ☎01 42 64 11 26 🖥 www.carajas.free.fr

There's something wrong about taking your wine in a baby bottle, but Le Carajas makes it feel right. A cozy, convenient location on rue des Trois Frères, Le Carajas serves up tasty traditional Brazilian dishes at somewhat steep prices. The service is warm and friendly; one cook and one waitress manage the small dining room. At non-peak hours, you might even snag a free entree if you chat them up a bit. The hours are flexible, but count on getting food at lunch and dinner hours.

✠ Ⓜ Anvers, Ⓜ Pigalle, or Ⓜ Abesses. Ⓢ *Entrees €5-12. Plats €12-25. Desserts €6. Menu €25.* ⏰ *Open M-F 7pm-midnight, Sa-Su noon-midnight.*

DJERBA CACHER CHEZ GUICHI

AFRICAN ❶

76 rue Myrha ☎01 42 23 77 99

Located in one of Paris's grittier neighborhoods, Djerba Cacher offers tasty Algerian food at very reasonable prices. Let's just say that tourists stick out around here. For the heartiest of the bunch, a visit to Djerba will give you a taste of the "real Paris," which doesn't welcome too many tourists. During the day, however, there's little danger of incident. The meat is freshly skewered and succulent, the condiments are tasty, and the service is friendly. There's no better time to go in than during an Algerian soccer match, so long as you don't mind that the service stops during exciting parts of the game.

✠ Ⓜ Barbès-Rochechouart. Ⓢ *Entrees €2.50-6.50. Sandwiches €6-11. Main Courses €8-25.* ⏰ *Open M-Th noon-4pm and 7-11pm, F noon-4pm, Su noon-4pm and 7-11pm.*

belleville and père lachaise

Belleville doesn't compare to the 19ème in terms of food quality. It would behoove you to to hop on the Metro for lunch after your cemetery visit.

LA BOLÉE BELGRAND

CRÊPERIE, CAFE ❶

19 rue Belgrand ☎01 43 64 04 03

Across the street from Ⓜ Gambetta, La Bolée Belgrand is a modest crêperie boasting American portions. A local crowd people watch through lace curtains and from outdoor tables while enjoying heaping crêpes and *galettes*. The La Totale, with cheese, eggs, tomatoes, onions, mushrooms, ham, bacon and salad, is a particular favorite.

✠ Ⓜ Gambetta. *i* 10% off takeout. Ⓢ *Galettes €7.50-9.50. Crêpes €5-7. Glaces €5.50-7.50.* ⏰ *Open Tu-Sa noon-2:30pm and 7-10:30pm.*

LE ZÉPHYR

🍴🍸 CAFE, BRASSERIE [3]

1 rue du Jourdain ☎01 46 36 65 81

A classic *brasserie du quartier* (neighborhood brasserie), Le Zéphyr offers a perfect example of the 20*ème*'s diverse population and relaxed vibe. The cafe's terrace looks out on the grand intersection of rue de Rigoles and rue du Jourdain; not grand in terms of exciting, but more in terms of strangely large. Food is only an option at lunchtime, but it's fresh, tasty, and reasonable as far as sit-down meals go.

⇆ [M]Jourdain. $ Lunch formule €9.90. Plats €10-20. Picnic €20. Cocktails €7-11. ⏰ Open daily 8am-2am.

LA MER À BOIRE

🍴🍸 CAFE [1]

1-3 rue des Envierges ☎01 43 58 29 43 💻www.la.meraboire.com

A three-, or, if you like a good view, four-in-one. This multi-purpose cafe/bar across from Parc de Belleville offers a spectacular view of Paris. Soak up the teenage revelry (accompanied by its unmistakable scent) across the street. Or check out the venue's occasional contemporary art exhibits and live music concerts. Simple tasty food is perfect for those *"petits faims,"* or small hungers, but won't suffice for a full meal. Hosts art exhibits and occasional concerts.

⇆ [M]Pyrénées. $ Snacks €5-10. Wine glasses €2.50-7.50. ⏰ Open M-Sa noon-1am. Kitchen open noon-2pm and 7:30-9pm.

NIGHTLIFE

Okay, real talk: you may have told your parents, professors, and prospective employers that you've traveled to Paris to take pictures of the Eiffel Tower, but after 50 years in the business we at Let's Go know why the young and the restless beeline for Europe. Parisians might not bathe or shave, but their city fosters one of the most sexually liberated cultures on earth. You didn't just come here for the museums. Accordingly, the City of Love boasts an exceptionally debaucherous night scene, and has something for everyone. Bars in Paris are either chic nighttime cafes bursting with people-watching potential, house-party-esque joints that are all about rock music and teenage angst, or laid-back neighborhood spots that often double as Anglo havens. In the 5ème and 6ème, bars draw French and foreign students, while the Bastille and Marais teem with Paris's young and hip, queer and straight. The Châtelet-Les Halles area draws a slightly older set, while the outer arrondissements cater to the full range of locals in tobacco-stained bungalows and yuppie drinking holes. Paris also harbors a ton of quality jazz bars, the best of which are listed in this guide.

greatest hits

- **OXYMORONIC MUCH?:** The ultimate Marais bar, **La Belle Hortense** is a haven of...wait for it...down-to-earth intellectuals.

- **VAGRANCY'S IN VOGUE:** Forget about the bars; pick up a bottle of something and picnic the **Champs de Mars** beneath the Eiffel Tower's canopy of lights. We apologize in advance for the excessive PDA of the teens that camp out there.

- **NOT MANY SPORTS ARE PLAYED ON THIS QUEEN'S COURT:** One of the most accessible gay clubs in town, **Le Queen** features regular drag nights.

- **BEST SOVIET BUNKER EVER:** Once you get past the concrete, the Bastille club **Wax** is a rare Parisian miracle—a place that is actually fun to dance in, and almost free.

- **PARISIAN GRUNGE:** One of the Bastille's most famous music venues, **Les Disquaires** cultivates a matured grunge vibe and hosts regular concerts.

Clubbing in Paris is less about hip DJs and cutting-edge beats than it is about dressing up, getting in, and being seen. Drinks are expensive, and Parisians drink little beyond the first round, included in most cover charges. Many clubs accept reservations, which means that on busy nights there is no available seating. It's best to dress well and be confident but not aggressive about getting in. Come early and bring or be in a group of girls if you can. Clubs are usually busiest 2-4am. One of Europe's most queer-friendly cities, Paris boasts a plethora of GLBT nightlife hotspots, both calm and cruisy. The Marais is the center of GLBT life in Paris. Most queer bars and clubs cluster around rue du Temple, rue Ste-Croix de la Bretonnerie, rue des Archives, and rue Vieille du Temple, in the 4ème.

student life

Paris nightlife has something for everybody. Stay out at a brasserie ordering wine, or hit up a neighborhood pub with you new backpacker friends. Parisian clubs are all about how you look - if you don't fit the look, you won't be getting in. Depending on the crowd, the gender dynamics of your group will also effect your chances with the doorman - kinda like getting into a frat party.

île de la cité and île st-louis

Far from a party spot, the islands are a bit of a nightlife wasteland. Still, there are a few overpriced brasseries that are worth a stop. The bars are a lot more fun and a lot less expensive on either side of the bank, in the neighboring 4ème and 5ème respectively.

LE LOUIS IX
CAFE, BRASSERIE
25 rue des Deux-Ponts ☎01 43 54 23 89
This is the place where the isle's men go to drink, probably because it has the cheapest beer around. As unpretentious as it gets in this neck of the woods.
✦ ⓂPont Marie. Ⓢ Wine €3.50-4.60. Beer €3.80-5. Aperatif €3.80-4.50. ◷ Open daily 7:30am-8:30pm.

LE SOLEIL D'OR
BRASSERIE
15 bd. du Palais ☎01 43 54 22 22
Its name doesn't quite make sense, but after paying this much for a beer on terrace, you'll certainly wish the sun weren't so damned golden come morning. The view of the sparkling Seine on a quiet evening makes it a nice place for a drink.
✦ ⓂCité. Ⓢ Aperitifs €2.20. Beer €2.20-€4.50. ◷ Open daily 7am-midnight. Happy hour 5-9pm.

L'ANNEXE
BRASSERIE
5 bd. du Palais ☎09 61 27 53 02
A neighborhood watering hole that remains as sequestered as possible from the dense troops of tourists in the areas. The €2 take-out beer is the only deal of note, otherwise you might consider drinking elsewhere.
✦ ⓂCité. Ⓢ Wine €3.80-4.20. Beer €4.20-5. Aperitifs €4-8. ◷ Open daily 7am-8pm.

ESMERALDA
BRASSERIE
2 rue du Cloître Notre-Dame ☎01 43 54 17 72 ▣www.lesmeralda.com
The most exciting thing about this brasserie is its romantic and literary name. Its overpriced beer and wine options are less exciting, though it does have a wider selection of cocktails than most places and is slightly cheaper than immediately surrounding brasseries.

SARL SAINT-REGIS
6 rue Jean de Bellay

✎ ♈️⛄ BRASSERIE
☎01 43 54 59 41

Less flashy than the nearby brasseries and about 2 in. further from the Seine, the Sarl St-Regis attracts Parisians willing to go the extra step and pay exorbitant prices for a cocktail just to avoid the twittering tourist mob.

⚹ ⓂPont Marie. Ⓢ Wine €4.30-5.60. Beer €4.90-6.50. Cocktails €9.50. 🕐 Open M-Th 7am-midnight, F-Sa 7am-1am.

---

as cool as ice

After walking around a bunch of museums and famous landmarks in Paris, one might need to cool off in a bar. What better way than going to the Ice Kube Bar on passage Ruelle? This ultra-hip bar is completely made out of ice and is situated inside the Kube hotel in the Goutte d'Or district. For a modest cover charge, you will be given gloves, a winter parka, and a half hour to drink an unlimited amount of vodka served at 5 degrees below zero Celsius. Having opened only a few years ago, the bar manages to be both modern and old school at the same time, satisfying everyone's desire for new age and retro. French artist, Laurent Saksik, a master at manipulating light and color, designed the interior's carved small lights in the walls of ice and even carved the glasses and furniture. Be sure to make a reservation, as this is one of the most popular spots in Paris and will definitely be full until the wee hours of the morning.

---

châtelet-les halles

▨ BANANA CAFÉ
13 rue de la Ferronerie

♈️✎▼ BAR, LGBT
☎01 42 33 35 31 🖥www.bananacafeparis.com

Situated in the heart of one of Paris's liveliest areas for nightlife, Banana Café is the self-declared, and rightly so, most popular GLBT bar in the 1er. The club suits a wide range of clientele, ranging from the somewhat reticent and straight patrons who occupy the outdoors terrace, to the pole/striptease dancers stationed outside on nice days. During the summertime, there's always some kind of hot deal on beer or drinks, and the party regularly spills out onto the rue de la Ferronerie. Head downstairs for a piano bar and more dancing space. There are weekly theme nights; "Go-Go Boys" takes place every Th-Sa midnight-dawn.

⚹ ⓂChâtelet i Happy hour pints €3, mixed drinks €4. Ⓢ Cover F-Sa €10; includes 1 drink. Beer €5.50. Mixed drinks €8. 🕐 Open daily 5:30pm-6am. Happy hour 6-11pm.

LE CLUB 18
18 rue Beaujolais

♈️✎▼ CLUB, LGBT
☎42 97 52 13 🖥www.club18.fr

Le Club 18 might be the oldest gay club in Paris, but the owners have certainly managed to keep up with today's LGBT partiers. Flashing lights and pop, house, and dance beats make for a wild night. Whether you partied at Studio 54 or you grew up on Gaga, the mixed crowd at Le Club 18 will welcome you with open arms. It's simply *fabuleux*.

⚹ ⓂPyramides. Ⓢ Cover €10; includes 1 drink. Mixed drinks €6-9. 🕐 Open W and F-Sa midnight-6am.

AU DUC DES LOMBARDS

♦ ✆ JAZZ CLUB

42 rue des Lombards   ☎01 42 33 22 88 🖳www.ducdeslombards.com

Murals of little-known jazz artists Duke Ellington and John Coltrane grace the facade of this well-known jazz joint. Still the best in French jazz, with occasional American soloists and hot items in world music. If you're in the mood for whisky, stay away; a bottle of Jack here costs €110 (!). Wine and beer are a bit more reasonable. Three sets each night—lower cover and concessions if you reserve in advance by phone.

✤ ⓂChâtelet. *i* Shows occasionally 8pm. Music 10pm-1:30am. Ⓢ Cover €19-25; students €12 if you call in advance. Couples €30 in advance. Shots €8.50-12. Short drinks €10. Long drinks €12. Wine by the bottle €27-45. ⓩ Open M-Sa 5pm-2am.

LE BAISER SALÉ

♦ ✆ 🖒 JAZZ CLUB, BAR

58 rue des Lombards   ☎01 42 33 37 71 🖳www.lebaisersale.com

A more modern take on the jazz bar; Cuban, African, and Antillean music featured alongside jazz and funk in a welcoming, mellow space. Mellow has its downside; sometimes the vibe here is so chill that the service on the terrace slows to a glacial pace. Expect cool funky music whether intensely grooving out in the club itself or lounging to ambient jazz/reggae with the commoners outside.

✤ ⓂChâtelet. *i* Free M night jam sessions at 10pm: 1-drink min. Ⓢ Cover varies, generally around €20, free very rarely. Beer €6.50-11.50. Mixed drinks €9.50; prices vary depending on show. At bar/terrace, beers €3.70-8.70, wine glass €5. ⓩ Open daily 5pm-6am. Happy hour 5:30-8pm.

O'SULLIVAN'S REBEL BAR

♦ ✆ 🖒 BAR

10 rue des Lombards   ☎01 42 71 42 72🖳www.osullivans-pubs.com

The next installment in a popular chain of Irish pubs, this O'Sullivan's is remarkable for its love of rebels and all things rebellious; pictures of Ché Guevara and James Dean grace the graffiti-covered walls. Unfortunately, the graffiti can make it a bit difficult to tell which bathroom is which. A little bit of dancing generally breaks out as the Guinness keeps flowing.

✤ ⓂChâtelet. *i* Happy hour daily from opening until 9pm; pints €3, drinks 2-for-1. Ⓢ Beer €3.30-6.90. Shots €5-7. Cocktails €8.50-16. ⓩ Open M-Th 5pm-2am, F 5pm-4am, Sa 2pm-4am, Su 2pm-2am.

LE SUNSIDE, LE SUNSET

♦ ✆ JAZZ CLUB, BAR

60 rue des Lombards   ☎01 40 26 21 25 🖳www.sunset-sunside.com

A jazz club with a great reputation, Le Sunside, Le Sunset is very popular with American and English expats and tourists. The bartender is always *dans la merde* (deep in shit) at this busy spot. Le Sunside and Le Sunset are in fact 2 separate, small jazz venues; Le Sunside is above Le Sunset, and opens 1hr. earlier. Sometimes both have concerts, sometimes only one does; check online. Acts range from traditional to experimental jazz.

✤ ⓂChâtelet. *i* Happy hour beer €3-5, mixed drinks €5. Concerts M-Sa 8pm-1am. ⓈBeer €5-6. Mixed drinks €9-10. Cover free or €22-25. ⓩ Open daily 6pm-2am. Happy hour 5-8 pm.

LA CHAMPMESLÉ

♦ ▼((•)) ✆ CLUB, LGBT

4 rue Chabanais   ☎01 42 96 85 20 🖳www.lachampmesle.com

This welcoming lesbian bar is Paris's oldest and most famous; the owner still works the bar and enthusiastically promotes the bar's late-night spectacles (they don't always happen, but when they do it's at 2am). The crowd is friendly; straight folks are warmly welcomed. The club hosts weekly cabaret shows (Sa 10pm) and monthly art exhibits.

✤ ⓂPyramides. *i* Wi-Fi, but don't bring your computer at night, you nerd. Ⓢ Beer €5 before 10pm, €7 after. Cocktails €8-10. ⓩ Open M-Sa 4pm-dawn.

FROG AND ROSBIF

●♥Ÿ(ŋ)⏚ BAR, BRASSERIE

116 rue St-Denis

☎01 42 36 34 73 ▇www.frogpubs.com

One of several Anglo-French "Frog and.." pubs in Paris. The Frog and Rosbif shows live rugby and soccer broadcasts; the floor gets sticky and loud. What makes this pub stand out in a neighborhood full of otherwise generic bars? Frog pubs brew their own beer; try the ginger twist and *parislytic* flavors. They're... interesting.

✚ ⓂÉtienne-Marcel. *i* Quiz nights Su 8pm. Free Wi-Fi. Happy hour pints €5; mixed drinks €5. Thirsty Thu students €4.50 beer and mixed drinks, €2 shots. Ⓢ Beer €6. Mixed drinks €7. ⏰ Open daily noon-2am. Happy hour 5:30-8pm.

LE REX CLUB

●♥Ÿ CLUB

5 bd. Poissonnière

☎01 42 36 10 96 ▇www.rexclub.com

Definitely the place to be if you're looking to get down on the floor or rock out to a phenomenal DJ set. The club hosts top-notch DJ's spanning pretty much any type of music that young people would have the slightest desire to dance to. The crowd is full of students, but due to the high quality of the DJs, there aren't too many Euro-trashy teenagers here. The large sweaty dance floor is surrounded by colorful booths.

✚ ⓂBonne Nouvelle. Ⓢ Cover €10-15. Mixed drinks €9-11. ⏰ Open W-Th 11:30pm-6am, F-Sa midnight-6am.

THE THISTLE PUB

●♥Ÿ⏚ PUB

112 rue Saint-Denis

☎01 40 26 33 20 ▇www.the-thistle.com

The self-proclaimed "most Scottish pub in Paris," the Thistle offers cheap drinks and a place to get super rowdy on sporting occasions. A small outdoors terrace is available for a more tranquil experience, but the party (including kilted Scottish men) often spills into the street.

✚ ⓂEtienne Marcel, Réaumur Sébastopol. *i* Happy hour pints €5. Ⓢ Generally, Verres €3.5 (plus the cost of getting evil eyes from the beer-drinking regulars). Cocktails €5. ⏰ Open M-F 3pm-2am, Sa-Su noon-2am. Happy hour M-F 3-8pm.

the marais

There are as many bars and clubs in the Marais as people. Indisputably the center of fun, Paris's GLBT nightlife scene and fashionable men's and women's bars and clubs crowd **rue Sainte Croix de la Bretonnerie.** Hot spots with outdoor seating are piled on top of one another on **rue Vieille du Temple,** from **rue des Francs-Bourgeois** to **rue de Rivoli.** The places on **rue des Lombards** have a more rough and convivial—though often touristy—atmosphere. The scene in the 3ème is a little more laid back—for the most part, women (and men, too) can leave their stiletto heels at home. There are a number of GLBT bars in the area on and around **rue aux Ours, rue Saint-Martin,** and **rue Michel Le Comte,** but mostly casual bars do live music, especially around the Pompidou.

▧ LE YONO

●♥⏚ BAR

37 rue Vieille du Temple

☎01 42 74 31 65

A rare find in Paris, Le Yono is a bar that's happy being just that, and with good reason. Devoid of an elaborately-themed decor or psychedelic lighting, Le Yono has it all with a mellow, table-filled area upstairs, and a DJ and dancing in the cave-like space below. A courtyard setting, stone interior, and hidden balcony up its cool factor.

✚ ⓂHôtel de Ville or ⓂSt-Paul. *i* Happy hour cocktails and pints €5. Ⓢ Beer €3.50. Wine €4-5. Cocktails €8.80-10. ⏰ Open Tu-Sa 6pm-2am. Happy hour 6-8pm.

ANDY WAHLOO
🍸 ☕ BAR

69 rue des Gravilliers   ☎01 42 74 57 81 ▣www.andywahloo-bar.com

Everything here is a twist on something else. Andy Wahloo, which means, "I have nothing" in a certain Moroccan dialect, serves delicious and ambitious cocktails (€10-14) to a fashionable Parisian clientele in an open courtyard and dark bar. The stop-sign tables and paint-can chairs are pushed aside for dancing later in the night. The incredibly attractive clientele will probably catch you staring.

✦ Ⓜ*Arts et Métiers.* ⓘ *A good place to wait for a table at 404 restaurant.* Ⓢ *Cocktails €10-14.* ⏰ *Open Tu-Sa 5pm-2am.*

RAIDD BAR
🍸 ▼ BAR, CLUB

23 rue du Temple   ☎01 42 77 04 88

If you want a penis or just want to see one, come here. Sparkling disco globes light up the intimate space, as do the muscular, topless torsos of the sexy bartenders. After 11pm, performers strip down in glass shower cubicles built into the wall (yes, they take it all off every hour on the hour starting at 11:30pm). Notoriously strict door policy—women are not allowed unless they are outnumbered by a greater ratio of (gorgeous) men.

✦ Ⓜ*Hôtel de Ville.* Ⓢ *Beer €4. Mixed drinks €10.* ⏰ *Open M-Th 5pm-4am, F-Sa 5pm-5am, Su 5pm-4am. Happy hour 5-9pm for all drinks, 5-11pm for beer.*

LA BELLE HORTENSE
✉🍸(♪) WINE BAR

31 rue Vieille du Temple   ☎01 48 04 71 60 ▣ www.cafeine.com

A literary bar/gallery/cafe, the intimate Hortense draws an older crowd of down-to-earth intellectuals. The walls are lined with books (literature, art, philosophy, and children's), and the mellow music will go with your Merlot. Frequent exhibits, readings, lectures, signatures, and discussions in the small back room filled with leather couches.

✦ Ⓜ*Hôtel de Ville.* Ⓢ *Varied wine selection from €3.50-8. Wine of the month €8.* ⏰ *Open daily 5pm-2am.*

OPEN CAFÉ
🍸✹☕▼ BAR

17 rue des Archives   ☎01 42 72 26 18

Popular almost to the point of absurdity, this GLBT-friendly bar draws a large crowd of loyal, mostly male customers to its corner. Though women are officially welcome, they might feel slightly uncomfortable in the ever-expanding sea of Y-chromosomes. Outdoor terrace seating, and sleek metal decor have (appropriately enough) rainbow accents.

✦Ⓜ*Hôtel de Ville.* ⓘ *Happy hour ½-price beer only.* Ⓢ *Beer €3.70. Wine €3.90.* ⏰ *Open Su-Th 11-2am, F-Sa 11-3am. Happy hour 6-10pm.*

STOLLY'S
✉🍸☕ BAR

16 rue Cloche-Perce   ☎01 42 76 06 76 ▣www.cheapblonde.com

This small Anglophone hangout takes the sketchy out of the dive bar and leaves behind the cool. The €13.50 pitchers of cheap blonde beer ensure that the bar lives up to its motto: "hangovers installed and serviced here." Come inside, have a pint, and shout at the TV with the decidedly non-trendy, tattoo-covered crowd.

✦ Ⓜ*St.Paul. On a dead-end street off rue du Roi de Sicile.* ⓘ *Happy hour mixed drinks and pints €5, pitchers €12. Occasional live music.* Ⓢ *Cocktails €6.50-8.* ⏰ *Open M-F 4:30pm-2am, Sa-Su 3pm-2am. Happy hour 5-8pm. Terrace open until midnight.*

LE PICK-CLOPS
✉ BAR

16 rue Vieille du Temple   ☎01 40 29 02 18

The diner-esque Pick-Clops draws kind of edgy 20-somethings day and night with its choice corner locale (perfect for people-watching and judging), rock and alternative music, and good food and drink. The waiters would probably

nightlife

go around on in-line skates if they knew how, but they settle at serving freshly made popcorn.

✦ Ⓜ Hotel de Ville. Ⓢ Beer €3.80-4.50. Mixed drinks €7-9.60. Salads €9.90-14.50. Add €0.50 for drinks after 10pm. ⏰ Open daily 7am-2am.

sure-fire ways to not get laid

The concurring opinion among the non-French that Paris harbors a certain romantic *je ne sais quoi* is indisputable, but the dating scene is still ambiguous. Some people reference the café and bar scene as a place to pick people up, but others scoff, claiming the land of Victor Hugo would never stoop to such a vulgar way of finding love. But even the French experience some bad luck in the seduction department now and then, and are forced to resort to desperate measures. Even when delivered in the international language of love, there's no excusing the following flops:

Est-ce que ton père a été un voleur? Parce qu'il a volé les étoiles du ciel pour les mettre dans tes yeux.

(Was your father a thief? Because he stole the stars from the sky to put them in your eyes.)

Tu dois être fatiguée parce que tu as trotté dans ma tête toute la journée.

(You must be tired, because you've been running through my head all day)

Est-ce que tu crois au coup de foudre au premier regard? Ou est-ce que je dois repasser?

(Do you believe in love at first sight? Or should I walk by again?)

Excuse-moi, est-ce que tu embrasses les inconnus ? Non ? Donc, je me présente.

(Excuse me, do you kiss strangers? No? Then let me introduce myself.)

Je viens d'arriver dans ta ville. Est-ce que tu pourrais m'indiquer le chemin jusqu'à ton appartement?

(I just arrived in this city. Could you tell me the way to your apartment?)

OKAWA
♥▼ BAR

40 rue Vieille du Temple ☎ 01 48 04 30 69 🖥 www.okawa.fr

Despite the fact that it glows red, Okawa never says stop; it says, "I'll be what you want me to be." Plop down on one of the leather tufted stools and ogle passersby or head down to a cabaret-concert in the basement *(W 8:30pm; €40 for dinner and show)*, which features chunky stone walls from the reign of Philippe-Auguste. Gay travelers welcome.

✦ Ⓜ Hôtel de Ville or Ⓜ St-Paul. *i* Happy hour beer €3.50-3.70, wine €3.50-4. ⏰ Open M-Th 10pm-2am, F-Sa 10pm-4am, Su 10pm-2am. Happy hour 7-9pm.

L'APPARREMMENT CAFÉ
♥ BAR, LOUNGE, CAFE

18 rue des Coutures St-Gervais ☎ 01 48 87 12 22

Dark and elegant, this beautiful red and wood-paneled lounge unexpectedly comes with board games and a chill, young crowd. Cocktails are a bit pricey *(€9.50)* but are interesting and cleverly named; topple over after Jenga, or ironically blackout after the Aide Memoire. Local artists' paintings are displayed on the walls.

✦ Ⓜ St-Paul or Ⓜ Chemin Vert. Ⓢ Cocktails €9.50. ⏰ Open M-Sa noon-2am, Su noon-midnight.

LE DÉPÔT 💵🍸▼ DANCE CLUB [3]

10 rue aux Ours ☎01 44 54 96 96 💻www.ledepot.com

A gay club that revolves around sex... literally. Winding passages with heavy walls lead to dance floors that shoot off into private rooms. Meanwhile, porn stars get off on mounted TVs. A steady stream of men and boys filter in at all hours, hoping for success in the designated "cruising" area. Women, as a rule, are not allowed.

⇞ ⓂÉtienne-Marcel. [$] Cover M-Sa before 9pm and Su before 4pm €8.50, increases incrementally after that. ⏰ Open daily 2pm-8am.

latin quarter and st-germain

Nightlife is a bit stronger in the fifth arrondissement; plenty of pricey bars and jazz clubs line the main streets and boulevards around St-Michel. What better way to walk off a few beers than a stroll down the promenade along the Seine? The 6*éme* is more of a bar and student-centered nightlife scene.

👍 **L'ACADÉMIE DE LA BIÈRE** 💵🍸 BAR

88bis bd. de Port Royal ☎01 43 54 66 65 💻www.academie-biere.com

With 12 beers on tap and over 300 more in bottles, this bar is as serious about beer as the Académie de La Langue Francaise is about the correct use of the subjunctive. According to this academy, "Hunger has no hour, nor does thirst"; accordingly, service of food, and obviously beer, is continuous throughout the night. Extensive menu featuring big portions of salads *(€10.50)*, tartines *(€6-10.50)*, and hot *plats (€9-15)*, among many other offerings.

⇞ ⓂVavin. [$] Aperos €4-9. Cocktails €7-9.10. Beer €4.20-5.50. ⏰ Open M-Th 10am-2am, F-Sa 10am-3am, Su 10am-2am.

👍 **LE CAVEAU DE LA HUCHETTE** 💵🍸 JAZZ BAR

5 rue de la Huchette ☎01 43 26 65 05 💻www.caveaudelahuchette.fr

In the past, the Caveau was a meeting place for secret societies and directors of the Revolution; downstairs, you can still see the prison cells and execution chambers occupied by the victims of Danton and Robespierre. World War II brought American soldiers, bebop, and New Orleans jazz to the establishment. Now an eclectic crowd of students, tourists, and locals comes prepared to listen, watch, and participate in an old-school jazz show in this affordable, popular club.

⇞ⓂSt-Michel. ℹ Live music 10pm-2am. [$] Cover M-Th €12, F-Sa €14, Su €12; students €10. Beers €6. Cocktails €8. ⏰ Open M-W 9:30pm-2:30am, Th-Sa 9:30pm-dawn, Su 9pm-2:30am.

LE CAVEAU DES OUBLIETTES 💵🍸 BEER CAVE

52 rue Galande ☎01 46 34 23 09

Divided into two main rooms and two divergent drinking experiences, Le Caveau des Oubliettes is a rare find in Paris. The upstairs bar (La Guillotine) has sod carpeting, ferns, and a real guillotine, creating a vibe that toes the line between Irish bog and French Revolution. The downstairs cellar or cave is an outstanding jazz club, and in those rare moments when there's no music playing, a good old-fashioned beer cave where dudes tend to bro and beer out. This cellar's previous use was as an actual *caveau des oubliettes* (literally "cave of the forgotten ones"), where criminals were locked up and forgotten.

⇞ ⓂSt-Michel. ℹ Jam sessions M-Th 10pm-1:30am, Su 10pm-1:30am. Free concerts F-Sa. [$] Cocktails €9. Beers €4-9. Liquor €7-12. ⏰ Open M-Th 5pm-2am, F-Sa 5pm-late, Su 5pm-2am. Happy hour 5-9pm.

LE PIANO VACHE

8 rue Laplace

✆♥♥ JAZZ BAR

☎01 46 33 75 03 ■lepianovache.com

This place certainly has character—once a butcher shop, Le Piano Vache ("The Cow Piano") is now a dim bar with an excess of cow paraphernalia and rockin' tunes nearly every night. A popular film site for music videos and movies, Piano Vache boasts a funky vibe, and a correspondingly eclectic crowd; patrons range from hipsters to nerds to older folks to Johnny Depp, who has been known to stop by.

⌗ Ⓜ Maubert Mutualité. *i* Live Jazz concerts on M. Gothic Night W, 80s Night Th, "Soirée Chewing-Gum des Oreilles" on F, Rock and Punk Night on Sa. Ⓢ Beers €5-6. Cocktails €6-7. ⌚ Open M-F noon-2am, Sa 6pm-2am.

LE WHO'S BAR

13 rue Petit Pont

♥♥ BAR

☎01 43 54 80 71

This bar stays open super late right in the swing of things—a stone's throw from the Seine and in the heart of the Latin Quarter's bar scene. Live pop and rock music every night at 10:30pm is not exactly original, but it certainly gets the job done. Old and young alike get down on the often sweaty dance floor; the old folks take the cake in terms of funkiness (smell and dancing abilities included).

⌗ Ⓜ St-Michel. *i* Disco in the basement W-Su 10:30pm-midnight. Ⓢ Beer €5.50-12. Cocktails €10-12. Aperos €6-10. ⌚ Open M-Th 5pm-5am, F-Sa 6pm-6am, Su 5pm-5am.

FINNEGAN'S WAKE

9 rue des Boulangers

Ⓦ IRISH PUB

☎01 46 34 23 65 ■www.finneganswakeparis.com

Claiming to be Paris's first and best Irish pub, Finnegan's has been around since 1989. The bar is a dark, renovated wine cellar with low ceilings and successfully combines a bougie French vibe with the unmistakeable feel of a gritty South Boston bar. Have a pint (€6) with the boisterous (i.e., as Irish as Paris can get) crowd of students and (drinking) professionals.

⌗ Ⓜ Jussieu. *i* Occasional live concerts of traditional Irish music in the downstairs cave from 5pm. Ⓢ Pints €5. Cocktails €6-7. ⌚ Open M-Th 6am-2am, F-Sa 6am-4pm. Happy hour daily 5-9pm.

AUX TROIS MAILLETZ

56 rue Galande

♥♥ JAZZ BAR

☎01 43 54 00 79, 01 43 25 96 86 before 5pm

The crowded basement cave features world jazz fusion (starting around 11pm), while the upper level buzzes with a mix of uncharacteristically chic students and older folks for cabaret or subdued piano concerts (starting around 10pm). Piano concerts come complete with personal serenades.

⌗ Ⓜ St-Michel. Ⓢ Cover for downstairs club F-Sa €20; no cover upstairs. Beer and wine €9-11.50. Mixed drinks €13.

LE PETIT JOURNAL

71 bd. St-Michel

♥ JAZZ BAR

☎01 43 26 28 59 ■www.petitjournalsaintmichel.com

A good hike up bd. St-Michel away from the Seine. Le Petit is one of the early jazz strongholds that consistently draws a mostly middle-aged crowd. Low ceilings, an old-fashioned bar right underneath the second floor of seating, and tables right next to the band create an intimate (or cramped, depending on your outlook) atmosphere. Top-rated New Orleans and Big Band acts frequently perform here.

⌗ Ⓜ Cluny-La Sorbonne or RER: Luxembourg. Ⓢ Concert with dinner €44-47. ⌚ Open Sept-May M-Sa 9pm-1:15am. Concerts at 9:15pm.

HORSE'S TAVERN

16 Carrefour de l'Odéon

♥♥⌂ BAR

☎01 43 54 96 91

Spread out on the lovely Carrefour de l'Odéon, Horse's Tavern serves up a wide variety of beers—the names of all the available beers line the terrace's

latin quarter and st-germain

awnings—and offers a relaxed bar experience. Waiters are tatted up and a bit severe, but the glasses are well-cleaned (relatively rare in Paris).

✦ ⓂMabillon. Ⓢ Wines €18.90-33.40. Aperitifs €4.50-12.50. Cocktails €9.50-10. Beers €2.60-11 ⧗ Open M-Th 7:30am-2am, F-Sa 7:30am-3am, Su 7:30am-2am.

LE 10 BAR
⊛ᵞ BAR

10 rue de l'Odéon ☎01 43 26 66 83 🖳 www.le10bar.com

A classic student hangout; the "facade" of the bar makes it look more like a flop-house than a pub. Precocious Parisian youths indulge in philosophical discussions while getting drunk. After several glasses of their famous spiced sangria (€3-3.50), anything can happen. Jukebox plays everything from Édith Piaf to Aretha Franklin.

✦ ⓂOdéon. Ⓢ Beers €3.50-5.50. Sangria €3-3.50. ⧗ Open daily 6pm-2am. Happy hour 4-8pm.

THE MOOSE
⊛ᵞ BAR

16 rue des Quatre Vents ☎01 46 33 77 00 🖳www.mooseheadparis.com

Hockey jerseys, Canadian license plates, and beer ads adorn this friendly Canadian bar popular among North American expats. The decor is luxurious, using wood and stone to create a deep winter feeling that crazy people yearn for during the summer time. Restaurant serves North American bar fare—nachos, burgers, and wings—until midnight.

✦ ⓂOdéon. ⓘ 2 for 1 beer deal on M, mixed drinks €5.50 on Tu. Ⓢ Cocktails €7.50-9.50. Beer €3.50-5.50 ⧗ Open M-Sa 4pm-2am, Su 11:30pm-2am. Happy hour 4-8:30pm.

FU BAR
⊛ᵞ BAR

5 rue St-Sulpice ☎01 40 51 82 00

This affordable multi-level bar boasts a ceaselessly boisterous Anglophone crowd. Great for impressing a date who has a martini sweet tooth, this hip bar serves quite the array of tantalizing martinis (€7.50) along with the regular bar fare.

✦ ⓂOdéon. ⓘ Occasional live music. Students get martinis €2 off on Tu. Ⓢ Beers €3-6. ⧗ Open M-Sa 5pm-2am.

invalides

If you want to party into the wee hours of the morn, stumble home to your affordable hotel room, and pass out after consuming another €1 bottle of wine, then you probably shouldn't stay in the 7ème. Filled with sights but devoid of personality, the neighborhood gets quiet early. The corner-cafe bars at **École Militaire** are packed almost exclusively with tourists, and the **rue-Saint-Dominique** has some brasseries frequented by locals. The following venues are a solid bet.

▨ CHAMPS DE MARS
PARK, ROMANTIC

Droves of French youngsters march over to the Champs de Mars with the setting sun, schlepping bottles of wine, cases of beer, and packs of cigarettes with them. You'll be thankful it's legal to drink outside in Paris as you approach this grassy stretch in front of the Eiffel Tower. Why? Because you'll find it overflowing with revellers playing guitar and bocce, exploring the subtleties of each other's faces (read: PDA) and generally being merry. The Eiffel Tower lights up on the hour and makes for a spectacular backdrop to the start of a good night.

✦ ⓂÉcole Militaire or ⓂLa Motte Picquet-Grenelle.

CLUB DES POÈTES
CLUB, POETRY

30 rue de Bourgogne ☎01 47 05 06 03 🖳www.poesie.net

If you want to drink and feel cultured, this restaurant by day and poetry club by night brings together an intimate community of literati for supper and sonnets. The hip patrons all seem to know each other and may seem intimidating at first, but you'll soon become fast friends as you cram in next to each other the L-shaped long table.

 # Ⓜ Varenne. i Poetry readings Tu 10pm, F-Sa 10pm. Come a little before then or wait for applause to enter. $ Prix-fixe entree-plat or plat-dessert €16. Lunch menu €16. Wine €4-8. ⏰ Open M-F noon-2:30pm and 8pm-1am. Kitchen open until 10pm.

O'BRIEN'S PUB

77 rue St-Dominique ☎01 45 51 75 87

This no-fuss, get-drunk Irish pub has landed incongruously in an otherwise posh neighborhood. Beers are reasonably priced, but most people come for the big-screen TV.

 # Ⓜ La Tour-Maubourg. $ Beers €5.60-7.40. ⏰ Open M-F 5pm-2am, Sa 2pm-2am, Su 5pm-2am; opens early on game days.

champs-élysées

Glam is the name of the game at the trendy, expensive bars and clubs of the *8ème*. Whether you're going for a mystical evening at **buddha-bar** or a surprisingly accessible evening at **Le Queen,** make sure to bring your wallet, dashing good looks, and if possible, a super-important and/or famous friend.

LE QUEEN 💳🍸▼ CLUB

102 Ave. des Champs-Élysées ☎01 53 89 08 90 🖥www.queen.fr

A renowned Parisian institution where drag queens, superstars, tourists, and go-go boys get down and dirty to the mainstream rhythms of a 10,000-gigawatt sound system. Her Majesty is one of the most accessible GLBT clubs in town, and has kept its spot on the Champs for a reason. Women have better luck with the bouncer if accompanied by at least one good-looking male.

 # Ⓜ Georges V. i M Disco, W Ladies Night, Su 80s. $ €20 cover includes first drink. All drinks €10 after that. ⏰ Open daily midnight-6am.

CHARLIE BIRDY 💳📶🍸 BAR, RESTAURANT

124 rue la Boétie ☎01 42 25 18 06 🖥www.charliebirdy.com

Charlie Birdy is dark and sexy, and that's just the way we like it. The restaurant-bar is enormous and checkered with flat-screen TVs, but still somehow manages to foster a warm, relaxed vibe. Drinks are mostly affordable with the exception of the aged liquors *(€12.50-14.50)*, but the fusion bar food will rack up your credit card bill.

 # Ⓜ Franklin D. Roosevelt. i Happy hour drinks half-price. $ Burgers €13-17. Salads €10.50-14.50. Wine €4.50-6.50. Beer €4-5.50. ⏰ Open daily noon-5am. Happy hour M-F 4-8pm.

BUDDHA-BAR 💳🍸 BAR, RESTAURANT

8 rue Boissy d'Anglas ☎01 53 05 90 00 🖥www.buddha-bar.com

Apparently too cool for overdone trends like capital letters, buddha-bar is billed as the most glamorous drinking hole in the city—Madonna tends to drop by when she's in town. If you're sufficiently attractive, wealthy, or well-connected, you'll quickly be led to one of the two floors of candlelit rooms, where your internal organs will gently vibrate to hypnotic "global" rhythms. A two-story Buddha watches over the chic ground-floor restaurant, while the luxurious upstairs lounge caters to those looking to unwind in style with one of the creative mixed drinks *(€16-21)*. A solid contingent of "atheist drinkers" think buddha is over-rated.

 # Ⓜ Madeleine or Concorde. $ Mixed drinks €16-21. ⏰ Open daily noon-2am.

LE SHOWCASE

🍸 CLUB

under Pont Alexandre III, Port des Champs Élysées ☎01 45 61 25 43 💻wwww.showcase.fr

The new kid on the block, or rather over the Seine. Built into the arches under the Pont Alexandre III, Le Showcase is only open two nights a week, but its odd hours appear to have only increased its popularity. Expect long lines of the lively, young and well-dressed after midnight.

 # [M]Champs-Elysées-Clémenceau. i Entrance typically free before midnight. $ Cover €10-15. Beer €8. Mixed drinks €10. ⏰ Open F-Sa 11pm-dawn.

opéra

CAFÉ LE BARON

🍸 BAR, RESTAURANT

11 rue de Châteaudun ☎01 48 78 13 68

A quintessential Parisian cafe, come here if you're really in the mood to receive some disdainful stares from behind sunglasses (if you're obviously American, that is), and cough up the fog of someone else's cigarette smoke. In a good way. Café Le Baron's sunny outdoors terrace is right in the thick of things near the Opéra district; the scene here is simply classic, and beautiful. Each cocktail looks like a work of art *(€2.20-7)*, and drinks are accompanied by a complimentary tasting plate of olives, veggies, and cheese. Tasteful modern decor graces the interior, with whitewashed walls lined with red wine bottles and an assortment of maroon sofas. The food here is also quite delectable, but expensive; just about everything on the menu is delicious, so you probably won't regret it.

 # [M] Notre Dame de Lorette, Cadette. i Happy hour cocktails and pints €5. $ Beers €2.60-7. Shots €5-18. Wine €2.60-5.50. Appetizers €14-19. Plats €17-26. Desserts €9-10. ⏰ Open M-Su 11am-1am. Happy hour 5:30pm-8pm

CORCORAN'S

🍸 CLUB, PUB

23 Bld. Poissonnière ☎40 39 00 16 💻www.corcorans.fr

Corcoran's is located smack dab in the center of all things touristy, and offers American drinks and bar food for reasonable prices by Opéra standards. A cavernous room boasts a pool table and several TVs, while the outdoors terrace generally fills up with eager people watchers on balmy summer evenings. Any Irish pub should have decent Guinness, and that Corcoran's does, but your waitress might take 10min. to get it to you, and then take another 5min. to add up your bill at the table. The party gets jumpin' on Th-Sa nights, when Corcoran's hires house, rock, and R&B DJs. On the whole a great destination for young people on weekend nights.

 # [M] Grands Boulevards. i Other locations at Bastille, St. Michel, and Clichy areas. Happy hour cocktails and pints €5. $ Shots €4. Cocktails €8.50-9.50. Beer €4-6.50. Whiskey €6.50-8.50. ⏰ Open M-Su 11am-2am. Happy hour M-F 5-8pm

HARD ROCK CAFE

🍸 BAR, RESTAURANT

14 bd. Montmartre ☎01 53 24 60 💻www.hardrock.com

American? Homesick? No? Wish you were American? The Hard Rock Cafe will make ex-pats feel right at home on Montmartre. Diner decor and rock memorabilia unabashedly decorate take center stage, while a big terrace boasts a view of one of the most happening boulevards in Paris. A good place to come drink at night, and possibly eat too—especially for some tasty, not-quite-absurdly-priced lunch formules.

 # [M] Grands Boulevards. $ Lunch formules €9.35-13.75. Entrées €12-22. Formule entrée, plat, and dessert €25. Drinks €7-15 ⏰ Open M-Th 8:30am-1am, F-Sa 8:30am-2am, Su 8:30am-1am.

Forget about the Opéra National—you can find music in Paris on the subway, in the Marais, or under the arches of the Place des Vosges. But on June 21, the evening of the summer solstice, Paris sounds out in full force as the city's corners and cafes, playgrounds and parks transform into a grand platform for musical discovery. **Fete de la Musique** (World Music Day) is a national event that promotes music, showcases young artists in a variety of free concerts, and fosters public appreciation for the arts. In Paris, the festival celebrates the eclectic population of the city and the vibrancy of a major French artistic center.

There are approximately 100 concerts and street performances ranging from classical renditions to techno experimental pieces. Even the most ambitious attendee will not see all of them; to take full advantage of this musical extravaganza, target the top ten events held in indoor venues, and then let the music guide you through the streets. But there is more to Fete de la Musique than just music. From the Brazilian drumming troupe, to the West African marching band, the festival celebrates of a unified French community, in a city that can still be defined by postcolonial divisions.

canal st-martin and surrounds

Try to stay on big streets and avoid heading to the Metro on back streets in the 10ème late at night. Pickpockets, muggers, and scumbags abound.

◼ CHEZ JEANETTE ◆♀ BAR

47 rue du Faubourg St-Denis ☎ 01 47 70 30 89 ▣www.chezjeanette.com

An old-school brasserie à la the 19th century, Chez Jeanette drips with authentic Parisian flavor, complete with candlelit tables and small red lamp chandeliers that hang from the cavernous white ceilings. Grab a seat at the marble counter or large windows of the spacious bar, though it tends to become standing room only at night. Given the old-school vibe here, the crowd is surprisingly down to earth and generally a pleasant mix of 20- and 30-somethings.

✦ Ⓜ Strasbourg St-Denis. Ⓢ *Aperos €2.50-7.60. Beers €2.50-6.40. Cocktails €6.50-8.* ⓩ *Open daily 8am-11:30pm.*

DELAVILLE CAFE ◆♀⌂ BAR, RESTAURANT

34 bd. Bonne Nouvelle ☎ 01 48 24 48 09 ▣www.delavillecafe.com

Situated in a historic building, Delaville successfully mixes cutting-edge design with classic Parisian architecture. If you start to feel cobwebby or old at the old-school, high-ceilinged bar, just slip into the ultra-modern lounge room, with its bright-red cylindrical stools and couches. The crowd's a bit touristy, but not sickeningly so. DJs take the reins Th-Sa, causing the building's old proprietors to roll over in their graves.

✦ Ⓜ Bonne Nouvelle. Ⓢ *Cocktails €8. Brunch €20.* ⓩ *Open M-Sa 11am-2am, Su noon-2am.*

L'ATMOSPHÈRE ◆♀ BAR

49 rue Lucien Sampaix ☎ 01 40 38 09 25

This delightful little bar looks out on the picturesque Canal St-Martin. There's no better place to watch the world—and the disappointing amount of trash in the canal—go by. The waitstaff somehow manages to combine characteristic Parisian efficiency with a warm and welcoming attitude, a real rarity in this city.

✦ Ⓜ Gare de l'Est. ⓘ *Live music some nights.* Ⓢ *Beers €2.50-5.* ⓩ *Open Tu-F 10am-2am, Sa 2pm-2am, Su 2-9:30pm.*

canal st-martin and surrounds

bastille

Nightlife in the 11ème has long consisted of Anglophones who drink too much and the Frenchies who hide from them. With a few exceptions, **rue de Lappe** and its neighbors offer a big, raucous night on the town dominated by expats and tourist-types, while **rue Oberkampf, rue Amelot,** and **rue Thaillandiers** are more eclectic, low-key, and local. Both streets are definitely worth your time, even if you have only one night in the area. **Rue Faubourg St-Antoine** is a world of its own, dominated by enormous nightclubs who only let in the well-dressed. **Rue du Faubourg St-Antoine** is the dividing line between the lively 11ème and the tamer 12th. The hotspots overflow into the streets, and you can hop from one club-lounge to another all night—but it won't be cheap.

▩ FAVELA CHIC
                                                     ● ⍦ BAR, CLUB
18 rue du Faubourg du Temple   ☎01 40 21 38 14 ▣www.favelachic.com

A self-proclaimed Franco-Brazilian joint, this place is light on the Franco and heavy on the brassy Brazilian. Wildly popular with the locals, this restaurant-bar-club has an eclectic decor and equally colorful clients. Dinner in the restaurant segues into unbridled and energetic table-dancing to Latin beats. Exceedingly crowded with sweaty (in a hot way) gyrating bodies during the weekend and a long line snaking out the door. Regulars report that groups high on estrogen and ethnic diversity will get you in more easily.

   ⚲ Ⓜ*République. Walk down rue du Faubourg du Temple, turn right into the arch at no. 18; the club is to your left.* Ⓢ*Mixed drinks €9, made strong enough to justify the cost. F-Sa Cover €10, includes a drink.* ⓣ*Open Tu-Th 8pm-2am, F-Sa 8pm-4am.*

▩ ZERO ZERO
                                                          ● BAR
89 rue Amelot   ☎06 68 84 28 57

A tiny, tiny bar covered from head to toe in stickers and graffiti, jammed with the artistic and the unpretentious. DJs spin hip-hop in the lowly-lit corner. The signature drink "Zero Zero," whose size you should not let deceive you, is a dangerously potent mix of dark rum, ginger, and lime (€3).

   ⚲ Ⓜ*Saint Sebastien Froissart.* Ⓢ*Beers €2.80-4. Cocktails €6.50-8.50.* ⓣ*Open daily 6pm-2am. Happy hour 6:30-8:30pm.*

▩ LE POP-IN
                                        ● BAR, ROCK CLUB
105 rue Amelot   ☎01 48 05 56 11 ▣www.popin.fr

Leaning more towards "popping" than "pop-in," this two-level bar/rock club/90s time warp boasts a basement that's a favorite all-night hangout for Paris' hipster crowd. Pop, rock, folk, and indie fold concerts almost nightly.

   ⚲ Ⓜ*St-Sebastien Froissart.* ⓘ*Check website for concerts.* Ⓢ*Beer €2.80-5.50.* ⓣ*Open daily 6:30pm-1:30am. Happy hour 6:30-9pm.*

▩ LE MÉCANIQUE (ONDULATOIRE)
                                               ● BAR
8 passage Thière   ☎01 43 55 16 74

Le Mécanique puts the booze back in bar, with over 90 kinds of whiskeys and 30 types of rum alone. A local hang out with a light-hearted sense of humor, pop-rocky vibe and rough-and-tumble aesthetic; a pair of skis, a gas pump, and a scooter are incorporated into the decor. Of course, rock is a religion here.

   ⚲ Ⓜ*Bastille.* Ⓢ*Beer €3-4. Aperos €3-5. Liquors €5-7.* ⓣ*Open M-Sa 6pm-2am, Su 7pm-2am. Live concerts every night at 9pm.*

▩ LES DISQUAIRES
                                ● ⍦(●)❄ BAR, MUSIC VENUE
6 rue des Taillandiers   ☎01 40 21 94 60 ▣www.lesdisquaires.com

Another one of Bastille's famous music venues, with a more matured grunge feel and a less poppy crowd. Tables are coated over in pliable black wax for initial carving, so that someone will remember your name even if you blackout.

⚐ Ⓜ Bastille or Ⓜ Ledru-Rollin. *i* *Live concerts every night at 8pm. Club W-Sa.* Ⓢ *Beer €3-4. Shots €3.5. Wine €3.50. Liquors €7.50-8.* ⏱ *Open daily 6pm-2am.*

▨ LE BARON ROUGE

1 rue Théophile-Roussel

⚐Ⓨ WINE BAR

☎01 43 43 14 32

A lively wine bar whose selection is not only breathtaking, but "yes I'll have another glass" cheap. A laid-back but cool crowd mingles around enormous wine barrels that double as tables, sipping steadily on the boisterous bartender's suggestions.

⚐ Ⓜ Ledru-Rollin. *i* *Credit card min. €15.* Ⓢ *Wine €1.50-3.20.* ⏱ *Open M and W-Th 10am-2pm and 5-10pm, F-Sa 10am-10pm, Su 10am-4pm.*

▨ MÉLAC

42 rue Léon Frot

⚐Ⓨ♨ WINE BAR, BISTRO

☎01 43 70 59 27 ▩www.melac.fr

A cozy, family-owned wine bar and bistro in the business of getting people tipsy since 1938. The menu features 35 wines, at least two of which are made in the vineyards of M. Mélac, a jovial Frenchie with an impressively upturned moustache. Mid-Sept., he lets children harvest, tread upon, and extract wine from grapes growing in the bar's storefront.

⚐ Ⓜ Charonne. Ⓢ *Wine €3.50-14 per glass.* ⏱ *Open Tu-Sa noon-3:30pm and 8-10:30pm. Closed in August.*

▨ WAX

15 rue Daval

⚐ DANCE CLUB

☎01 40 21 16 16 ▩www.lewax.fr

A rare Parisian miracle—a place that is actually fun to dance in and almost free (you have to buy at least one drink to stay, though). Set up in a concrete bunker with retro orange, red, yellow, and white couches, this mod dance club is packed with a mix of locals and tourists recreating the disco days.

⚐ Ⓜ Bastille, Take bd. Richard Lenoir, then make a right on rue Daval. *i* *No cover. Mandatory coat check on weekends. W and Su disco/funk, Th R&B, Sa-Su house.* Ⓢ *Beer €5.50. Aperos €5.50-10. Liquors €8-9.50, €0.50 mixers. Cocktails €10.* ⏱ *Open W-Sa 10pm-dawn.*

LE BAR SANS NOM

49 rue de Lappe

⚐Ⓨ LOUNGE

☎01 48 05 59 36

Le Bar Sans Nom and the people sitting there, may not look like much at first glance, but this quiet bar serves some of the best mixed drinks *(€9-10)* around. The dim, seductive lounge area's tall ceilings and huge, Bohemian wall hangings makes the slightly older clientele look cooler.

⚐ Ⓜ Bastille. *i* *Credit card min. €12. Free tarot-card reading Tu 7-9pm.* Ⓢ *Beer €5-6.50. Shots €6.50.* ⏱ *Open Tu-Th 6pm-2am, F-Sa 6pm-4am.*

LE KITCH

10 rue Oberkampf

⚐ BAR

☎01 40 21 94 14

This might be the most random collections of objects that we've ever seen hung on a wall—we're talking rainbow broomsticks, marble mosaics, fish nets. Well, this is Le Kitch, after all. Priding itself on the nonsense factor, this kitschy bar named its signature drink, a mojito-come-slushy, Shrek *(€7.50)*. Laid-back atmosphere and welcoming weirdos, the loveable kind.

⚐ Ⓜ Oberkampf or Ⓜ Filles du Calvaire. *i* *Credit card min. €20.* Ⓢ *Beer €3. Liquors €8. Cocktails €7.50.* ⏱ *Open daily 5:30pm-2am. Happy hour 5:30-9pm.*

LA QUILLE

111 rue St-Maur

⚐ BAR, BILLIARDS, BOWLING

☎01 43 55 87 21 ▩laquille.net

Knowing that Parisians were not going to bowl if they had to wear dumb shoes, this bar opted for a mini-version with no footwear specifications. Fashionable bowling and billiards complete with neon lights and a Top 40 playlist.

⚐ Ⓜ Parmentier. Ⓢ *Beer €2.20-3. Pint €4. Bowling €4 per person. Billards €13 per hr.* ⏱ *Open daily 2pm-2am.*

SANZ SANS

📧 BAR, CLUB, RESTAURANT

49 rue du Faubourg St-Antoine ☎01 44 75 78 78 🖳www.sanzsans.com

A popular bar/restaurant/club that takes classy and brings it down to earth. The red interior is decked out in velvet, with chandeliers and knock-offs of famous paintings. For the voyeuristic, narcissistic or prowlistic, a baroque-framed screen projects scenes from the bar like a black-and-white movie.

‡ ⓂBastille. *i* M funk/groove, Tu R and B, W mix, Th hip hop and reggae, F-Sa house. Ⓢ Cover €5 on weekends. Beer €3-3.50. Cocktails €12. Mixed drink €9. ⏲ Bar open M-Th 9am-3am, F-S 9am-5am. Club M-Th midnight-3am, F-Sa 8:30pm-5am.

LE BAR À NENETTE

📧♈ BAR

26bis rue de Lappe ☎01 48 07 08 18

A bistrot-like bar with a wooden facade, wall-sized mirrors, and a cool casual vibe. Its happy hour keeps going and going *(cocktails €5)*. Friendly owner and pretty bartenders complement the welcoming atmosphere.

‡ ⓂBastille. Ⓢ Wine €4. Liquors €5-7. ⏲ Open daily 5pm-2am. Happy hour 5-10pm.

BARRIO LATINO

📧♈((•)) DANCE CLUB

46/48 rue du Faubourg St-Antoine ☎01 55 78 84 75

Barrio Latino is bigger up close than you'd expect. With an impressive 5 floors, the richly decorated bar/restaurant/night club is stylish, sexy and warm. Enthusiastic and aspiring salsa dancers shake it like a polaroid picture in various corners, well into their third, slightly overpriced drink. The giant dance floor heats up around 11pm. Dress to get laid. Come to dance.

‡ ⓂBastille. Ⓢ Cover €20 Th-Sa. Beer €6.50-9. Cocktails €12-13.50. Shooters €6.50 ⏲ Open M-Th 10pm-2am, F 10pm-2:30am, Sa 10pm-3am, Su 10pm-2am. DJ arrives at 10pm.

CHINA CLUB

♈❄ CLUB, RESTAURANT

50 rue Charenton ☎01 43 46 08 09 🖳www.lechina.eu

Squeezing class out of fake bamboo, all three levels of this bar/club/restaurant drip with elegance. The first and second floors feature a restaurant/piano bar/smoking lounge vibe, with high ceilings, marble floors, oriental carpets, and luxurious lounge chairs; downstairs in Club Chin Chin, things get more intimate, but stay classy, with red velvet and dimmed lights. Beware that being sophisticated is expensive *(mixed drinks €10-15)*.

‡ ⓂLedru-Rollin or ⓂBastille. *i* Piano bar M, Su 8pm-midnight. Nightly concerts at 8:30pm. Ⓢ 3-course dinner menu €40-45. ⏲ Restaurant open daily 8pm-2am. Bar/club open daily 6pm-2am.

NOUVEAU CASINO

📧 CLUB, CONCERT HALL

109 rue Oberkampf ☎01 43 57 57 40 🖳www.nouveaucasino.net

The party center of the uber-hip countercultural scene that most of the young people along rue Oberkampf buy into. The old movie-theater-turned-concert-venue and club only tolerates underground music, ranging from electro pop to hip-hop to pop to rock. The crowd spills into the attached Café Charbon to liquor up before and after events or chills near the bar designed to look like an iceberg.

‡ ⓂParmentier or ⓂMénilmontant. Ⓢ Check the website or call for a weekly schedule. Cover €5-15, usually free before 1am. Concerts €5-20. Tickets cheaper in advance, available through FNAC. ⏲ Open midnight-dawn when there are events.

nightlife

butte-aux-cailles and chinatown

Blessed with a young and unassuming crowd, the 13ème's local haunts are cluttered with vintage instruments, overflow onto maritime concert venues floating along the Seine, and maintain a chill atmosphere you never knew that a city as conscientiously chic as Paris could keep up. Walk down to the Porte de la Gare, grab a bottle of wine with some friends and watch the Seine go by.

LE MERLE MOQUER
● BAR

11 rue de la Butte-aux-Cailles ☎01 45 65 12 43

Capturing the spirit of the neighborhood with its eclectic mix of African art, uneven stools, and spray-painted doors, this bar is a little funky, not at all fussy, and the best place on the street to dance. Homemade, flavored rum punches are well worth the €6. Ginger-apple-pear-cinnamon is the bartender's choice.

⚡Ⓜ*Place d'Italie.* Ⓢ*Drinks €4-6.* 🕐 *Open M-Su 5pm-2am.*

LA FOLIE EN TETE
● BAR

33 rue de la Butte-aux-Cailles ☎01 45 80 65 99 ▤www.lafolieentete.blogspot.com

This hole-in-the-wall is packed with the neighborhood's chillest residents. Instruments hang from the ceiling, shaking gently to reggae tunes. Strangers are greeted with a friendly smile. The house punch is poured with home-made syrup (€4.50).

⚡Ⓜ*Place d'Italie.* Ⓢ *Cocktails €7. Punch €5.50.* 🕐 *Open M-Sa 5pm-2am, Su 6pm-midnight. Happy hour daily 6-8pm.*

LA DAME CANTON
● BAR, CONCERT VENUE

Porte de la Gare ☎01 45 84 41 71 ▤www.dame-decanton.com

A quirky alternative to all those passé land-locked watering holes, this floating bar is deliberately odd in the extreme, even by Butte-aux-Cailles standards. A seizure-inducing collection of fishing nets, musical instruments, books on Australia, postmodern takes on the Mona Lisa, and small Chinese lamps decorate the walls and ceiling. The floor slopes, the patrons rock dreds, and the owner's been known to wear jean suits. The burly bartenders will serve you Pirate Punch (€3) and cocktails (€7.50) in plastic cups or out of cans. The lolling waters of the Seine make La Dame Canton a little less than stable, so we advise you avoid getting plastered on board. But the view of the Seine is spectacular, and the mix of soul funk, hip hop, and reggae demonstrate excellent taste. Live concerts every night, starting at about 8:30pm.

⚡Ⓜ*Quai de la Gare.* ⓘ *Cover T-Th €8, students €6; F-Sa €10.* Ⓢ *Cocktails €7.50.* 🕐 *Open Tu-Th 7pm-2am, F-Sa 7pm-5am.*

BATEAU EL ALAMEIN
◉ BAR ❷

Port de la Gare ☎01 45 86 41 60 ▤elalamein.free.fr

Between El Alamein's pet parrots and its jungle of potted plants, this bar feels more like a floating garden than a bar on a boat. The floral still lifes that line the walls and the Chinese cabinet of pottery add a feminine touch, but the names of the house cocktails—a Marijuana Rum, anyone?—suggest that this bar errs towards the raunchier side of the ▨**madonna-whore complex** *(marijuana rum; €6).* Downstairs stage features performers at 9pm.

⚡ Ⓜ*Quai de la Gare.* Ⓢ *Wine €3, cocktails €6-8.* 🕐 *Open daily 8:30pm-2am.*

LE SPUTNIK
● BAR ❷

14 rue Buttes-aux-Cailles ☎01 45 65 19 82

Named for the first artificial satellite, this multi-purpose cafe/bar attracts a student crowd (read: bookish girls with guitars) for its cheap drinks and free Wi-Fi, not to mention its hypnotizing circle. Russian murals and screaming orgasm posters decorate the walls, providing an appropriate backdrop for political conversations among the decidedly left of center.

⌖ [M]Place d'Italie. ℹ Shots €3. Happy hour cocktails €5. ⏰ Open M-Sa 2pm-2am, Su 4pm-midnight, holidays 4pm-2am.

montparnasse

Montparnasse doesn't have much in terms of nightlife; at night, most of its younger residents are busy partying it up in other *arrondissements.* Older crowds frequent the bars along the main boulevards and avenues.

L'ENTREPÔT 🍸 BAR, RESTAURANT, CINEMA

7-9 rue de Francis Pressenc ☎01 45 40 07 50 💻www.lentrepot.fr

L'Entrepôt offers the potential for a quadruple-dip, boasting an art gallery, a three-screen cinema, a restaurant with garden seating, and a bar that hosts regular concerts. The young and nerdy clientele enjoys free lectures and discussions on topics ranging from modern literature to hip-hop. Until the end of 2010, the venue will host Ciné-Philo, a screening, lecture, and discussion cafe, held every other Sunday at 2:20pm *(€8);* check the monthly schedule in the main foyer. Thursday jazz nights, and Friday and Saturday world music nights *(€7-10).* Free improv theater with audience participation third Sunday of each month at 7:30pm. Check website for other special events, including jam sessions, scholarly debates, and slam poetry.

⌖ [M] Pernety. [$] Lunch formule €15; brunch formule €25. Movie tickets €7, students €5.60, under 12 €4. Costs of other events vary. ⏰ Gallery open M-F 11am-7pm. Brunch Su 2:30-6:30pm. Bar open daily 9pm-midnight. Restaurant M-W noon-3pm and 7:30-10:30pm, Th-Sa noon-3pm and 7:30-11pm, Su noon-3pm and 7:30-10:30pm.

LE REDLIGHT 🍸 BAR, CLUB

34 rue du Départ ☎01 42 79 85 49 💻www.leredlight.com

Formerly known as Enfer, Le Redlight is located at the foot of the Tour Montparnasse. Cozy red booths surround a disco-lit dance floor. DJs generally fall under the electro/dance/house genre, but they mix it up with R and B every once in a while. The party doesn't get jumping 'til late, and drinks are expensive, so start your night early and then head here; make-up you caked on will be quickly sweat off. Fauxhawks and fitted hats alike nod to the music.

⌖ [M] Montparnasse-Bienvenue. [$] Cover €20; includes 1 drink. ⏰ Open only on weekends, opening time varies with DJ set, generally until 2am. Check website for specifics.

passy and auteuil

The 16*ème* isn't the hottest spot in town, but it does feature a few stylish bars with reasonably priced drinks. You'll be hanging out with the chic and the too-cool-for-school, so leave those frayed sneakers at home.

SIR WINSTON 🍸 BAR, CLUB

5 rue de Presbourg ☎01 40 67 17 37

This cafe/salon/bar/club is a sophisticated hotspot of the young Parisian Bobos (that's bohemian bourgeoisie, for those not in the know). Lean back into a leather chair and sip on a glass of wine *(€5)* or smoke attractively alongside a pensive Buddha. After all, Buddha would have totally done the same. There's a dance space downstairs, though the music is mainly jazz and lounge tunes.

⌖ [M]Kleber. [$] French fries €5. Caesar salad €5. ⏰ Open daily 9am-4am.

LA GARE

🍸 BAR

19 Chausee de la Muette ☎01 42 15 15 31 🖥www.restaurantlagare.com

Once a train station, La Gare is now a trendy bar and the favored hang-out spot of the wealthy young things who live in surrounding apartments. The drinks aren't always as strong as they could be, but there is a wide selection of elaborate cocktails *(€10)*; the ginger mojito and French fizz (absinthe, ginger, vanilla, syrup, and lemonade) are particularly mouth-watering. The terrace is a nice place to sit, and the inner lounge is warmed by a raging fire, though you'll probably want to move on before the night ends.

‡ [M]Muette. [$] Red wine €5.50. Martini €5.50. ⏰ Open daily, noon-1am.

THE HONEST LAWYER

🍸 BAR

176 rue de la Pompe ☎01 45 05 14 23 🖥www.honest-lawyer.com

An unpretentious place to liquor up in the 16*ème* is about as hard to find as an honest lawyer, but The Honest Lawyer is just that. The wood paneling, brass lamps, and free Wi-Fi are reminiscent of a law library; the '80s pop, large-screen TVs, and the large painting of a judge nursing a tankard of beer, not so much. A regular and largely male crowd of disheveled grad student types schlep their laptops and briefcases here for a relaxed and reasonably priced drink. Our intrepid researcher-writers report that the Stella here is "bomb-ass" *(€3.50)*.

‡ [M]Victor Hugo. [$] Martini €4. Beer €3-5. Cocktail €8. ⏰ Open M-F 7:30am-2am, Sa 10am-2am, Su 7:30am-2am.

FROG XVI

🍸 BAR

110bis ave. Kleber ☎01 47 27 88 88 🖥www.frogpubs.com

Frog XVI is what happens when Englishmen move to Paris. All beers are home-brewed and fairly cheap *(2.3L jugs €24)*. Neon lights, leather stools, hopping music, and an uncommonly attractive clientele make for a classy place to get drunk. Might be one of the few places in Paris where quesadillas, nachos *(€7)* and chicken wings are served up with a shot of tequila *(€4)*.

‡ [M]Trocadero. [$] Wine €5. Cocktails €6. Fish and chips, €14.50. Smoked salmon and cream cheese bagel €13. ⏰ Open daily noon-2am. Happy hour M-Fri 5:30-8pm.

DUPLEX

🍸 CLUB

2bis av. Foch ☎01 45 00 45 00 🖥www.leduplex.com

One of the few "hot" nightlife options in the 16th, Duplex shines as a legitimate club. Each of the three dance floors plays different music, ranging from R and B to house. Theme nights cater to every kind of partier.

‡ [M]Charles de Gaulle-Etoile. i Ladies enter free before midnight on F. [$] Cover and first drink Tu-Th, Su €15, F-Sa €20. Drinks M €8, Tu-Th €9, F-Sa €11, Su €9. ⏰ Open Tu-Su 11pm-dawn.

batignolles

If you're thinking of a wild night on the town in the 17*ème*, forget it. If the people who live here drink here, they do it by themselves; the craziest it'll get is a few drinks with old friends and maybe a couple of new ones. Sometimes, though, that's all you need.

LE BLOC

CAFE, BAR

21 rue Brochant ☎01 53 11 02 37

Like a good mistress, Le Bloc is always open, accommodating, and kind of cool. This former clinic turned industrial cafe/bar caters to the neighborhood's turtleneck-wearing types from morning till dawn, and will be whatever you want it to be. The food is decent enough *(penne au pisto; €8.80)*, and drinks range from whatever to shocking *(kir €2.90, cosmo €7.50)*. Look for the little nook under the stairs with the brown couch, pink walls, and fake skeleton.

⌗ ⓂBrochant. *i* Free Wi-Fi. Ⓢ Salads €9-10.20. Most cocktails €6.50. ⌚ Open daily 8:30am-2am.

L'ENDROIT
BAR, CAFE

74 rue Legendre ☎01 42 29 50 00

Set at the center of the tree-lined Place du Dr.Felix Lobligeois, l'Endroit attracts a mixed crowd. But its almost indecent opening hours, expansive terrace, and revolving liquor display make it a consistently good place to sit for a drink French-style: over food and into the wee morn.

⌗ ⓂRome . *i* Brunch Sa-Su 11am-4:30pm. Ⓢ Mojitos €9-15. Burger €16. Wine €23 ⌚ Open Su-Th 11am-2am, F-Sa 11am-5am.

SANS GÊNE
BAR

122 rue Oberkampf ☎01 46 27 67 82 ▓www.sansgene.fr

Like many of the hotspots in the 17ème, Sans Gene is a good place for casual after-dinner drinks. Hot pink and black interior attracts a bigger crowd than neighboring bars, probably because it manages to be both punk and cutesy.

⌗ ⓂBrochant. *i* Brunch Sa-Su noon-4pm. Ⓢ Cheese ravioli €14.50. Lamb with gratin dauphinoise €19. Cocktails €8.50. Wine €4. ⌚ Open M-Su 9am-2am.

JAMES JOYCE PUB
♥♿♼⚅ BAR

71 Bld. Gouvion-St-Cyr ☎01 44 09 70 32 ▓www.kittyosheas.com

One of the few typically English pubs in Paris, the James Joyce attracts just about every older English speaker in a 1-mile radius. Anglophones would probably be better served drinking the French way, seeing as this is Paris, but if you're homesick this is one of the best places to go. The most interesting drink on the menu is definitely the "g-string" *(vodka, Triple Sec liquor, and banana juice; €10)*.

⌗ ⓂPorte Maillot. Ⓢ Wine €4. Guinness €4.50. Burger and fries €10. ⌚ Open daily noon-2am.

JAZZ CLUB ÉTOILE
JAZZ CLUB

81 Boulevard Gouvion-St-Cyr ☎01 40 68 30 42 ▓www.jazzclub-par.com

Disclaimer: this is probably the kind of place your parents would go to. Older crowd aside, the club gets the atmosphere right with high-quality jazz performances every night. Before being bought by the Hotel Meridien, this used to be one of Paris's premier clubs, bringing in big names like BB King and Ike Turner.

⌗ ⓂPorte Maillot. *i* Daily shows. Ⓢ Plats €14-27. Wine €29-59. ⌚ Bar open T-Sa 5:30-10pm.

buttes chaumont

Buttes Chaumont doesn't have the most popping nightlife scene, and this is definitely not the safest neighborhood in Paris. That being said, drinks are generally cheap, and the company can get rowdy at the more student-ish bars. If you can only hit up one place, it has to be the Ourcq. The beer goes for only €2.50 and keeps the locals coming.

📑 OURCQ
♥♼ BAR, TEA HOUSE

68 quai de la Loire ☎01 42 40 12 26

Where the students, hipsters, hippies, and other budget-conscious folks go to get down. There's always a party going on, whether it's a Tuesday or a Saturday night. During the day, this classic brasserie doubles as a tea salon and provides its customers with a wide selection of board games and books to go along with their hot beverage of choice *(€2-3)*.

⌗ ⓂLaumière. Ⓢ Wine by the glass €2-3. Beers €2.50-4. Cocktails €5. ⌚ Open W-Th 3-midnight, F-Sa 3pm-2am, Su 3pm-10pm.

ABRACADABAR

🎵♀ BAR, CONCERT HALL

123 ave. Jean Jaurès ☎01 42 03 18 04 🖳www.abracadabar.fr

Hip hop, trip hop,'70s soul, and generally hot beats blast through the speakers on weeknights, while patrons are treated to live concerts on Fridays and Saturdays (OK, not actually treated; prices vary). Munchies aside, the crowd is fun, albeit a bit aged-out punk/hip hop. Drinks are steep—beer and cocktails are a good €1.50-2 more expensive than anything you'll get at Ourcq.

🚇 Ⓜ*Laumière.* Ⓢ *Beers €3.50-7. Cocktails €7.* 🕐 *Open daily 6pm-6am.*

CAFE ROZIER

♀🍴🌿 BAR

14 quai de la Loire ☎01 42 39 68 98

About half of the people at Rozier might be finishing up their dinner, but that shouldn't stop you from taking advantage of its lovely terrace and relatively cheap drinks. The vibe seems disproportionately yuppie for the neighborhood. A good spot to have an appetizer before dinner or a digestif after, but don't plan on getting krunked here without drawing some sideward glances.

🚇 Ⓜ*Laumière.* Ⓢ *Beers €3-3.20. Wine by the glass €3.60-5.80. Shots €4.* 🕐 *Open M-F noon-2am, Sa 5pm-2am, Su noon-2am.*

LE FAITOUT

♀♀ BAR

23 av. Simon Bolivar ☎01 42 08 07 09 🖳www.lefaitout.fr

A cozy, relaxed bar located on the residential avenue Simon Bolivar. The decor is classic, the drinks are affordable, and the crowd is rowdy on weekends (a bit subdued on weeknights). The kitchen is open late, so you can grab a quick snack if you feel the need to wash something down besides your sorrows. Plenty of students, as is most often the case at bars in Buttes.

🚇 Ⓜ*Laumière.* Ⓢ *Shots €3. Wine by the glass €2.60-6.50.* 🕐 *Open daily 7am-2am.*

montmartre

Nightlife in Montmartre comes, of course, with the burden of not getting too drunk and staying away from the shady cabarets/strip clubs. The best way to stay safe is to keep your wits about you.

🏛 LE RENDEZ-VOUS DES AMIS

♀♀ BAR ❸

23 rue Gabrielle ☎01 46 06 01 60 🖳www.rdvdesamis.com

You know that you're in for a night of debauchery when the bar's owners and bartenders drink harder than their customers, pounding shots and beers at random. A true Montmartre institution, Le RVDA has been around for 17 years, and it's not hard to see why. Convivial and untouristed, this bar has a live-free-or-die ethos. Patrons rock out to house music, experimental hip hop, and occasionally live music. The mixed drinks are a rip-off, so stick to the beer, though that can also get pricy. Welcome to Montmartre. Cigarettes are sold out front on an informal basis, but don't bring your drink outside—the burly but friendly bouncer will have words for you. Small appetizers are available to help you stomach the beer.

🚇 Ⓜ*Abbesses.* Ⓢ *Beers €2.30-7. Pitchers €7.* 🕐 *Open daily 8:30am-2am.*

🏛 L'ESCALE

♀♀ BAR

32bis rue des 3 Freres ☎01 46 06 12 38

A very popular spot among the students of Montmartre, this restaurant serves up famously strong cocktails for just €4.50. Young folks huddle around cozy, small tables, and the owner proudly proclaims on the website that L'Escale and its strong drinks are the number-one enemy of the police. There's generally a guest DJ playing house music, or whatever else is super hip at the moment, on Sunday nights.

🚇 Ⓜ*Abbesses.* Ⓢ *Beers €3.50-8. Cocktails €4.50.* 🕐 *Open daily 2pm-2am. Happy hour 4-10pm.*

montmartre

CHEZ JULIEN

👁🍸 BAR

2 rue Lepic

☎01 42 64 21 20

The vibe is, like, totally relaxed here, dude. Old records and images of '60s celebrities decorate the walls. Locals flock here for the martinis served in beer glasses. While the attached restaurant is a bit pricey, the drinks are affordable by Red Light District standards. A nice spot to start out the night, but it closes at midnight, so don't get too comfortable.

⧣ ⓜBlanche. ⓢ Aperos €2.60-6. Wine €2.50-5. Cocktails €7.50. ⏰ Open daily 7:30am-midnight.

BRASSERIE L'EPOQUE

👁🍸 BAR

38 bd. de Clichy

☎01 42 52 36 00

Looking for a Euro-trash vibe with a characteristically snooty French welcome? You've found the right place. Disco lights flash and techno pulses from the speakers at this bar in the heart of the Red Light District. Drinks get pretty expensive (shots start at €9, and don't get us started on cocktails), and the bartenders constantly hassle customers to either drink faster or more. A place to visit if you're looking for a bearable, but classically Red Light District experience.

⧣ ⓜPigalle. ⓢ Aperos €5-11. Shots €9-11. Cocktails €11-18. ⏰ Open M-F 10am-4am, Sa-Su 10am-5am.

THE HARP

👁🍸 SPORTS BAR

118 bd. de Clichy

☎01 43 87 64 99

Feel like starting the day off wrong with a beer or two? The Harp's got your back. Open till 9am on weekends, this sports bar revolves around rugby, soccer, and booze and hosts plenty of late-night partiers. Boasting a great selection of beers on tap, a pint costs only €6, a hell of a deal for the Red Light District. If the Harp had an anthem, it'd be James Brown and Betty Newsome's "It's a Man's World"; expect lots of bros and the women who love them. Several big-screen TVs make this the ideal spot to watch the game.

⧣ ⓜBlanche. ⓢ Beer €4-6. ⏰ Open M-W 5pm-4am, Th-Sa 5pm-9am, Su 5pm-4am.

LA FOURMI

👁🍸🍽 BISTRO, BAR

74 rue des Martyrs

☎01 42 64 70 35

This chic option seems to have attracted the young, wealthy, and classy Parisian crowd, along with a bunch of Montmartre's other non-creeps. Wine bottles decorate the dimly lit interior. We recommend drinking here in the summer, when the outdoor terrace buzzes with progressively emphatic French and conversation as the bar's collective BAC begins to rise.

⧣ ⓜPigalle. ⓢ Cocktail €9.50. Wine €2.50-3.20. ⏰ Open M-Th 6pm-2am, F-Sa 6pm-4am.

L'ART SCENIK CAFÉ

👁🍸🍽 BAR

48 bd. Clichy

☎01 42 57 38 70

A variety of potted plants hang in a canopy that rings L'Art Scenik Café's low-ceilinged bar, generating a Parisian-jungle vibe (if that's even possible?). Bartenders are most likely getting down behind the bar; come here if you want to get down with them and some incredibly rowdy, sweaty soccer fans. The happy hour prices are off the chain; don't miss 'em. Look for the bright neon sign hanging over the terrace.

⧣ⓜPigalle. *i* Happy hour daily €2.20 for a 40cL beer. ⓢ Beer €3. Cocktails €8. ⏰ Open M-Th 5pm-5am, F-Sa 5pm-6am, Su 5pm-5am. Happy hour daily 5-9pm.

LE BEL-AIR

👁🍸 BAR

6 rue Germain Pilon

☎01 42 54 92 68 🖥www.myspace.com/lebelair

This little mom-and-pop operation is on the first floor of what used to be an apartment; the old family pictures are still on the wall. There's always some type of entertainment going on here, even if it's just chill reggae flowing in the back-

nightlife

ground. Weeknights often feature a movie on the big-screen TV, while weekends can get a bit rowdier, with small rock concerts.

✚ Ⓜ*Abbesses.* Ⓢ *Wine €2.80-3.50. Cocktails €4-7.* ☒ *Open daily 5pm-2am.*

LE DOLL
◆ ⴹ BAR

104 bd. de Clichy ☎01 82 09 47 42 🔲www.ledoll.com

A newcomer to the Pigalle neighborhood, Le Doll is new, sleek, and shiny. Fashion-conscious Parisians sidle up to the bar, lit up a striking shade of pink, then settle onto cube-shaped orange stools or into plush black leather couches. Come here if you like to live (or look like you live) the fast life. This is the spot to be on weekends after 10pm, when house and guest DJs get Le Doll jumping with house and techno.

✚ Ⓜ*Anvers.* Ⓢ *Cover prices vary, but most events are free.* ☒ *Open M-Sa noon-3:30am.*

JUST BE
ⴹ ◆ BAR

46 rue Caulaincourt ☎01 42 55 14 25 🔲www.justbe-paris.com

A warm maroon exterior invites you into this cozy neighborhood bar and bistro. The warm walls are brick and painted purple. While nothing too crazy ever happens here, this is a meditative spot to grab a drink before or after dinner. Younger and older crowds mix together, vying for one of Just Be's extremely comfy arm chairs. Some couples interpret these to be love seats. A very small terrace is available for those who need some fresh air.

✚ Ⓜ*Lamarck-Caulaincourt.* 𝒊 *DJs show up on Saturday nights.* Ⓢ *Vodka shots €3.50. Glasses €7. Aperos €4-8. Beer €3-5.* ☒ *Open Tu-Su 11am-2am.*

belleville and père lachaise

Given that it's mostly a residential neighborhood, Belleville has very few nightlife options. Crowds tend to be exclusively local, so this is a great place to see how Parisians really get down.

[✓] LOU PASCALOU — BAR

14 rue des Panoyaux — ☎01 46 36 78 10

The uncontestable number-one hotspot of the 20th arrondissement. On summer nights, a crowd floods out of the bar and vies for chairs on the terrace. The friendly staff handles drink orders en masse and somehow keeps their wits about them.

Ⓜ Ménilmontant. $ Beers €2-6.50. Wine glasses €2-4.60. Cocktails €5-6.50. ⏰ Open daily 9am-2am.

CAFÉ MÉNILMONTANT — BAR

143 bd. Ménilmontant — ☎01 47 00 08 98

This *cafe du quartier* offers great happy-hour deals on wine glasses and pints. Locals share tables with strangers as they angle for one of the coveted terrace seats on summer nights; grab an empty chair and make some new friends.

Ⓜ Ménilmontant. $ Happy-hour wine glasses €1.15-1.30, pints €3.30-3.80, bottles €15.50-39.50. Bar meal formule €8. ⏰ Open daily 7am-2am.

LE MIROIR — BAR

111 bd. du Ménilmontant

Cheap beer and strong cocktails attract a local crowd. There's no pretension here; the bar definitely worth checking out, but only come if you don't mind standing out among a crowd of regulars.

Ⓜ Ménilmontant. $ Beers €2.70-3. Cocktails €5. ⏰ Open M-Sa 9am-1am.

ARTS AND CULTURE

They may have ripped off the Italians for a few hundred years in there (cough Renaissance painting cough), but the beloved neurotics of Paris have been the single most innovative force in the art world since the Enlightenment, and the city's creative energies show no signs of slowing down. You're obviously going to visit the Pompidou, but if you want a window into what Paris's artists are up to today, check out the following venues. A note on this section: because most of them are indispensable sights in and of themselves, Paris's cutting-edge art galleries are distributed throughout the Sights chapter by neighborhood, as opposed to being listed here. **Fait and Cause** in the Marais and **Galerie Loevenbruck** in St-Germain are both must-sees.

greatest hits

- **ENCORE!: Odéon Théâtre de l'Europe** is indisputably the big fish of Paris's theater scene. That's really saying something.
- **VOULEZ-VOUS COUCHEZ AVEC MOI?:** Forget about the Moulin Rouge—**Le Lapin Agile** is one of the best cabarets in the city, with plenty of fishnets and feathers to go around.
- **PARTY IN DA CLUB: Elysée Montmartre** is one of the better known hip hop clubs in Western Europe. And maybe the world.

student life

The city of Paris has inspired countless artistic, theatrical, and literary masterpieces. *The Hunchback of Notre Dame, Les Misèrables,* and *The Da Vinci Code*—what more do you need?

theater

ODÉON THÉÂTRE DE L'EUROPE
LATIN QUARTER AND ST-GERMAIN

2 rue Corneille ☎ 01 44 85 40 40 www.theatre-odeon.fr

The big fish in a theater-themed neighborhood, the streets leading towards the Odéon Théâtre are named after some of France's most famous playwrights, including Corneille and Racine. The Odéon itself is a classically beautiful theater; gold lines the mezzanine, and muted red upholstery covers the chairs. Considering that this is the mecca of Parisian theatre, the prices are stunningly reasonable. Works range from the classical to the avant-garde.

Odéon. $ Shows €5-32. Limited number of extremely cheap rush tickets available right before the show. ⏰ Performances generally M-Sa 8pm, Su 3pm.

THÉÂTRE DE LA VILLE
CHÂTELET-LES HALLES

2 pl. du Châtelet ☎01 42 74 22 77 www.theatredelavilleparis.com

Built in 1862, the Théâtre de la Ville underwent a rapid number of name changes (and identity crises) in the 1870s. It has since come of age and is now one of the most renowned theaters in Paris—in the '80s it became a major outlet for avant-garde contemporary dance and, therefore, its attendant younger artists. A soiree here should fit into most travel budgets. Bravo!

Châtelet. $ Tickets €17-23, students €15. ⏰ Box office open M 11am-7pm, Tu-Sa 11am-8pm.

LE VIEUX COLOMBIER
LATIN QUARTER AND ST-GERMAIN

21 rue de le Vieux Colombier ☎ 01 44 39 87 00 vieux.colombier.free.fr

Located in one of Paris' snobbiest areas, Le Vieux Colombier almost closed in the 1970s; the city brought it back in 1986 and classified it as a historical monument. It now puts up a wide range of plays, made possible by the Vieux Colombier's in-house production team, for one-to-two month runs. Widely considered one of Paris's preeminent contemporary theatres, their performances are definitely worth an evening.

St.-Sulpice. $ Tickets €27-32. ⏰ Shows W-Sa 7-8pm, Su 4pm.

THÉÂTRE DE LA HUCHETTE
LATIN QUARTER AND ST-GERMAIN

23 rue de la Huchette ☎ 01 43 26 38 99 www.theatre-huchette.com

Théâtre de La Huchette has produced the same two plays six days a week since 1957: La Cantatrice and La Lecon, Ionesco's first two works. Other modern plays rotate through Huchette's repertoire as well. Of course, you'll have to elbow your way through the droves of tourists around St. Michel to get there.

St. Michel. $ Tickets €22 per show, €32 for 2 on the same night. Students under €15, except on Sa and holidays. ⏰ Shows M-Sa, La Cantatrice at 7pm, La Lecon at 8pm.

THÉÂTRE DU CHÂTELET
♿ CHÂTELET-LES HALLES

15 ave. Montaigne ☎01 49 52 50 50 www.chatelet-theatre.com

A staple of the 1st arrondissement since 1862, the majestic Théâtre du Châtelet is now under the direction of Jean-Luc Choplin, and hosts opera, ballet, and classical performances. It also is home to the annual Cesar French film awards. If you're not a student (or probably even if you are one), get ready to fork over some serious change for an opera here.

⇟ Châtelet. *i* Call ahead for wheelchair access. $ Tickets €10-120. Last-minute discounts if shows haven't sold out. ⏰ Box office open daily 11am-7pm, open 1hr before show on Su and holidays.

gotta get them tix

TICKET AGENCIES: FNAC (*74 av. des Champs-Èlysées, 8éme ☎01 53 53 64 64 💻www.fnac.fr [M]Franklin D. Roosevelt. ⏰ Open M-Sa 10am-11:45pm, Su noon-11:45pm. i Also at 77-81, bd. St-Germain; 109 Porte Berger; 30 av. d'Italie, 13éme; 136 rue de Rennes, 6éme; 109 rue St-Lazare, 9éme; 26-30 av. de Ternes, 17éme.*) **Virgin Megastore** (*52 av. des Champs-Elysées, 8éme ☎01 49 53 50 00 💻www.virginmegastore.fr [M] Franklin D. Roosevelt. ⏰ Open M-Sa 9am-6pm.*)

cabaret

★ LE LAPIN AGILE

🎫 MONTMARTRE

22 rue des Saules ☎01 46 06 85 87 💻www.au-lapin-agile.com

Halfway up a steep, cobblestoned hill that American tourists describe as "just like San Francisco," Le Lapin Agile has been around since the late 19th century, providing savvy Parisians and tourists with a venue for music, dance and theatre. The tiny pink, green-shuttered theater was a hotspot of the 20th-century bohemian art scene in Paris—Picasso and Max Jacob are on the list of people who cabareted (is that a word?) there.

⇟ [M]Lamarck-Coulaincourt. *i* Ticket price includes first drink. $ Tickets €24, students under 26 €17. ⏰ Shows Tu-Su, 9pm-2am.

BAL DU MOULIN ROUGE

🎫 MONTMARTRE

82 bd. de Clichy ☎ 01 53 09 82 82 💻www.moulin-rouge.com

Ever since Christina & Co's music video, the only thing people associate with "Moulin Rouge" is that universal question: *"Voulez-vous couchez avec moi?"* But the world-famous cabaret and setting for the song and film isn't just about sex; it's also about glam and glitz. Since its opening in 1889, the Moulin Rouge has hosted international superstars like Ella Fitzgerald and Johnny Rey, and now welcomes a fair crowd of tourists for an evening of sequins, tassels, and skin. The shows remain risqué, but the price of admission is prohibitively expensive. The late show is cheaper, but be prepared to stand if it's a busy night.

⇟ [M]Blanche. *i* Elegant attire required; no shorts, sneakers, or sportswear permitted. $ Ticket for 9pm €102, 11pm show €92; includes half-bottle of champagne. Combo 7pm dinner and 9pm show €150-180. Occasional lunch shows €100-130; call for more info. ⏰ Dinner at 7pm. Shows nightly 9, 11pm.

CAVEAU DE LA RÉPUBLIQUE

🎫 THE MARAIS

1 bd. St-Martin ☎01 42 78 44 45 💻www.caveau.fr

It's mostly Parisians at this 100-year-old venue for political satire, and understandably so—the comedians are ruthlessly witty, and talk extra fast. If you don't really speak French and think Sarkozy's a popular president, then you'll probably find the *tour de champs*—comprised of six separate comedy and song acts—excruciatingly long, and not very funny. Those who speak French, laugh the best.

⇟ [M]République. $ Tickets Tu-Th €34, F-Su €41. student discount available. ⏰ Tickets sold up to 6 days in advance; Box office open M noon-6pm, Tu-Sa noon-7pm, Su noon-4pm. Shows Jan-June and mid-Aug-Dec Tu-Sa 8:30pm, Su 3:30pm.

cinema

L'ARLEQUIN — LATIN QUARTER AND ST-GERMAIN

76 rue de Rennes ☎01 45 44 28 80

A proud revival theater, L'Arlequin goes heavy on the Hitchcock, mixing in other classic European films and some more modern French selections. The same three films are featured each week, undoubtedly decreasing the prevalence of adolescent movie-hopping. Some films are in English, but beware of certain dubbed selections.

[M]Saint-Sulpice. $ Full price €9.50, reduced price €6.50 for 60+, students, 18-under, and big families. Only under 18 receive discount F-Su nights.

ACTION CHRISTINE — LATIN QUARTER AND ST-GERMAIN

4 rue Christine ☎01 43 33 86 86 www.actioncinemas.org

This small theater plays mostly American flicks from the 1930s-1960s for the tourist circus at Saint-Michel, but some more modern productions occasionally sneak into the program. Christine also hosts lectures and discussions with local film scholars; check out the website or visit the theater itself for listings. This is a nice way to escape the heat of the day or wind down after a long day from Saint Michel; despite its proximity to the tourist factory, you would think Action Christine was in a small village in the northeastern part of France.

[M]Odéon. i Films in English, French subtitles. $ Full price €8, under 20 €6, group price €4.50, students 14-26 €3.50, student groups €3. ⏰ First show at 2pm, last show 10pm.

CINÉMATHÈQUE FRANÇAISE — BASTILLE

51 rue de Bercy ☎01 71 19 32 00 www.cinematheque.fr

Though it's had some problems settling down (it's moved over five times, most recently in 2005), the Cinémathèque Française is committed to sustaining film culture. A must for film buffs, the theater screens four-to-five classics, near-classics, or soon-to-be classics per day; foreign selections are usually dubbed. The Française also features multiple movie-related exhibits, which include over 1,000 costumes, objects, and apparatuses from the past and present world of film.

[M]Bercy. i Buy tickets 20min. early. $ €6.50, under 26 and seniors €5, under 18 €3. ⏰ Temporary and permanent collections open M and W-Sa noon-7pm, Su 10am-8pm. Ticket window open from noon-last showing M and W-Sa, from 10am-last showing on Su.

LA PAGODE — INVALIDES

57 Bis rue de Babylone ☎01 45 55 48 48 www.etoile-cinemas.com

See **Sights,** p. 101.

[M]St-François-Xavier. $€8.50; over 60, under 21, students, and M and W €7. ⏰Screenings from 1:30-10:30pm.

LES TROIS LUXEMBOURG — LATIN QUARTER AND ST-GERMAIN

67 rue Monsieur-le-Prince ☎08 92 68 93 25 www.lestroisluxembourg.com

The first multiplex in Paris and the first art house theatre in the Latin Quarter, Les Trois Luxembourg is an old cinema devoted to contemporary film culture. They pay special attention to "auteur" cinema, including documentaries. Independent, classic, American, and foreign films are shown with French subtitles.

[M]Luxembourg. $ €7, reduced ticket price M-Tu.

music

ELYSÉE MONTMARTRE — MONTMARTRE

72 bd. Rochechouart ☎01 44 92 45 36 www.elyseemontmartre.com

Any hip-hop nerd will remember this historic music hall in the Roots' hit song, "You Got Me": "She said she loved my show in Paris at Elysée Montmartre/and that I stepped off the stage and took a piece of her heart." Catch various hip-hop, soul, reggae, rock, indie, and underground acts here.

✳ Ⓜ Anvers. Ⓢ *Prices vary, but generally €13.80-45.* ⓘ *Hall opens at 11:30pm for all shows.*

LE BATACLAN

🡒 BASTILLE

50 bd. Voltaire   ☎01 43 14 00 30 ▣www.le-bataclan.com

In French slang, *bataclan* means stuff or junk. In French music culture, Bataclan means a 1,500-person concert space and cafe-bar that used to be a Chinese pagoda and now hosts the likes of Metallica, Oasis, Blur, Prince, MGMT, and indie rock bands.

✳ Ⓜ Oberkampf. ⓘ *Go for the hipster in you.* Ⓢ *Tickets start at €15 and vary with each show.* ⓘ *Open Sept-July. Call or look online for schedules and reservations.*

LA CIGALE

🡒 BASTILLE

120 bd. Rochechouart   ☎01 49 25 89 99 ▣www.lacigale.fr

La Cigale is a historic stop for most contemporary music (rock, indie, hip-hop, soul, etc.) tours. Inaugurated in 1887 and classified as a historical monument in 1981, the theater's past artists have included French mega-mogul Johnny Halladay, Radiohead, Cypress Hill, and the Red Hot Chili Peppers. Capacity is a little under 1,400, so buy tickets online if you want a spot.

✳ Ⓜ Pigalle. Ⓢ *Prices vary, but generally €22.70-84.* ⓘ *Hours vary depending on concert.*

POINT EPHÉMÈRE

🡒 CANAL ST-MARTIN AND SURROUNDS

200 quai de Valmy   ☎01 40 34 02 48 ▣www.pointephemere.org

A continuously changing, grungy bar/restaurant/concert hall/dance studio/artist residence, where non-conformity and cigarettes reign supreme. Music acts are usually lesser known. On a concert night, the 300-seat space is packed with guys who collect tattoos and girls who tote helmets instead of purses.

✳ Ⓜ Jaures. ⓘ *Don't walk back late alone.* Ⓢ *Tickets prices vary per show.* ⓘ *Open M-Sa noon-2am, Su 1-9pm.*

music

CITÉ DE LA MUSIQUE

BUTTES CHAUMONT

221 ave. Jean-Jaurès · ☎01 44 84 45 00 · 🖳www.cite-musique.fr

Cité de la Musique was opened in 1995 as one of Mitterand's Grands Projets; today, this modern venue hosts everything and anything, from lute concerts to American gospel, in its enormous *salle des concerts* and smaller amphithéâtre.

✈ Ⓜ️Porte de Pantin. Ⓢ Tickets €8-40. ⌚ Shows at 8pm. Box office open Tu-Sa noon-6pm, Su 10am-6pm.

opera and dance

OPÉRA DE LA BASTILLE

BASTILLE

pl. de la Bastille · ☎08 92 89 90 90 · 🖳www.operadeparis.fr

The Opéra Garnier's "ugly" other half, the Opéra de la Bastille tends to do pieces with a more modern spin. Though the building's decor is somewhat questionable, the operas and ballets tend to be breathtaking enough to compensate. There may not be gilded columns, but you'll still feel like you're at the opera. The 2010-2011 season will include the operas *Siegfried* and *Akhmatova*, and the ballets *Romeo and Juliet* and *Swan Lake*.

✈ Ⓜ️Bastille. 𝒊 For wheelchair-access, call 2 weeks ahead. ☎01 40 01 18 50. Tickets can be purchased by Internet, mail, phone, or in person. Rush tickets 15min. before show for students under 25 and seniors. Ⓢ Tickets €5-200. ⌚ Box office open M-Sa 10:30am-6:30pm.

OPÉRA GARNIER

OPÉRA

pl. de l'Opéra · ☎08 92 89 90 90 · 🖳www.operadeparis.fr

Imagine The Opera (capital T, capital O) in Paris; now go to the Opéra Garnier. Hosts mostly ballet, chamber music, and symphonies.

✈ Ⓜ️Opéra. 𝒊 Tickets usually available 2 weeks before the show. Last-minute discount tickets go on sale 1hr. before show. For wheelchair access call 2 weeks ahead. Ⓢ Ticket prices vary; operas €7-160, ballets €6-80. ⌚ Box office open M-Sa 10:30am-6:30pm.

OPÉRA COMIQUE

CHÂTELET-LES HALLES

5 rue Favart · ☎01 42 44 45 46 · 🖳www.opera-comique.com

Opéra Comique is opera lite for drama dieters. Founded in 1714 to give theatergoers an alternative to the predominantly Italian operas of the time, the company has produced operas composed by Berlioz and Bizet and premiered Debussy's only opera back in the day.

✈ Ⓜ️Richelieu-Drouot. Ⓢ Tickets €6-108. Cheapest tickets with limited visibility usually available until the show starts. ⌚ Box office open M-Sa 9am-9pm.

guignol

MARIONNETTES DU LUXEMBOURG

LATIN QUARTER AND ST-GERMAIN

in the Jardin du Luxembourg · ☎01 43 26 46 47 · 🖳guignolduluxembourg.monsite-orange.fr

Dance, puppets, dance! In the fictional battle of the marionettes, this one comes out on top. The best *guignol* in Paris has played the same classics since its opening in 1933, including *Le Petit Chaperon Rouge (Little Red Riding Hood)* and *Pinocchio*.

✈ Ⓜ️Vavin. Ⓢ €4.50. ⌚ Run time approx. 40min. Arrive 30min. early for good seats. Performances W 4pm, Sa-Su 11am, 4pm. Performances during the summer daily at 4pm, matinée performance Sa-Su 11am.

SHOPPING

Depending on who you're talking to, shopping and Paris are almost synonymous. It can be hard to keep yourself from going crazy, but you probably should. The excessive wealth of Champs-Élysées and Shopping and Ile St-Louis are not for the faint of heart; they're for the rich. The many antique shops, rare books, and tempting tourist trappings could easily empty pockets. No one likes credit card debt, so we recommend the vintage shops and quirky boutiques in the youth-centric Marais and Bastille. Thrift stores in Paris are the anti-Salvation Army—good-as-new or clearance Oscar de la Renta and Chanel are severely marked down to high but managable prices (think Nordstrom or Anne Taylor), and make for ridiculous finds. Despite the snobby maitre d's and constant critiques of American foreign policy, the French are about as fascinated by US culture as the US is by theirs; perhaps because of this, Paris has a higher concentration of jazz music stores and vintage record shops than most American cities. It you take your music like you take your men (retro and coated in vinyl), then you'll be right at home.

greatest hits

- **THE MALL OF AMERICA'S NOT AMERICAN:** Pick up basic essentials and then some at the world's first shopping mall, **La Samaritaine.**

- **DRESS LIKE CRUELLA DE VILLE: Come on Eileen** is a vintage shopper's paridise, and features a wide selection of fur coats for non-PETA cardholders.

- **HEY, WE HATE NAZIS TOO:** The original location of the famed bookstore **Shakespeare and Co.** was allegedly forcably closed in WWII, when the owner refused to sell a Nazi officer the store's final copy of *Finnegan's Wake*. It remains the most famous (and politically active) bookstore in the city.

books

shopping

◼ SHAKESPEARE AND CO.
37 rue de la Bûcherie

◆ LATIN QUARTER AND ST-GERMAIN
☎01 43 25 40 93 ▣www.shakespeareco.org

Shakespeare & Co. is an absolutely lovable English-language bookshop and miniature socialist utopia. Scenes from the film *Before Sunset* were shot here. Allegedly, the owners allow passing "tumbleweeds" to sleep for free, provided they volunteer in the shop and read a book a day. An adjacent storefront holds an impressive collection of first editions, with emphasis on the Beat Generation.

✠ Ⓜ*St-Michel.* *i* *Bargain bins outside include French classics translated into English.* ⌚ *Open M-F 10am-11pm, Sa-Su 11am-11pm.*

◼ ABBEY BOOKSHOP
29 rue de la Parcheminerie

◉ LATIN QUARTER AND ST-GERMAIN
☎01 46 33 16 24 ▣www.abbeybookshop.net

Clear your afternoon; if you're going to Abbey Bookshop, you'll need the time. Set in a back alley, you'll need a few minutes to get used to the sheer number of books surrounding you. With a collection that includes everything from *Why Sex is Fun*, to *Bin Laden: Behind the Mask of a Terrorist*, this Canadian-owned shop probably has what you're looking for, and if not they'll order it for you. Plus they carry ◼**Let's Go**—they've obviously got the right idea.

✠ Ⓜ*St-Michel or Cluny.* *i* *Books in English and other languages available.* ⌚ *Open M-Sa 10am-7pm.*

◼ LES MOTS À LA BOUCHE
6 rue Ste-Croix de la Bretonnerie

◆ THE MARAIS
☎01 42 78 88 30 ▣www.motsbouche.com

A two-story bookstore offering mostly queer literature, photography, magazines, and art, with everything from Proust to guides on lesbian lovemaking. The international DVD collection is somewhat hidden in the corner of the bottom level (€10-€28); titles range from artistic to pornographic. Also a small English section.

✠ Ⓜ*Hôtel de Vile.* ⌚ *Open M-Sa 11am-11pm, Su 1-9pm.*

◼ L'HARMATTAN
16, 21 bis, 24 rue des Ecoles

◆ LATIN QUARTER AND ST-GERMAIN
☎01 40 46 79 10 or 01 40 46 79 14 ▣www.librarieharmattan.com

You might not immediately recognize that you're in a bookstore when you walk into L'Harmattan. With maps of different countries on the walls, and books from all over the world, it has a War Room feel to it that might make you want to talk military strategy.

✠ Ⓜ*Cluny-La Sorbonne.* *i* *2 other locations in Paris.* ⌚ *Open M-Sa 10am-12:30pm and 1:30-7pm.*

LADY LONG SOLO
38 rue Keller

◉ BASTILLE
☎09 52 73 81 53 ▣www.ladylongsolo.com

An odd assortment of counter-cultural books that includes communist pamphlets and guides to the wonders of medical marijuana. Basically, where the druggies who decide to write books sell them. Hours unreliable at best. Pamphlets advocating for the legalization of pot lying about.

✳ Ⓜ*Bastille.* Ⓢ *Books as low as €2.* ⌚ *Open M, Tu 11am-4pm, W 2-8pm, Th, F, Sa 11am-4pm, sometimes Sunday.*

LE MANOEUVRE
◆ BASTILLE

58 rue de la Roquette Paris ☎01 47 00 79 70

A small French-language bookstore stacked with international literature on translation, from Central European to North African.

✳ Ⓜ*Bastille.* ⌚ *Open Su-M 3-8pm, Tu-Sa 10:30am-8pm.*

THE VILLAGE VOICE
◆ LATIN QUARTER AND ST-GERMAIN

6 rue Princesse ☎01 46 33 36 47 🖥www.villagevoicebookshop.com

When The Village Voice opened in 1982, the narrow streets of this neighborhood were still lined with 16th- and 17th-century homes. Named both as a tribute to the local artistic community and to the New York publication, the Village Voice's guest lecturers have included John Ashbery, Margaret Atwood, and David Sedaris.

✳ Ⓜ*Mabillon.* ✦ *Often hosts authors for readings and book signings.* ⌚ *Open M 2-7:30pm, Tu-Sa 10am-7:30pm, Su noon-6pm.*

GIBERT JEUNE
◆❄ LATIN QUARTER AND ST-GERMAIN

5 pl. St-Michel ☎01 56 81 22 🖥www.gibertjeune.fr

If you're studying abroad in Paris this is probably where you'll want to buy your textbooks—Gibert Jeune carries over 300,000 titles. The selection is organized by academic subject—we were particular fans of their social sciences section. By the time you're through shopping here, you'll be set to look like a real *savant parisien*. Plus it's air conditioned, which can be a welcome change from the heat of a Parisian summer.

✳ Ⓜ*St-Michel.* ✦ *Will buy back books.* ⌚ *Open M-Sa 9:30am-7:30pm.*

SAN FRANCISCO BOOK CO.
◆ LATIN QUARTER AND ST-GERMAIN

17 rue Monsieur le Prince ☎01 43 29 15 70 🖥www.sanfranciscobooksofparis.com

San Francisco Book Co. certainly has a laid back Cali feel to it. Selling everything from trashy English crime lit to the classics like Chaucer and Flaubert, San Francisco Book Co. has things under control.

✳ *Odéon.* ⌚ *Open M-Sa 11am-9pm, Su 2-7:30pm.*

apparel

CLOTHES AND ACCESSORIES

▨ LA SAMARITAINE
◆ CHÂTELET-LES HALLES

67 rue de Rivoli ☎08 00 01 00 15 🖥www.lasamaritaine.com

Spanning three blocks of the city's prime real estate, La Samaritaine is one of the oldest and most obnoxiously large department stores in Paris, and offers 48,000 square meters of shopping space. The department store was founded in 1869 when Ernest Cognacq, a street salesman who had tired of selling his gentlemen's ties on the often rainy and windy Pont Neuf, decided to bring his operation indoors. La Samaritaine helped usher in the age of conspicuous consumption with an unforgettable slogan: "One finds everything at La Samaritaine." The roof cafe, accessible by a quick elevator ride, has a fantastic, free view of the city. Although the building was renovated in 1928, it closed indefinitely in 2006 for security renovations; murmurs of a reopening in late 2011 have been heard, but those are about as reliable as any other construction timeline in France (read: very unreliable). Check online for progress.

FORUM LES HALLES
📍 CHÂTELET-LES HALLES

Les Halles   ☎08 25 02 00 20 🖳www.forumdeshalles.com

Like most of Paris' monuments, Les Halles history is closely tied to the whims of French royalty and, later on, its politicians. The mall began as a small food market in 1135; Philippe Auguste and, later, Louis-Philippe and François I all considered Les Halles a sort of pet project, and its expansion soon surpassed their expectations. The forum and gardens above ground attract a large crowd. Descend into the pits of one of Paris's storied historical sites to discover its bastard American child; a 200-boutique shopping mall (plus three movie theaters), the Gap, H&M, and Franck Provost.

♯ ⓜ Les Halles. 🕐 Open M-Sa 10am-8pm.

ATELIER 33
📍 BASTILLE

33 rue du Faubourg St-Antoine   ☎01 43 40 61 63

This boutique caters to the kind of people who wear studded jeans jackets

look, but no touchy

Below you'll find a list of the big names that you automatically associate with the Paris shopping scene. Unless you found a Parisian 🎴sugar daddy (and props to you if you did) you probably won't be leaving with much, but who doesn't like looking at pretty things? Salespeople won't be jumping to help you, but they'll gladly answer your questions if you ask nicely.

- **CARTIER** (*23 place Vendôme* ☎01 44 55 32 20 🖳www.cartier.com ⓜ*Tuileries*)

- **CHANEL** (*42 avenue Montaigne* ☎01 47 23 74 12 🖳www.chanel.com ⓜ*Franklin D. Roosevelt*)

- **CHRISTIAN LOUBOUTIN** (*19 rue Jean-Jacques Rousseau* ☎01 42 36 05 31 🖳www.christianlouboutin.com ⓜ*Les Halles or Louvre Rivoli*)

- **DIOR** (*8 Place Vendôme* ☎01 42 96 30 84 🖳www.dior.com ⓜ*Tuileries*)

- **GIVENCHY** (*56 rue François 1er* ☎01 43 59 71 25 🖳www.givenchy.fr ⓜ*George V*)

- **GUCCI** (*60 avenue Montaigne* ☎01 56 69 80 80 🖳www.gucci.com ⓜ*Franklin D. Roosevelt*)

- **HERMÈS** (*24 rue du Faubourg Saint-Honoré* ☎01 40 17 47 17 🖳www.hermes.com ⓜ*Madeleine*)

- **JEAN-PAUL GAULTIER** (*44 avenue George V* ☎01 44 43 00 44 🖳www.jeanpaulgaultier.com ⓜ*Charles de Gaulle - Étoile*)

- **LOUIS-VUITTON** (*101 avenue des Champs-Elysées* ☎01 53 57 52 00 🖳www.louisvuitton.com ⓜ*Charles de Gaulle - Étoile*)

- **VALENTINO** (*27 rue Faubourg Saint-Honoré* ☎01 42 66 95 94 🖳www.valentino.com ⓜ*Madeleine*)

- **VERSACE** (*45 avenue Montaigne* ☎01 47 42 88 02 🖳www.versace.com ⓜ*Franklin D. Roosevelt*)

- **YVES SAINT-LAURENT** (*32 rue du Faubourg Saint-Honoré* ☎01 53 05 80 80 🖳www.ysl.com ⓜ*Madeleine*)

shopping

(€34), or order custom-made dresses to be worn with diamonds (*€300-€3,000*). Occasional sales.

✦ ⓂBastille. Ⓢ T-Shirts from €9. 🕑 Open M-Sa 10:30am-7:30pm.

LE GRAIN DE SABLE
🌂 THE MARAIS

79 rue St.Louis-en-l'Île ☎01 46 33 67 27 💻www.legraindesable.fr

Absolutely exquisite hats (*€155*) and head pieces (*€45*) that any 20-something probably can't pull off and certainly can't afford. The beautiful works are hand-made, often at a wood table in the boutique. If you do spring for one, you'll attract admiring double-takes all day.

✦ ⓂPont Marie. Ⓢ Hats €30-155. 🕑 Open M and W-Su 11am-7pm, Tu 3-7pm.

SOBRAL
🌂 THE MARAIS

79 rue St. Louis-en-l'Île ☎01 43 25 80 10 💻www.sobraldesign.com

Chunky and colorful earrings, necklaces, and bracelets (*€10-100*) inspired by pop art, but kept classy with a retro touch.

✦ ⓂPont Marie. Ⓢ Bracelets €45. Necklaces up to €110. 🕑 Open daily 11am-7:30pm.

TOTAL ECLIPSE
🌂 BASTILLE

40 rue de la Roquette ☎01 48 07 88 04

Select one of a kind pieces with large stones and funky colors, all handmade by a man named Simon.

✦ ⓂBastille. ⓈHandmade jewelry €8-50. 🕑Open M-F 11am-7:30pm, Sa 10:30am-8pm.

VINTAGE

▨ COME ON EILEEN
🌂 BASTILLE

16-18 rue des Taillandiers ☎01 43 38 12 11

A little known vintage shopper paradise, with three sparkling floors (literally: the ground is patterned in glitter). Designer labels and other high quality pieces are readily available. Friendly staff is happy to help you find hidden treasures. Large fur coat selection (*€30-50*).

✦ ⓂVoltaire. Ⓢ Prices starting at €10. 🕑 Open M-F 11am-8:30pm, Su 2-8pm. In winter closed on F from 4-6pm.

▨ FREE 'P' STAR
🌂 THE MARAIS

8 rue Ste-Croix de la Bretonnerie ☎01 42 76 03 72 💻 www.freepstar.com

Enter as Plain Jane and leave a star—from the '80s or '90s, that is. Wide selection of vintage dresses (*€20*), velvet blazers (*€40*), boots (*€30*), and military-style jackets (*€5*) that all seem like a good idea when surrounded by other antiquated pieces, but require some balls to be worn out in the open. There's no way to go wrong with the €10 jean pile and €3 bin. Second location at 61 rue de la Verrerie (☎01 42 78 0 76).

✦ ⓂHôtel de Ville. *i* Credit card min. €20. 🕑 Open M-Sa noon-11pm, Su 2-11pm.

▨ MAMIE BLUE
🌂 OPÉRA

69 rue de Rochechouart ☎01 42 81 10 42 💻www.mamie-vintage.com

This vintage store does more than sell old clothes for reduced prices—it transports shoppers back through the decades. A vintage boutique in both decor and spirit, Mamie Blue specializes in clothing from the '20s-'70s. Each piece is hand chosen by the owner.

✦ ⓂAnvers or Barbès. *i* Also does restorations. Ⓢ Dresses €40-175. 🕑 Open M 2:30-7:30pm, Tu-Sa 11:30am-1:30pm and 2:30-7:30pm.

COIFFEUR
🌂 THE MARAIS

32 rue de Rosiers

Right next door to L'As du Falafel, Coiffeur brings in the type of people who are just as willing to battle a crowd in the name of a good bargain. High quality vintage clothing is sold at a such fair price that nothing stays in the store for very long. The sweater rack (€10-€15) is a local fave.

✻ Ⓜ*Hotel de Ville.* Ⓢ *Dresses €10-€22. Jackets from €25.* ⏰ *Open daily 11am-9pm.*

ADOM
🛒 BASTILLE

35 and 56 rue de la Roquette   ☎01 48 07 15 94 or 01 43 57 54 92

Think of every canonical high school film you've ever seen: *Fast Times at Ridgemont High*, *The Breakfast Club*, *Napolean Dynamite*. The selection at Adom seems to be made up of the wardrobe department from all of them. Cowboy boots, acid wash jeans, and letterman jackets are in ample supply here. It's like totally awesome, duh.

✻ Ⓜ*Bastille.* Ⓢ *Boots from €35. Cut-offs €15.* ⏰ *Open M-Sa 11am-8pm and Su 3-8pm.*

FRIP'IRIUM
🛒 THE MARAIS

2 rue de la Verrerie   ☎01 40 29 95 57

Another vintage shop in the Marais? *Quelle bonne suprise!* Frip'irium has a large collection of vintage bathing suits, lace shirts, and scandalous booty shorts; all the things you'd expect in this arrondissement. A friendly staff and chill music playing make your vintage shopping experience here enjoyable, even if you buy something a little skanky.

✻ Ⓜ*Hôtel de Ville* Ⓢ *Jackets €25-€30.* ⏰ *Open Tu-Sa 1-9pm, Su 2-9pm.*

FRIPES STAR
🛒 THE MARAIS

61 rue de la Verrerie   ☎01 42 78 00 76

This store is like the Jan to Free 'P' Star's Marsha; it's fine, but not nearly as cool. They offer a huge selection of shirts, dresses and skirts, though they do have more browsing room than Free 'P' Star. Prices are pretty comparable, and the loft area has a €1 bin. At the end of the day though, Marsha was just cooler (read: go to Free 'P' Star).

✻ Ⓜ*Hôtel de Ville.* Ⓢ *Dresses €10-€15.* ⏰ *Open M-Sa 11am-9pm, Su 2-9pm.*

VERTIGES ET RAG
🛒 THE MARAIS

83-85 rue St. Martin   ☎01 48 87 36 64

The prices here are amazing—you can find Ralph Lauren button-down shirts for €5. On the Rag side of the store, you'll find Converses and handkerchiefs. Watch out for the guys breakdancing in the aisles to Hammertime.

✻ Ⓜ*Rambateau or Hotel de Ville.* 𝒊 *Mostly men's wear.* Ⓢ *Mostly €5-€15. Jackets from €60.* ⏰ *Open daily 10:30am-8pm.*

music

🎵 CROCOJAZZ
🔖 LATIN QUARTER AND ST-GERMAIN

64 rue Ste Geneviève   ☎01 46 34 78 38

Everything is all about jazz here, from the books on Miles Davis to the DVDs on Louis Armstrong. With the faint smell of slow burning cigars and stacks of old records, Crocojazz sets the mood right. Extremely knowledgeable employees can help you find almost anything.

✻ Ⓜ*Maubert Mutualité.* Ⓢ *Records €10-22. CDs €10-18* ⏰ *Open Tu-Sa 11am-1pm and 2-7pm.*

🎵 LA CHAMUMIÈRE À LA MUSIQUE
🔖❄ LATIN QUARTER AND ST-GERMAIN

5 rue de Vaugirard   ☎01 43 54 07 25 🖥www.chaumiereonline.com

Mozart lovers will feel right at home at La Chamumière à la Musique. Come here to buy and exchange your classical CDs, stock up about books on your favorite composers, and stay up to date on the *hot hot hot* contemporary classical music scene.

✻ Ⓜ*Odéon.* Ⓢ *CDs from €2.* ⏰ *Open M-F 10am-7:30pm, Sa 10am-8pm, Su and holidays 2-8pm.*

shopping

CROCODISC

40-42 rue des Ecoles

LATIN QUARTER AND ST-GERMAIN
☎01 43 54 47 95 or 01 43 54 33 22

It's the kind of shop that makes you feel like going out and buying cool sneakers to match your new record. Stretching across two storefronts, Crocodisc runs the genre gamut, carrying rock, reggae, Italian, '60s, North African, garage, psyche/acid, trip hop and soul music. Listening stations are interspersed between random objects.

✣ ⓂMaubert-Mutualité. Ⓢ Records €10-20. CDs €8-15. ⌚ Open Tu-Sa 11am-7pm.

LA DAME BLANCHE

47 rue Montagne Ste Geneviève

LATIN QUARTER AND ST-GERMAIN
☎01 43 54 54 45

"Music is a gift." This is the message that greets you as you walk into La Dame Blanche, and they certainly seem to think so. Be sure to duck your head to avoid hitting the low ceilings as you peruse their jazz, classical, and avante-garde music collection.

✣ ⓂMaubert-Mutualité. Ⓢ CDs €10-23. ⌚ Open M-Sa 10:30am-8pm, Su 11:30am-8pm.

BOULINIER

20 bd. St-Michel

LATIN QUARTER AND ST-GERMAIN

Are you old enough to miss cassette tapes? We're not, but luckily for you 40-somethings, Boulinier still carries them. This multi-level music shop is your go-to for records, CDs, DVDs, and yes, cassette tapes. Unfortunately, they don't carry 8-tracks (sorry Disco Stu).

✣ ⓂCluny or Odéon. Ⓢ Records €12-14. ⌚ Open M 10:30am-midnight, T-W 1:30-8:30pm, F-Sa 10:30am-midnight.

MONSTER MELODIES

9 rue des Décharges

CHÂTELET-LES HALLES
☎01 40 28 09 39

From jazz to ska, from Bieber to Ziggy Marley, Monster Melodies probably carries what you're looking for. The lower level houses well over 10,000 used CDs, while the upstairs sells those vinyl things your parents are always talking about.

✣ ⓂLes Halles. ⌚ Open M-Sa noon-7pm.

BORN BAD RECORD SHOP

17 rue Keller

BASTILLE
☎01 43 38 41 78 🖥 www.bornbad.fr

Vintage records from a variety of genres, including soul, funk, garage, punk, and ska, sold in a slightly funky-smelling shop (€10-29). You might have to throw a few elbows to get to the good stuff at the bottom of the discount bin.

✣ ⓂBastille. Ⓢ CDs €13. Records €10-29. ⌚ Open M-Sa noon-8pm.

OCD

26 rue des Ecoles

LATIN QUARTER AND ST-GERMAIN
☎01 43 25 62 93 🖥 www.ocd.net

OCD: Obsessive Compulsive DVDs. With 3 locations around Paris, OCD carries music and movies, as well as shows like Lost and Grey's Anatomy dubbed in French. Just when you thought McDreamy couldn't be any hotter...

✣ ⓂJussieu or Maubert-Mutualité. ⌚ Open M-Sa 11am-8pm, Su 1-7pm.

specialty

🎁 PYLÔNES

57 rue St-Louis-en-l'Île

THE MARAIS
☎01 46 34 05 02 🖥 www.pylones.com

An adult version of a toy store with the kind of spunky things you'll impulsively buy, never need, but always marvel at. Like graters topped with doll heads (€18). More useful, but just as fun items include cigarette cases (€12) — you're in Paris now, tobacco's a part of growing up — and espresso cups (€6). The playful, artful objects are fun to look at even if you don't get any.

✴ Ⓜ*Pont Marie.* *i* *5 other locations around the city.* Ⓢ *Cups €6, wallets €24.* ⏰ *Open daily 10:30am-7:30pm.*

🖼 LA GRANDE ÉPICERIE DE PARIS ☛ INVALIDES

38 rue de Sèvres

The butcher actually has a thin twirled mustache. We thought only cartoon French people looked like that.

✴ Ⓜ*Vaneau.* *i* *No pets allowed.* Ⓢ *Water €30. This place is way too expensive for you.* ⏰ *Open M-Sa 8:30am-9pm.*

LA PETITE SCIERIE ☛ ÎLE DE LA CITÉ AND ÎLE ST-LOUIS

60 rue St-Louis-en-l'Île ☎01 55 42 14 88 🖥lanetitescierie.fr

Committed to true French artisanship, Cathérine Duoy's high-quality specialties have been sold on the Île de la Cité for the last 25 years.

✴ Ⓜ*Pont Marie.* Ⓢ *Foie-gras 180g €32, 320g €60.* ⏰ *Open Th-M 11am-7pm. Open daily in December.*

LE MARCHÉ AUX FLEURS ☛ THE MARAIS

pl. Louis-Lépine

This covered flower marketplace is a pretty place to stop for lilacs, orchids and any other flower variety for you, yourself and the honey you may not have. Parisians have been ducking under dangling wicker baskets, wandering through blooming bushes, and picking up quaint garden knick-knacky from here for years.

✴ Ⓜ*Cité.* *i* *Turns into Marché aux Oiseaux (bird market) on Su.* ⏰ *Open daily 8am-7pm.*

BARTHÉLÉMY ☛ INVALIDES

51 rue de Grenelle ☎01 45 48 56 75

A cheese lover's dream.

✴ Ⓜ*Rue de Bac.* Ⓢ *Boulamour raisins €6.50.* ⏰ *Open Tu-F 8:30am-1 pm and 4-7:15pm, Sa 8:30am-1:30pm and 3-7pm.*

EXCURSIONS

You know how celebrities and Wall Street suits who'd rather not look at poor people flee to the world's Wisteria Lanes? Well, France's well-moneyed aristocracy did it first, and their opulent chateaus outside Paris make Warren Buffet look like a struggling entrepreneur. Appropriated by the masses during a certain Revolution, the palaces of France's former elite have since been turned into illustrious museums and public parks, and make for a relaxing daytrip from the bustle of the city. Hike through the forests of Fontainebleau, sample some *chantilly* at Chantilly, and witness evidence of the Sun King and Napoleon's respective inferiority complexes at Versailles. The train and bus systems around Paris run pretty smoothly, so accessing most of these sights shouldn't be a problem.

greatest hits

- **MARIE ANTOINETTE HAD IT GOOD.** Versailles is as great as you've heard. Actually, no, it's probably better. The ◩**Hall of Mirrors** (p. 209) is one of the only places where it's okay to check yourself out non-stop.

- **WHIP IT GOOD.** Cool Whip ain't got nothin' on *chantilly*. Try the *chantilly* at **Le Hameau** (p. 223) for a much classier dessert than that sundae you had at Friendly's last week.

- **MAJOR IN BEER.** Boozin' is all you'll study at **L'Academie de la Bière** (p. 215) in Chartres, with an impressive curriculum of Irish brews.

- **DINE LIKE A DUKE.** That's the theme at **Le Caveau des Ducs** (p. 219), where you might spend a little more than you're used to, but you'll leave happy.

versailles ☏01 30

If you descend the great steps of the Versailles garden slowly enough, you might just feel like royalty. A whopping 580m long, this crib won't fit in your camera frame. To be fair, the palace did house all 6,000 members of the royal court and serve as the seat of government, after **Louis XIV** (1643-1715) decided in 1661 that his father's old brick and stone chateau needed an upgrade. No less than four men were needed to get it done. Louis XIV, or the Sun King, or the self-aggrandizing narcissist, commissioned two architects, Lous Le Vau and Jules Hardouin-Mansart, painter Charles Le Brun, and landscape designer André Le Nôtre to create an unquestionable symbol of the awesome power of the French monarchy. Later, with the 1789 Revolution, Louis XVI and Marie-Antoinette would learn just how contestable that power was when set under a guillotine blade. In 1837, King Louis-Phillipe initiated a clever piece of PR, opening up parts of the palace to the public and dedicating it to "all the glories of France." Since then, the chateau has remained largely unaltered, though a €370 million renovation and restoration campaign was launched in 2003, and visitors now are hardly ever of royal blood.

ORIENTATION

As the Sun King demanded, a visit to the 800-hectare property must begin at the **terrace.** To its left, the **Parterre Sud** opens up to the **Orangery,** which once boasted 2000 orange trees. The fresh-squeezed orange juice stands scattered throughout the sight today recall the orangery's historical production. The **Parterre d'Eau**, the first of many ponds and lakes on the premises, stands in the middle of the terrace. Past the **Bassin de Latone** and to the left is the **Jardin du Roi**, a fragrant, flower-lined sanctuary only accessible from the easternmost side facing the **Bassin du Miroir.** Near the grove's southern gate lies the **Bassin de Bacchus,** one of four seasonal fountains, which portrays the Roman god of wine, crowned in vine branches, reclining on a bunch of grapes. Some traveler's report having taken swigs of wine there in honor of the great god. Behind it, the **Bosquet de la Salle de Ball** is a semicircle of cascading waterfalls and torch holders, where royals once late-night bacchanalias of their own.

Moving north to the center of the garden leads to the **Bosquet de la Colonnade,** an impressive arrangement of 32 violet and blue marble columns, sculptures, and white marble basins, created by Hardouin-Mansart in 1864. The northern gate to the Colonnade opens onto the 330m long **Tapis Vert,** the main walkway leading to the garden's most ostentatious fountain, the **Bassin d'Apollo,** in which the god himself charges out of the water on bronze horses. On the garden's northern side, you'll find the **Bosquet de l'Encelade.** When the fountain is on, a 25m jet bursts from Titan's enormous mouth, which is plated, as all mouths should be, with shimmering gold.

The **Bassin de Flore** and the **Bassin de Cérès** show ladies, busts out, reclining in their natural habitats—a bed of flowers and wheat sheaves, respectively. The **Parterre Nord** overlooks some of the garden's most spectacular fountains. The **Allée d'Eau,** a fountain-lined walkway, provides the best view of the **Bassin des Nymphes de Diane.** The path slopes toward the sculpted **Bassin du Bragon,** where a beast slain by Apollo spurts water 27m into the air. Next to it, 99 jets of water issue from sea horns encircling Neptune in the **Bassin de Neptuune,** the gardens' largest fountain; make your way here at 5:20pm for a truly spectacular fountain finale.

If you get tired of the grandeur of the main gardens and groves, head up to Marie-Antoinette's Estate, where the quiet, flower-filled paths are much less of an ego display.

SIGHTS

CHATEAU

☎01 30 83 78 89 💻www.chateauversailles.fr

Though the Sun King's palace boasts a whopping 51,200 square meters of floor space, the public is granted access to only a small percentage of it. With over ten million visitors per year, the Versailles staff is practiced in the art of shuttling tourists through. After a walk through the **Musée de l'Histoire de France,** which briefly recounts French history in chronological order, visitors are shepherded down the halls in a single direction. The museum's 21 rooms feature stunning portraits of the royal family, including a smaller copy of Rigaud's famous **depiction of Louis XIV** with red-heeled shoes. Up the main staircase to the right is the two-level chapel where the King heard Mass, built in 1710. Here God competed with the Sun King for attention while the court gathered to watch him pray.

Through the hallway, where the ceiling is covered with marvelous frescoes (don't forget to look up!), are the luxurious **State Apartments,** which include both the king's bedroom, the **Room of Abundance,** the **Apollo Salon,** and the famed **Hall of Mirrors.** Note how tiny the bed is; like Napoleon, Sarkozy, and other French leaders that followed him, Louis XIV was a man of less than average height, with an ensuing inferiority complex, and was known to wear shoes with 5 in. heels. The Apollo Salon houses the Sun King's throne; 3m tall, the throne enabled the King to tower over his subjects and enjoy the view of the beautiful fresco of himself on the ceiling, which compares him to Apollo and portrays him as the bearer of Enlightenment. When they weren't trying to figure out how to kill him, French citizens showed great deference to the king, and ritualistically bowed or curtsied when they passed the throne, even when great Louis wasn't there. As if the Apollo Salon wasn't elaborate (or pathological) enough, the sumptuous Hall of Mirrors exemplifies the King's opulent taste. Lined with the largest mirrors 17th-century technology could produce, and windows that overlook to the grand gardens outside, the room served as a reception for great ambassadors. Today it can be rented out for a hefty sum.

The **Queen's Bedchamber,** where royal births were public events in order to prove the legitimacy of heirs, is much less ornate than the king's, but almost exactly as the queen last left it on October 6, 1789. A rendition of *Le Sacre de Napoleon* by French neo-classicist David depicts Napoleon's self-coronation, and dominates the **Salle du Sacré,** also known as the **Coronation Room.** David painted Napoleon's mother, Letizia, into the scene even though she refused to be there. The more honest painting of **Battle of Aboukir** is positioned on the wall next to it, and portrays the gore of war—and perhaps the price of all the royal splendor that surrounds it.

Ⓢ *Admission to palace and audio guide €15, reduced price €13. The "passport" one-day pass allows entry to the palace, Trianon palace and Marie-Antoinette's estate €18. Day of Les Grands Eaux Musicales €25. Trianon palace and Marie Antionette's Estate €10, reduced price €6.* 🕐 *Chateau open Tu-Su Apr-Oct 9am-6:30pm; Nov-Mar 9am-5:30pm. Last entry 30min. before close.*

GARDENS

Gardening *à la française* is nothing short of neurotic. The park of Versailles, with its parterres, groves, status, fountains, pools and trees boxed in metal frames, is no exception. Meticulously designed by André Le Nôtre in 1661 and completed by **Jules Hardouin-Mansart,** the chateau gardens are an impressive 800 hectares. During **Les Grand Eux Musicales,** almost all the fountains are turned on at the same time, and chamber music booms from among the groves. Wandering through the gardens' many walks, you will find a number of marble statues and bursting fountains.

TRIANONS AND MARIE ANTOINETTE'S HAMEAU

Contrary to what officials will tell you, the walk up to **Trianons** and **Marie Antoi-nette's Hameau** does not take 25min. Less ambitious sightseers are overwhelmed by the prospect of leaving the main area, which makes for a quieter and infinitely more pleasant Versailles experience. The garden surrounding Petit Trianon and Marie Antoinette's hameau is one of the most beautiful and tranquil areas of the park. Inspired by Jean-Jacques Rousseau's theories on the goodness of nature, the Queen wanted a simple life, and so commissioned Richard Mique to construct a 12-building compound comprised of a dairy farm, gardener's house, and mill around a pristine, swan-filled lake. Complete with lilac beds, flower pots, and thatched roofs, Marie Antoinette played the peasant and held intimate parties in her **Temple of Love.** We doubt the irony of this idealized pastoralism escaped the Parisian masses of the time. **Petit Trianon** was built between 1762 and 1768 for Louix XV and his mistress Mme. de Pompadour. Some ways away from the palace, the more homey chateau was intended to serve as a love den. Unfortunately, Pompadour died before it was completed. The **Grand Trianon** was intended to be a chateau-away-from-chateau for Louix XIV, who reached the mini chateau by boat from the Grand Canal. Both the Petit and Grand Trianon provide a less ostentatious view of royal life and allow one to imagine the life of a man rather than the life of a king.

FOOD

Eating in Versailles is less expensive than you would expect, considering the three million tourists that visit the town each year. Restaurants and vendors jack up the price about €1-2 for the privilege of eating where the kings once did, but prices outside of the gilded gates are more reasonable. The royal feasts rolled right out with Louis XVI's head; today, options are pretty much limited to sandwiches, crêpes and pizza. Wise visitors—that means you, fair Let's Go traveler—know that packing a long baguette, some fruit and a bottle of wine and spreading out on the grass is the best way to do it.

ESSENTIALS

Getting There

RER trains beginning with "V" run from Invalides or any stop on RER Line C5 to the **Versailles Rive Gauche station.** (**i** Buy a round-trip ticket, as ticket lines are long at Versailles station. Ⓢ Round-trip €5.80.☑ 30-40min., every 15min.) Buy your RER ticket before going through the turnstile to the platform; when purchasing from a machine, look for the **Ile-de-France ticket option.** While a Metro ticket will get you through these turnstiles, it won't get you through RER turnstiles at the other end and could ultimately result in a significant fine. From RER: Versailles, turn right down **av. du General de Gaulles,** walk 200m, and turn left at the big intersection on av. de Paris. You'll know it when you see it.

Getting Around

The **tourist office** is on the left before the chateau courtyard. Info on local accommodations, events, restaurants, and sightseeing buses. Also sells tickets for historical guided tours of the town. Not to be confused with office that sells guided tours of the chateau. (2bis av. de Paris ☎01 39 24 88 88 ▧www.versailles-tourisme.com ☑ Open M 11am-5pm, Tu-Sa 9am-6pm, Su 11am-5pm.)

Were it not for a scrap of fabric, the cathedral and town of Chartres might still be a sleepy hamlet. But the cloth that the Virgin Mary supposedly wore when she gave birth to Jesus made Chartres a major medieval pilgrimage center. The majestic cathedral that towers over the city isn't the only reason to visit; the *vieille ville* is also a masterpiece of medieval architecture, which almost makes you forget the zooming highways that have encroached upon it. Chartres's medieval tangle of streets can be confusing but getting lost here is enjoyable.

ORIENTATION

To reach the **Cathedral** from the train station, walk straight ahead down **Avenue Jehan de Beauce** to **Place de Châtelet,** then look up. You'll see the Cathedral and the **Place de la Cathédrale,** and quickly begin to comprehend that the Cathedral isn't the only show in town. Don't make the mistake of asking a local where the Cathedral is; you'll get laughed at or severely snarked. The **Musée des Beaux-Arts** and other prominent sights are located nearby. **The Maison Picassiette** is a little farther, about 10min. away from the *vieille ville* by **taxi.**

SIGHTS

Is the cathedral the best show in town? Yes. The only one? No, absolutely not. Check out a few of these recommended spots before, during, or after your tour of the massive Cathedral.

Chartres Cathedral

THE CATHEDRAL CHURCH

18 Cloitre Notre Dame ☎02 37 21 75 02 www.cathedrale-chartres.com

The Cathédrale de Chartres is quite possibly the best-preserved medieval church in Europe, having miraculously escaped major damage during its nearly 1,000 years of existence; while Notre Dame's statues were beheaded, those architectural wonder survived the French Revolution and WWII unscathed. The Church features some Romanesque elements, but has the Gothic aspects of its design to thank for its stunning stained glass and enormous size. The mélange of the two architectural periods is easily visible in its dramatic and subtly lopsided towers. The one on the left was finished in 1513, and built in the Late Gothic, or Flamboyant, style; the one on the right was built just before the 1194 fire, and is characterized by an octagonal Romanesque design. It is also the tallest tower of its kind still standing. The Cathedral's spires are visible from most locations in the town, and the beauty and complexity in the Cathedral's stained glass windows are truly unbelievable. It has stood here for nearly a millennium, and has hosted such momentous events as Henri IV's coronation in 1594.

The only English-language tours of the Cathedral are given by **Malcolm Miller,** an authority on Gothic architecture, and the Chartres Cathedral specifically, who has been leading visitors through the church for over 40 years. His presentations on the Cathedral's history and symbolism are interesting, witty, and enjoyable for visitors of all ages; after covering the historical and architectural highlights of the monument, he selects individual stained glass tableaux from among the church's 176 windows to examine more closely. If you can afford it *($ Tours €10. ⏰ M, W-Su twice a day, once in morning and once in afternoon)*, take both his morning and afternoon tour—no two are alike. If you're the sensitive type, you might want to stay away. If you can take only one of his tours, visitors who took both recommend the morning one. He's in his seventies, so fatigue is a factor; some visitors even suspected that he'd had a few **cocktails at lunch.**

If it weren't for the **Sancta Camisia,** Chartres wouldn't be what it is today. The year after he became emperor in 875 CE, Charlemagne's grandson—Charles the Bald—donated the Sancta Camisia, the cloth believed to have been worn by the Virgin Mary when she gave birth to Christ, to Chartres. Thousands of Catholics journeyed to the church to kneel before the sacred relic, in hopes that it would heal them and answer their prayers. The sick who journeyed to the Cathedral were nursed in the crypt below the sanctuary, and the cloth's powers were "confirmed" in 911 CE, when it supposedly saved the city from invading Goths and Vikings; the Viking leader Rollon converted to Christianity and became the first Duke of Normandy. Today, the relic is on display in the back of the church on the left-hand side, and alternates between the three chapels. Don't worry, this isn't some repeat of the **Monty Hall problem;** just look for the chapel with the large cloth hanging in front of it, and a mob of non-praying tourists parked in front. The Cathedral doesn't get too crowded on weekdays, so you can generally get some nice face time with the shroud then.

At a time when books were rare and the vast majority of people were illiterate, the cathedral's **stained glass windows** served as religious literature. Most of the 176 windows date from the 13th century, and were preserved through both World Wars by the heroic and extremely savvy town authorities, who carefully dismantled all the windows and stored them in Dordogne until the wars were over. The original associations of medieval merchants who paid for the windows are represented in their lower panels, ranging from bakers and fur merchants. The glass designs are characterized by a stunning color known as **"Chartres blue,"** which has not been successfully reproduced in modern times. The center window depicts the story of Christ, from the Annunciation to the ride into Jerusalem. An important detail: stories read from bottom to top, left to right. If you take the Malcolm Miller tour, he guides you through a couple of the windows; this is invaluable, as there's no way a non-expert could ever decipher the windows alone.

The windows of Chartres often distract visitors from the treasure below their feet: a winding **labyrinth** pattern that is carved into the floor in the rear of the nave. Designed in the 13th century, the labyrinth was a pilgrimage substitute; by following this symbolic journey on their hands and knees, the devout would enact a symbolic voyage to Jerusalem. Now the labyrinth is uncovered on Fridays only, so if you're really into this kind of thing, you'll have to delay your visit until then. Upon request, Miller will talk about the labyrinth on Fridays.

 # Place de la Cathédrale. i English-language audio guides available at the gift shop require a piece of identification as a deposit. 1 hr. English tours of the cathedral by Malcolm Miller begin outside the gift shop in the cathedral. Easter to early Nov. M-Sa noon and 2:45pm; call ☎02 37 28 15 58 for tour availability during winter months. [$] English tours €10, students and children €5. Audio guides €3.50, €4.50, €6.50, depending on tour.

TOUR JEHAN-DE-BEAUCE

☎02 37 21 75 02

Only the athletic and non-claustrophobic can climb the narrow staircase to the cathedral's north tower, Tour Jehan-de-Beauce (named after its architect), for a stellar view of the cathedral's roof, its flying buttresses, and the city below. If you don't make it all the way to the top, the first viewing platform offers a slightly obstructed but nonetheless impressive sight.

[$] €7, ages 18-25 €4.50, under 18 free. ⏰ Open May-Aug M-Sa, 9:30am-12pm and 2-5:30pm, Su 2-5:30pm. Sept-Apr M-Sa, 9:30am-12:30pm and 2-5pm, Su 2-5pm. Last entrance 30min. before close. Access to roof structure May-Aug starting at 4pm, Sept-Apr, Sa-Su and school holidays starting at 3pm. Tours of the upper stained-glass windows available upon request. Closed Jan 1 and 5 and Dec 25.

CRYPT

☎02 37 21 56 33

Visitors may enter the 110m long subterranean crypt only as part of a guided tour. Parts of the crypt, including the well which Vikings tossed the bodies of their victims into during raids, date back to the ninth century.

i *Information sheets in English available. Tours in French leave from store, opposite the cathedral's south entrance at 18 Cloître Notre Dame. French-language tours 30min. English leaflets at the La Crypte store. Groups should call ahead: ☎02 37 21 75 02.* ⑤ *€2.70, students €2.10, under 7 free.* ⌚ *Apr-Oct M-Sa 2:15, 3:30, 4:30pm, Su 11am; Nov-Mar M-Sa 4:15pm, Su 11am. Additional 5:15pm tour June 22-Sept 21.*

Other Sights

⬛ MAISON PICASSIETTE
⬗ MUSEUM

22 rue du Repos
☎02 37 34 10 78

This fascinating museum was owned, operated, and created by Chartres resident Raymond Isidore. After buying the plot of land at 22 Repos, Isidor decided to start making intricate mosaics out of pieces of all broken and discarded glass that he could find; he mosaic-ed every surface he could find, including each wall and floor in his house. While crafting the masterpiece open to visitors today, he worked odd jobs, including as a cemetery sweep. The art is somewhat of an Impressionist/Mosaic fusion, but words really don't suffice: you just have to visit. Unfortunately, Mr. Isidore has left us; if he was still around, maybe you could pay your entry fee in broken glass.

⌗ *22 rue du Repos. Most accessible by taxi, which can be found in pl. de la Cathédrale or pl. Pierre Sémard.* ⑤ *€5.10, €2.60 reduced.* ⌚ *Open April-Oct M and W-Su 10am-noon and 2-6pm.*

CENTRE INTERNATIONALE DU VITRAIL
⬗ MUSEUM

5 rue du Cardinal Pie
☎02 37 21 65 72 ▣www.centre-vitrail.org

Founded by Pierre Firmin Didot in 1980, the Centre Internationale du Vitrail is strangely located in a medieval tithing barn dating from the 12th century. The Center, however, has nothing to do with tithes or barns; it's all about the stained glass. Exhibits explain the process behind crafting a stained glass window, and the evolution of these processes from the Middle Ages up until the modern day. There's also an exhibit analyzing the stained glass at the neighboring cathedral. The Center offers guided tours and workshops for groups; call ahead for details.

⌗ *5 rue du Cardinal Pie. Across the street from Cathedral.* ⑤ *Prices vary for exhibition viewing, but standard prices apply for guided group visits: €6.50-7.* ⌚ *Open M-F 9:30am-12:30pm, 1:30-6pm, Sa 10am-12:30pm and 2:30-6pm, Su and holidays 2:30-6pm.*

MUSÉE DES BEAUX-ARTS
⬗ MUSEUM

29 Cloître Notre-Dame
☎02 37 90 45 80

Located in the former Bishop's Palace, the beautiful and creaky building which the Beaux Arts is now situated in is a little more impressive than the museum itself. The museum itself is still very... eclectic. A recent temporary exhibit on sculptures, tools, and masks from West Africa, complete with a bale of hay and tribal music, doesn't have much to do with the 15th-19th-century European paintings in the permanent collection upstairs, or the harpsichord room downstairs. Nonetheless, the Museum is manageably sized and worth a visit if you have a little more touristing in you.

⌗ *29 Cloître Notre-Dame. Across the street from Cathedral.* ⑤ *Permanent collection €3.10, €1.60 reduced. Permanent and temporary exhibits €5.10, reduced €2.60.* ⌚ *Open May-Oct M and W-Sa 10am-noon and 2-6pm, Su 2-6pm; Nov-Apr M and W-Sa 10am-noon and 2-5pm, Su 2-5pm. Last entry 30min. before close. Closed Jan 1, May 1 and 8, Nov 1 and 11, and Dec 25.*

www.letsgo.com ⑫ **213**

ÉGLISE SAINT-AIGNAN CHURCH

Pl. Saint-Aignan

A largely Gothic structure; from outside, it definitely looks unremarkable until you see the ceiling frescoes, a true rarity in French churches. A historical monument since 1840, the church suffered some serious damage during the siege of Chartres in 1568; its stained glass windows, unlike those of the Cathedral, did not hold up. The ceiling frescoes have stayed remarkably fresh and colorful despite all the light that flows in from the Church's large Gothic-style windows.

🧭 Pl. Saint-Aignan. Facing the Cathedral in the pl. de la Cathédrale, turn right on Rue des Grenets. Walk down street 5-6 blocks, for about 5min. Place Saint-Aignan will be on your left. $ Free. ⏰ Open M-F 10-noon and 2-5:30pm, Sa 2-5pm. Mass M 9am, Tu-F 7am, Sa 9am, Su 10:30am.

FOOD

Food in Chartres services pretty much only the tourist population, so falling into a tourist trap is, by definition, inevitable. Some falls, however, can be easier to take than others; try these particularly pleasant ones. If you're looking for cheap stuff, there are several kebab joints right around the train station.

ÉPICERIE DE LA PLACE BILLARD GROCERY STORE [1]

19 rue des Changes ☎02 37 21 00 25

A friendly, inexpensive grocery store that sells all the basics that you might need for a picnic on a park bench (not much green space in Chartres). The store also sells over 40 flavors of "*limonade*" soda (€5).

⏰ Open M-Sa 6:30am-7:30pm, Su 6am-6pm.

LE MOULIN DE PONCEAU TRADITIONAL [3]

21/23 rue de la Tannerie ☎02 37 35 30 05 💻www.lemoulindeponceau.fr

Situated a 5min. walk from the Cathedral along the tranquil Eure River, Le Moulin de Ponceau features quite possibly the most divine outdoors seating arrangement known to man; about 20 tables snake along the river around the restaurant's back side and up rue de la Tannerie. If you're so unlucky as to miss one of these tables, the indoors' red walls and wooden beams are quite cozy. But the restaurant would be nowhere if the food didn't live up to the restaurant's divine situation; regulars vie for reservations to break up their Cathedral visits. In short, the food may not be worth every penny (at these prices, that's kind of impossible), but the dining experience is, on the whole, entirely worth it.

$ Entrees €14-17. Plats €18-24. Desserts €11. Menus €23, €38, and €51 (tasting). ⏰ Open daily 12:15-2pm, 7:30-9:30pm. Closed Su dinner in the summer. Oct 1-Mar 31 closed W and Sa lunch as well as Su dinner.

IL TÉATRO ITALIAN [2]

18 bd. Chasles ☎02 37 36 69 70 💻restaurant-ilteatro.com

Lots of red, coupled with pictures of Robert De Niro, make this fine establishment unmistakably Italian. The food is quite tasty, reasonably priced, and whipped up with fresh ingredients. Selections are predictable, in a good way: pizzas, pastas, meats, and fish, and even some gelato.

$ Menus Midi €10-15. Pasta €8-14. Pizzas €8-11. ⏰ Open M-F noon-2:30pm and 7-11pm, Sa-Su noon-2:30pm and 7-11:30pm.

NIGHTLIFE

Not much "pops off" in Chartres at night, especially during the week. Tourists are generally a bit older than the lively ex-pat crowd in Paris, so don't expect much beyond a refreshing drink before your train ride back.

L'ACADEMIE DE LA BIÈRE

🍺🍸 BAR

8 rue du Cheval Blanc ☎02 37 36 90 07

One of the only viable hotspots in Chartres. With a Guinness sign hanging high, the priorities of this Irish tavern are clear....beer, beer, and beer! Boasting a cozy interior bar room and an outdoors beer garden for the warmer months of the year, this is a favorite weeknight and weekend spot for locals; tourists welcome as well. Choose from a wealth of bottled beers and whiskies.

 # On place de la Cathédrale, across the street from the Cathedral. $ Beers €4-6. ⏰ Open M-Th 6pm-1am, F-Sa 6pm-2am.

ESSENTIALS

[i]

Getting There

Chartres is accessible by frequent **trains** from **Gare Montparnasse, Grandes Lignes,** on the **Nogent-le-Rotrou line.** About 1 train per hr. runs during the summer; pick up a schedule ahead of time in both summer and winter, as times are irregular. *($ round-trip €27.20, under 25 and seniors €20.40, under 12 €13.60. Discount of 20-40% available if bought up to 2 weeks ahead of time. ⏰ 55-75min.)*

Getting Around

Chartes is an obscenely walkable city, with most of its worthwhile sights clustered around the Cathedral. The Maison Picassiette is the main exception to this, and is most accessible by **cab.** We suggest **Taxi 2000** *(Place Pierre Sémard, 28000 Chartres ☎ 02 37 36 00 00.)* Located in front of the cathedral's main entrance at **Pl. de la Cathédrale,** the **tourist office** should be your first stop (☎ *02 37 18 26 26* 💻*www.chartres-tourisme.com. ⏰ Apr-Sept M-Sa 9am-7pm, Su and holidays 9:30am-5:30pm. Oct-Mar M-Sa 9am-6pm, Su and holidays 9:30am-5pm. Closed Jan 1 and Dec 25.)* The office can help you find **hotel accommodations** *(€2 surcharge),* and supplies visitors with a free and helpful map that includes a walking tour and a list of restaurants, hotels, and sights. While the entire city is accessible by foot for those in good physical condition, there are several options for those who need to take a breather. A tourist train **Chart'train** runs during the tourist season and features narrated tours of the old city in French and English *(☎02 37 25 88 50 $ €6, under 12 €3. ⏰ Mar-Nov 35min., every hr. on the hr., 10:30am-6pm.)* English-language **walking tours** are also available *($ €5, under 14 €3.50, young children free. ⏰ July-Aug Sa, 1hr., 4:15pm.).* Audio guides of the *vieille ville* are a decent option for groups ($ *€5.50.* ⏰ *1hr.*).

fontainebleau ☎01 60

Almost as splendid and much less touristed than Versailles, the Chateau de Fontainebleau offers a thrilling window into the rich history of the French monarchy, from the political intrigue of the 12th century to the material excesses of the 18th. The palace served as a country retreat for monarchs dating back to the 12th century, but it really took on its modern character during the rule of Francis I, who transformed the modest compound into a fantastical display of wealth and decadence. Leonardo Da Vinci and other Renaissance Italian artists were employed to paint its galleries and frescoes. Like most symbols of the French aristocracy, the castle was appropriated by the French Revolution; in July 1815, the Fontainebleau was the scene of Napoleon's abdication. Today, the sedimented wealth of 600 years' worth of kings makes for a spectacular day in the French countryside. The chateau remains home to the strikingly well preserved royal quarters, a beautiful chapel, several sprawling gardens, and a park.

ORIENTATION

To get oriented in Fontainebleau, make your first stop at the Tourism Office, right across from the Chateau, and the Chateau bus stop.

SIGHTS

The **Chateau**, its **Gardens**, and **the Forest** constitute the sights in Fontainebleau. It's a good idea to read up a bit on the history of the gardens and area surrounding the Chateau itself before coming, since the explanation placards are only in French.

▨ GRANDS APPARTEMENTS ♦Ġ MUSEUM

pl. du Général de Gaulle ☎01 60 71 50 60 ▣www.musee-chateau-fontainebleau.fr

While Fontainebleau's lush grounds are blissfully open to the public, access to the Chateau's apartments and various museums is not free of charge. For the record, though, the prices are worth it. The Chateau's main attractions can be divided into its apartments, museums, and theaters. Located on the first floor of the Chateau, the Grands Appartements offer a striking perspective on the luxury the French royalty enjoyed throughout their period of rule. Don't fear paying a significant entry fee just to look at apartments; the apartments at Fontainebleau, Grands or Petits, bear no resemblance to the studios or cheap flats you might be thinking of. At their height, these "apartments" were the royal quarters, containing the sleeping chambers, library, galleries, ballrooms, and place of worship for members of the monarchy. Given their broad scope, you should devote the lion's share of your visit to them. There are a few areas in particular that are not to be missed. The beginning of the exhibit consists of the **Celebration Gallery** and the **Gallery of Plates,** and offers some background on the fascinating history of the Chateau. The Celebration Gallery boasts expansive fresco depictions of some of the Chateau's historically significant events, while the Gallery of Plates' 128 porcelain plates illustrate other important events. A particularly wondrous plate depicting a sea of people flooding into Fontainebleau documents the marriage of the duke of Orléans to Princess Helen of Mecklenburg; it's a must-see.

The royal quarters speak volumes about their past residents, beyond the obvious realization that they lived in extreme luxury. Napoleon had two bedrooms, each reflecting one side of his personality. The first boasts mirrors on two opposite walls, a testimony to Napoleon's extreme vanity and insecurity, while the other room, furnished with a monk-ish narrow bed, reveals the serious, business-oriented demeanor that presided over the precipitous rise and fall of the French Empire. The richly decorated **Empress' Bed Chamber** was inhabited by Marie Antoinette, Josephine and Empress Eugenie; within are a set of wardrobes where the queens were to keep their "valuables"—as if the Chateau wasn't itself a successive set of valuable possessions. Easily the funniest of the Castle's rooms is Napoleon's **Throne Room,** that Napoleon constructed out of what used to be the King's main bedchambers. Designed by Charles Percier and Pierre Fontaine, the Room is decorated and outfitted with rich maroon and yellow chairs. The comedy of the room, however, lies in its disproportionately and deliberately small throne. Napoleon must have worried about looking dwarfed by his own chair before his courtly sycophants; little did he know that the pathetic size of his throne would immortalize his insecurities.

Moving on from the infinite neuroses of France's Emperor, Francois I left a significant mark on the Fontainebleau with the **Renaissance Rooms,** consisting of the Galerie de Francois I, La Chambre de la Duchesse d'Etampes, and the Salle de Bal. The castle's most famous room is the **Galerie de Francois I.** The 210 ft. long gallery displays his extreme egotism alongside some fantastic Renaissance Italian artwork. F's (for Francois, fool) and Francois' salamander emblem unabashedly adorn the gallery. If you can get past the pretension, then you'll be able to enjoy an awe-inspiring display of artwork; the frescoes of Rosso Riorentino, a pupil of Michelangelo, pay homage to Francois' desire to create a second Rome.

La Salle de Bal, or the ballroom, is less famous than the Galerie, but cooler if you like to combine partying and tourism. The place where the royal parties raged is decorated with frescoes by Nicollo dell'Abbate. The floor is open to guests, so take a special someone for a spin on the floor. The tour ends with the utterly jaw-dropping **Trinity Chapel.** Contained in the Grands Appartements to facilitate convenient worship for the royal families, the Trinity Chapel features frescos painted under Henri IV by Martin Fréminet. It also lays claim to two important events: Louis XV's wedding to Marie Leszczinska in 1725 and Louis Napoleon's baptism in 1810. The feeling of this Chapel is distinctly intimate; for tourists who have probably tired of cavernous cathedrals, the chapel is a pleasant switch-up.

$ *"Visite libre" (i.e. unaccompanied, encompassing the Big Apartments and the Renaissance Rooms) €8, €6 reduced. To visit the small apartments, the Museum of Napoleon, or the Hunting Apartment and the Furniture Gallery alone, you must arrange a group visit: €6.50, €5 reduced.* ⏰ *Open Apr-Sept W-M 9:30am-6pm, Oct-Mar W-M 9:30am-5pm.*

THE GARDENS

GARDENS

Surrounding the Chateau 💻www.fontainebleau-tourisme.com/pays-fontainebleau

Free to the public charge year-round, the Chateau's three main Gardens exhibit a wide variety of styles, and therefore serve a variety of modern-day uses. The most formidable of the gardens is without a doubt the **Grande Parterre.** Located on the south side of the Chateau, it was designed and realized by Louis XIV's preferred gardener, Andre Le Notre, the man responsible for just about every famous French garden that was landscaped in this period. This was Le Notre's largest creation, spanning about 14 hectares. The garden was constructed from 1660-1664, and was lucky enough to receive a few last-minute additions before the collapse of France as the proprietors of the castle had known it. Luckily, the Fontainebleau grounds crew has kept up with Le Grand Parterre; the grass is divinely manicured, recalling the gluttonous visual perfection of some of Le Notre's other creations. By contrast, the **Jardin Anglais,** a relatively recent creation in 1812, looks like it might have been designed by Le Notre's three-times bastarded great-grandson. In fact, it was created by Hutault. Its asymmetrical, rather average-looking (upon first glance) appearance was very stylish at the time; the English Garden format was a reaction against Le Notre's hypersymmetrical and ordered gardens at Versailles and Vaux-le-Vicomte. In a moment of rare deference to anything, Napoleon begrudgingly submitted to the trend and commissioned Hutault to start work on the garden. Hutault searched high and low for rare plants and trees to plant the grounds with; tree admirers will be eager to check out the garden's rare spruce, Japanese sophora, and Virginia tulip trees. Today, the garden is remarkably unkempt. The grass runs tall and messy around the edges; this neglect has, of course, encouraged the tourists to use the garden as a recreational "chill spot." Within the Jardin Anglais is the **Etang des Carpes,** a pond filled with carp fish. If you want to conquer both the land and the water of Fontainebleau, you can experience all four hectares of the carp-filled lake in a kayak *(€4 per 15 min., €7 per 30min., €12 per hr.).* The **Jardin Diane,** the last of the castle's major surrounding gardens, is smaller than the vast Grande Parterre and the sprawling Jardin Anglais. It takes its name from a fountain statue of the huntress Diana, installed in the center of the garden under Henri IV. Originally the queen's personal garden, the garden was closed to the public until the 19th century, when the purchase of some nearby buildings and land up the garden's borders to the town. Today, its inhabitants are the royally-inclined among Fontainebleau's youth; the beach has become a friendly zone for rowdy games of tag and rowdier rounds of teen drinking.

ⓢ *Free.* ☒ *Parterre open May-Sept 9am-7pm. Mar-Apr and Oct 9am-6pm; Nov-Feb 9am-5pm. Jardins Anglais and Diane open at the same time, close one hour prior.*

MUSÉE NAPOLEON
➥& MUSEUM

Place du Général de Gaulle ☎01 60 71 50 60 ▣www.musee-chateau-fontainebleau.fr

Located in the Louis XV wing of the Chateau, this exhibition of Napoleon's personal items debuted in 1986. It features some fantastic pieces, including jackets and uniforms Napoleon wore in battle, plates and serving platters used for royal occasions, gifts he received at his weddings, and even a recreated tent from his hunting trips, complete with Indian cotton.

ⓢ *Same as Chateau.* ☒ *Open Apr-Sept W-M 9:30am-6pm; Oct-Mar W-M 9:30am-5pm.*

MUSÉE CHINOIS DE L'IMPÉRATRICE
MUSEUM

A fantastic collection of vases and furniture; the most impressive piece is probably the chandelier in the Grand Salon. At the command of the Empress Eugenie, Napoleon set aside four rooms on the ground floor of the Great Pavilion to house the Musée Chinois de l'Impératrice Eugénie. The museum exhibits pieces from the Summer Palace in Beijing taken during a French military action in China in 1860. The rest of the collection was given by the ambassadors of Siam in 1861 when they came to visit the Chateau at Fontainebleau.

i Group entry only.

LE PARC AND LA FORET DE FONTAINEBLEAU
& PARK

The Park and the Forest are both located outside of the Fontainebleau grounds. The Park is across the street from the Grande Parterre, and boasts a canal that runs through its main thoroughfare, a few benches, and plenty of overgrown grass to partially shelter the sometimes questionably appropriate activities of its visitors. While the park is often a bit PG-13 (or R, depending on your level of curiosity) around the edges, it's a great shady retreat for a picnic. It's also a long enough walk back to the Chateau to safely burn off a luxuriously fatty midday picnic. The Forest of Fontainebleau is located around the perimeter of the town. Given the 300km of cleared paths, it's definitely worth dedicating a whole day or two to hiking it or biking through it. The Chateau visit, like all touristy activities, is surprisingly tiring. Anybody who isn't a voracious adventurer will be more inclined to fall into one of the tourist trap brasseries or catch the train back to Paris than head out into the Forest after their visit. Should you be up for the challenge, it's best to rent a bike and take one of the Office of Tourism's six suggested paths, which range in length from about an hour to 6hr., and also range widely in difficulty. Several guides are also available, which detail paths in the forest explorable by foot (€9-12). Don't, however, plan to take an extended break on the trail. While the forest is palatial and impossible to fully patrol, Let's Go recommends that you stay on the path and don't camp in the forest; a recent initiative has strictly prohibited camping on the Forest's property. Getting busted can lead to hefty fines.

⚘ *Office of Tourism located across from Chateau bus stop at 4 rue Royale. i Bike rental available at the Office of Tourism. Guides to different paths €9-12, available at Office of Tourism.* ⓢ *Bike rental €5, €15 for half-day, €19 for full day.* ☒ *Open Apr-Oct M-Sa 10am-6pm, Nov-Mar 10am-1pm only, Su and holidays 10am-1pm and 2-5:30pm.*

FOOD

When eating in Fontainebleau, you don't have to go far to find the good stuff at good prices. Walk into town a bit; when you hit **rue Ferrare,** which is adjacent to the tourist office, you'll find some tasty options frequented more by locals than by tourists. It just so happens that our two favorite restaurants are next to each other; take your pick.

LA PETITE ALSACE

ALSATIAN [2]

26 rue de Ferrare ☎01 64 23 45 45

A cheap and tasty option for those who want a stick-to-your-ribs meal before, during, or after a tiring museum visit. One of the *flammekeuches* is enough for two, and other dishes are fantastically copious. FYI, a *flammekeuches* is basically the Alsatian take on pizza, minus the tomatoes, plus onions (lots of them!). The help is friendly, and eager to chat with French-speaking customers.

$ *Lunch formules €9.70, €12.50. Flammekeuches €8-11.50. Big salads €9-14.50. Main courses €9.50-21. Desserts €6-9. Dinner formule €15.* ⏰ *Open daily noon-10pm.*

LE CAVEAU DES DUCS

TRADITIONAL [3]

24 rue de Ferrare ☎01 64 22 05 05 🖥www.lecaveaudesducs.com

A bistro with a slightly expensive yet gastronomically sound menu. In the summertime, guests can enjoy the Caveau's selections underneath luxurious canopy. The fare is traditionally French, as is the staff; you know the drill, foie gras, *magret de canard*, etc. The portions are copious, so this is a good spot to hit for lunch before or in the middle of your Chateau visit (your ticket lasts all day).

$ *Menu du jour €20 (entrée and plat and dessert). From the menu, formules €19.40, €25, and €33. Salad and verre de vin €13-19.* ⏰ *Open daily noon-2pm and 7-10:30pm.*

ESSENTIALS

Practicalities

The tourist office provides maps of Fontainebleau, guides for your visit to the forest, and audio tours for visits outside the Chateau itself (*4 Rue Royal* ☎*01 60 74 99 99* 🖥*www.fontainebleau-tourisme.com* ⏰ *Open May-Oct M-Sa 10am-6pm, Su 10am-1pm and 2-5:30pm; Nov-Apr M-Sa 10am-6pm, Su 10am-1pm.*).

Getting There

Trains from Gare de Lyon on the *banlieue sud-est* line *(direction Montargis* $ *€15.80 round trip* ⏰ *45min. every hr.)*. At Gare de Lyon, follow the signs towards the Grandes Lignes, and buy your ticket from the **billets Ile de France counter,** located around the corner from the long succession of SNCF ticket windows. Don't get confused: this train is NOT operated by SNCF. From the station, follow signs (or the masses of people) to the **buses. Veolia** *(☎ 01 64 22 23 88* $ *€1.70)* runs buses right after each train arrival from Paris. Take bus A (dir. Chateau-Lilas), and get off at the Chateau stop. You'll hop off right across the street from the tourist office and, in the other direction, the Chateau.

chantilly ☎03 44

The French don't call whipped cream "chantilly" for nothing—this 14th- to 19th-century château is as whimsical as the delicious dessert topping allegedly invented on its grounds. A gorgeous mix of Gothic extravagance, Renaissance geometry, and flashy Victorian ornamentalism, the triangular-shaped château is surrounded by a moat, lakes, canals, and the elegantly simple Le Nôtre gardens. Between the architecturally masterful and slightly smelly Grandes Écuries (stables) and the world-class Musée Condé, it's a wonder that Chantilly has stayed a hidden treasure for so long. The whole package makes for a delightful foray into the French countryside; just 30min. from the city, visitors can stroll through the dense woodland surrounding the castle and hear nothing but the melodious singing of the *tilleul*, the bird from which the town derives its name.

ORIENTATION

Chantilly's **tourist office** is about 50m. up **rue des Otages** from the **train station.** Across the street from the office, there's a well-worn and well-marked **path** that will take you on a 25min. scenic walk through the woods to the castle. The path does sort of trail off toward the end, but by that point the chateau will be clearly visible, and you can forge your own way there. Alternatively, upon exiting the train station, walk up rue des Otages, take a left on ave. du Marcehal Joffre and a right on rue du Connetable. This route will lead you past most of the town's restaurants, Le Potager des Princes and straight on to the stables. The **chateau grounds** consist of the **hippodrome,** the **Grandes Écuries,** the **castle** and the surrounding **gardens.**

Though giant castles generally tend to overshadow small towns, a world does exist outside of Chateau Chantilly, albeit a tiny and generally less impressive one. Due to its wonderfully soft soil, which goes easy on the fragile legs of thoroughbreds, Chantilly is one of the biggest horse training centers in the world. Just opposite the stables, horses race April through October at the chateau's hippodrome. Besides equestrian activities, Chantilly is known for its black lace, porcelain, and most notably, whipped cream. **Rue du Connétable** is Chantilly's main commercial street, and sports several cafes, a few restaurants, and a tabac; it runs through the center of town and dead ends into the chateau's Grandes Écuries.

SIGHTS

CHÂTEAU DE CHANTILLY

CHATEAU

☎03 44 62 62 62 www.domainedechantilly.com

A Roman citizen named Cantilius originally built his villa here, and since then an almighty sequence of kings and medieval lords have successively upstaged him. In the 17th century, Louis XIV's cousin, the Grand Condé, commissioned a château and wisely employed landscape artist André Le Nôtre, an expert in all things grass-related and the mastermind behind the gardens of Versailles, Vauex-le-Vicomte, and other studies in excess from this period. The castle itself was built upon a rock so that it would be elevated above the surrounding marshland. It was while the Grand Condé played at peasantry in these magnificent grounds that the now-famed *crème chantilly* was invented. Though the original castle was destroyed during the revolution, the Duc d'Aumale, King Louis-Philippe's fifth son, rebuilt it in the 1870s, complete with the eclectic facade, modern wrought-iron grillwork, copies of Michelangelo marbles, lush greenery, and the extravagant entrance hall.

From train station, turn right on rue Victor Hugo, and continue to rue de Gouvieux, turn right. Turn left at rue de Paris, then turn right at Petite Place Omer Vallon. Continue onto rue do Connétable, turn left at château. $ Château and park €12, children under 18 accompanied by an adult free. The chateau, park and Grand Stables with equestrian demonstration €19/8. Audio tours €3/2. Guided visit of private apartments 2-3 times per day, reserved ahead €5. Petit trains with 40min. tour of gardens and grounds in French and English on the hour from 11am-6pm €5. ⏰ Château open Apr-Nov M and W-Su 10am-6pm, gardens until 8pm; Nov-Mar M and W-F 10:30am-12:45pm and 2-5pm, Sa-Su and holidays 10:30am-5pm, gardens until 6pm. Program of daily children's activities available at ticket office.

MUSÉE CONDÉ

MUSEUM

Château

Despite having one of the fluffiest desserts in history named after it, Chantilly is a sight of substance. The impressive Musée Condé, which lies inside the château's fortified walls, is oft considered one of the most important French collections, second only the Louvre. It's the only other museum in France to boast five Raphaels, in addition to its Poussins, Delacroixs and Ingres'. The Duc d'Aumule was a bibliophile who later became interested in 16th-19th century art, specifically French, Italian, and Dutch paintings. The result of his interest is a rambling series of exhibits that display a stunning 800 paintings; 3000 drawings; and hundreds of engravings, sculptures, and tapestries, among them works by Titian, Corot, Botticelli, Greuze, Reynolds, Watteau and Van Dyck. The only movement that is notably excluded from the collection is Impressionism, which the Duke detested. Marble busts and drawings of royals and nobles attest to the château's illustrious litany of owners: the powerful, noble Montmorency family, and the royal Bourbon and Condé princes. The Duke literally left his own mark on the place by stamping his initials on random doors and plates throughout the castle (look for the superimposed H on the O). In accordance with his will, the paintings and furniture are arranged as they were over a century ago, in the distinctively 19th-century frame-to-frame (academic) style, notwithstanding the 5% of the art that had to be re-arranged due to sun damage. The Musée's absolute gem is the tiny velvet-walled sanctuary. This hidden gallery contains what the Duke himself considered the finest works in his collection: illuminated manuscripts by Jean Fouquet, a painting by Fra Filippo Lippi, and two Raphaels. Alas, the museum's two most valuable pieces, a Gutenberg Bible and the illuminated manuscripts of the Très Riches Heures (1410), are too fragile to be kept in public view—but a near-perfect digitized facsimile of the latter can be seen in the illustrious library, second only to the Bibliothèque Nationale in prestige. The rest of the château's *appartements* can be visited only by taking a guided tour in French.

⇟ Located within château grounds. $ Included in château admission. ⏰ Same as château.

GARDENS

GARDEN

Château

Castle officials suggest mapping your way through Château de Chantilly's grounds—a sprawling 240 hectares, 170 of which is open to the public. Directly in front of the château, the gardens' central expanse is designed in the French formal style, with neat rows of carefully pruned trees, statues, and geometric pools which are rely entirely on natural water pressure. To the left, hidden within a forest, the Romantic English garden attempts to re-create an untamed wilderness. Paths meander around pools where lone swans glide across the surface. Windows carved into the foliage allow you to see fountains in the formal garden as you stroll through. To the right, the Anglo-Chinese gardens hide an idyllic play-village *hameau* (hamlet), the inspiration for Marie-Antoinette's hamlet at Versailles. Farther in, a statue of Cupid reigns over the "Island of Love." Recent additions include the **kangaroo** enclosure—15 or so are wallabies gathered in the far right corner of the formal gardens—and a 4,000-square-meter floral and osier labyrinth, near the hamlet; both represent a move back toward former royal flair.

*⇟ Located within Château grounds. **i** Boating on the Grand Canal on weekends from 11am-6pm. 4 persons max per boat. $ Admission €6, under 18 accompanied by an adult free. Boats €12 per hour. ⏰ Open M and W-Su 10am-8pm. Last entry 6pm.*

GRANDES ÉCURIES — HISTORIC SIGHT

On rue Connétable ☎ 03 44 57 13 13 🖥www.domainedechantilly.com

Another great, if pungent, draw to the château is the Grandes Écuries (stables), whose immense marble corridors, courtyards, and facades are masterpieces of 18th-century French architecture. Commissioned by Louis-Henri Bourbon, who hoped to live here when he was reborn as a horse (seriously), the Écuries boast extravagant fountains, domed rotundas, and sculptured patios that are enough to make even the most cynical believe in reincarnation. From 1719 to the Revolution, the stables housed 250 horses and hundreds of hunting dogs, and now are home to the Musée Vivant du Cheval, an extensive collection, supposedly the largest in the world, of all things equine.

⇟ Entrance is through the Jeu de Paume gate, to the right. $ €4, children free. Grand stables and equestrian demonstration €11. Equestrian show €21-22; check website or call for details. ⏰ Open Jan 9-Apr 2 M and W-Su 2-5pm, Apr 3-Nov 7 M and W-Su 10am-5pm, Dec M and W-Su 2-6pm.

THE HIPPODROME — RACETRACK

Opposite the Grand Stables, just outside the forest, the Hippodrome is a major racetrack built in 1834. Two of France's premier horse races are held here in June. The ground's soft soil is especially suitable for the delicate legs of thoroughbreds.

$ Hippodrome matches €3, schedule upon request at the tourist office. ⏰ Open Apr-June.

LE POTAGER DES PRINCES — ♿ GARDEN

17 rue de la Faisanderie ☎03 44 57 39 66 🖥www.potagerdesprinces.com

The Prince's Kitchen Garden is a cultivated two-hectare expanse of greenery, modeled on the château's original 17th-century working garden. First designed by Le Nôtre as a pheasantry for the Grand Duke Condé in 1682, it was later converted into a "Roman pavilion" of terraced gardens. Abandoned during the Revolution's pruning of excess, the gardens were restored in 2002 to their former verdant glory, this time as a public attraction. Catering mostly to children, the garden is arranged in themed areas, including a fantasy region replete with bridges and grottoes, a romantic and aromatic rose garden, and a ménagerie that features goats, squabbling chickens, and over 100 varieties of pheasant. It also hosts occasional concerts and plays by the likes of Shakespeare and Marivaux in the summer months; check website for details.

⇟ 300m from the stables down rue Connétable toward the town, turn on rue des Potagers; garden is at end of road. $ Admission €7.50, children €6.50. ⏰ Open Mar 20-Oct 31 M and W-F 2-5:30pm, Sa-Su 2-6pm. Park closes at 7pm. Puppet shows W, Sa, Su 3:30pm.

FOOD 🍴

Kings may have once feasted here, but then they could afford to; if you want to dine in Chantilly cost-effectively, we recommend packing a sandwich and a *bouteille*. **Rue de Connétable** offers a number of reasonably priced cafes, crêperies, pizzerias and boulangeries. There are some decent ice cream and sandwich stands near the entrance to the château grounds, and the château itself hosts a pricey restaurant.

LE BOUDOIR — TEA HOUSE, EPICERIE ❷

100 rue du Connétable ☎03 44 55 44 49

A cute delicatessen with puffy chairs and tables interspersed between cans of *foie gras* and shelves of jam. Compensating for the fact that it's slightly farther away (by about 30 seconds) from the château than other restaurants on the street, the *salon de thé* is also cheaper, and as an added bonus, quieter. Selection includes quiches, assorted plates, tartines and a daily plat.

⇟ From train station, follow rue Victor Hugo until rue de Gouvieux and turn right. Turn left at rue de Paris, then right at Petite Place Omer Vallon. $ Entrees €5-7.50. Plats du jour, salad, and espresso €13. ⏰ Open M 11am-6pm, Tu-Sa 10am-7pm, Su 11am-7pm.

LE HAMEAU 🍴 TRADITIONAL [3]

Château ☎03 44 57 46 21 or 03 44 56 28 23

Tucked away on the hamlet that inspired Marie-Antoinette's fake peasant village at Versailles, this rustic restaurant is the only sanctioned eating option on château grounds. The menu offers fresh cheese, salads, *gesiers*, *magret de canard*, paté, terrines and *foie gras* in a variety of combination plates *(€11.90-23)*. For dessert *(€5-11)*, try the *chantilly* with fruit, *chantilly* with ice cream, *chantilly* with pie, or just plain *chantilly*. The outdoor terrace is so pleasant, you might be tempted to forget about the bills you're dropping.

From the château, bear left and go down the stairs toward the fountains; turn right and walk along canal des Morfondus. Cross the canal by one of the two wood-planked bridges and you'll see the restaurant on your right once you clear the woods. $ Assiette gourmande €23. ⏰ Open mid-Mar to mid-Nov daily noon-6pm. No lunch after 3pm.

ESSENTIALS

Getting There

Trains leave from Gare du Nord RATP to Chantilly Gouvieux *($ Round-trip €14, under 25 €11 ⏰ up to 35min., every hr. 6am-10pm)*. Schedule varies with season. From the **train station,** walk straight up **rue des Otages** about 50m. to the **tourist office,** which offers brochures and maps. The tourist office can also call you a **taxi** *($ €6 ☎03 44 57 10 03)* or rent you a **bike** with which to explore the town and castle grounds *($ €10 per ½-day, €15 per day)*.

Getting Around

The best way to get from the **train station** to the chateau is to follow the signs. The **Tourist Office** is particularly helpful, offering additional information on tours, ticket purchases, and various rentals *(60 av. du Maréchal Joffre ☎03 44 67 37 37 💻www.chantilly-tourisme.com ⏰ Open May-Sept M-Sa 9:30am-12:30pm and 1:30-5:30pm, Su 10am-1:30pm. Oct-Apr M-Sa 9:30am-12:30pm and 1:30-5:30pm)*. For the lazy and/or tired traveler, there is also a free but irregular **navette** (shuttle) service; catch one just to the left as you exit the train station *(⏰ Approximately every hr. M-Sa until 6pm)*.

vaux-le-vicomte ☎01 64

It's occurred to us more than once that the trials and tribulations of the French monarchy actually make daytime TV look plausible, and the saga of Vaux-le-Vicomte is no exception. The palatial monument grants invaluable insight into 17th-century French architecture, horticulture, and politics, and played a pivotal role in 17th-century French history. Originally a modest hunting retreat, it was purchased in 1641 by Jean-Michel Fouquet, an ambitious 26-year-old member of Parliament who would soon become Louis XIV's Minister of Finance. Ever the modest type, Fouquet oversaw the château's transformation into one of the most lavish castles in France. Upon its completion 20 years later, he threw an extravagant party in honor of the Sun King. Novelties included elephants wearing crystal jewelry and whales in the canal, and the evening concluded with an exhibition of fireworks that featured the king and queen's coat of arms and **pyrotechnic squirrels** (Fouquet's family symbol). Despite the extensive debauchery, the highlight of the fête was undoubtedly when its host was arrested. Fouquet's lavish lifestyle had sparked rumors of embezzlement at court, which were then nourished by jealous underlings; the Sun King ultimately sentenced him to life, and he died in Pignerol in 1680. The best way to see Vaux's gardens is during the *visites aux chandelles*, when the château and grounds are lit up by thousands of candles, and classical music plays through the gardens in homage to Fouquet's last bacchanalian party; arrive around dusk on Saturday evenings during the summer to see the grounds in all their glory.

ORIENTATION

As you head to Vaux-le-Vicomte for your daytrip, you should understand that you're here for the château, and pretty much nothing else. There's not much to see in Melun, the neighboring small town; restaurants are owned and run by the château, and there are no other tourist sights or nearby hotspots to speak of. The glorious castle itself can basically be broken down into four parts, listed in terms of progressively increasing awesomeness: the **kitchens and cellars** in the basement, the **private quarters** of the castle, the **dining room** on the main floor, and the **dome** at the top of the castle. In order to progress through the Museum without having to double-back or wander aimlessly though the hallways, make sure to enter through the entrance facing the **garden.**

SIGHTS

CHÂTEAU VAUX-LE-VICOMTE

CHATEAU

77950 Maincy ☎01 64 14 41 90 www.vaux-le-vicomte.com

The massive renovation of Fouquet's chateau was the brainchild of master architect Louis Le Vau and painter-decorator Charles Le Brun. It was the first time that the two men had collaborated, and the castle they produced was so magnificent that the Sun King repeatedly employed them to build palaces of his own; Le Vau and Le Brun later designed both Versailles and the Louvre. Today, the Vaux remains entirely furnished, and even features wax figures in certain of the apartments and basement facilities which serve to act out scenes (in French) from the Chateau's height of prestige prior to Fouquet's arrest and exile. The château is home to many beautiful rooms and *chef d'oeuvres*, of which a few bear special notice. **Madame Fouquet's Closet,** once lined with tiny mirrors, was the decorative precedent for Versailles' Hall of Mirrors, while the **Room of the Muses** constitutes one of Le Brun's strongest and most famous decorative efforts. The artist had planned to crown the cavernous, Neoclassical **Oval Room** (or Grand Salon) with a fresco entitled **The Palace of the Sun,** but Fouquet's arrest halted all decorating activity, and only a single eagle and a patch of sky were painted in to fill the space. It's unclear how highly Fouquet actually thought of the King, given that he was ultimately convicted of embezzling his funds; nonetheless, the study in excess that is the **King's Bedchamber** boasts lavish marble and gold ceilings, and includes one of Le Notre's masterpieces, *Time Bearing Truth Heavenward.* Tours of the château are mainly conducted in French, and some of the tour guide's literal English translations of the different sights are a bit, shall we say, awkward. We advise that you purchase the portable handheld audio tour in English instead *(€3).* The program's historical context includes an analysis of Fouquet and Louis XIV's relationship, and enriches a visit to the Vaux.

i Check website for specific opening dates, as they vary year to year. $ "Simple Visit" (includes access to garden, main floor of chateau, and the basement) €14, students and ages 6-16 €11, families of four or more €44. "Complete Visit" (same as simple visit, plus access to chateau's private apartments) €16/€13/€52. ⏰ Open Mar 27-Nov 7 10am-6pm, Dec 18-Dec 31 11am-6pm. Open 11am-11pm.

THE GARDENS

♿ GARDENS

Château

When Fouquet decided to rebuild the previously unremarkable Vaux-Le Vicomte after purchasing it in 1641, he chose to employ the services of a budding master of shrubbery, geometry, and all things grass-related, Andre Le Notre. Thanks in great part to his convincing effort at Vaux, Le Notre became the landscaper behind France's most extravagant gardens, including the grounds of Versailles, the Tuileries, Chantilly, and Fontainebleau. It was at Vaux that Le Notre first put to test his style of sculpting nature into symmetrical geometric patterns, and constructed the grounds to appear to be endless by applying the laws of perspective. The architectural and design-based feats it showcases are impressive, and the techniques Le Notre debuted at Vaux became the standard for 17th-century French gardens. The **Water Mirror,** for example, was designed to reflect the castle perfectly. From the back steps of the chateau, it looks as if you can see the entire landscape at a glance, but, as you walk toward the far end of the garden, the grottoes at the back appear to recede, revealing a sunken canal known as **La Poêle** (the Frying Pan) which is invisible from the chateau itself. The ascent to the **Farnese Hercules** rewards the heartiest of chateau visitors with the best vista of the grounds. Seeing the whole garden takes some effort, or a little extra change. The topiary mazes and shimmering ponds make for a meditative, if long, walk. If physical exertion's not really your style, you can always rent one of the chateau's golf carts.

i *Check website for specific opening dates, as they vary year to year. Golf carts €20 per hr, €15 per 45min.* Ⓢ *Garden visit €8. Garden visit also included in "Simple Visit" and "Complete Visit" packages to the chateau.* ⌚ *Open daily Mar 27-Nov 7 10am-6pm, Dec 18-Dec 31 11am-6pm.*

FOOD

Food at the Chateau is limited to the two restaurants provided by the chateau, **L'Ecureuil** and **Les Charmilles.** L'Ecureuil is a self-service cafeteria that's open whenever the château is; the swanky Les Charmilles is only open on Saturday evenings and Sunday afternoons. If you're up for the preparation it requires, you can pack a picnic lunch and eat in one of the many secluded spots of Fouquet's tremendous gardens.

L'ECUREUIL

Château

♥ ♈ ⌂ SELF-SERVICE ❷

Named after Fouquet's "emblem" (*ecureuil* means squirrel; personally, we'd want our emblem to be a lion or something), this restaurant serves tasty, relatively well-priced, traditional cuisine right next to the Chateau's welcome center and gift shop. The service is cafeteria-style; you pick out your pre-made desserts, salads, and drinks, and order up main courses to be cooked by the chef while you wait in line. The food is fresh and delicious, despite the set-up. Indoor and outdoor seating available; the mood is relaxed, so take in a bottle of wine after, or preferably before, you take in the Chateau. It'll make your visit, or the shuttle ride back, all the more fun.

⚑ *Next to the Chateau's gift shop.* Ⓢ *Entrées €3-7.50. Plats €9.40-12. Desserts €1.50-3.20. Beer €3-4.20. Wine bottles €13-45.* ⌚ *Open daily 11:30am-6pm, Sa candlelight soirées 11:30am-11pm.*

ESSENTIALS

Getting There

By Car

From Paris, take the **highway A4 or A6** and then follow the direction of Troyes via the A5. Take the first exit **Saint Germain Laxis** off the A5. Vaux-le-Vicomte is just 1km away; signs will lead you there. With GPS, enter "Maincy" as the name of the city, and you will find the château de Vaux-le-Vicomte on the D215 road.

By Rail

You can either take a nonstop **SCNF** train from Gare de Lyon to Melun, or take the **RER** line D through some of Paris' northern banlieues and suburbs. There are a lot more stops on the RER train ride, but you see more, which has its advantages for those who tend to prefer the scenic route. The RER also leaves more frequently, and from a greater variety of stops (Chatelet, Gare de Lyon, and Saint-Lazare) than the nonstop train. The chateau is 6km away from the **train station,** and accessible by **taxi** *(€17)*. On weekends, a **shuttle** runs from the Melun train station to Vaux-le-Vicomte *(round trip €7)*. Check on the château's website for seasonally variable shuttle times.

Getting Around

For information on tours, train schedules, accommodations, or additional sightseeing during your stay, contact the local tourist office, **Service Jeunesse et Citoyenneté,** conveniently located by the Melun train station *(18 rue Paul Doumer* ☎ *01 64 52 64 52* 🖥*www.ville-melun.fr* 🕐 *Open M 1:30-6pm, Tu-Sa 10am-12:30pm and 1:30-6pm).*

ESSENTIALS

You don't have to be a rocket scientist to plan a good trip. (It might help, but it's not required.) You do, however, need to be well prepared, and that's what we can do for you. Essentials is the chapter that gives you all the nitty-gritty you need to know for your trip: the hard information gleaned from 50 years of collective wisdom (and that phone call to Paris the other day that put us on hold for an hour). Planning your trip? Check. Staying safe and healthy? Check. The dirt on transportation? Check. We've also thrown in communications info, meteorological charts, and a 🖳phrasebook, just for good measure. Plus, for overall trip-planning advice from what to pack (money and as little underwear as possible) to how to take a good passport photo (it's physically impossible; consider airbrushing), you can also check out the Essentials section of 🖳www.letsgo.com.

We're not going to lie—this chapter is tough for us to write, and you might not find it as fun of a read as 101 or Discover. But please, for the love of all that is good, read it! It's super helpful, and, most importantly, it means we didn't compile all this technical info and put it in one place for you (yes, YOU) for nothing.

greatest hits

- **GET A VISA.** Put it on your spring-cleaning list, since you'll need to apply six to eight weeks in advance (p. 228).

- **DOLLAR DOLLAR BILLS Y'ALL.** Need them? We all do. Need them from across the ocean? Here's how (p. 229).

- **BUY A RAIL PASS.** Comfortable cabins, new friends, not walking—what's better (p. 235)?

- **SHIP SOUVENIRS HOME BY SURFACE MAIL.** Our scintillating "By Snail Mail" section will tell you how. You'll laugh, you'll cry (p. 237).

- **PHONE HOME.** ET did it, you should do it. You should also try and save money while doing it. We can help (p. 236).

- **FRENCH IS FOR LOVERS.** And Francophiles; our phrasebook will have you professing love and stomach pains in no time (p. 241).

planning your trip

DOCUMENTS AND FORMALITIES

You've got your visa, your invitation, and your work permit, just like Let's Go told you to, and then you realize you've forgotten the most important thing: your passport. Well, we're not going to let that happen. **Don't forget your passport!**

entrance requirements

- **PASSPORT:** Required for citizens of all countries.
- **VISA:** Required for citizens of any country for stays longer than 90 days.
- **WORK PERMIT:** Required for all foreigners planning to work in France.

Visas

EU citizens do not need a visa to globetrot through France. Citizens of Australia, Canada, New Zealand, and the US do not need a visa for stays of up to 90 days, but this three-month period begins upon entry into any of the countries that belong to the EU's **freedom of movement** zone. For more information, see **One Europe**. Those staying longer than 90 days may purchase a visa at a French consulate. A visa costs €99 and allows the holder to spend 90 days in France.

one europe

The EU's policy of freedom of movement means that most border controls have been abolished and visa policies harmonized. Under this treaty, formally known as the Schengen Agreement, you're still required to carry a passport (or government-issued ID card for EU citizens) when crossing an internal border, but, once you've been admitted into one country, you're free to travel to other participating states. Most EU states are already members of Schengen (excluding Cyprus), as are Iceland and Norway.

Double-check entrance requirements at the nearest embassy or consulate of France for up-to-date information before departure. US citizens can also consult ▣http://travel.state.gov.

Entering France to study requires a special visa. For more information, see the **Beyond Tourism** chapter.

Work Permits

Admittance to France as a traveler does not include the right to work, which is authorized only by a work permit. For more information, see **Beyond Tourism** .

TIME DIFFERENCES

Paris is 1hr. ahead of Greenwich Mean Time (GMT) and observes Daylight Saving Time. This means that it is 6 hr. ahead of New York City, 9hr. ahead of Los Angeles, 1 hr. ahead of the British Isles, 8 hrs. behind Sydney, and 10hr. behind New Zealand.

- **AUSTRALIAN CONSULAR SERVICES IN PARIS: Embassy.** (4 rue Jean Rey 75015 Paris ☎+01 40 59 33 06 🖳www.france.embassy.gov.au ⏰ Open M-F 9am-5pm.)

- **CANADIAN CONSULAR SERVICES IN PARIS: Embassy.** (35 Avenue Montaigne, 75008 Paris ☎01 44 43 29 00 🖳www.france.gc.ca ⏰ Open M-F 9am-noon and 2-5pm.)

- **IRISH CONSULAR SERVICES IN PARIS: Embassy.** (4 rue Rude, 75116 Paris ☎01 44 17 67 00 🖳www.embassyofireland.fr ⏰ Open M-F 9:30am-noon.)

- **NEW ZEALAND CONSULAR SERVICES IN PARIS: Embassy.** (7ter rue Léonard da Vinci, 75116 Paris ☎01 45 01 43 43 🖳www.nzembassy.com/france ⏰ Open M-Th 9am-1pm and 2-5:30pm, F 9am-1pm and 2-4pm. July and August M-Th 9am-1pm and 2-4:30pm, F 9am-2pm.)

- **UNITED KINGDOM CONSULAR SERVICES IN PARIS: Embassy.** (2 Avenue Gabriel 75382 Paris ☎01 43 12 22 22 🖳ukinfrance.fco.gov.uk/en ⏰ Open M-F 9:30am-1pm, 2:30-6pm.)

- **UNITED STATES CONSULAR SERVICES IN PARIS: Embassy.** (35, rue du Faubourg St Honoré 75363 Paris ☎01 44 51 31 00 🖳french.france.usembassy.gov ⏰ Open M-F 9:30am-1pm, 2:30pm-6pm.)

- **FRENCH CONSULAR SERVICES IN AUSTRALIA: Consulate.** (Level 26, St-Martins Tower, 31 Market St., Sydney, Australia NSW 2000 ☎02 9268 2400 🖳www.ambafrance-au.org ⏰ Open M-F 9am-1pm.)

- **FRENCH CONSULAR SERVICES IN CANADA: Consulate.** (1 pl Ville Marie Montréal, QC H3B 4S3, Canada ☎514 878 3485 🖳www.consulfrance-montreal.org ⏰ Open M-F 9:30am-4:30pm.)

- **FRENCH CONSULAR SERVICES IN IRELAND: Embassy.** (36 Ailesbury Road, Dublin 4, Ireland ☎+353 1 277 5000 🖳www.ambafrance.ie/ ⏰ Open M-F 9:30am-noon.)

- **FRENCH CONSULAR SERVICES IN NEW ZEALAND: Embassy.** (34-42 Manners Str. PO Box 11-343, Wellington, New Zealand ☎43 84 25 55 🖳www.ambafrance-nz.org ⏰ Open M-Th 9am-6pm, F 9am-4pm.)

- **FRENCH CONSULAR SERVICES IN UNITED KINGDOM: Consulate.** (21 Cromwell Road, London SW2 2EN ☎020 7073 1250 🖳www.ambafrance-uk.org/ ⏰ Open M-Th 8:45am-noon, F 8:45-11:30am.)

- **FRENCH CONSULAR SERVICES IN UNITED STATES: Consulate.** (4101 Reservoir Road Northwest, Washington DC 20007-2151 ☎202 944 6000 🖳www.ambafrance-us.org ⏰ Open M-F 8:45am-12:45pm.)

money · getting money from home

money

GETTING MONEY FROM HOME

Stuff happens. When stuff happens, you might need some money. When you need some money, the easiest and cheapest solution is to have someone back home make a deposit to your bank account. Otherwise, consider one of the following options.

Wiring Money

Arranging a **bank money transfer** means asking a bank back home to wire money to a bank in Paris. This is the cheapest way to transfer cash, but it's also the slowest and most agonizing, usually taking several days or more. Note that some banks may only release your funds in local currency, potentially sticking you with a poor exchange rate; inquire about this in advance. In Paris, bank transfers can be performed at post office banks (*La Banque Postale*). **Banque de France** has some of the most competitive rates for international transfers in Paris. Money transfer services like **Western Union** are faster and more convenient than bank transfers—but also much pricier. Western Union has many locations worldwide. To find one, visit ◼www.westernunion.com or call the appropriate number: in Australia ☎800 173 833, in Canada and the US ☎800 325 6000, in the UK ☎0800 735 1815, or in France ☎01 48 26 64 91. To wire money using a credit card in Canada and the US, call ☎800-CALL-CASH; in the UK, ☎0800 833 833. Money transfer services are also available to **American Express** cardholders and at selected **Thomas Cook** offices.

US State Department (US Citizens only)

In serious emergencies only, the US State Department will forward money within hours to the nearest consular office, which will then disburse it according to instructions for a US$30 fee. If you wish to use this service, you must contact the Overseas Citizens Services division of the US State Department. (☎1 202 501 4444, from US ☎888-407-4747)

TIPPING AND BARGAINING

By law in France, a service charge is added to bills in bars and restaurants, called *"service compris."* Most people do however, leave some change (up to 2€) for drinks and food, and in nicer restaurants it is not uncommon to leave 5% of the bill. For other services, like taxis and hairdressers, 10-15% tip is acceptable.

TAXES

As a member of the EU, France requires a value added tax (VAT) of 19.6%, which is applied to a variety of goods and services (e.g. food, accommodations), though it is less for food (5.5%). Non-European Economic Community visitors to France who are taking these goods home may be refunded this tax for purchases totaling over €175 per store. When making purchases, request a VAT form, and present them at the *détaxe* booth at the airport. These goods must be carried at all times while traveling, and refunds must be claimed within 6 months.

money · taxes

---

the euro

Despite what many dollar-possessing Americans might want to hear, the official currency of 16 members of the European Union—Austria, Belgium, Cyprus, Finland, France, Germany, Greece, Ireland, Italy, Luxembourg, Malta, the Netherlands, Portugal, Slovakia, Slovenia, and Spain—is the euro.

Still, the currency has some important—and positive—consequences for travelers hitting more than one eurozone country. For one thing, money-changers across the eurozone are obliged to exchange money at the official, fixed rate and at no commission (though they may still charge a small service fee). Second, euro-denominated traveler's checks allow you to pay for goods and services across the eurozone, again at the official rate and commission-free. For more info, check a currency converter (such as www.xe.com) or www.europa.eu.int.

To use a debit or credit card to withdraw money from a cash machine (ATM) in Europe, you must have a four-digit Personal Identification Number (PIN). If your PIN is longer than four digits, ask your bank whether you can just use the first four or whether you'll need a new one. Credit cards don't usually come with PINs, so if you intend to hit up ATMs in Europe with a credit card to get cash advances, call your credit card company before leaving to request one.

Travelers with alphabetic rather than numeric PINs may also be thrown off by the absence of letters on European cash machines. Here are the corresponding numbers to use: 1 = QZ; 2 = ABC; 3 = DEF; 4 = GHI; 5 = JKL; 6 = MNO; 7 = PRS; 8 = TUV; 9 = WXY. Note that if you mistakenly punch the wrong code into the machine multiple (often three) times, it can swallow (gulp!) your card for good.

safety and health

GENERAL ADVICE

In any type of crisis, the most important thing to do is **stay calm.** Your country's embassy abroad is usually your best resource in an emergency; registering with that embassy upon arrival in the country is a good idea. The government offices listed in the **Travel Advisories** feature at the end of this section can provide information on the services they offer their citizens in case of emergencies abroad.

Local Laws and Police

La Police Nationale is the branch of French law enforcement that is most often seen in urban areas like Paris. To reach the Parisian police, call ☎17.

Drugs and Alcohol

There is no drinking age in Paris, but to purchase alcohol one must be at least 18 years old. The legal blood-alcohol level for driving in France is .05%, which is less than it is in countries like the US, UK, New Zealand and Ireland so exercise appropriate caution when driving in France.

Disabled and GLBT Travelers

Fear not—Paris loves you.

L'Association des Paralysées de France, Délégation de Paris is an organization devoted to helping people with disabilities in Paris. In addition to promoting individuals' fundamental rights to state compensation, public transportation, and handicapped-conscious jobs, the association also organizes international vacations. (17-19 bd. Auguste Blanqui, 13ème ☎01 40 78 00 00)

Centre Lesbien Gai Bi and Trans-Paris Ile-de-France functions both as a counseling agency in and of itself, offering counseling and reception services for limited times during the week, and as the umbrella organization and formal location for many other GBLT resource organizations in Paris.. (63 rue Beaubourg ☎01 43 57 21 47 ⓂRambuteau ⓂLes Halles. ⌚ Administrative reception hours open M 1-8pm, Tu 10am-1pm, 2-6pm, W 1pm-7m, Th 1pm-6pm, F 1pm-6pm. Psychologist available Tu, W, F 6pm-8pm, Sa 5-7pm.) **Clan Natur** is a GLBT nudist society that organizes nudist soirées, if you're into that sort of thing. (5 Place de l'Adjudant Vincenot ☎01 56 53 90 26 🖳www.clannature.citegay.com)

essentials

travel advisories

The following government offices provide travel information and advisories by telephone, by fax, or via the web:

- **AUSTRALIA: Department of Foreign Affairs and Trade.** (☎61 2 6261 1111 ■www.dfat.gov.au/index.html)
- **CANADA: Department of Foreign Affairs and International Trade (DFAIT).** Call or visit the website for the free booklet Bon Voyage...But. (☎800 267 8376 ■www.dfait-maeci.gc.ca)
- **NEW ZEALAND: Ministry of Foreign Affairs.** (☎64 4 439 8000 ■www.mfat.govt.nz)
- **UK: Foreign and Commonwealth Office.** (☎44 20 7008 1500 ■www.fco.gov.uk)
- **US: Department of State.** (☎888 407 4747 from the US, 1 202 501 4444 elsewhere ■http://travel.state.gov)

SPECIFIC CONCERNS

Demonstrations and Political Gatherings

The French Revolution may have been in 1789, but the spirit of the revolution certainly hasn't died. Protests and strikes are frequent in Paris over anything from the minimum wage to Sarkozy's wardrobe choices, but violence does not often occur (unless he wears white after Labor Day). You may find yourself in the city on the day of a transit strike (as one LG researcher did) but who hasn't always wanted to travel France by Vespa? Transit strikes can be some of the most disruptive, but they generally don't last more than a week.

emergency!

- **EMERGENCY NUMBERS: Police** ☎17. *i* For emergencies only. **Ambulence (SAMU)** ☎15. **Fire** ☎18. **Poison** ☎01 40 05 48 48. *i* In French, but some English assistance available. **Rape** ☎08 00 05 95 95. *i* Open M-F 10am-7pm. **SOS Help!** ☎17 An emergency hotline for English speakers in crisis.
- **CRISIS LINES: AIDES** First French association against HIV/AIDS and viral hepatitis. (☎0 800 84 08 00 ■www.aides.org ⏰ Open 24hr.) **Alcoholics Anonymous (AA)** (☎01 46 34 59 65 ■www.aaparis.org.) **Red Cross France** Provides HIV testing. (43 rue de Valois, 1er ☎01 42 61 30 04 ■www.croix-rouge.fr Ⓜ Palais-Royal or Ⓜ Bourse.) **International Counseling Service (ICS).** (☎01 45 50 26 49 ■www.icsparis.com.)
- **HOSPITALS/MEDICAL SERVICES: American Hospital of Paris** (63 bd. Hugo, Neuilly ☎01 46 41 25 25 ■www.american-hospital.org Ⓜ Port Maillot, then bus #82.) **Hôpital Bichat** (46 rue Henri Buchard, 18ème ☎01 40 25 80 80 Ⓜ Port St-Ouen)

PRE-DEPARTURE HEALTH

Matching a prescription to a foreign equivalent is not always easy, safe, or possible, so if you take **prescription drugs,** carry up-to-date prescriptions or a statement from your doctor stating the medications' trade names, manufacturers, chemical names, and dosages. Be sure to keep all medication with you in your carry-on luggage.

The names in French for common drugs are: *aspirine* (aspirin), *acétaminophène* (acetaminophen), *ibuprofène* (ibuprofen), *antihistaminiques* (antihistamines), and *pénicilline* (penicillin).

IMMUNIZATIONS AND PRECAUTIONS

Travelers over two years old should make sure that the following vaccines are up to date: MMR (for measles, mumps, and rubella); DTaP or Td (for diphtheria, tetanus, and pertussis); IPV (for polio); Hib (for *Haemophilus influenzae* B); and HepB (for Hepatitis B). For recommendations on immunizations and prophylaxis, check with a doctor and consult the **Centers for Disease Control and Prevention (CDC)** in the US or the equivalent in your home country. (☎1 800 CDC INFO 🖳www.cdc.gov/travel)

budget airlines

The recent emergence of no-frills airlines has made hopscotching around Europe by air increasingly affordable. Though these flights often feature inconvenient hours or serve less popular regional airports, with ticket prices often dipping into single digits, it's never been faster or easier to jet across the continent. The following resources will be useful not only for crisscrossing France but also for those ever-popular weekend trips to nearby international destinations.

- **BMIBABY:** Departures from multiple cities in the UK to Paris, Nice, and other cities in France. (☎0871 224 0224 for the UK, 44 870 126 6726 elsewhere 🖳www.bmibaby.com)

- **EASYJET:** London to Bordeaux and other cities in France. (☎44 871 244 2366, £0.10 per min. 🖳www.easyjet.com Ⓢ UK £50-150.)

- **RYANAIR:** From Dublin, Glasgow, Liverpool, London, and Shannon to destinations in France. (☎0818 30 30 30 for Ireland, 0871 246 0000 for the UK 🖳www.ryanair.com)

- **SKYEUROPE:** Forty destinations in 19 countries around Europe. (☎0905 722 2747 from the UK, 421 2 3301 7301 elsewhere 🖳www.skyeurope.com)

- **STERLING:** The first Scandinavian-based budget airline connects Denmark, Norway, and Sweden to 47 European destinations, including Montpellier, Nice, and Paris. (☎70 10 84 84 from Denmark, 0870 787 8038 from the UK 🖳www.sterling.dk)

- **TRANSAVIA:** Short hops from Krakow to Paris. (☎020 7365 4997 from the UK 🖳www.transavia.com Ⓢ From €49 one-way.)

- **WIZZ AIR:** Paris from Budapest, Krakow, and Warsaw. (☎0904 475 9500 from the UK, £0.65 per min. 🖳www.wizzair.com)

essentials

STAYING HEALTHY

Medical Care

A booming metropolis, Paris has numerous hospitals, and non-French speaking travelers will be pleased to find that often the staff will speak English. While treatment can be expensive, French healthcare is more than adequate.

getting around

For information on how to get to Paris and save a bundle while doing so, check out the Essentials section of **www.letsgo.com.** (In case you can't tell, we think our website's the bomb.) For information on how to get around Paris, tips on how to navigate the Metro can be found in the Orientation section.

BY PLANE

Commercial Airlines

For small-scale travel on the continent, *Let's Go* suggests **budget airlines** for budget travelers, but more traditional carriers have made efforts to keep up with the revolution. The **Star Alliance Europe Airpass** offers low economy-class fares for travel within Europe to 220 destinations in 45 countries. The pass is available to non-European passengers on Star Alliance carriers, including Lufthansa, BMI, Spanair, and TAP Portugal (www.staralliance.com). **EuropebyAir's** snazzy FlightPass also allows you to hop between hundreds of cities in Europe and North Africa. (☎888 321 4737 www.europebyair.com $ Most flights US$99.)

In addition, a number of European airlines offer discount coupon packets. Most are only available as tack-ons for transatlantic passengers, but some are standalone offers. Most must be purchased before departure, so research in advance. For example, **Oneworld,** a coalition of 10 major international airlines, offers deals and cheap connections all over the world, including within Europe. (www.oneworld.com)

BY TRAIN

Trains in France are generally comfortable, convenient, and reasonably swift. Second-class compartments, which seat from two to six, are great places to meet fellow travelers. Make sure you are on the correct car, as trains sometimes split at crossroads. Towns listed in parentheses on European train schedules require a train switch at the town listed immediately before the parentheses.

rail resources

- **WWW.RAILEUROPE.COM:** Info on rail travel and railpasses.
- **POINT-TO-POINT FARES AND SCHEDULES:** www.raileurope.com/us/rail/fares_schedules/index.htm allows you to calculate whether buying a railpass would save you money.
- **WWW.RAILSAVER.COM:** Uses your itinerary to calculate the best railpass for your trip.
- **WWW.RAILFANEUROPE.NET:** Links to rail servers throughout Europe.
- **FOR CHUNNEL TICKETS:** **Eurostar** reservations (☎0843 2186 186 www.eurostar.com.uk.) **Eurotunnel** (☎0810 63 03 04 www.eurotunnel.com.)
- **WWW.LETSGO.COM**

You can either buy a **rail pass,** which allows you unlimited travel within a particular region for a given period of time, or rely on buying individual **point-to-point** tickets as you go. Almost all countries give students or youths (under 26, usually) direct discounts on regular domestic rail tickets, and many also sell a student or youth card that provides 20-50% off all fares for up to a year.

BY BUS

Though European trains and rail passes are extremely popular, in some cases buses prove a better option. In France however, bus travel is often a hassle. Travelers generally opt for bus travel only for short trips between destinations that are not served by trains. However, often cheaper than rail passes, **international bus passes** allow unlimited travel on a hop-on, hop-off basis between major European cities. **Busabout,** for instance, offers three interconnecting bus circuits covering 29 of Europe's best bus hubs. (☎44 8450 267 514 🖳www.busabout.com $ 1 circuit in high season starts at US$579, students US$549.) **Eurolines,** meanwhile, is the largest operator of Europe-wide coach services. We get misty-eyed just thinking about their unlimited 15- and 30-day passes to 41 major European cities. (☎0 892 89 90 91, €0.34 per min 🖳www.eurolines.com $ High season 15-day pass €345, 30-day pass €455; under 26 €290/375. Mid-season €240/330; under 26 €205/270. Low season €205/310; under 26 €175/240.)

BY BICYCLE

Some youth hostels rent bicycles for low prices, and in some parts of Paris, it is possible to rent bikes from street locations and drop them off elsewhere. In addition to **panniers** (US$40-150) to hold your luggage, you'll need a good **helmet** (US$10-40) and a sturdy **lock** (from US$30). For more country-specific books on biking through France, try **Mountaineers Books.** (1001 SW Klickitat Way, Ste. 201, Seattle, WA 98134, USA ☎206 223 6303 🖳www.mountaineersbooks.org)

keeping in touch

BY EMAIL AND INTERNET

Hello and welcome to the 21st century, where you can check your email in most major European cities, though sometimes you'll have to pay a few bucks or buy a drink for internet access. Although in some places it's possible to forge a remote link with your home server, in most cases this is a much slower (and thus more expensive) option than taking advantage of free **web-based email accounts** (e.g., 🖳**www.gmail.com**). **Internet cafes** and the occasional free internet terminal at a public library or university are listed in the **Practicalities** section. For lists of additional cyber cafes in Paris, check out specific websites—examples include 🖳www.cybercaptive.com and 🖳www.netcafeguide.com.

Wireless hot spots make internet access possible in public and remote places. Unfortunately, they also pose security risks. Hot spots are public, open networks that use unencrypted, unsecured connections. They are susceptible to hacks and "packet sniffing"—the theft of passwords and other private information. To prevent problems, disable "ad hoc" mode, turn off file sharing and network discovery, encrypt your email, turn on your firewall, beware of phony networks, and watch for over-the-shoulder creeps.

BY TELEPHONE

Calling Home from Paris

Prepaid phone cards are a common and relatively inexpensive means of calling abroad. Each one comes with a Personal Identification Number (PIN) and a toll-free access number. You call the access number and then follow the directions for dialing your PIN. To purchase prepaid phone cards, check online for the best rates;

■www.callingcards.com is a good place to start. Online providers generally send your access number and PIN via email, with no actual "card" involved. You can also call home with prepaid phone cards purchased in Paris.

If you have internet access, your best—i.e., cheapest, most convenient, and most tech-savvy—bet is probably our good friend **Skype.** (■www.skype.com) You can even video chat if you have one of those new-fangled webcams. Calls to other Skype users are free; calls to landlines and mobiles worldwide start at US$0.021 per minute, depending on where you're calling.

Another option is a **calling card,** linked to a major national telecommunications service in your home country. Calls are billed collect or to your account. Cards generally come with instructions for dialing both domestically and internationally.

Placing a collect call through an international operator can be expensive but may be necessary in case of an emergency. You can frequently call collect without even possessing a company's calling card just by calling its access number and following the instructions.

international calls

To call France from home or to call home from France, dial:

- **1. THE INTERNATIONAL DIALING PREFIX.** To call from **Australia,** dial ☎0011; **Canada** or the **US,** ☎011; **Ireland, New Zealand, France,** or the **UK,** ☎00.
- **2. THE COUNTRY CODE OF THE COUNTRY YOU WANT TO CALL.** To call **Australia,** dial ☎61; **Canada** or the **US,** ☎1; **Ireland,** ☎353; **New Zealand,** ☎64; the **UK,** ☎44; **France,** ☎33.
- **3. THE CITY/AREA CODE.** Let's Go lists the city/area codes for cities and towns in France, opposite the city or town name, next to a ☎, as well as in every phone number. If the first digit is a zero (e.g., ☎01 for Paris), omit the zero when calling from abroad (e.g., dial ☎1 from Canada to reach Paris).
- **4. THE LOCAL NUMBER.**

Cellular Phones

The international standard for cell phones is **Global System for Mobile Communication (GSM).** To make and receive calls in France, you will need a GSM-compatible phone and a **SIM (Subscriber Identity Module) card,** a country-specific, thumbnail-size chip that gives you a local phone number and plugs you into the local network. Many SIM cards are prepaid, and incoming calls are frequently free. You can buy additional cards or vouchers (usually available at convenience stores) to "top up" your phone. For more information on GSM phones, check out ■www.telestial.com. Companies like **Cellular Abroad** (■www.cellularabroad.com) and **OneSimCard** (■www.onesimcard.com) rent cell phones and SIM cards that work in a variety of destinations around the world. In France, **Orange** is a great cell phone option for travelers, offering affordable phones (~€35) that come pre-loaded with minutes and can be recharged at most supermarkets and tobacco shops. (■www.orange.co.uk)

BY SNAIL MAIL

Sending Mail Home from Paris

Airmail is the best way to send mail home from Paris. **Aerogrammes,** printed sheets that fold into envelopes and travel via airmail, are available at post offices. Write "airmail" and *"par avion"* on the front. Most post offices will charge exorbitant fees or simply refuse to send aerogrammes with enclosures. Surface mail is by far the cheapest and slowest way to send mail. It takes one to two months to cross the Atlantic and one to three to cross the Pacific—good for heavy items you won't need for a while, like souvenirs that you've acquired along the way.

Sending Mail to Paris

In addition to the standard postage system, **Federal Express** handles express mail services from most countries to France. (☎800 463 3339 🖳www.fedex.com) Sending a postcard within France costs €0.56, while sending letters (up to 20g) domestically requires €0.56.

There are several ways to arrange pickup of letters sent to you while you are abroad. In France, you can request that a FedEx package be held for pickup at the FedEx office, rather than having it sent to an address. Mail can also be sent via **Poste Restante** (General Delivery) to almost any city or town in France with a post office, but it is not very reliable. Address Poste Restante letters like so:

Napoleon BONAPARTE
Poste Restante
Paris, France

The mail will go to a special desk in the central post office, unless you specify a post office by street address or postal code. It's best to use the largest post office, since mail may be sent there regardless. It is usually safer and quicker, though more expensive, to send mail express or registered. Bring your passport (or other photo ID) for pickup; there may be a small fee. If the clerks insist that there is nothing for you, ask them to check under your first name as well. *Let's Go* lists post offices in the **Practicalities** section for each city.

American Express has travel offices throughout the world that offer a free **Client Letter Service** (mail held up to 30 days and forwarded upon request) for cardholders who contact them in advance. Some offices provide these services to non-cardholders (especially AmEx Travelers Cheque holders), but call ahead to make sure. For a complete list of AmEx locations, call ☎800 528 4800 or visit 🖳www.americanexpress.com/travel.

climate

As pleasantly romantic as it is to think of Springtime in Paris, *le printemps* doesn't last forever. Paris has a temperate climate, with four seasons. The Northern Atlantic current keeps weather from approaching any extremes. Winters in Paris can be cold, but heavy snow is not characteristic of the City of Lights. Springtime in Paris is definitely a lovely time of year; flowers bloom, trees grow leaves—it's everything you've read about. Summers are comfortable for the most part, though some days in August will have you wishing you had picked a city convenient to a beach. Fall is brisk, but enjoyable as the city's foliage changes before your eyes.

MONTH	AVG. HIGH TEMP.		AVG. LOW TEMP.		AVG. RAINFALL		AVG. NUMBER OF WET DAYS
January	6°C	43°F	1°C	34°F	56mm	2.2 in.	17
February	7°C	45°F	1°C	34°F	46mm	1.8 in.	14
March	12°C	54°F	4°C	39°F	35mm	1.4 in.	12
April	16°C	61°F	3°C	43°F	42mm	1.7 in.	13
May	20°C	68°F	10°C	50°F	57mm	2.2 in.	12
June	23°C	73°F	13°C	55°F	54mm	2.1 in.	12
July	25°C	77°F	15°C	59°F	59mm	2.3 in.	12
August	24°C	76°F	14°C	57°F	64mm	2.5 in.	13
September	21°C	70°F	12°C	54°F	55mm	2.2 in.	13
October	16°C	61°F	8°C	46°F	50mm	1.9 in.	13
November	10°C	50°F	5°C	41°F	51mm	2.0 in.	15
December	7°C	45°F	2°C	36°F	50mm	1.9 in.	16

essentials

measurements

Like the rest of the rational world, France uses the metric system. The basic unit of length is the meter (m), which is divided into 100 centimeters (cm) or 1000 millimeters (mm). One thousand meters make up one kilometer (km). Fluids are measured in liters (L), each divided into 1000 milliliters (mL). A liter of pure water weighs one kilogram (kg), the unit of mass that is divided into 1000 grams (g). One metric ton is 1000kg.

MEASUREMENT CONVERSIONS	
1 inch (in.) = 25.4mm	1 millimeter (mm) = 0.039 in.
1 foot (ft.) = 0.305m	1 meter (m) = 3.28 ft.
1 yard (yd.) = 0.914m	1 meter (m) = 1.094 yd.
1 mile (mi.) = 1.609km	1 kilometer (km) = 0.621 mi.
1 ounce (oz.) = 28.35g	1 gram (g) = 0.035 oz.
1 pound (lb.) = 0.454kg	1 kilogram (kg) = 2.205 lb.
1 fluid ounce (fl. oz.) = 29.57mL	1 milliliter (mL) = 0.034 fl. oz.
1 gallon (gal.) = 3.785L	1 liter (L) = 0.264 gal.

language

You'll be surprised to learn that the official language in Paris is French. Shocking, we know. English speakers will be happy to note that English is the most commonly taught foreign language in France, followed by Spanish and German.

PRONUNCIATION

What you've heard is true: the French resent tourists who don't speak their language. They are quite good at turning their noses up at you (centuries of snootiness can do that). However, what you probably don't know is that the French people are more than happy to help if you at least attempt French. Reading French can be tricky, but the table below should help you out.

PHONETIC UNIT	PRONUNCIATION	PHONETIC UNIT	PRONUNCIATION
au	o, as in "go"	ch	sh, as in "shoe"
oi	ua as in "guava"	ou	oo, as in "igloo"
ai	ay as in "lay"	à	ah, as in "menorah"

PHRASEBOOK

ENGLISH	FRENCH	PRONUNCIATION
Hello!/Hi!	Bonjour!	bohn-jhoor
Goodbye!	Au revoir!	oh ruh-vwah
Yes.	Oui	wee
No.	Non	nohn
Sorry!	Désolé!	day-zoh-lay
EMERGENCY		
Go away!	Allez-vous en!	ah-lay vooz on
Help!	Au secours!	oh sek-oor
Call the police!	Appelez les flics!	apple-ay lay fleeks
Get a doctor!	Va chercher un médecin!	vah share-shay un mayd-sin
Police station	Poste de Police	Exactly like you'd think.
Hospital	Hôpital	Ho-pee-tal
Liquor store	Magasin d'alcool	Maga-zin dal-cool
FOOD		
Waiter/waitress	Serveur/Serveuse	server/servers
I'd like...	Je voudrais	Je voo-dray
Thank you!	Merci!	mare-see
Check please!	La facture, s'il-vous-plait!	La fact-tour, seal-voo-play
Where is...	Où est...	Oo ay...

language · phrasebook

ENGLISH	FRENCH	ENGLISH	FRENCH
I am from (the US/ Europe).	Je suis des Etats-Unis/de l'Europe	What's the problem, sir/ madam?	Quelle est la problème, monsieur/madame?
I have a visa/ID.	J'ai un visa/de l'identification.	I lost my passport/ luggage	J'ai perdu mon passeport/ baggage
I will be here for less than six months.	Je serai ici pour moins de six mois.	I have nothing to declare.	Je n'ai rien à déclarer.
You are the woman of my dreams.	Vous êtes la femme de mes rêves.	Perhaps I can help you with that?	Puis-je vous aider avec ça?
Your hostel, or mine?	Votre hôtel, ou le mien?	Do you have protection?	Avez-vous un préservatif?
I would like a round-trip ticket.	Je voudrais un billet aller-retour.	Where is the train station?	Où est la gare?
Can I see a double room?	Puis-je voir un chambre pour deux?	How much does this cost?	Combien ça coûte?
Where is the bathroom?	Où est la salle de bain?	Is there a bar near here?	Est-ce qu'il y a un bar près d'ici?
What time is the next train?	A quelle heure est la prochaine train?	Do you have this bathing suit in another size?	Avez-vous cette maillot de bain dans une autre taille?
Can I have another drink please?	Puis-je prendre un autre boisson s'il vous-plait?	Please don't arrest me!	S'il vous plait, ne m'arretez pas!

I'm in a committed relationship.	Je suis dans une relation engagée.	You talkin' to me?	Vous me parlez?
It was like this when I got here.	C'était comme ça quand je suis arrivé(e).	I don't speak much French.	Je ne parle pas beaucoup de Français.
I feel sick.	Je me sent malade.	Leave me alone!	Laissez-moi tranquille!
What time does reception close?	A quelle heure est-ce que la réception ferme?	I don't understand.	Je ne comprends pas.
Actually, I'm from Canada.	Actuellement, je suis Canadien(ne).	I didn't vote for him, I swear.	Je n'ai pas voté pour lui, je el jure.

let's go online

Plan your next trip on our spiffy website, ▇www.letsgo.com. It features full book content, the latest travel info on your favorite destinations, and tons of interactive features: make your own itinerary, read blogs from our trusty Researcher-Writers, browse our photo library, watch exclusive videos, check out our newsletter, find travel deals, follow us on Facebook, and buy new guides. Plus, if this Essentials wasn't enough for you, we've got even more online. We're always updating and adding new features, so check back often!

essentials

PARIS 101

history

PARISIANS OF YORE

A haven for artsy eccentrics even in prehistoric times, it was the limestone quarries at the site of modern Paris that originally lured budding artists, providing them with optimal rock drawing materials. By the third century BCE, Paris— then called Lutetia—found itself settled by the **Parisii,** a Celtic tribe of Gaul who settled on what is now the tiny islet of **Île de la Cité.** The settlement did not turn out as planned. **Caesar's** armies swiftly conquered the city in 53 B.C., and the town was destroyed by a horde of barbarians a century later. This (first) demolition of Paris marks the beginning of what is perhaps the most enduring and treasured of all French traditions: military defeat.

In a wise PR move, the town officially changed its name to Paris in the fourth century A.D., and conditions on Île de la Cité seemed to improve. Legend has it that man-beast **Attila the Hun** was fast approaching Paris as he ravaged through Gaul in the mid-400s, when out of the dust rose a sweet-faced peasant girl named Geneviève, whose mighty prayer repelled Attila. It is worth noting that Attila the Hun did not actually attack Paris; be that as it may, Geneviève was instated as the city's patron saint in 509.

facts and figures

- **LIGHT BULBS ON THE EIFFEL TOWER:** 20,000
- **ARRONDISSEMENTS:** 20
- **PUBLIC BICYCLES:** 20,000
- **PUBLIC BICYCLES THAT HAVE BEEN STOLEN:** 8,000
- **WEEKS IT WOULD TAKE TO SEE EVERY PIECE OF ART IN THE LOUVRE:** 7

FRANKLY, MY DEAR, THEY DIDN'T GIVE A DAMN

Sadly, no amount of hallelujahs could spare the town from the **Franks.** Paris became the center of the kingdom of Clovis in 508, but power shifted out of Paris to the north of France after **Charlemagne** became king of the Franks in the eighth century. Weak and disunited, Paris was left exposed to attacks from the ◢**Vikings.** Settlements on the banks of the Seine were again in ruins, and Parisians retreated back to Île de la Cité.

As Charlemagne's Carolingian dynasty was destabilized by infighting throughout the 10th century, the counts of Paris ruled the city with increasing autonomy. In 987, they elected Hugues Capet king, and the cultural juggernaut that is Paris finally got moving under the **Capetian dynasty.** With Paris as their capital, Capetian monarchs renovated and adopted the stunning Roman Palais de la Cité. **Philippe Auguste** was easily the most successful of these medieval French kings. His reign fostered dramatic progress in architecture, education, and urban expansion, and Paris became the richest city in the West. Unfortunately, diseased rats and ill-behaved Englishmen loomed on the horizon. The plague of 1348 and rampant political instability ushered in the **Hundred Years' War with England**, and in 1420, England seized Paris. Despite the valiant antics of a teenage and possibly schizophrenic girl named **Joan de Arc**, who led a failed seige of Paris in 1429, the occupation held until **Charles VII** finally recaptured the city in 1436, booting out the English.

OUT OF THE DARK

By the late 15th century, Paris had thrown itself headlong into the **Renaissance. Francis I** founded the Collège de France in this period, which joined the long-established University of Paris and Sorbonne and breathed new life into French intellectualism. The city's attempts at civilized progress were somewhat undermined by the **Wars of Religion**, a conflict between Roman Catholics and Protestant Huguenotes which resulted in a series of genocidal massacres that took place over the course of 30 years. Out of the chaos rose gallant **Henry IV,** who guaranteed the Huguenots religious freedom through the **Edict of Nantes** in 1598. Henry IV had his priorities straight: he converted to Catholicism because "Paris is well worth a mass." He paid the price when a radical Catholic knifed him to death just at the height of his glory in 1610. In the spirit of brotherly love, a Parisian mob executed the assassin by scalding and then quartering him.

LOVIN' THOSE LOUEYS

Henry was succeeded by a long line of Louis's, the first being his son, nine-year-old Louis XIII. Despite a nasty stutter, little Louis did an adequate job maintaining Paris as an economic and artistic stronghold, but approval ratings plummeted once his successor, **Louis XIV**, came along. After series of civil wars called the **Fronde**, which stemmed from major discontent between nobility and the bourgeoisie, the "Sun King" tightened his grip to maintain the peace. Parisians in this period were overcome by despair—horrifically, the death rate in the city at the time was higher than the birthrate. In addition to his megalomaniacal and sociopathic tendencies, Louis XIV was also a wuss and fled to his ridiculously extravagant palace in **Versailles** out of fear of his citizens in 1682. Under the following two Louis's (XV and XVI), health conditions in the city improved, but **Enlightenment thinkers** began to probe society with ideas of *liberté, egalité,* and *fraternité.* ◢**Revolution** began in 1789, culminating in the fall of the **Bastille** on July 14th, 1792, and the beheading of Louis XVI and his cake-eating wife Marie Antoinette.

BEAUCOUP COUPS

The Jacobins of the **First French Republic** began the **Reign of Terror**—an execution campaign spearheaded by Maximilein Robespierre. He and his henchmen guillotined thousands of so-called counterrevolutionaries, terrorizing the city and the countryside. Eventually, his lesser council members decided enough was enough and led a coup, called the Thermidorian Reaction, giving him a taste of his own guillotine. A government called the Directory was established in Paris, but coups were all the rage back then, and **Napoleon Bonaparte** took over several years later in 1804.

Between the Directory, Napoleon, and the line of kings that followed his downfall, politics were messy in France for several decades. Parisian citizens were left out to dry as a result, and a growing, poverty-stricken underclass lashed out again in the **Revolution of 1848**. They ousted the Orleans monarchy and created the **Second French Republic,** led by elected president **Napoleon III**, the former emperor's nephew. Unsurprisingly, he was also a glutton for power and soon turned himself into emperor of the Second Empire in 1851. During Napoleon III's twenty-year reign, **Baron Haussman,** the biggest urban planning badass of the 19th century, transformed Paris' economy and infrastructure. Under Napolean, Parisian industrial, artistic, and intellectual influence spread, until 1870, when the **Franco-Prussian War** brought poverty and despair to Paris once again.

The surrender of Paris in 1871 to Prussia marked the end of the imperial regime in France. The **Third Republic** did not do much politically for France, but ushered in an era fondly known as the **Belle Epoque,** a period characterized by flourishing modern art, entertainment, fashion, and an epic ▓**World's Fair.** Paris undeniably earned a worldwide reputation as a capital of the arts. Popularity of the **risqué cabaret show** also soared during the Époque, and brothels attracted as many thrill-seekers as the newly erected **Eiffel Tower** did.

THE WAR YEARS

Like most places 'round the world, Paris suffered considerably during World War I and the postwar years. Postwar Paris was the unofficial home of expatriates, drawn to the **bohemian lifestyle** of Paris that was absent from most war-stricken cities. Despite a dismal economy, and probably aided by the abundance of wine available for Prohibition-fleeing Americans, Surrealism, Existentialism, and Expressionism arose in the city. The onset of World War II, however, was soon followed by a terrible **Nazi** occupation in Paris that lasted from 1940-1944. A resistance movement led by **General Charles de Gaulle** helped liberate Paris after the Allied forces landed in Normandy in 1944. Most of Paris's historical buildings and monuments were spared from the destruction of the war. Over half a million French citizens were not as lucky.

PROTESTS, BAD HYGIENE, AND EYESORES, OH MY

Catching its breath after the Nazis, the city saw little action until the global ▓acid trip that was the 1960s. In 1961, a peaceful demonstration by North Africans protesting the **Algerian War** turned into a bloody massacre, with over 100 killed by police and dumped into the Seine River. In 1968, nine million workers staged strikes to protest big business, and that same year demonstrations by students against university policy seem to balance Paris on the brink of anarchy. De Gaulle took on the Nazis, but he couldn't handle angry hippie kids. He retired, and **George Pompidou** became president in 1969.

The end of the Algerian War brought thousands of immigrants to the city, prompting the construction of new suburbs (*banlieues*, or "outskirts") that soon became notorious for poverty, crime, and, most unforgivably, ugly architecture. Despite various swings in French politics and more controversial construction over the next few decades, Paris remained a relatively calm spot until the mid-1990s, when Muslim extremists bombed the city's subways. Today, racial tensions between the ethnic French and North Africans still occasionally disrupt the city's cosmopolitan flow. In 2005, **violent riots** broke out in the city's streets and chaos soon spread around the country as rioters, mostly frustrated children of North African immigrants, razed the streets and attacked police.

PARIS—SO IN RIGHT NOW

Despite the sporadic political violence of the past half-century, Paris has steadily continued to serve as a beacon of unparalleled cosmopolitan culture, as any Parisian will be more than happy to remind you. Political and cultural leaders continue to actively nurture the fashion, art, and architecture that has defined the city's history; since taking office in 2007, President **Nicolas Sarkozy** has personally maintained the city's reputation for elegance through his refined eye for accessories, such as third wife Carla Bruni. After centuries of such artistic endeavors, "The City of Lights" has remained a glamorous haven of avant-garde thinkers, intellectuals, and romantics, and will for years to come.

arts

LITERATURE AND PHILOSOPHY

So Much for Renaissance

An oasis for egotistical visionaries, ennui-ridden madmen, and their ensuing authority issues, Paris has been an intellectual epicenter since its more sensitive cavemen discovered rock drawing. Due to the French predisposition towards joining mobs and executing monarchs, however, it took a few centuries for the city to stop trying to kill off its own protégés. After immersing himself in **humanism** at the University of Paris, **John Calvin** was forced to flee the city and its Wars of Religion in 1533. In 1588, famed essayist **Michel de Montaigne** was imprisoned twice in the same brief trip to Paris by the League of Protestants and was almost prevented from publishing a revised addition of his *Essais*.

Enlightened Guillotines

Conditions in Paris improved in the 17th and 18th centuries when the city played host to the **Enlightenment**, an intellectual movement which championed human reason over dogmatism. As with all things in Paris, the Enlightenment quickly turned political. **Moliere** provided the 17th century's comic relief by parodying (and enraging) the city's prudish bourgeoisie. As a young man, **Voltaire** spent most of his time in Paris pretending to go to law school, getting locked up in the Bastille, and promoting social reform through satire. Both writers struck a cord with the city's historically murderous dislike for its ruling class, and the philosophies of **Jean-Jacques Rousseau** only fanned the flames. In 1792, the Enlightenment's political theories catalyzed the **French Revolution**, and Parisians expressed their commitment to rational discourse via guillotine.

Realists and Romantics

19th-century Paris was defined by crosscurrents of **Realism**, **Romanticism**, and perpetual social upheaval. Referring to Paris as his "dear old hell," **Honore de Balzac** gregariously slept his way through the city while writing his *Comedie Humaine*. The work established the novel as the pre-eminent literary medium of the age, a position which **Victor Hugo**'s wildly popular *The Hunchback of Notre Dame* confirmed. Though immediately acclaimed, Romantics and Realists often ran afoul of French censorship laws. **Gustave Flaubert** was prosecuted for immorality in 1858 due to the detailed descriptions of the adulterous *Madame Bovary*.

Surrealism and Social Upheaval

If 19th-century Paris was characterized by a conflation of intellectual movements, early 20th-century Paris was characterized by an eruption of them. In rebellion against the "rationalism" of prior centuries, **Surrealism** explored the intersections of the subconscious with everyday reality through melting clocks and illogical gibberish; **Andre Breton** was the author of its Manifesto. Attracted by the city's intellectualism, jazz and liquor, alienated ex-pats from around the world flocked to Paris throughout the 1920s and '30s. **F. Scott Fitzgerald, Ernest Hemmingway, Gertrude Stein** and other writers of the **"Lost Generation"** produced groundbreaking works of American literature at a safe distance from the country they criticized. **Aime Cesaire, Leopold Sedar Senghor,** and other intellectuals from France's African and Caribbean colonies founded the **Negritude** movement, a precursor to the postcolonial nationalist movements in decades to come. The home to the most progressive theories of the age, Paris' intellectual tolerance was considerably undermined by the **Dreyfuss Affair**, a tour de force of anti-Semitism which foreshadowed France's none-too-impressive resistance to the Holocaust to come.

Bra Burning and the Post-Folks

Those dense books about "power" and "knowledge" that your liberal arts class forced you to read? Yeah, products of postwar Paris. When they weren't busy getting busy, **Jean-Paul Sartre** and **Simone de Beauvoir** spent their time dominating Parisian academic circles with theories of **Existentialism** and **Second Wave Feminism**, respectively. **Postmodernists** of the 1970s such as **Michel Foucault** and **Jacques Derrida** revolutionized academic thought and brought the transparency of philosophical writing to new lows. All three of these intellectual movements intersected heavily with **Postcolonialism**, as nationalist forces chafed against French colonial rule.

FINE ARTS AND ARCHITECTURE

Church v. Nudists

Exchanging the **homoerotic nudes** of the Classical age for excessive portrayals of passion, religion maintained a stranglehold on the art world throughout the Middle Ages. **Saint-Denis Basilica,** considered the first Gothic building ever built, was finished in 1144 in what is now a suburb of Paris. The **Notre Dame,** sans hunchback, followed soon after, as did the wondrous **Sainte-Chapelle.** By the 15th century, Gothic art and architecture morphed into an Italian-influenced **Renaissance** style, which recovered both realistic linear perspective and an appreciation for very naked people.

Baroque and Rococo

Drawing on the raw emotion of Italian artwork, a unique French Baroque style emerged under the reign of Louis XIII. The art form reached its height with Louis XIV's flamboyant renovations of **Versailles,** an exorbitant spectacle which the prols of Paris were rumored to have issues with. By the 1720s, the light-hearted and asymmetrical **rococo** began to supersede Baroque style, and was much preferred by Louis XV. Paintings of debaucherous fetes and **naughty shepardesses** abounded.

Neoclassicism

After the Revolution and the rise of Napoleon I, neoclassicism emerged as a reaction to the aristocratic Baroque and rococo styles. Ancient Greek and Roman forms were once again depicted on canvas and in sculpture, and landmarks such as the **Arc de Triomphe** and the **Pantheon** were erected as odes to ancient architecture. Napoleon, in his infinite modesty, hired period artist **Jacques-Louis David** to paint gigantic portraits of him, idolizing the emperor as hero and god.

arts · fine arts and architecture

Make a Good Impression

After marrying his father's mistress, Parisian **Édouard Manet** started experimenting with color, texture, and nudity in ways that had never been dreamed of. The seeds of **Impressionism** were thus sewn. The miraculous works of **Claude Monet, Pierre-Auguste Renoir,** and **Edgar Degas** soon graced Paris, capturing and focusing on light and color in ways that have yet to be surpassed. **Post-Impressionists** took their techniques to a new level: **Vincent van Gogh** (actually a Dutchman, but give him credit for living in Paris) delved into emotional **expressionism, Georges Seurat's** bold **Pointilist** style rocked the art world in 1884, and **Paul Cézanne** experimented with dimension.

Romantics Unite

The vivid and sometimes shocking scenes depicted by **Eugène Delacroix** and **Jean-Auguste-Dominique Ingres,** both of whose ceiling paintings you can crane your neck to admire in Hotel de Villes and the Louvre repectively, captured the raw passion of the Romanticism that characterized the late 19th century. In **Saint-Jean-Cap-Ferrat**, you can see a perfect example of the beginning of the **Belle Époque** in the **Villa Ephrussi de Rothschild**. In Nice, the **Hotel Negresco** is another example of the Belle Époque. Built in 1912 by then-famous architect **Eiffel,** the hotel has every extravagant feature you can hope for to attract wealthy clients, including the 16,309 crystal chandelier commissioned by **Czar Nicholas II**. He did not get to deliver it due to the **October Revolution**.

Hip To Be a Square

The rise of Cubism in Paris was marked by exalted Cubist Pablo Picasso's painting *Les Demoiselles d'Avignon*, which he painted in Paris in 1907. Using pure, brilliant color and strong expression, Picasso's rival, **Henri Matisse**, whose collection can be found in **Cimiez**, squeezed his paint from the tube directly onto the canvas in a bid against Cubism known as **Fauvism** (from *fauves*, or wild animals).

Contemporary Art

After WWII, French art diverged, with some artists joining the **Abstract Expressionsim** movement, others getting involved in **pop art,** and still others creating innovative works. Today, the Centre Pompidou in Paris houses the **Musée National d'Art Moderne,** the largest collection of modern art in Europe. The building itself is an ode to modern architecture with all the stuff usually hidden by walls—electrical lines, piping, etc.—exposed on the outside of the building in brightly colored tubes.

culture

FOOD AND DRINK

A French **breakfast** typically consists of light fare—a quick stop for coffee and a *croissant* at the nearest café, or a few *tartines* (slices) of bread with jelly. Stop at a *boulangerie* to pick up a pastry or a baguette that was made mere minutes before the shop opened. **Lunch** is a longer affair, but it is becoming less leisurely as even Parisians adjust to the busy workday of a globalized world. Simple yet savory lunch chow found in cafés and *brasseries* includes salads, *quiche*, and tasty *croque-monsieur*, otherwise known as a grilled ham and cheese. Eating out for lunch can be more intimidating for non-French speakers, but it's just a matter of bucking up and testing out your throaty *s'il vous plait*, no matter how big the waiter's scowl is.

The same goes for **dinner,** where tourists subject themselves to confusion and anxiety as an intimidating *maître'd* recites the menu in rapid fire French. Stay strong. The food's worth it. A traditional French meal consists of five courses: *hors d'oeuvre*, soup, a main course, salad, cheese, and dessert, each paired with a wine. Except for the most extravagant five-star establishments, however, a restaurant meal is typically two or three courses depending on your appetite and budget. Some economical travelers may opt to skip the food and just indulge in the ✦vin, but we suggest you skip nothing. Most restaurants open around 7:30 or 8 and take orders until 11; keep a look out for classic French dishes such as *cassoulet*, a meat stew, or *coq au vin*, wine-cooked chicken. By law, restaurants must have a prix-fixe menu, so if they aren't showing you one, do not hesitate to inquire.

people and customs

FIRST IMPRESSIONS

The first time you meet in France, shake hands, although friends will greet one another with a kiss on the cheek. Women are expected to kiss twice. If you're planning on fine dining, dress it up – the easiest way to stand out as a tourist is to wear shorts and a T-shirt out to dinner. Don't expect to be let into the club wearing sneakers. At restaurants, the tip is included in the bill, but feel free to leave a 5-10% tip for exceptional service.

WHAT NOT TO SAY

Don't discuss money in private or public company. It's seen as tasteless. In restaurants, arguing over who had what when the bill comes up is even more shameless. The host usually is expected to pay; however, among friends it is more common to split the bill by the number in your party. In addition to money, talking about business is also seen as boring.

DEMAIN

If you're invited to dinner at someone's house, you'll find them unprepared if you show up "on time." Try aiming for 15 to 30 minutes late. The attitude of "do it later/ tomorrow" is one that France, and Southern Europe generally, embraces. While the punctual Germans might do it differently, a café rendezvous typically never starts on time.

WE'RE CLOSED

In France, services usually reserved for Sunday, such as restaurants and cafés generally are closed the day after rest, on Monday. Keep in mind if you're planning a hot date on a Monday, make sure to reschedule for later in the week. Plus, who wants to go on a date on Monday night?

USE YOUR CRAPPY FRENCH

When entering any sort of establishment, remember that it is the patron's (your) job to initiate conversation. Using French is crucial; it's a sign that you're trying to adapt to the culture and that you're willing to embarrass yourself to do so. French appreciate the struggle and, as most know a few words of English themselves, will often bail you out and start talking in English.

balls and bikes

Although known more for its catwalks and museums, Paris is home to people who don't mind breaking a sweat, too. The **Parc des Princes,** a spectacular stadium in the middle of the city, seats 50,000 and is home to the city's soccer team, **Paris St. Germain F.C.** Every May, the **French Open** draws thousands of people from around the world to watch tennis elite grunt it out on the clay courts of **Stade Roland Garros,** and the 3,500 competitors of the **Tour de France** bicycle race end in Paris at the **Arc d'Triomphe.** For those without iron lungs and massive calves, **Vélib bikes** are handy for tootling around the city, and for an even less stressful outing, one can spend a leisurely afternoon boating on the Seine or strolling through one of Paris's thirty-five parks and gardens.

paris 101

things you should know

THE CITY

The **Seine River**—one of the favorite spots of young romantics—flows through Paris, dividing the city between the *Rive Gauche* (Left Bank) on the south and the *Rive Droite* (Right Bank) to the north. Paris is subdivided into twenty *arrondissements*, or districts (abbreviated **"ème"**). Starting with the *premier* (first) arrondissement in the heart of Paris, the rest follow a clock-wise pattern that spirals around to the city's outermost areas. A ring highway called the *périphérique* encircles the arrondissements, separating them from the *banlieues* (the 'burbs). Within the city, each arrondissement has a local mayor and council, but the head honcho is really the **City Mayor,** who is elected by the city council and serves six-year terms. The current mayor is prominent socialist **Bertrand Delanoë,** France's first openly gay high-ranking politician.

Apart from the arrondissements, Paris is divided by a diverse number of neighborhoods that are sometimes comprised of more than one arrondissement. These neighborhoods have distinct features and feels that make each unique against the city backdrop. Here's a quick break down of Paris' seventeen neighborhoods:

Châtelet-Les Halles (1er, 2ème)

From the immense art collection at the **Musée du Louvre** to the couture shopping and extravagant hotels on the place **Vendôme,** high culture abounds in Châtelet-Les Halles. Neighboring the Louvre is the magnificent **Jardin des Tuileries,** landscaped by Louis XIV's very own Andre Le Nôtre. Head over to rue St. Honoré to gawk at the pricey boutiques and the people who can afford their clothes. Farther east is Les Halles, the former rat-infested food market district of Paris that is now home to the cavernous underground mall, **Forum des Halles,** jazz clubs, and a pleasant park.

The Marais (3ème, 4ème)

Called "The Swamp" in French, the lively, funky Marais district bears no resemblance to its wet, marshy beginnings. Glorious 17th-century architecture, including the breathtaking **Place des Vosges** blends in with the plethora of modern galleries, hip restaurants, and bars that are popular amongst the younger crowd. Paris' most gay-friendly district is also home to the bakeries and delis of Paris's oldest Jewish neighborhood along **rue de Rosiers.** The wildly colored **Centre Pompidou** is situated towards the western edge.

Île de la Cité and Île St-Louis (4ème)

Right at the center of the city, these two islands are the beating heart of old Paris. Île de la Cité was the site of the first settlement of Paris and has the historic landmarks to prove it. Here you'll find the **Notre Dame,** the stunning **Sainte-Chapelle** church, and the **Palais de Justice.** Across the bridge is its sister island Île St-Louis, once a pasture-

land but now home to many small shops, eateries, and 17th-century mansions.

Latin Quarter (5ème)

Boasting the prestigious **Sorbonne** built in 1257, the Latin Quarter was the intellectual heart of Paris and played host to a number of geniuses including Descartes, Sartre, and Hemingway. No longer teeming with as many students, the Quarter has actually become quite schlocky in some parts, with its main drag **boulevard St-Michel** crowded with blasé eateries and chain clothing stores. Head off onto the quieter side streets, however, and the wonderful bookstores, ethnic restaurants, and even the occasional heated debate over coffee bring back the feel of days gone by.

St-Germain (6ème)

St-Germain has a similar intellectual history to that of the Latin Quarter, and these days it is as well known for its upscale apartments as it is its charming cobblestone streets. Stop for lunch to people watch at a cafe on **boulevard St-Germain** and peruse luxurious boutiques where most everything costs a pretty penny. Then stroll through the 59 exquisite acres of the **Jardin du Luxumbourg** before heading to the **Musée d'Orsay.** Within the towering walls of the Orsay, a revamped Époque train station, are the works of famous Impressionist artists, including Monet, Cézanne, and Rodin.

Champs-Élysées (8ème)

The **Champs-Élysées boulevard,** is perhaps Paris's most visited shopping district, but it is by no means its best. Ridiculously expensive stores, ho-hum chain restaurants, and absurd auto showrooms line the streets, and the sophisticated air of its fashion heyday is gone. At night, the street comes alive with bass pumping out of tourist-filled clubs. Those who can afford the opulent hotels and apartments on the **rue du Faubourg St-Honoré** and **avenue Montaigne** probably enjoy them, but for most of us they are simply eye candy.

Opéra (9ème)

With nightclubs, porn shops, high-end department stores, and famous opera houses, this area has something for just about everyone. The rococo **Opéra Garnier,** with ceilings painted by Chagall, is a gorgeous landmark in the lower 9ème and is not too far from the colossal department store **Galeries Lafayette.** Yet the upper region of Pigalle, once the stomping grounds of World War II soldiers needing some TLC, is home to strip joints and X-rated cinemas.

Canal St-Martin (10ème)

In the days of Napoleon III, the 10ème was a hotbed for revolutionary zeal, but these days the area has become lackluster. Two train stations bring the most foot traffic to its streets, and currently its most prominent artistic feature is the graffiti. If you find yourself there, take a stroll along the **Canal St-Martin** or try one of its underrated restaurants.

Bastille (11ème, 12ème)

This youthful, somewhat raucous neighborhood's history lies in beginning of the Revolution when restless Parisians stormed the Bastille fortress. The club goers and pub patrons of today keep this vivacious attitude alive, especially on the eve of the commemorative national holiday (July 14th). **Bastille Square** is also site of the modern **Opéra Bastille,** which, amongst the funky fun, can seem out of place. The area is home to may immigrants and blue-collar *artistes*, giving it a bohemian feel. Affordable lodging enhances its allure for budgeted travelers.

Butte-Aux-Cailles and Chinatown (13ème)

From overcrowding to pollution, the 13ème has not been the most reputable of Parisian neighborhoods, but it is certainly not without merit. Since the influx of refugees during the Vietnam War, Paris's **Chinatown** has grown to 13 square blocks, a thriving cultural addition to the largely working class neighborhood. Today it is the focus of development with the contemporary **Bibliothèque de France,** built in 1996, and other construction projects undertaken since then.

Montparnasse (14ème, 15ème)

Café life reigned supreme here for the first half of the 20th century, and in the 1920s it would have been completely normal to see Hemingway and Fitzgerald getting *tré* deep in conversation (and *très* drunk). Expat culture declined abruptly after World War II, and today Paris's only skyscraper, **Tour Montparnasse,** is the focus of much hatred from aesthetically concerned Parisians. The area is generally uninviting and industrial, but its lack of tourists makes lodgings and restaurants are relatively ▓**cheap.** You can also check out thousands of dead Parisians in the **catacombs.** Yum.

Passy and Auteuil (16ème)

Once little 12th-century woodland suburbs, the villages of Passy, Auteuil, and Chaillot were eventually integrated into the city and are now known for their posh, bourgeois inhabitants and picturesque boulevards. It's a rather exclusive, but refreshingly peaceful, residential area with the best view of the Eiffel Tower at the **place de Trocadéro.**

Batignolles (17ème)

Diverse is the best way to describe the 17ème. Bourgeoisie and working class residents living mere minutes perhaps they're attracted by the delicious ethnic restaurants. Its upper crust lives closer to the 8ème and 16ème, while the western section features the same rough-around-the-edges vibe of neighboring Montmartre and Pigalle.

Montmartre (18ème)

Can, can you do the can-can? Cabaret performers in Montmartre can. The historic bohemian area of Paris, whose steep, windy streets were once populated by artists galore, is now frequently overwhelmed with sweaty families clambering up the hill to the stunning **Sacré-Coeur** basilica or snapping photos outside of the **Moulin Rouge.** On less busy days, the charm and comfort of the neighborhood is more evident, especially in the less-well-trodden areas; but at night you'll mostly find unsavory brothel clients.

Buttes Chaumont (19ème)

This working-class region has the feel, but not the maddening crowds, of neighboring Montmartre. Immigrants of all backgrounds call it home, and different ethnic communities have sprung up over the years drawing travelers, hungry from watching a play or browsing a gallery, to their restaurants and markets. The 19ème also offers fans of science a nerdy (and incredible) recluse in the **Cité des Sciences et de l'Industrie.**

Belleville and Père Lachaise (20ème)

A history of violence and suppression has shaped the 20ème into a tough yet charismatic area with a large immigrant population from France's old colonies. Visitors don't usually frequent the 20ème, but it is home to the burial grounds of famous figures, such as Edith Piaf, Jim Morrison, and Oscar Wilde, in the **Père Lachaise Cemetery.**

holidays and festivals

Hit Paris at certain times of the year and enjoy spirited parades, crazy celebrations, and mouth-watering events. Paris kicks off every New Year in ☿ **champagne-drenched style,** with fireworks off the Eiffel Tower and the truly spectacular **Grande Parade.** May is a busy month for public holidays (a.k.a. ◪**three-day weekends**) including **Victory Day** on May 8th (celebrating the liberation of Paris in 1945), **Ascension Day, Whit Sunday,** and **Whit Monday. Bastille Day** on July 14th commemorates the French Revolution of 1792 with picnicking in parks all over the city, loads of fireworks, and an impressive military parade. Summer festivals draw the music crowd with the **Paris Jazz Festival** happening every weekend in June and July and the **Fête de la Musique,** a huge free music festival in June that has professional and amateur indie crooners singing all over Paris' streets. Paris is home to various other art and film festivals, but the fête that takes the cake is the **Salon du Chocolat in October.** Yes, it is an entire festival devoted to the finest chocolate in the world.

media

Le Monde is the most widely read French newspaper and the most readily available, but copies of *Le Figaro* and the *International Herald Tribune,* the global edition of the *New York Times,* are easy to pick up as well. Popular magazines include the weekly *Paris Match* and *Le Point,* which cover local and world news, and fashion magazines *Elle* and *Vogue.* The **France 24** television channel broadcasts current affairs and international news in French and English, as does **Radio France Internationale (RFI)** on the airwaves. *Agence France-Presse* (◪www.afp.com), *Connexion* (◪www.connexionfrance.com), and *French News* (◪www.france24.com) are other English newspapers.

BEYOND TOURISM

The American in Paris is the best American.
  -F. Scott Fitzgerald

If you're reading this section, then chances are you believe, deep down, that you and Paris were made for each other. You're an idealist taking a gap year to save the trees, the whales, or the French economy, one exorbitant tuition payment at a time. You're a budding existentialist who wears Tina Fey glasses and unnecessary scarves, and are destined to write subversive poetry in smoky cafes. You could spend that semester abroad building latrines in the Third World, but let's be honest: adultery, *ennui*, and other French traditions are totally your thing. We at *Let's Go* are just a little bit jealous of you. If you're still looking for the right university, volunteer program, or work placement that will whisk you away to the land of love, lust, and the Louvre, read on.

greatest hits

- **FOSTER YOUR FOODIE SIDE** at the planet's most prestigious culinary school in the world's most culinary city at the **Cordon Bleu Paris Culinary Arts Institute** (p. 258).

- **GET TO KNOW DELACROIX BETTER THAN HIS MOTHER DID** with some art history classes at **L'École du Louvre** (p. 259).

- **INDULGE YOUR INNER ARISTOCRAT** while paying tribute to the proleteriat by restoring castles and learning medieval masonry with the **Club du Vieux Manoir** (p. 260).

studying

We know, we know, it's become a cliché: the American college student heading off to France to discover Proust, Parisian men, and the perfect croissant. But there's a reason more than 15,000 students study abroad in France each year. Paris, obviously the most popular destination, provides a Mecca for the art and architecture-inclined with its world-famous cultural landmarks, while smaller cities make it easy to meet local students and practice your French. If you speak decent French, don't be afraid to enroll directly in the French university system. Navigating the bureaucracy of course enrollment can be a nightmare, and that first *exposé oral* may be terrifying, but there's no better way to immerse yourself in French life. Otherwise, there are dozens of American-run study-abroad programs, so you can make your fautes and faux-pas in the company of fellow foreigners.

UNIVERSITIES

The French higher education system operates very differently from the American system. Unlike in the States, where high school seniors agonize over SATs and college applications, any French student who has obtained their Baccalaureate is eligible to enroll in university. (The weeding-out process doesn't happen until later, when students who don't pass their final exams are forced to redo the previous year or just drop out.) Given that education is heavily subsidized (one year at the prestigious Sorbonne costs a mere €400) and that most students live at home rent-free throughout their college years, it's no surprise that almost everyone at least starts university.

visa information

If you're lucky enough to have an EU passport, stop reading and count your blessing. Non-EU citizens hoping to study abroad in France, on the other hand, must obtain a **special student visa** from the French consulate. The process of applying for and obtaining a visa can take time, so give yourself at least two and a half months. **Short-stay visas** are good for up to 90 days, but if you're studying abroad, chances are you'll be there at least a semester, in which case you'll need one of two **long-stay visas.** Prospective long-term travelers must fill out **two to four applications**—depending on the consulate—for the appropriate visa and provide a **passport** valid for at least three months after the student's last day in France, plus two extra **passport photos.** Additionally, students must give **proof of enrollment** in or admission to a French learning institute, a **letter** from the home university or institution certifying current registration as a student, a **financial guarantee** with a monthly allowance of US$600 per month during the intended stay, and **proof of medical insurance.** Finally, there is a visa **application fee** of €60 for short-stay visas and €99 for long-stay. When in France, students with long-stay visas must obtain a **carte de séjour** (residency permit) from the local Préfecture de Police; students should file to obtain the card as soon as possible upon arrival. They will be required to undergo a **medical examination** (including x-rays) in addition to providing proof of residency (if your name's not on the electricity/gas bill, the bill of your host family or landlord and a copy of their French identity card will do). You'll also need to bring two passport photos, proof of financial resources, and €55, which is the cost of the carte de séjour.

International Programs

- **AMERICAN INSTITUTE FOR FOREIGN STUDY (AIFS):** With programs in 17 different countries and over 50,000 participants each year, AIFS is one of the oldest and largest cultural exchange organizations out there. In France, AIFS offers semester, year-long, and summer programs in Paris, Cannes, and Grenoble (term-time only) in both French and English. (☎800 727 2437 ■www.aifs.com Ⓢ *Semester $13,695-16,495; summer $6495-8495.*)

- **COUNCIL ON INTERNATIONAL EDUCATIONAL EXCHANGE (CIEE):** With programs in Paris and Rennes, CIEE offers students a range of options in terms of length of stay (semester, year-long, and summer programs), housing arrangements, and expected language experience. (☎800 407 8839 ■www.ciee.org Ⓢ *Semester $13,800-16,800; three-week summer $3375, six-week $6550.*)

- **ARCADIA UNIVERSITY:** Arcadia's semester study abroad program in Paris is based around an interdisciplinary seminar entitled "History, Politics, and Diplomacy of France and Europe" in which students are expected to develop an individual research project. The six-week summer program has a similar focus on "Intensive French and Politics: Economics, Diplomacy, and the European Union." Students are housed in residence dorms in Paris. (☎866 927 2234 or 215 572 2901■www.arcadia.edu/abroad Ⓢ *Semester $16,990. Estimate does not include meals.*)

- **INSTITUTE FOR THE INTERNATIONAL EDUCATION OF STUDENTS (IES):** IES offers a summer program in Arles, a semester or academic year program in Nantes, and summer, semester, and academic year programs in Paris. Business students can earn a Certificate in International Management by enrolling in a full-time master's program with French and international students. Otherwise, students take some of their classes on-site at the IES Abroad Center but are encouraged to take one or two courses at one of the French IES's partner institutions. (☎800 995 1750 or 312 994 1750 ■www.iesabroad.org Ⓢ*Semester $16,700-18,215; summer $6500-6675.*)

- **EXPERIMENTAL LEARNING INTERNATIONAL (ELI):** ELI's semester-long study and internship program, based in Paris, involves academic coursework, an internship where students work alongside French professionals, and a final research project. The goal is to help students begin to build a professional network in France in their area of interest. (☎303 321 8278 ■www.eliabroad.org Ⓢ *Semester €6500.*)

- **CULTURAL EXPERIENCES ABROAD (CEA):** CEA offers summer, semester, trimester, short-term, or academic-year programs in Paris, Aix-en-Provence, Grenoble, and the French Riviera. Most students live in shared apartments, but there is the option to "upgrade" to a homestay or independent living arrangement.(☎800-266-4441 ■www.gowithcea.com Ⓢ *Fees range from $4395 for a 4-week session to $25,995 for an academic year.*)

- **THE COLLEGE CONSORTIUM FOR INTERNATIONAL STUDIES (CCIS):** CCIS is a partnership of colleges and universities that sponsors a number of study-abroad programs around the world. In France, students can choose between Aix-en-Provence (which offers an intensive studio art option), Avignon, Chambéry, and Annecy (in the French Alps), Nice, Paris, and Angers (summer only). (☎800 453 6956 or 202 223 0330 ■www.ccisabroad.org Ⓢ *Semester $6490-10,861; summer $2617-5484. Estimates do not include room and board and vary depending on length and location of program.*)

French Programs

- **CENTER FOR UNIVERSITY PROGRAMS ABROAD (CUPA):** CUPA specializes in study abroad exclusively in Paris. The program is geared toward those very comfortable in French; after a three-week orientation, students are enrolled directly in French universities and expected to do the same work as their Parisian peers. (☎413 549 6960 ■www.cupa-paris.org Ⓢ *Semester $16,950; academic year $23,250. Optional host family housing and meals $6450 per semester or $11,700/year.*)

studying . universities

- **MIDDLEBURY SCHOOLS ABROAD:** Open to students from all universities, Middlebury Schools Abroad are known for their rigorous immersion experience; all students take courses at one of Middlebury's partner universities and are required to sign a language pledge attesting that they will only speak French with one another. Independent housing is not permitted; students either live with local families or in French residence halls. Semester and year-long programs are offered in Bordeaux, Poitiers, and Paris. *(☎802 443 5745 💻www.middlebury.edu/sa [$] Semester $11,200. Estimate does not include room and board.)*
- **COLUMBIA-PENN PROGRAM IN PARIS AT REID HALL:** The Columbia-Penn Program at Reid Hall offers students the choice of taking courses in French in-house at Reid Hall or in the French university system. All participants are required to take a course on French academic writing in the humanities and social sciences. *(☎212 854 2559 💻www.columbia.edu/cu/ogp [$] Semester $16,300. Estimate does not include room and board.)*
- **VASSAR-WESLEYAN PROGRAM IN PARIS (VWPP):** Heavily populated by Vassar and Wesleyan folk (read: leggings and scarves a must), the Vassar-Wesleyan program is nevertheless open to students from all colleges and universities for semester or full-year study abroad. Students stay with host families and take most of their courses in-house at the Reid Hall facility, but are encouraged to take at least one course at one of the French partner universities. Fall semester begins with a two-week intensive language program in Bordeaux, while spring semester orientation takes place in Paris. *(☎860 685 2550 💻www.wesleyan.edu/ois/programs/paris/intro.html [$] Semester $23,800. Fee includes most meals.)*

LANGUAGE SCHOOLS

As renowned novelist Gustave Flaubert once said, "Language is a cracked kettle on which we beat out tunes for bears to dance to." While we at *Let's Go* have absolutely no clue what he was talking about, we do know that the following are good resources for learning French.

- **ALLIANCE FRANÇAISE:** The Alliance Française offers classes for all levels, from beginner to advanced, as well as evening workshops on topics like pronunciation or written French and professional courses on Business French, Legal French, Tourism French, and Medical French for those looking to work in France long-term. Private and group lessons and self-guided learning courses using the Multimedia Resource Center are also available. *(101 Bld. Raspail ☎01 42 84 90 00 💻www.ccfs-sorbonne.fr)*
- **COURS DE CIVILISATION FRANÇAISE DE LA SORBONNE:** A popular option for Americans looking for an excuse to be eligible for a student visa, the Cours de Civilisation Française de la Sorbonne offers sessions ranging in length from three to 12 weeks. Regular language and civilization classes meet 12hr. per week, intensive courses meet 25hr. per week. *(☎01 44 10 77 00 💻www.ccfs-sorbonne.fr)*
- **EUROCENTRES:** With sites in Paris, La Rochelle, and Amboise, Eurocentres offers French classes mostly in the mornings, with an option for business French. The schools all provide recreation rooms and free internet access, and organize a variety of outings and social activities. *(☎+41 4 44 85 50 40 💻www.eurocentres.com)*

CULINARY SCHOOLS

- **CORDON BLEU PARIS CULINARY ARTS INSTITUTE:** There's no more prestigious training academy for the serious aspiring chef than the original Paris branch of the Cordon Bleu. Certificate and degree programs available. More tourist-friendly options include two- to four-hour workshops and short courses that range in length from two days to one week. Price of a one-day taste of Provence workshop? €175. Bragging rights? Priceless. *(☎01 53 68 22 50 💻www.cordonbleu.edu [$] €175 for one-day cooking class.)*
- **PROMENADES GOURMANDES:** If the corporate Cordon Bleu is too impersonal for

you, Paule Caillat's cooking classes and market tours are just the opposite. Capped at eight students, classes are scheduled on request and take place in a home kitchen in the Marais in either French or English. Every class includes a three-course lunch that you will have prepared and a cheese tasting. *(☎01 48 04 56 84 💻www.fmeunier.com $ Half-day cooking classes €270 per person.)*

ART SCHOOLS AND COURSES

- **L'ÉCOLE DU LOUVRE:** Installed in the Louvre in 1882, the École du Louvre, dedicated to "making the Louvre into a living center of study," offers degree-granting undergraduate, graduate, and post-graduate classes in art history and museum studies, as well as evening and summer classes and an art auctioneer training program. Looking for less of a commitment? Every Monday, Tuesday, and Thursday from 6:30-7:45pm, the École organizes free lectures by academics, curators, and other museum professionals. *(☎01 55 35 18 35 💻www.ecoledulouvre.fr $ Tuition fee undergraduate studies €350.)*
- **MUSÉE DES ARTS DÉCORATIFS:** The Musée des Arts Décoratifs offers year-long day and evening classes and intensive holiday workshops in studio art. Topics range from the conventional (oil painting, sculpture, figure drawing) to the more esoteric (*trompe l'oeil* painting, engraving, and comic book-making). *(☎+33 1 44 55 59 02 💻www.lesartsdecoratifs.fr $ Free.)*
- **FONDATION CARTIER POUR L'ART CONTEMPORAIN:** The Fondation Cartier, housed in a unique Jean Nouvel building, offers a variety of different courses designed to initiate students in modern and contemporary art. Classes take place on Tuesdays from 7:30-9pm, and are organized into eight-week sessions. Students can choose between 13 different sessions on topics such as architecture, photography, fashion, design, and gardening. *(☎01 42 18 56 67 💻 www.fondation.cartier.fr .)*

volunteering

"When good Americans die, they go to Paris," Oscar Wilde once famously said. Well, we're here to help you earn your place in French heaven by being a "good" American tourist and leaving the country in better shape than you found it.

Despite being the fifth-richest country in the world by GDP, France faces a variety of social issues, and so there is no shortage of aid organizations looking for volunteers. Whether you want to devote yourself to wildlife conservation, raise awareness about AIDS among urban youth, or take part in archaeological restoration, France abounds with organizations and volunteer opportunities to suit every interest and commitment level.

If you're interested in part-time or relatively short-term volunteer work, get in touch with one of the volunteer centers listed below. For travelers looking for a much longer or more immersive volunteer experience, volunteer companies are often the way to go, especially for younger or less-experienced travelers looking for community and support. These parent organizations will charge a fee in most cases, but in exchange they will usually take care of all the logistical details, arrange your airfare, room, and board if necessary, and provide you with a group environment. Of these, the **International Volunteer Program** *(💻www.ivpsf.org)*, which places volunteers in French non-profits for six weeks during the summer, and **Volunteers for Peace** *(💻www.vfp.org)*, which runs International Voluntary Service projects ranging from historic preservation work to AIDS/HIV education are among the best. Websites like www.transitionsabroad.com, www.volunteerabroad.com, www.volunteerinternational.org, and www.idealist.org are also great places to start your search for jobs, internships, or volunteer opportunities abroad.

YOUTH AND COMMUNITY

- **GROUPEMENT ÉTUDIANT NATIONAL D'ENSEIGNEMENT AUX PERSONNES INCAR-CERÉES (GENEPI):** Founded by students after the violent riots over the prison system in the early '70s, GENEPI pairs student volunteers with inmates in French prisons to promote social rehabilitation. (☎01 45 88 37 00 🖳www.genepi.fr)

- **SECOURS POPULAIRE FRANCAIS:** A humanitarian organization created in 1945, Secours Populaire Français helps to combat poverty by providing food, clothing, health care, and temporary housing and organizing sporting and cultural activities for poor children and families. (☎01 44 78 21 00 🖳www.secourspopulaire.asso.fr)

CONSERVATION AND ARCHAEOLOGY

- **CLUB DU VIEUX MANOIR:** Club du Vieux Manoir arranges projects of various lengths to restore castles and churches and teach young people about the importance of protecting the *patrimoine national*. (☎01 44 72 33 98 🖳www.clubduvieuxmanoir. asso.fr *i* Most programs 14 and older. Ⓢ Membership and insurance fee €16 per year. Program fee €14 per day, includes food and lodging.)

- **MINISTRY OF CULTURE, SOUS-DIRECTION DE L'ARCHÉOLOGIE:** This government department that oversees archaeological digs on French soil publishes a list of summer excavations that accept volunteers in May. (☎ 01 40 15 77 81 🖳www.culture.gouv.fr)

- **REMPART:** A union of nearly 170 nonprofit organizations throughout France that accept volunteers for restoring historic sites and monuments, including military heritage sites, religious heritage sites, civic heritage sites, industrial heritage sites, and natural heritage sites. (☎01 42 71 96 55 🖳 wwww.rempart.com *i* 18 and older. Basic French knowledge recommended. Ⓢ Room and board vary by camp. Registration fee covers accident insurance.)

working

If you're looking to stay in France for longer than just a vacation, you'll probably need to find a way to *gagne de l'argent*. As with volunteering, work opportunities tend to fall into two categories. Some travelers want long-term jobs that allow them to integrate into a community, while others seek out short-term jobs to finance the next leg of their travels. With France's 7.4% unemployment rate, long-term jobs are currently hard to come by. Travelers without EU citizenship face a particular challenge when searching for a job in France: only employers who cannot find qualified workers in the EU may petition to bring in a long-term worker who is not an EU citizen. If you're undeterred by the less-than-welcoming attitude toward foreign workers, you may want to try a job that requires English-language skills, as bilingual candidates have a better chance of finding work. Working as an au pair or teaching English are both popular long-term employment options. If you're in the market for a short-term stint, be on the lookout for a service or agricultural job.

Classified advertisements in newspapers and online are good resources for international job-seekers. Agence Nationale pour l'Emploi (🖥www.anpe.fr) has listings for many skilled and unskilled jobs alike, while Agence pour l'Emploi de Cadres (🖥www.apec.fr) catalogues professional job listings. Michael Page (🖥www.michaelpage.fr) is another job recruiting agency with offices in major French cities as well as international locations. The American Chamber of Commerce (🖥www.amchamfrance.org), located in Paris, fosters Franco-American business relations, and is currently generating an online job and internship directory. Note that working abroad often requires a special work visa.

more visa info

EU citizens have the right to work in France without a visa, and can easily obtain a **carte de séjour** (residency permit) by presenting a passport, proof of employment, and other identification documents. Visit www.infomobil.org for a complete list of requirements. Non-EU citizens hoping to work in France for less than 90 days must apply for an Autorisation Provisoire de Travail at a local branch of Direction Départementale du Travail, de l'Emploi et de la Formation Professionnelle (D.D.T.E.F.P.). A passport and proof of short-term employment are necessary to secure authorization; a short-term, or Schengen visa (US$82) is also sometimes required. Non-EU citizens wishing to work in France for more than 90 days must have an offer of employment authorized by the French Ministry of Labor (🖥www.travail.gouv.fr/) before applying for a long-stay visa (US$136) through their local French consulate. Within 8 days of arrival in France, holders of long-stay visas must apply for a carte de séjour. International students hoping to secure a job must possess a **carte de séjour d'étudiant** (student residency card) and apply for an Autorisation Provisoire de Travail at a D.D.T.E.F.P. office. Students in France are permitted to work up to 19½hr. per week during the academic year, and full time during summer and holidays. Special rules apply for au pairs and teaching assistants; see www.consulfrance-washington.org for more info.

LONG-TERM WORK

As we mentioned, it can be tricky finding long-term work in France. American firms, however, are a more likely bet. A listing of American firms in France is available for purchase from the American Chamber of Commerce in France. Go to www.amchamfrance.org or e-mail amchamfrance@amchamfrance.org for more information.

Teaching English

Teaching in French public schools and universities is largely restricted to French citizens. One of the only exceptions is the French government's foreign language assistants program, coordinated by the French embassy in your home country. Teaching assistants commit to teaching for 7-9 months in public schools throughout metropolitan France, as well as overseas in Guadeloupe, Martinique, French Guiana, and Reunion. Assistants work 12 hours per week in an elementary school (ages 8-11) or secondary school (ages 11-18). The salary is approximately €780 per month, which includes mandatory health insurance and French social security. No prior teaching experience necessary, but some background in French language is required. Applicants must be 20-29 years of age and have completed a bachelor's degree. Interested American citizens and permanent residents should contact the embassy in Washington at least six months prior to the start of the academic year. For more information, visit www.ambafrance-us.org.

It is also sometimes possible to find jobs independently, but in most cases you'll need a Teaching English as a Foreign Language (TEFL) certificate. ESL Base (www.eslbase.com) posts notices for schools seeking native English speakers as teachers, then you contact the school directly. Full-time and part-time opportunities.

University fellowship programs can be a great way to find a teaching job. Some people have also found jobs by contacting schools directly. If you want to try your luck, the best time to do so is several weeks before the start of the academic year.

au pair sites

- **ACCUEIL INTERNATIONAL SERVICES** (☎01 39 73 04 98 www.accueil-international.com)
- **AGENCE AU PAIR FLY** (☎03 34 37 65 70 83 www.aupairfly.com)
- **INTEREXCHANGE** (☎212 924 0446 www.interexchange.org)
- **CHILDCARE INTERNATIONAL** (☎+44 20 89 06 31 16 www.childint.co.uk)
- **INTERNATIONAL AU PAIR ASSOCIATION** (☎+31 20 421 2800 www.iapa.org)

Au Pair Work

Au pairs in France are typically paid between €50 and €75 per week. Much of the au pair experience depends on the family with which you are placed. There is a database for au pair agencies at www.europa-pages.com/au_pair/france.html.

Short-Term Work

Scouting the flyers at famed Parisian English-language bookstore Shakespeare & Co. can be a great way for English speakers to find short-term jobs like tutoring or babysitting. Websites like www.craigslist.com and www.franglo.com are good virtual equivalents.

- **EASY EXPAT:** Easy-to-navigate with summer, seasonal, and short-term jobs as well as volunteer opportunities and internships. Options range from teaching ski lessons to working at Disneyland Paris. (www.easyexpat.com/paris_en.htm)
- **FÉDÉRATION UNIE DES AUBERGES DE JEUNESSE:** Offers short-term work in member youth hostels, from catering to reception. Submit application to individual hostels. (☎+33 1 40 15 77 81 www.fuaj.org)

tell the world

If your friends are tired of hearing about that time you saved a baby orangutan in Indonesia, there's clearly only one thing to do: get new friends. Find them at our website, www.letsgo.com, where you can post your study-, volunteer-, or work-abroad stories for other, more appreciative community members to read.

INDEX

index

MAP INDEX

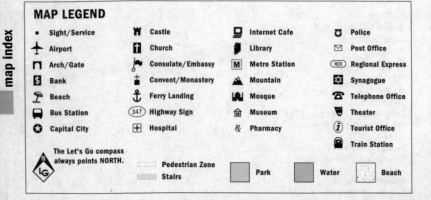

MAP LEGEND

- ▪ Sight/Service
- ✈ Airport
- ⋂ Arch/Gate
- 💲 Bank
- 🏖 Beach
- 🚌 Bus Station
- ✪ Capital City

- 🏰 Castle
- ✝ Church
- 🏴 Consulate/Embassy
- ✝ Convent/Monastery
- ⚓ Ferry Landing
- (347) Highway Sign
- ✚ Hospital

- 💻 Internet Cafe
- 📖 Library
- Ⓜ Metro Station
- ⛰ Mountain
- 🕌 Mosque
- 🏛 Museum
- ℞ Pharmacy

- ⛉ Police
- ✉ Post Office
- (RER) Regional Express
- ✡ Synagogue
- ☎ Telephone Office
- ♥ Theater
- ⓘ Tourist Office
- 🚂 Train Station

The Let's Go compass always points NORTH.

- Pedestrian Zone
- Stairs
- Park
- Water
- Beach

map index

LET'S GO!

THE STUDENT TRAVEL GUIDE

These Let's Go guidebooks are available at bookstores and through online retailers:

EUROPE
Let's Go Amsterdam & Brussels, 1st ed.
Let's Go Berlin, Prague & Budapest, 2nd ed.
Let's Go France, 32nd ed.
Let's Go Europe 2011, 51st ed.
Let's Go European Riviera, 1st ed.
Let's Go Germany, 16th ed.
Let's Go Great Britain with Belfast and Dublin, 33rd ed.
Let's Go Greece, 10th ed.
Let's Go Istanbul, Athens & the Greek Islands, 1st ed.
Let's Go Italy, 31st ed.
Let's Go London, Oxford, Cambridge & Edinburgh,
    2nd ed.
Let's Go Madrid & Barcelona, 1st ed.
Let's Go Paris, 17th ed.
Let's Go Rome, Venice & Florence, 1st ed.
Let's Go Spain, Portugal & Morocco, 26th ed.
Let's Go Western Europe, 10th ed.

UNITED STATES
Let's Go Boston, 6th ed.
Let's Go New York City, 19th ed.
Let's Go Roadtripping USA, 4th ed.

MEXICO, CENTRAL & SOUTH AMERICA
Let's Go Buenos Aires, 2nd ed.
Let's Go Central America, 10th ed.
Let's Go Costa Rica, 5th ed.
Let's Go Costa Rica, Nicaragua & Panama, 1st ed.
Let's Go Guatemala & Belize, 1st ed.
Let's Go Yucatán Peninsula, 1st ed.

ASIA & THE MIDDLE EAST
Let's Go Israel, 5th ed.
Let's Go Thailand, 5th ed.

ACKNOWLEDGMENTS

TERESA THANKS: Veggie Planet pizzas and Petsi Pies coffee, Liza Flum's kitchen and bootleg TV and the rickety machines at the Central Square Y. I thank Joe Gaspard and my pod-mates for having my back, and my parents, bad music, and David Foster Wallace for getting me through. My uncle's '80s comic books and my grandpa's Chicago sundaes helped too.

JOE THANKS: the Let's Go office team and his RWs for their hard work. Special thanks go out to the Starbucks staff for keeping me well caffeinated, to Bolt Bus for taking me back to Dix Hills, to my brother and sisters for always being down to party, and to my mother for her continued support. The ladies of Harem Pod never failed to make me laugh, even when I was pulling my hair out. Lady Gaga should also be thanked for her part in keeping me happy; we could definitely have a bad romance.

LET'S GO masthead

DIRECTOR OF PUBLISHING   Ashley R. Laporte
EXECUTIVE EDITOR   Nathaniel Rakich
PRODUCTION AND DESIGN DIRECTOR   Sara Plana
PUBLICITY AND MARKETING DIRECTOR   Joseph Molimock
MANAGING EDITORS   Charlotte Alter, Daniel C. Barbero, Marykate Jasper, Iya Megre
TECHNOLOGY PROJECT MANAGERS   Daniel J. Choi, C. Alexander Tremblay
PRODUCTION ASSOCIATES   Rebecca Cooper, Melissa Niu
FINANCIAL ASSOCIATE   Louis Caputo

DIRECTOR OF IT   Yasha Iravantchi
PRESIDENT   Meagan Hill
GENERAL MANAGER   Jim McKellar

ABOUT LET'S GO

THE STUDENT TRAVEL GUIDE

Let's Go publishes the world's favorite student travel guides, written entirely by Harvard students. Armed with pens, notebooks, and a few changes of clothes stuffed into their backpacks, our student researchers go across continents, through time zones, and above expectations to seek out invaluable travel experiences for our readers. Because we are a completely student-run company, we have a unique perspective on how students travel, where they want to go, and what they're looking to do when they get there. If your dream is to grab a machete and forge through the jungles of Costa Rica, we can take you there. If you'd rather bask in the Riviera sun at a beachside cafe, we'll set you a table. In short, we write for readers who know that there's more to travel than tour buses. To keep up, visit our website, www.letsgo.com, where you can sign up to blog, post photos from your trips, and connect with the Let's Go community.

TRAVELING BEYOND TOURISM

We're on a mission to provide our readers with sharp, fresh coverage packed with socially responsible opportunities to go beyond tourism. Each guide's Beyond Tourism chapter shares ideas on responsible travel, study abroad, and how to give back to the places you visit while on the road. To help you gain a deeper connection with the places you travel, our fearless researchers scour the globe to give you the heads-up on both world-renowned and off-the-beaten-track opportunities. We've also opened our pages to respected writers and scholars to hear their takes on the countries and regions we cover, and asked travelers who have worked, studied, or volunteered abroad to contribute first-person accounts of their experiences.

FIFTY-ONE YEARS OF WISDOM

Let's Go has been on the road for 51 years and counting. We've grown a lot since publishing our first 20-page pamphlet to Europe in 1960, but five decades and 60 titles later, our witty, candid guides are still researched and written entirely by students on shoestring budgets who know that train strikes, stolen luggage, food poisoning, and marriage proposals are all part of a day's work. Meanwhile, we're still bringing readers fresh new features, such as a student-life section with advice on how and where to meet students from around the world; a revamped, user-friendly layout for our listings; and greater emphasis on the experiences that make travel abroad a rite of passage for readers of all ages. And, of course, this year's 16 titles—including five brand-new guides—are still brimming with editorial honesty, a commitment to students, and our irreverent style.

THE LET'S GO COMMUNITY

More than just a travel guide company, Let's Go is a community that reaches from our headquarters in Cambridge, MA, all across the globe. Our small staff of dedicated student editors, writers, and tech nerds comes together because of our shared passion for travel and our desire to help other travelers get the most out of their experience. We love it when our readers become part of the Let's Go community as well—when you travel, drop us a postcard (67 Mt. Auburn St., Cambridge, MA 02138, USA), send us an email (feedback@letsgo.com), or sign up on our website (www.letsgo.com) to tell us about your adventures and discoveries.

For more information, updated travel coverage, and news from our researcher team, visit us online at www.letsgo.com.

THANKS TO OUR SPONSORS

- **HOTEL DU LION D'OR.** 5 rue de la Sourdiere, 75001 Paris. ☎33 (0)1 4260 79 04. ✉www.hoteluliondor.com.

thanks to our sponsors

HELPING LET'S GO. If you want to share your discoveries, suggestions, or corrections, please drop us a line. We appreciate every piece of correspondence, whether a postcard, a 10-page email, or a coconut. Visit Let's Go at **www.letsgo.com** or send an email to:

feedback@letsgo.com, subject: "Let's Go Paris"

Address mail to:

Let's Go Paris, 67 Mount Auburn St., Cambridge, MA 02138, USA

In addition to the invaluable travel advice our readers share with us, many are kind enough to offer their services as researchers or editors. Unfortunately, our charter enables us to employ only currently enrolled Harvard students.

Distributed by Publishers Group West.
Printed in Canada by Friesens Corp.
Maps by © Let's Go and Avalon Travel
Design Support by Jane Musser, Sarah Juckniess, Tim McGrath

ISBN-13: 978-1-59880-709-7
Seventeenth edition
10 9 8 7 6 5 4 3 2 1

Let's Go Paris is written by Let's Go Publications, 67 Mt. Auburn St., Cambridge, MA 02138, USA.

Let's Go® and the LG logo are trademarks of Let's Go, Inc.

quick reference

YOUR GUIDE TO LET'S GO ICONS

☎	Phone numbers	♿̸	Not wheelchair-accessible	❄	Has A/C
🖥	Websites	📶	Has internet access	✥	Directions
💳	Takes credit cards	⛅	Has outdoor seating	*i*	Other hard info
🚫	Cash only	▼	Is GLBT or GLBT-friendly	$	Prices
♿	Wheelchair-accessible	🍸	Serves alcohol	⏰	Hours

PRICE RANGES

Let's Go includes price ranges, marked by icons ❶ through ❺, in accommodations and food listings. For an expanded explanation, see the chart in How To Use This Book.

FRANCE	❶	❷	❸	❹	❺
ACCOMMODATIONS	up to €25	€25-€40	€40-€60	€60-€80	€80 or above
FOOD	up to €15	€15-€25	€25-€35	€35-€45	€45 or above

IMPORTANT PHONE NUMBERS

EMERGENCY: POLICE ☎17, FIRE ☎18, MEDICAL EMERGENCY ☎15			
European emergency	☎112	Directory assistance	☎118 218
English-language crisis line	☎01 47 23 80 80	SNCF train reservations and information	☎08 92 30 83 08

To call France from home or to call home from France, dial the international dialing prefix (from Australia ☎0011; Canada or the US ☎011; New Zealand, France, or other European countries ☎00) + country code for the country you're calling (Australia 61; Canada or the US 1; Ireland 353; the UK 44; France 33) + area code (omit initial zeroes if calling from abroad) + local number.

USEFUL FRENCH PHRASES

ENGLISH	FRENCH	PRONUNCIATION
Hello!/Hi!	Bonjour!	bohn-jhoor
Do you speak English?	Parlez-vous anglais?	par-lay voo ong-lay
Yes.	Oui	wee
No.	Non	nohn
Help!	Au secours!	oh sek-oor
I'm lost	Je suis perdu(e)	jh'swee perh-doo
I don't understand	Je ne comprends pas	jh'ne kom-prahn pa

TEMPERATURE CONVERSIONS

°CELSIUS	-5	0	5	10	15	20	25	30	35	40
°FAHRENHEIT	23	32	41	50	59	68	77	86	95	104

MEASUREMENT CONVERSIONS

1 inch (in.) = 25.4mm	1 millimeter (mm) = 0.039 in.
1 foot (ft.) = 0.305m	1 meter (m) = 3.28 ft.
1 mile (mi.) = 1.609km	1 kilometer (km) = 0.621 mi.
1 pound (lb.) = 0.454kg	1 kilogram (kg) = 2.205 lb.
1 gallon (gal.) = 3.785L	1 liter (L) = 0.264 gal.